THE DAYS ARE JUST PACKED

A Calvin and Hobbes Collection by Bill Watterson

IS THE COAST CLEAR? GIVE ME A BOOST!
WHAT'S THE PLAN?
WE WAIT FOR SUSIE TO WALK UNDERNEATH THIS TREE AND THEN WE DROP THE WATER BALLOON ON HER!
WHAT IF SHE DOESN'T WALK BY?
THEN WE JUST SIT IN THE TREE ALL DAY.
I LOVE SUMMER.
THE DAYS ARE JUST *PACKED*.
WATERSON

Andrews and McMeel
A Universal Press Syndicate Company
Kansas City

Calvin and Hobbes is distributed internationally by Universal Press Syndicate.

ISBN: 0-8362-1735-7 paperback
0-8362-1736-5 hardback

Library of Congress Catalog Card Number: 93-71863

MOMMM
WHAT'S THE MATTER??
HOW DO UGLY THINGS LIKE OCTOPUSES AND HAIRY BUGS REPRODUCE? ARE THEY ACTUALLY ATTRACTED TO EACH OTHER?
IT'S 3 AM! GO TO SLEEP!
COME TO THINK OF IT, I WONDER HOW PEOPLE ARE ATTRACTED TO EACH OTHER.
I'LL BET THAT'S WHY THEY CLOSE THEIR EYES WHEN THEY SMOOCH.

LOOK AT WHAT THIS DUMB TOASTER DID TO MY TOAST!
IT DIDN'T COOK IT ENOUGH THE FIRST TIME, SO I PUSHED IT DOWN AGAIN AND NOW ONE SIDE'S BURNED AND THE OTHER'S HARDLY SINGED! THAT TOASTER RUINED MY TOAST!
AND YET ...SOMEHOW... LIFE GOES ON.
BENEATH THAT LARGER PERSPECTIVE IS A GUY WHO DOESN'T WANT TO SPRING FOR A NEW TOASTER.

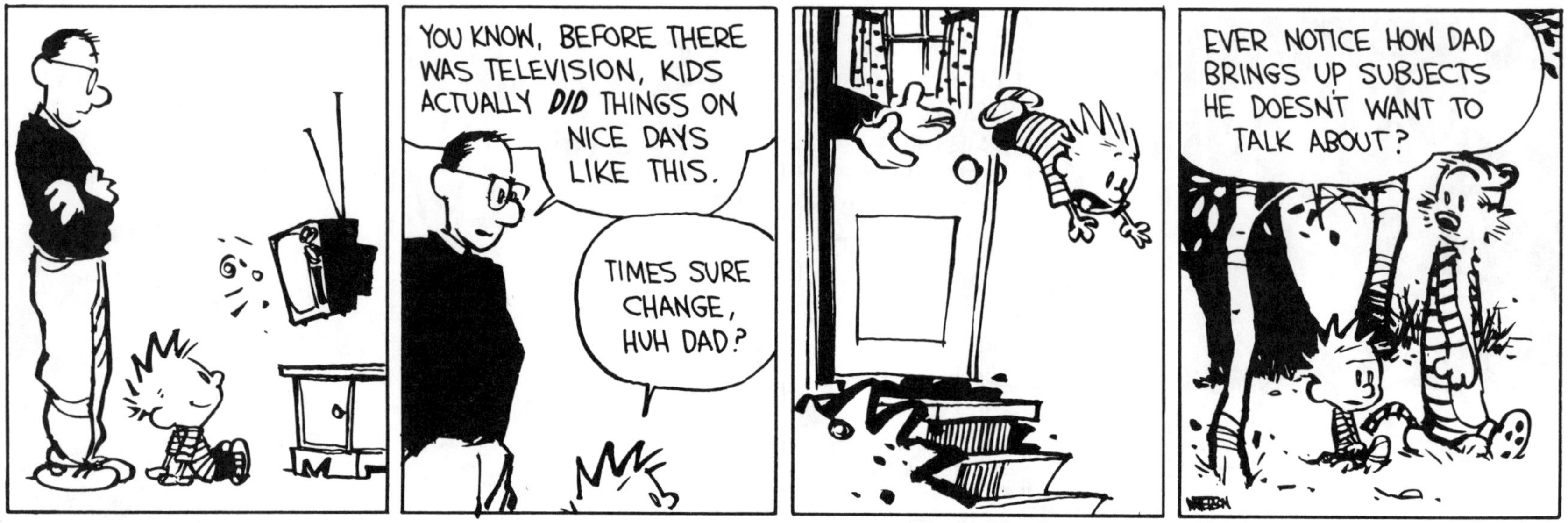
YOU KNOW, BEFORE THERE WAS TELEVISION, KIDS ACTUALLY *DID* THINGS ON NICE DAYS LIKE THIS.
TIMES SURE CHANGE, HUH DAD?
EVER NOTICE HOW DAD BRINGS UP SUBJECTS HE DOESN'T WANT TO TALK ABOUT?

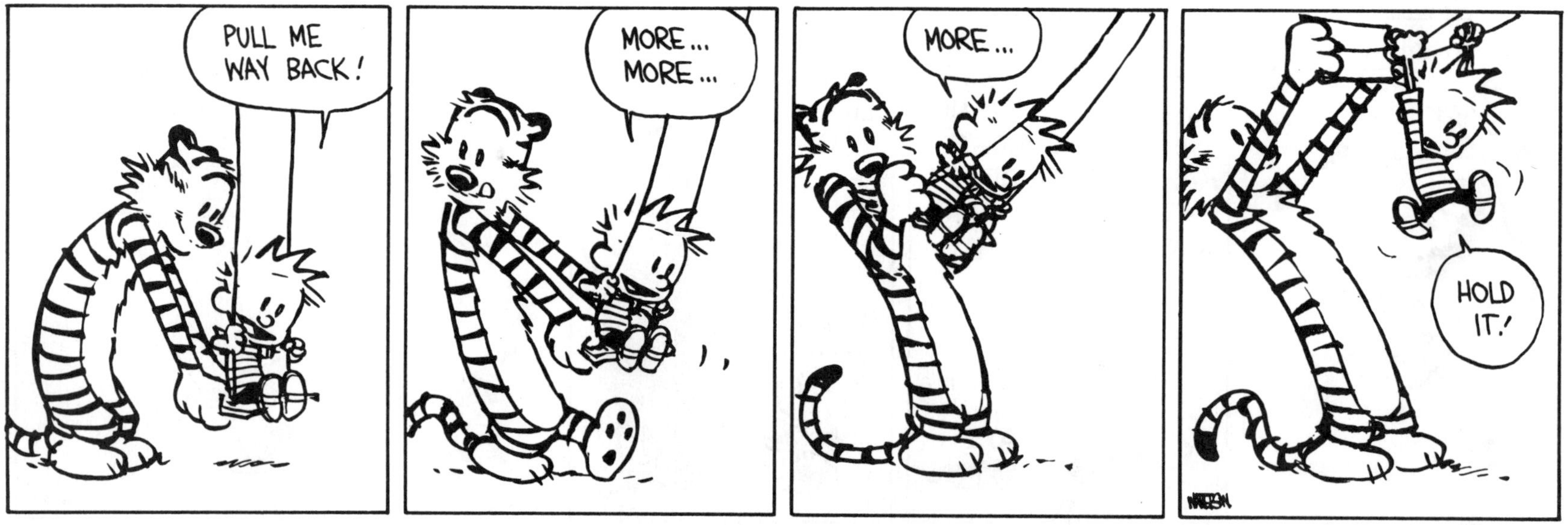
PULL ME WAY BACK!
MORE... MORE...
MORE...
HOLD IT!

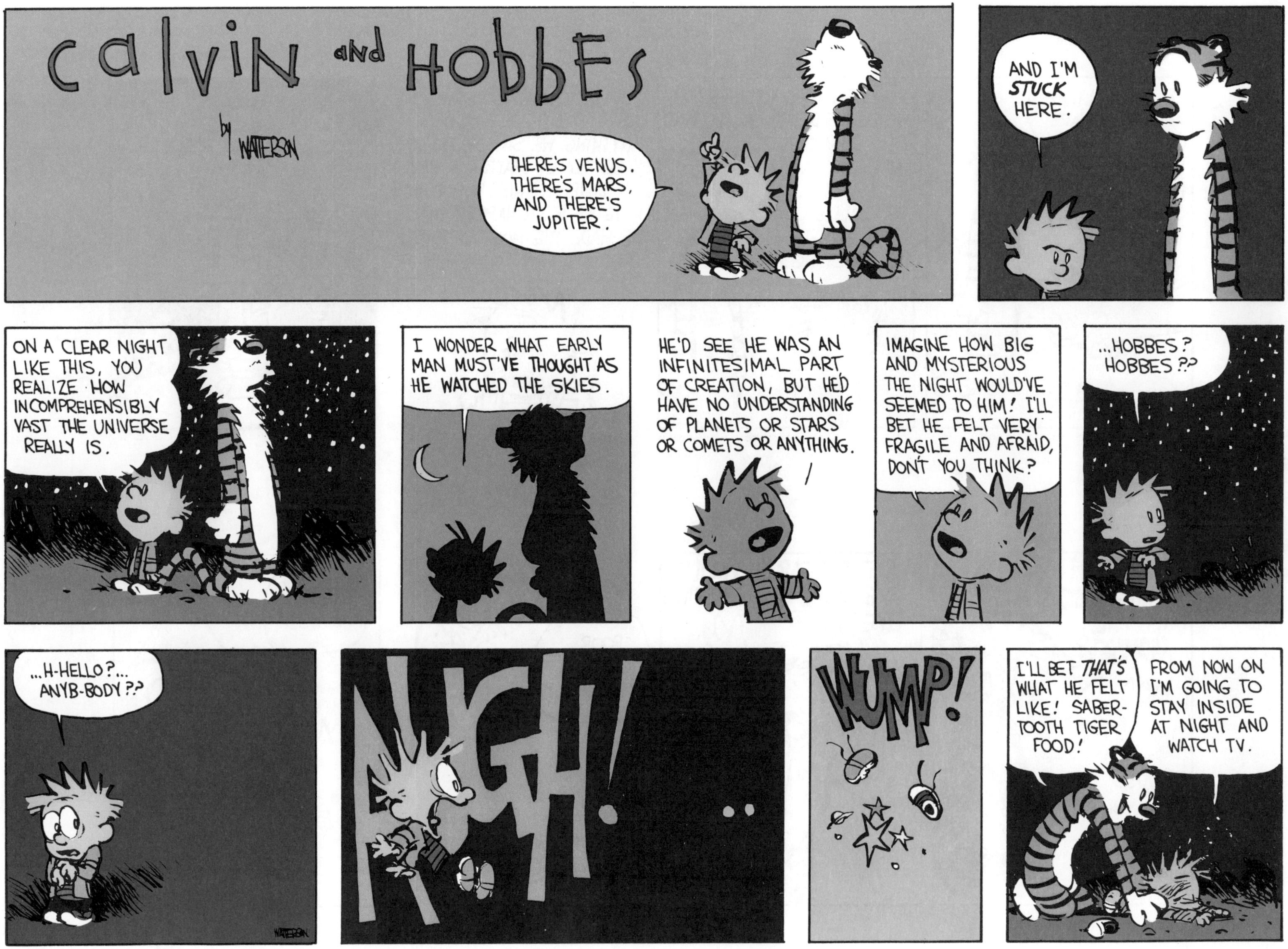
calvin and HOBBES
by WATTERSON
THERE'S VENUS. THERE'S MARS, AND THERE'S JUPITER.
AND I'M *STUCK* HERE.
ON A CLEAR NIGHT LIKE THIS, YOU REALIZE HOW INCOMPREHENSIBLY VAST THE UNIVERSE REALLY IS.
I WONDER WHAT EARLY MAN MUST'VE THOUGHT AS HE WATCHED THE SKIES.
HE'D SEE HE WAS AN INFINITESIMAL PART OF CREATION, BUT HE'D HAVE NO UNDERSTANDING OF PLANETS OR STARS OR COMETS OR ANYTHING.
IMAGINE HOW BIG AND MYSTERIOUS THE NIGHT WOULD'VE SEEMED TO HIM! I'LL BET HE FELT VERY FRAGILE AND AFRAID, DON'T YOU THINK?
...HOBBES? HOBBES??
...H-HELLO?... ANYB-BODY??
WATTERSON
AUGH!
WUMP!
I'LL BET *THAT'S* WHAT HE FELT LIKE! SABER-TOOTH TIGER FOOD!
FROM NOW ON I'M GOING TO STAY INSIDE AT NIGHT AND WATCH TV.

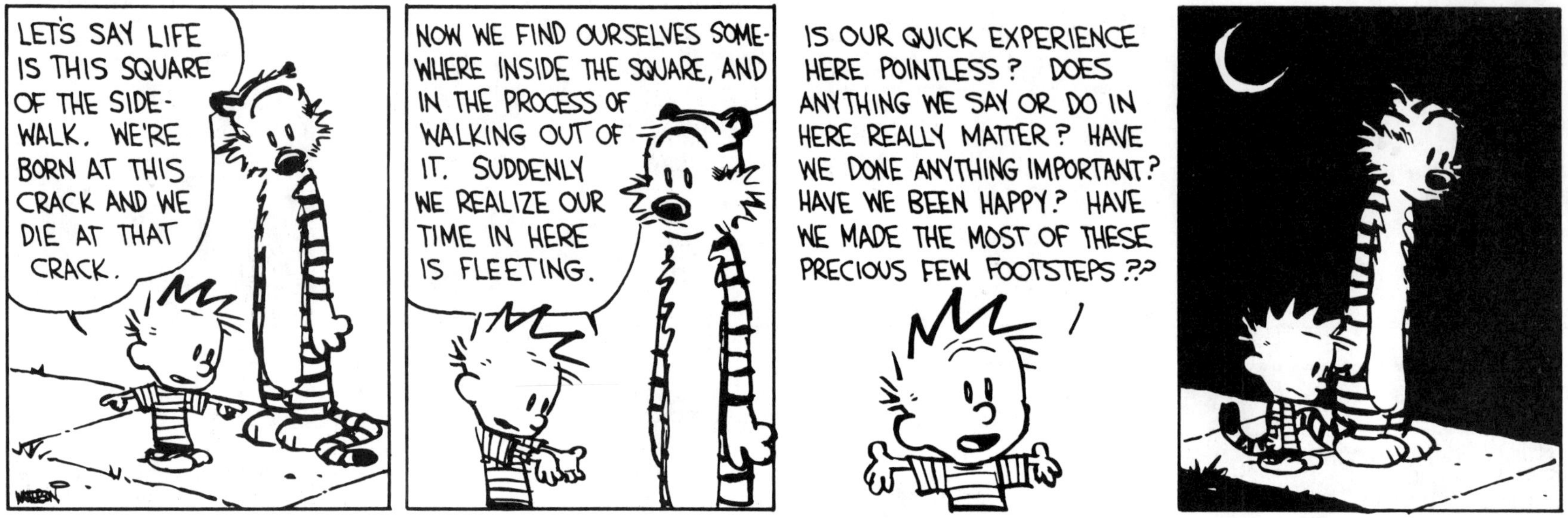
LET'S SAY LIFE IS THIS SQUARE OF THE SIDE-WALK. WE'RE BORN AT THIS CRACK AND WE DIE AT THAT CRACK.
NOW WE FIND OURSELVES SOME-WHERE INSIDE THE SQUARE, AND IN THE PROCESS OF WALKING OUT OF IT. SUDDENLY WE REALIZE OUR TIME IN HERE IS FLEETING.
IS OUR QUICK EXPERIENCE HERE POINTLESS? DOES ANYTHING WE SAY OR DO IN HERE REALLY MATTER? HAVE WE DONE ANYTHING IMPORTANT? HAVE WE BEEN HAPPY? HAVE WE MADE THE MOST OF THESE PRECIOUS FEW FOOTSTEPS??

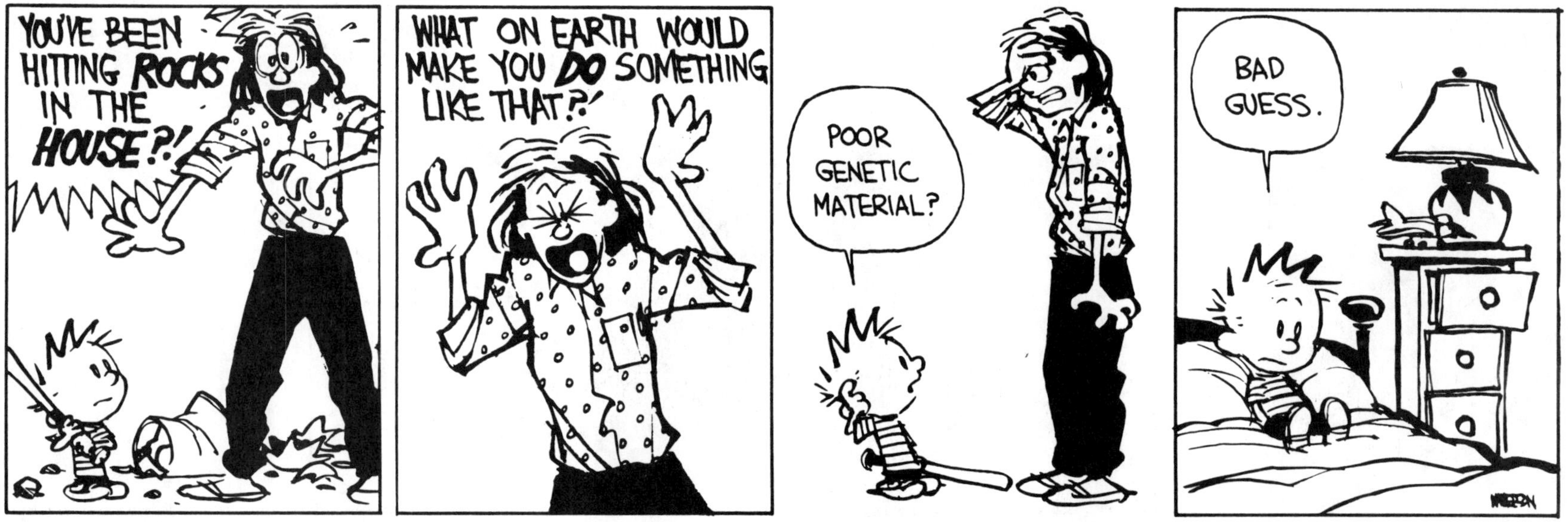
YOU'VE BEEN HITTING ROCKS IN THE HOUSE?!
WHAT ON EARTH WOULD MAKE YOU DO SOMETHING LIKE THAT?!
POOR GENETIC MATERIAL?
BAD GUESS.

WANT TO SEE A GREAT IDEA IN ACTION?

FIRST YOU DRINK HALF THE MILK IN YOUR THERMOS. THAT LEAVES ENOUGH ROOM SO YOU CAN WAD THE REST OF YOUR LUNCH IN THERE. SEE, HERE GOES MY JELLY SANDWICH AND A BANANA!

LET IT SOAK FOR A MINUTE, THEN SHAKE IT ALL UP INTO SLUDGE AND CHOKE IT DOWN! YOUR STOMACH WON'T KNOW THE DIFFERENCE, AND IT SAVES YOUR TEETH UNDUE WEAR AND TEAR!

NOBODY LIKES MY GREAT IDEAS IN ACTION.

I'D SAY I'VE HAD A PRETTY GOOD LIFE SO FAR.

IN FACT, LOOKING BACK, I HAVE ONLY ONE REGRET.

WHAT'S THAT?

I REGRET I WASN'T BORN WITH OPPOSABLE TOES.

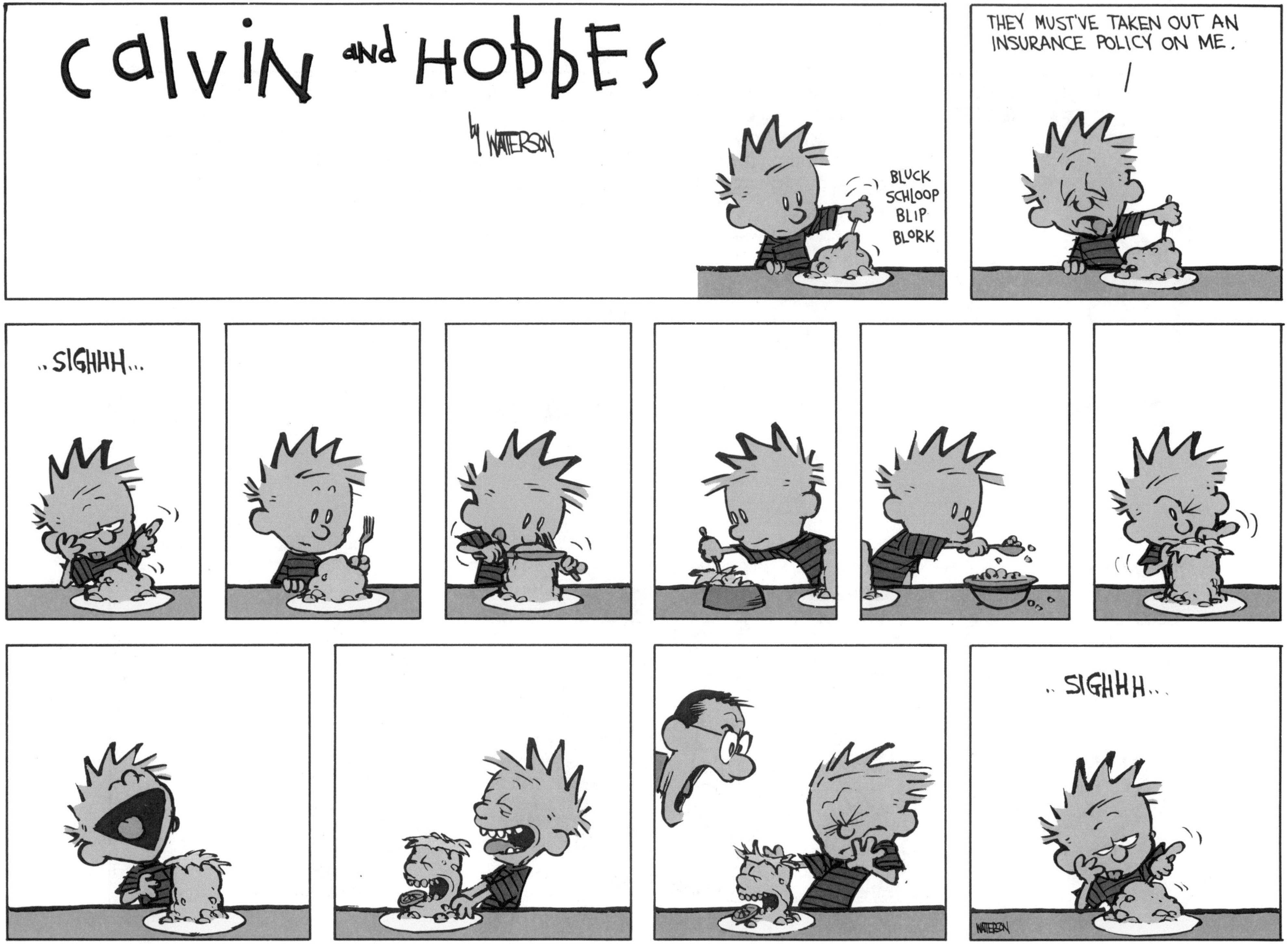

Calvin and HOBBES
by WATTERSON
BLUCK
SCHLOOP
BLIP
BLORK
THEY MUST'VE TAKEN OUT AN INSURANCE POLICY ON ME.
.. SIGHHH...
.. SIGHHH...
WATTERSON

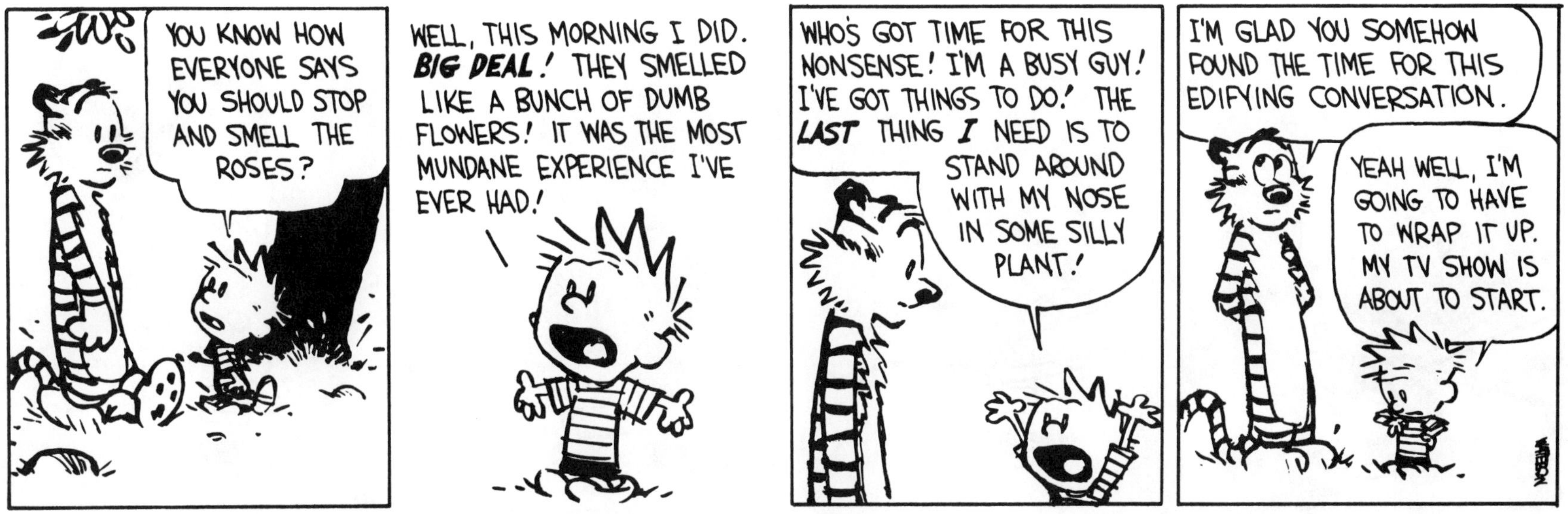
YOU KNOW HOW EVERYONE SAYS YOU SHOULD STOP AND SMELL THE ROSES?
WELL, THIS MORNING I DID. BIG DEAL! THEY SMELLED LIKE A BUNCH OF DUMB FLOWERS! IT WAS THE MOST MUNDANE EXPERIENCE I'VE EVER HAD!
WHO'S GOT TIME FOR THIS NONSENSE! I'M A BUSY GUY! I'VE GOT THINGS TO DO! THE LAST THING I NEED IS TO STAND AROUND WITH MY NOSE IN SOME SILLY PLANT!
I'M GLAD YOU SOMEHOW FOUND THE TIME FOR THIS EDIFYING CONVERSATION.
YEAH WELL, I'M GOING TO HAVE TO WRAP IT UP. MY TV SHOW IS ABOUT TO START.

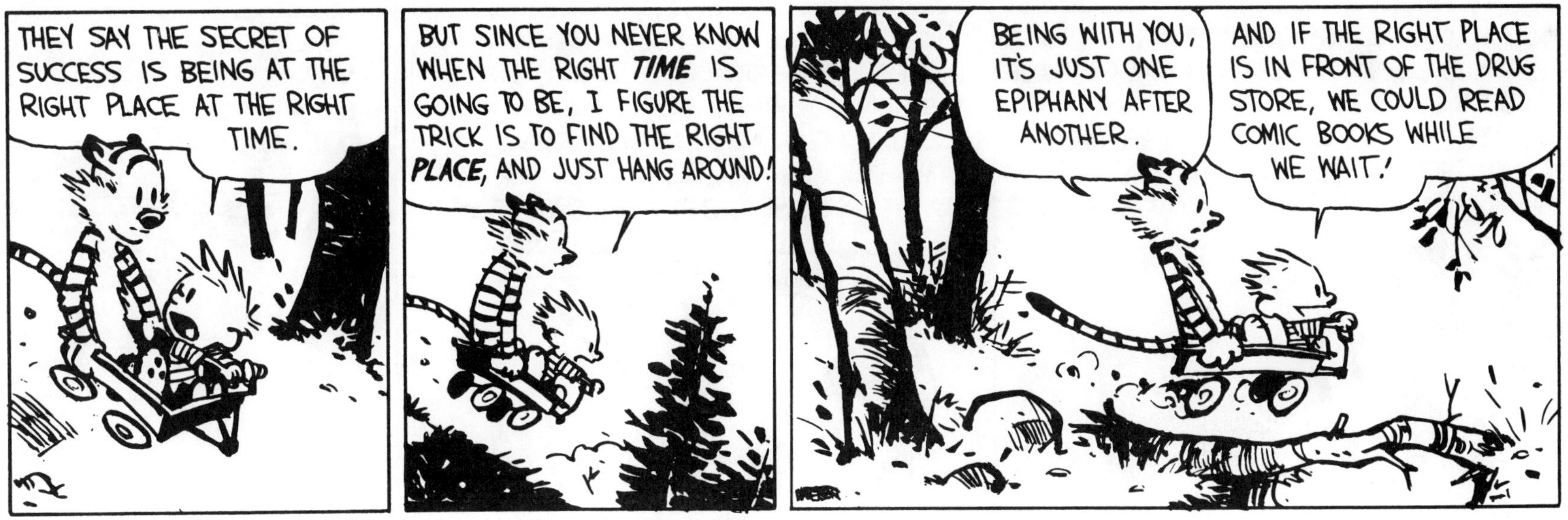
THEY SAY THE SECRET OF SUCCESS IS BEING AT THE RIGHT PLACE AT THE RIGHT TIME.
BUT SINCE YOU NEVER KNOW WHEN THE RIGHT TIME IS GOING TO BE, I FIGURE THE TRICK IS TO FIND THE RIGHT PLACE, AND JUST HANG AROUND!
BEING WITH YOU, IT'S JUST ONE EPIPHANY AFTER ANOTHER.
AND IF THE RIGHT PLACE IS IN FRONT OF THE DRUG STORE, WE COULD READ COMIC BOOKS WHILE WE WAIT!

ATTENTION! ALL RISE! THIS MEETING OF G.R.O.S.S. IS NOW CALLED TO ORDER BY THE GREAT GRANDIOSE DICTATOR-FOR-LIFE, THE RULER SUPREME, THE FEARLESS, THE BRAVE, THE HELD-HIGH-IN-ESTEEM, CALVIN THE BOLD! YES, STAND UP AND HAIL HIS HUMBLENESS NOW! MAY HIS WISDOM PREVAIL!
THREE CHEERS FOR FIRST TIGER AND EL PRESIDENTE, HOBBES, THE DELIGHT OF ALL COGNOSCENTI! HE'S SAVVY! HE HAS A PRODIGIOUS IQ, AND LOTS OF PANACHE, AS ALL TIGERS DO! IN HIS FANCY CHAPEAU, HE'S A LEADER WITH TASTE! MAY HIS ORDERS BE HEEDED AND HIS VIEWS BE EMBRACED!
YOU CAN TELL THIS IS A GREAT CLUB BY THE WAY WE START OUR MEETINGS!

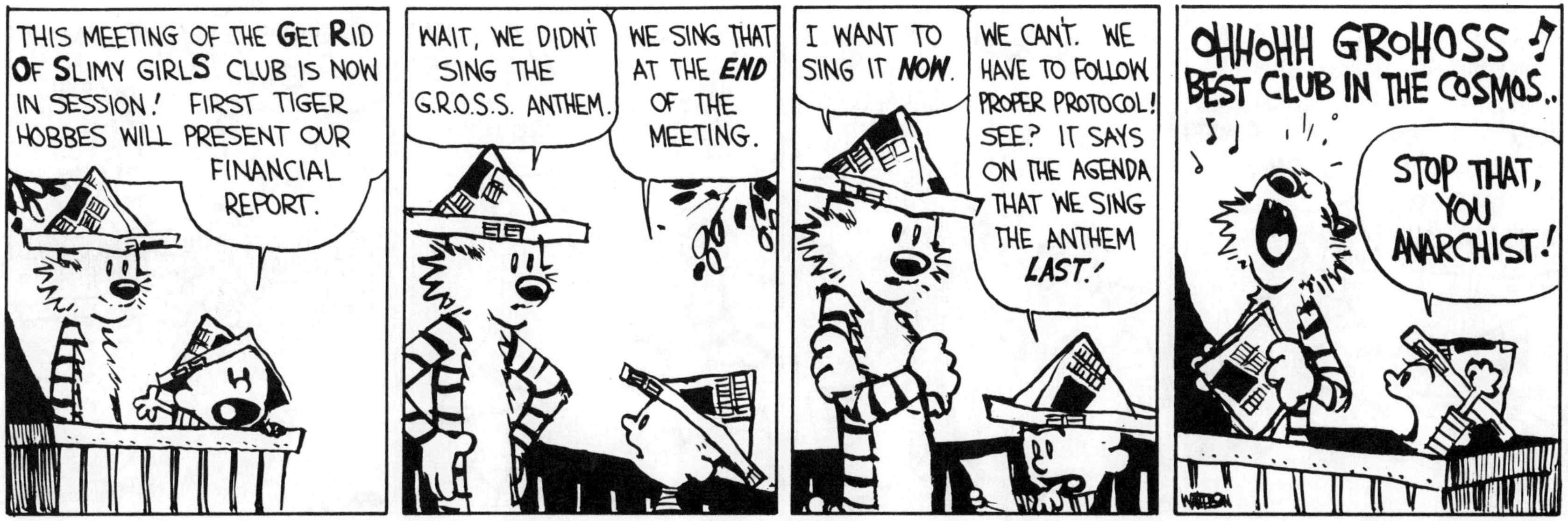
THIS MEETING OF THE GET RID OF SLIMY GIRLS CLUB IS NOW IN SESSION! FIRST TIGER HOBBES WILL PRESENT OUR FINANCIAL REPORT.
WAIT, WE DIDN'T SING THE G.R.O.S.S. ANTHEM.
WE SING THAT AT THE *END* OF THE MEETING.
I WANT TO SING IT *NOW*.
WE CAN'T. WE HAVE TO FOLLOW PROPER PROTOCOL! SEE? IT SAYS ON THE AGENDA THAT WE SING THE ANTHEM *LAST*!
OHHOHH GROHOSS ♪ BEST CLUB IN THE COSMOS..
STOP THAT, YOU ANARCHIST!

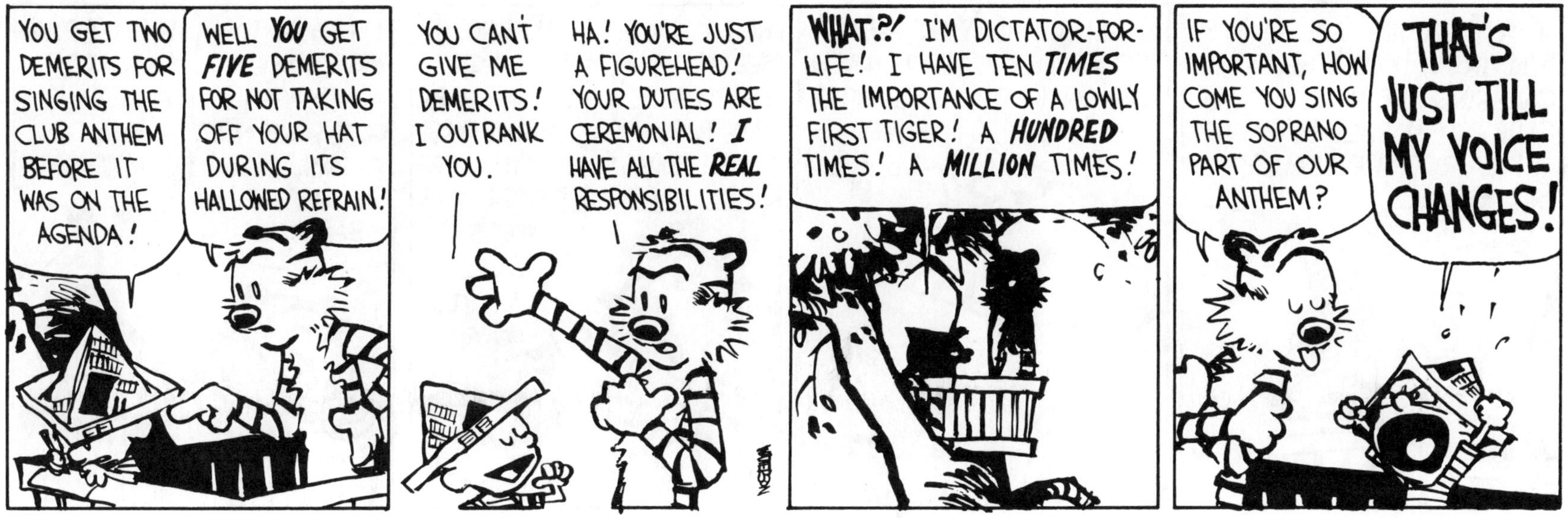
YOU GET TWO DEMERITS FOR SINGING THE CLUB ANTHEM BEFORE IT WAS ON THE AGENDA!
WELL *YOU* GET *FIVE* DEMERITS FOR NOT TAKING OFF YOUR HAT DURING ITS HALLOWED REFRAIN!
YOU CAN'T GIVE ME DEMERITS! I OUTRANK YOU.
HA! YOU'RE JUST A FIGUREHEAD! YOUR DUTIES ARE CEREMONIAL! *I* HAVE ALL THE *REAL* RESPONSIBILITIES!
WHAT?! I'M DICTATOR-FOR-LIFE! I HAVE TEN *TIMES* THE IMPORTANCE OF A LOWLY FIRST TIGER! A *HUNDRED* TIMES! A *MILLION* TIMES!
IF YOU'RE SO IMPORTANT, HOW COME YOU SING THE SOPRANO PART OF OUR ANTHEM?
THAT'S JUST TILL MY VOICE CHANGES!

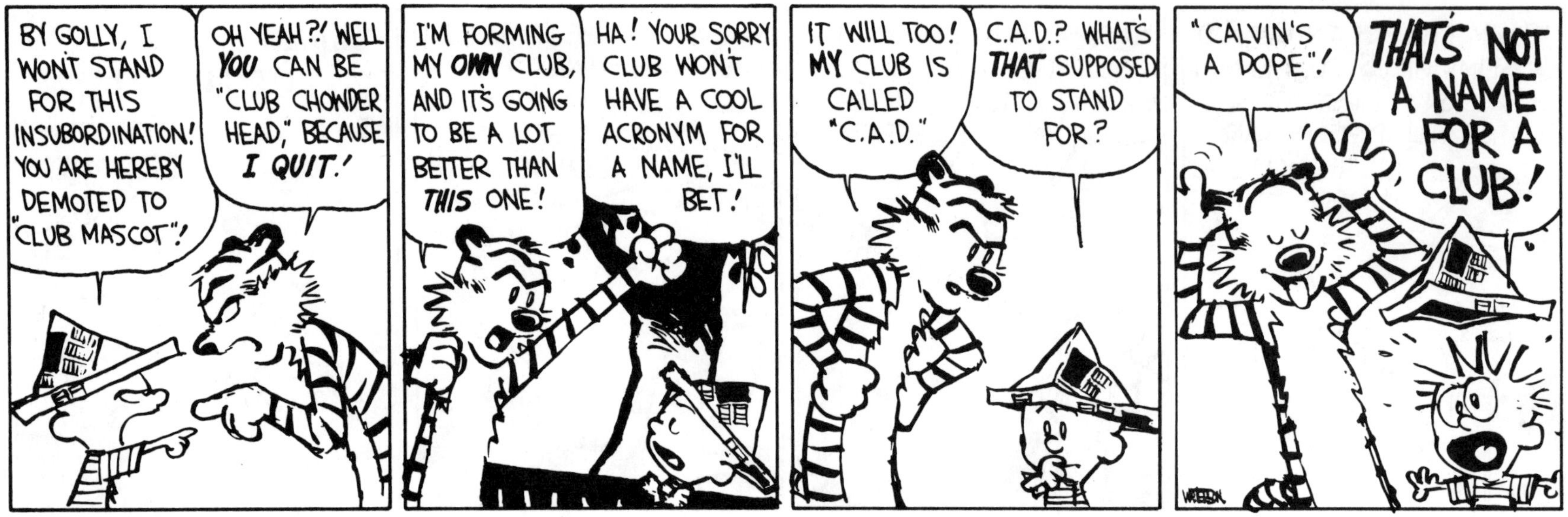
BY GOLLY, I WON'T STAND FOR THIS INSUBORDINATION! YOU ARE HEREBY DEMOTED TO "CLUB MASCOT"!
OH YEAH?! WELL YOU CAN BE "CLUB CHOWDER HEAD," BECAUSE I QUIT!
I'M FORMING MY OWN CLUB, AND IT'S GOING TO BE A LOT BETTER THAN THIS ONE!
HA! YOUR SORRY CLUB WON'T HAVE A COOL ACRONYM FOR A NAME, I'LL BET!
IT WILL TOO! MY CLUB IS CALLED "C.A.D."
C.A.D.? WHAT'S THAT SUPPOSED TO STAND FOR?
"CALVIN'S A DOPE"!
THAT'S NOT A NAME FOR A CLUB!

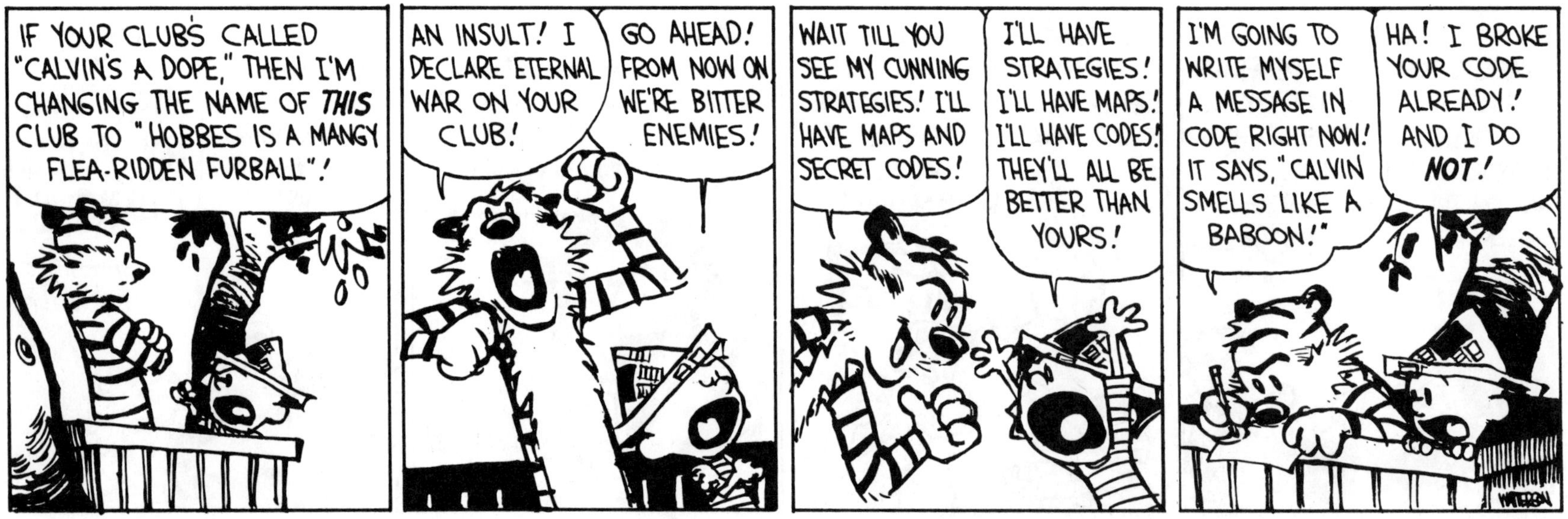
IF YOUR CLUB'S CALLED "CALVIN'S A DOPE," THEN I'M CHANGING THE NAME OF THIS CLUB TO "HOBBES IS A MANGY FLEA-RIDDEN FURBALL"!
AN INSULT! I DECLARE ETERNAL WAR ON YOUR CLUB!
GO AHEAD! FROM NOW ON WE'RE BITTER ENEMIES!
WAIT TILL YOU SEE MY CUNNING STRATEGIES! I'LL HAVE MAPS AND SECRET CODES!
I'LL HAVE STRATEGIES! I'LL HAVE MAPS! I'LL HAVE CODES! THEY'LL ALL BE BETTER THAN YOURS!
I'M GOING TO WRITE MYSELF A MESSAGE IN CODE RIGHT NOW! IT SAYS, "CALVIN SMELLS LIKE A BABOON!"
HA! I BROKE YOUR CODE ALREADY! AND I DO NOT!

WHEN YOU SEE HOW COOL MY CLUB IS, YOU'LL BEG TO BE IN IT, BUT I WON'T LET YOU!
WHO NEEDS YOUR STINKY CLUB?! I'VE GOT MY OWN CLUB!
MY CLUB DEDICATES ITSELF TO THE DESTRUCTION OF YOUR CLUB!
GOOD! IT'S A BATTLE TO THE FINISH! THIS IS TOTAL WAR!
OH YEAH? WE'LL SEE ABOUT THAT! WHAT? ONLY IN YOUR DREAMS, FUZZ FACE!
?
HEY CALVIN! WHO ARE YOU YELLING AT UP THERE?
YIKES! SHH! IT'S SUSIE!

HOBBES, IT'S SUSIE! SHE'S RIGHT UNDER US! IT'S THE CHANCE OF A LIFETIME! REAL SMOOTH, PASS THE BAG OF ROTTEN APPLES WE'VE BEEN SAVING! QUICK! QUICK!
WHAT ABOUT OUR WAR? I THOUGHT I WAS OUT OF THE CLUB!
ALL CHARGES ARE DROPPED! YOU'RE BACK IN! YOU'RE BACK IN!
MAYBE I WANT A PROMOTION FIRST.
IT'S YOURS! NAME IT! JUST GIVE ME THE MUSHY APPLES!
MUSHY APPLES? WHO ARE YOU TALKING TO?
SUSIE, DON'T MOVE, OK? STAY EXACTLY WHERE YOU ARE.

YAA! YAA! GET RID OF SLIMY GIRLS! HA HA!
OOH, IS SHE MAD AT YOU!
HA HA HA! OUR CLUB IS A SUCCESS!
I THINK SHE'S RUNNING OFF TO TELL ON US.
WHO CARES! IT WAS WORTH IT! WHAT A PERFECT PLAN!
TALK ABOUT SOMETHING WE'LL LOOK BACK ON WITH PRIDE IN OUR DECLINING YEARS!

SUSIE DERKINS SAYS YOU WERE THROWING MUSHY APPLES AT HER!
WE WERE GETTING RID OF SLIMY GIRLS! THAT'S OUR CLUB!
WELL **STOP** IT! YOU KNOW BETTER THAN THAT! I THINK YOU'D BETTER COME INSIDE.
YOU CAN TELL THIS IS A GREAT CLUB BECAUSE WE ALWAYS GET IN TROUBLE FOR FOLLOWING OUR CHARTER!

caLViN aND HObbEs by WATTERSON

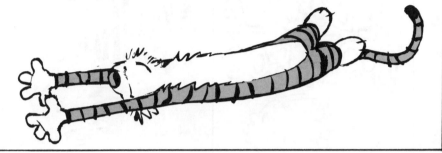

I'M HOOOAAGHHH!

AAAAAAAA!

IF YOU ACHE, IT'S BECAUSE YOU DON'T PROPERLY STRETCH BEFORE EXERCISING.

I DIDN'T KNOW I WAS GOING TO *BE* EXERCISING!!

17

oooOOEEE
EEBOOEE BOOEEBOO
WAHHHOOooo
THAT'S MY SIREN SO YOU KNOW I'M COMING!
KIDS DON'T **NEED** SIRENS.

WHEN A KID GROWS UP, HE HAS TO **BE** SOMETHING. HE CAN'T JUST STAY THE WAY HE IS.
BUT A TIGER GROWS UP AND STAYS A TIGER. WHY IS THAT?
NO ROOM FOR IMPROVEMENT.
OF ALL THE LUCK, MY PARENTS HAD TO BE HUMANS.
DON'T TAKE IT TOO HARD. HUMANS PROVIDE SOME VERY IMPORTANT PROTEIN.

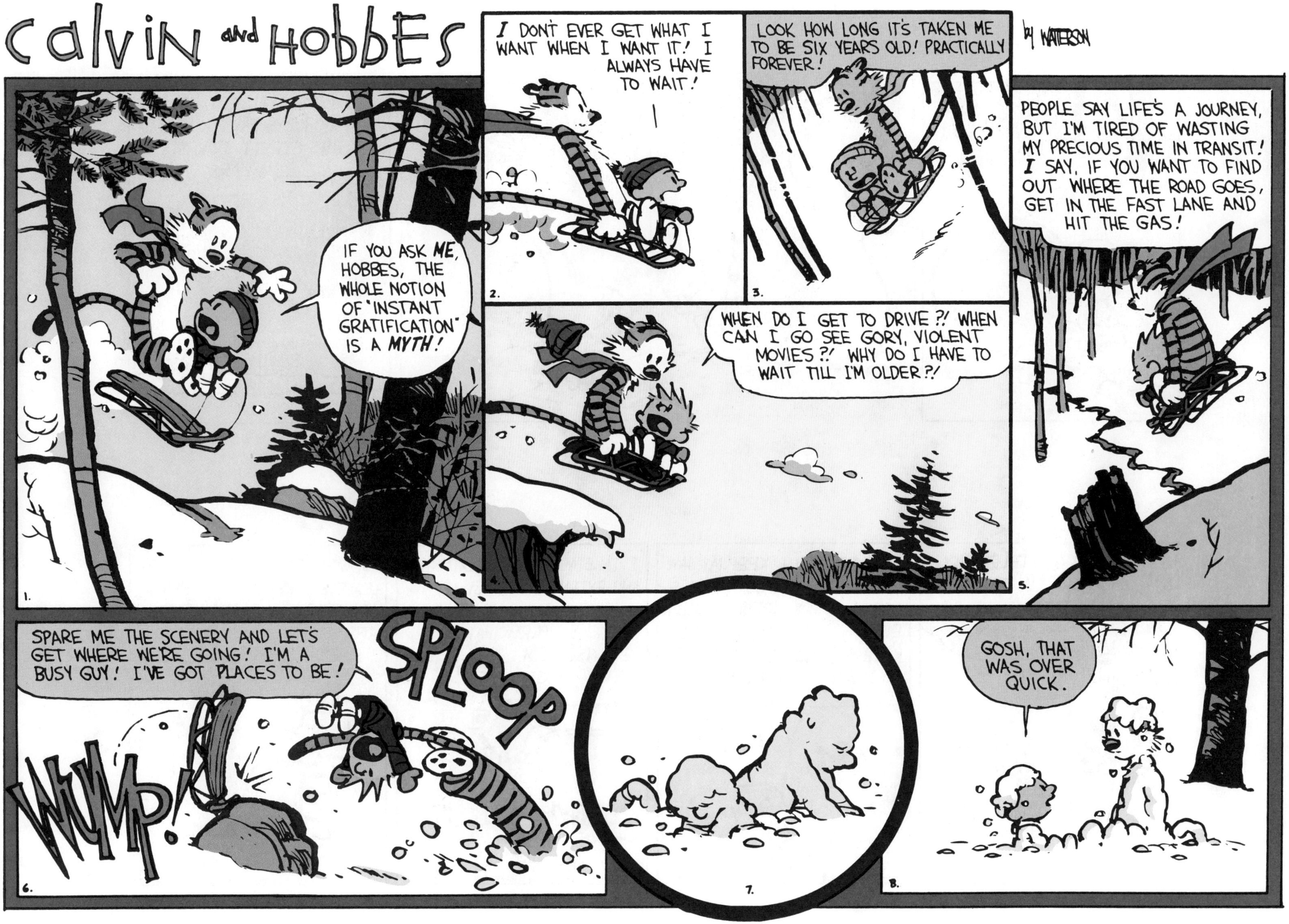

Calvin and Hobbes
by Watterson
IF YOU ASK ME, HOBBES, THE WHOLE NOTION OF "INSTANT GRATIFICATION" IS A MYTH!
I DON'T EVER GET WHAT I WANT WHEN I WANT IT! I ALWAYS HAVE TO WAIT!
LOOK HOW LONG IT'S TAKEN ME TO BE SIX YEARS OLD! PRACTICALLY FOREVER!
WHEN DO I GET TO DRIVE?! WHEN CAN I GO SEE GORY, VIOLENT MOVIES?! WHY DO I HAVE TO WAIT TILL I'M OLDER?!
PEOPLE SAY LIFE'S A JOURNEY, BUT I'M TIRED OF WASTING MY PRECIOUS TIME IN TRANSIT! I SAY, IF YOU WANT TO FIND OUT WHERE THE ROAD GOES, GET IN THE FAST LANE AND HIT THE GAS!
SPARE ME THE SCENERY AND LET'S GET WHERE WE'RE GOING! I'M A BUSY GUY! I'VE GOT PLACES TO BE!
SPLOOP
WUMP!
GOSH, THAT WAS OVER QUICK.

IT'S NO SURPRISE TO *ME* THAT NOBODY'S SOLD A HOUSE ON THIS STREET FOR SIX YEARS.

I TRY TO MAKE TELEVISION-WATCHING A COMPLETE FORFEITURE OF EXPERIENCE.
NOTICE HOW I KEEP MY JAW SLACK, SO MY MOUTH HANGS OPEN. I TRY NOT TO SWALLOW EITHER, SO I DROOL, AND I KEEP MY EYES HALF-FOCUSED, SO I DON'T USE ANY MUSCLES AT ALL.
I TAKE A PASSIVE ENTERTAINMENT AND EXTEND THE PASSIVITY TO MY ENTIRE BEING. I WALLOW IN MY LACK OF PARTICIPATION AND RESPONSE. I'M UTTERLY INERT.
I'M GOING TO LEAVE BEFORE YOU START ATTRACTING FLIES.
I CAN ALMOST FEEL MY NEURAL TRANSMITTERS SHUTTING DOWN.

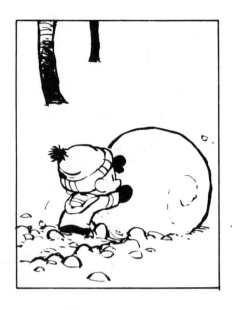

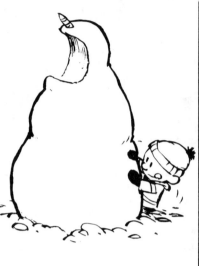

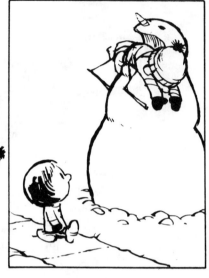

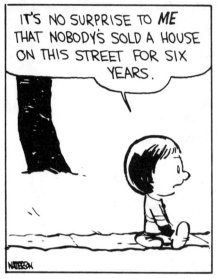

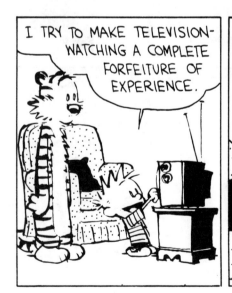

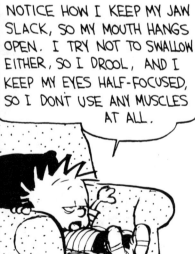

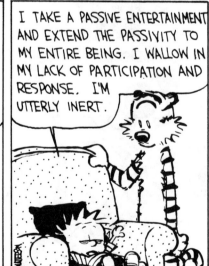

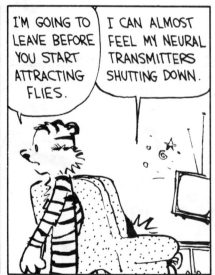

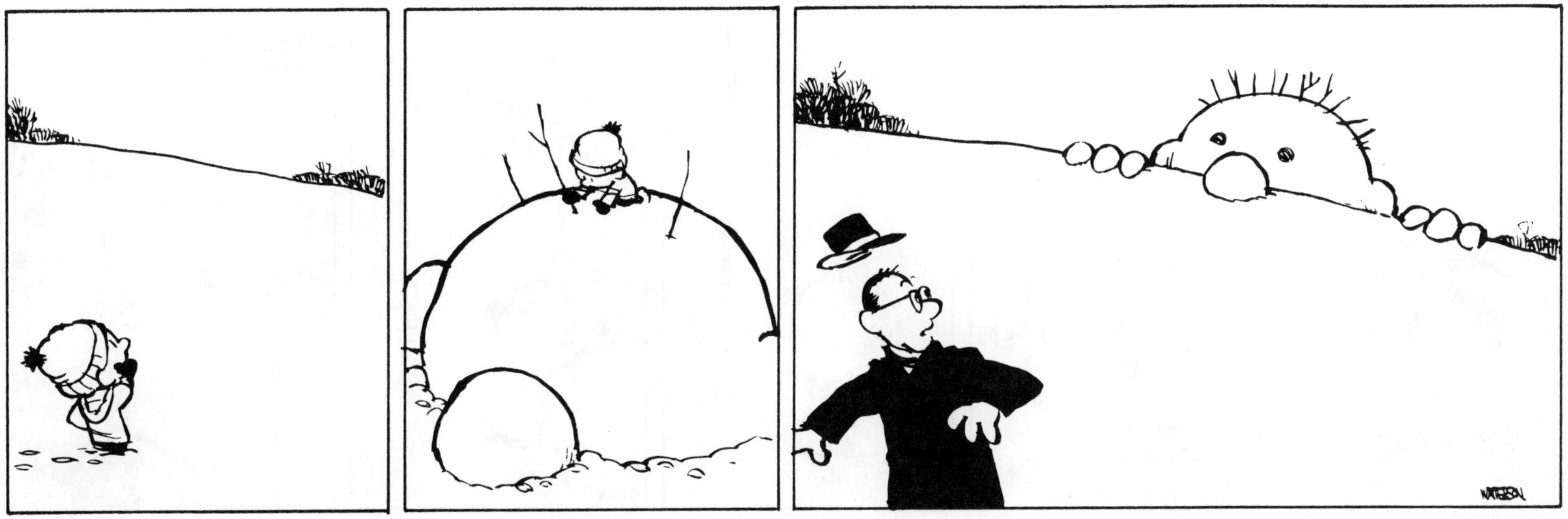

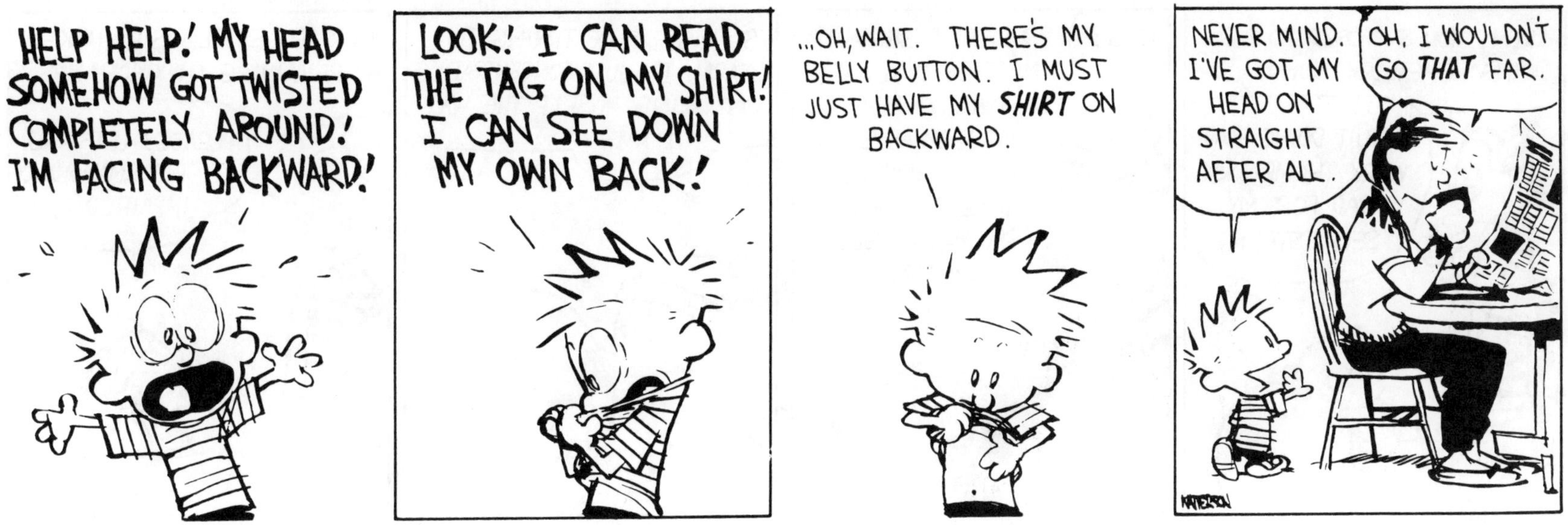
HELP HELP! MY HEAD SOMEHOW GOT TWISTED COMPLETELY AROUND! I'M FACING BACKWARD!
LOOK! I CAN READ THE TAG ON MY SHIRT! I CAN SEE DOWN MY OWN BACK!
...OH, WAIT. THERE'S MY BELLY BUTTON. I MUST JUST HAVE MY SHIRT ON BACKWARD.
NEVER MIND. I'VE GOT MY HEAD ON STRAIGHT AFTER ALL.
OH, I WOULDN'T GO THAT FAR.

PULL
PULL
OH SURE! NICE TRY!
PULL
WATTERSON
DARN, DARN, DARN DARN, DARN!

AREN'T YOU SUPPOSED TO BE DOING HOMEWORK NOW?
I QUIT DOING HOMEWORK. HOMEWORK IS BAD FOR MY SELF-ESTEEM.
IT IS?
SURE! IT SENDS THE MESSAGE THAT I DON'T KNOW ENOUGH! ALL THAT EMPHASIS ON RIGHT ANSWERS MAKES ME FEEL BAD WHEN I GET THEM WRONG.
SO INSTEAD OF TRYING TO LEARN, I'M JUST CONCENTRATING ON LIKING MYSELF THE WAY I AM.
YOUR SELF-ESTEEM IS ENHANCED BY REMAINING AN IGNORAMUS?
PLEASE! LET'S CALL IT "INFORMATIONALLY IMPAIRED."
WATTERSON

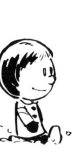

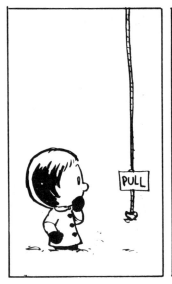

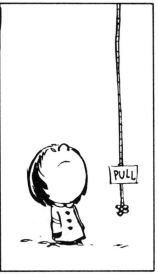

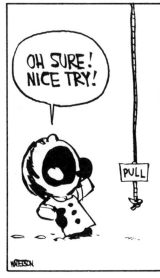

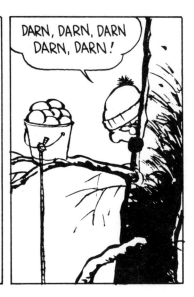

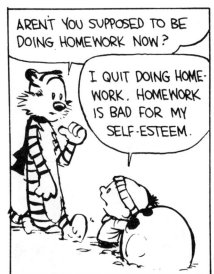

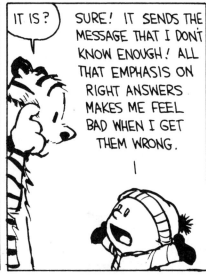

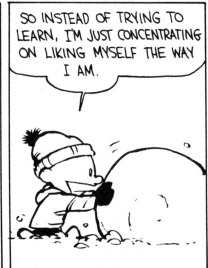

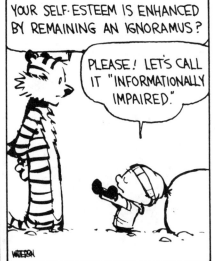

SEE, HOBBES, WE SHOULDN'T NEED ACCOMPLISHMENTS TO FEEL GOOD ABOUT OURSELVES. SELF-ESTEEM SHOULDN'T BE CONDITIONAL.

THAT'S WHY I'VE STOPPED DOING HOMEWORK. I DON'T NEED TO LEARN THINGS TO LIKE MYSELF. I'M FINE THE WAY I AM.

SO THE SECRET TO GOOD SELF-ESTEEM IS TO LOWER YOUR EXPECTATIONS TO THE POINT WHERE THEY'RE ALREADY MET?

RIGHT. WE SHOULD TAKE *PRIDE* IN OUR MEDIOCRITY.

REMIND ME TO INVEST OVERSEAS.

I THINK THIS SNOWMAN IS GOOD ENOUGH, DON'T YOU?

LOOK, DAD MADE ME DO MY HOMEWORK!

HE SAID, WHEN I'M OLDER, I'LL DISCOVER THAT THERE ARE FEW PLEASURES GREATER THAN LEARNING.

SO I SAID, *FINE*, I'LL LEARN WHEN I'M *OLDER!*

WHAT DID *HE* SAY?

HE SAID, IF I DIDN'T START CRACKING BOOKS *NOW*, THIS WOULD BE AS OLD AS I'D GET.

SOUNDS LIKE YOU LEARNED SOMETHING ALREADY.

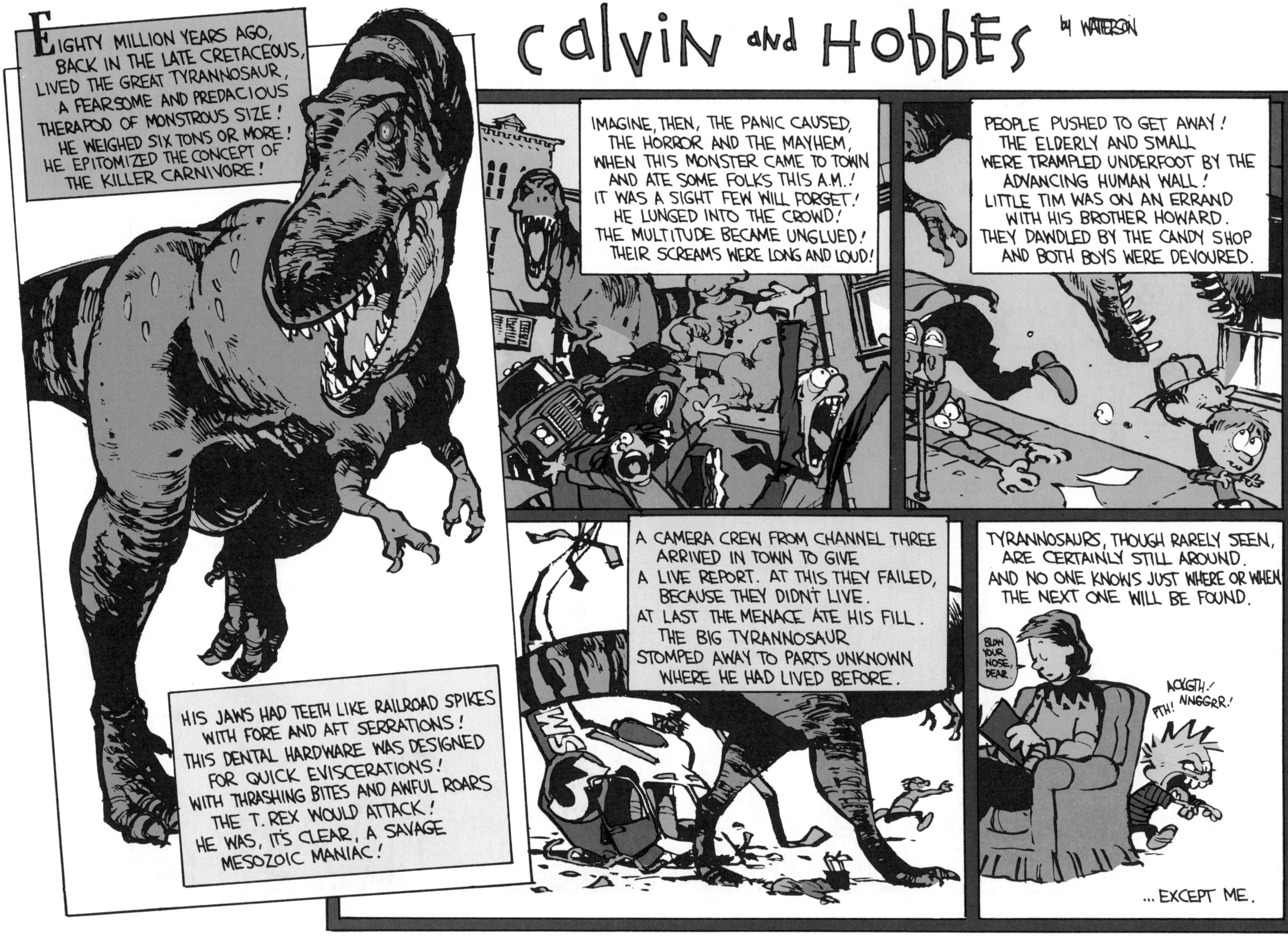
Calvin and Hobbes
by Watterson
EIGHTY MILLION YEARS AGO, BACK IN THE LATE CRETACEOUS, LIVED THE GREAT TYRANNOSAUR, A FEARSOME AND PREDACIOUS THERAPOD OF MONSTROUS SIZE! HE WEIGHED SIX TONS OR MORE! HE EPITOMIZED THE CONCEPT OF THE KILLER CARNIVORE!
HIS JAWS HAD TEETH LIKE RAILROAD SPIKES WITH FORE AND AFT SERRATIONS! THIS DENTAL HARDWARE WAS DESIGNED FOR QUICK EVISCERATIONS! WITH THRASHING BITES AND AWFUL ROARS THE T. REX WOULD ATTACK! HE WAS, IT'S CLEAR, A SAVAGE MESOZOIC MANIAC!
IMAGINE, THEN, THE PANIC CAUSED, THE HORROR AND THE MAYHEM, WHEN THIS MONSTER CAME TO TOWN AND ATE SOME FOLKS THIS A.M.! IT WAS A SIGHT FEW WILL FORGET! HE LUNGED INTO THE CROWD! THE MULTITUDE BECAME UNGLUED! THEIR SCREAMS WERE LONG AND LOUD!
PEOPLE PUSHED TO GET AWAY! THE ELDERLY AND SMALL WERE TRAMPLED UNDERFOOT BY THE ADVANCING HUMAN WALL! LITTLE TIM WAS ON AN ERRAND WITH HIS BROTHER HOWARD. THEY DAWDLED BY THE CANDY SHOP AND BOTH BOYS WERE DEVOURED.
A CAMERA CREW FROM CHANNEL THREE ARRIVED IN TOWN TO GIVE A LIVE REPORT. AT THIS THEY FAILED, BECAUSE THEY DIDN'T LIVE. AT LAST THE MENACE ATE HIS FILL. THE BIG TYRANNOSAUR STOMPED AWAY TO PARTS UNKNOWN WHERE HE HAD LIVED BEFORE.
TYRANNOSAURS, THOUGH RARELY SEEN, ARE CERTAINLY STILL AROUND. AND NO ONE KNOWS JUST WHERE OR WHEN THE NEXT ONE WILL BE FOUND.
BLOW YOUR NOSE, DEAR.
PTH! ACKGTH! NNGGRR!
... EXCEPT ME.

MOM AND DAD DRIVE ME CRAZY.

THEY DON'T UNDERSTAND *ME* AND I DON'T UNDERSTAND *THEM.* IT'S HOPELESS!

I'M RELATED TO PEOPLE I DON'T RELATE TO.

HERE WE STAND, PEERING DOWN THE DIZZYING DEPTHS OF DOOM DROP! DO WE TURN AROUND AND RETREAT TO THE STUPEFYING SECURITY OF HOME AND HEARTH?

OR DO WE BRAVE THE DESCENT, RISK DEMISE, AND EXPERIENCE THE FLOOD OF SOMATIC SENSATION THAT SCREAMS WE ARE ALIVE, GLORIOUSLY ALIVE, HOWEVER TEMPORARILY??

...HOBBES?

I THOUGHT THE QUESTION WAS RHETORICAL. THE OTHER WAY, THOUGH!

HERE'S THE LATEST POLL ON YOUR STANDING AS "DAD."

WONDERFUL.

THE GOOD NEWS IS THAT YOU HAVE A HIGH NAME-RECOGNITION FACTOR. ALL THE HOUSEHOLD SIX-YEAR-OLDS POLLED WERE ABLE TO IDENTIFY YOU AS "DAD."

THIS RECOGNITION, HOWEVER, IS LINKED TO THE FACT THAT YOUR POLICIES ARE UNIVERSALLY DEPLORED. THERE'S TALK ABOUT VOTING YOU OUT OF OFFICE AND MAKING MOM "DAD."

I SEE. AND WHAT DO *YOU* KNOW ABOUT THIS?

MY FIRST ACT WILL BE TO MAKE YOU DO THE COOKING.

WHOA! THAT CHANGES EVERYTHING!

DAD'S CALLING YOU.

HE WASN'T? HUH! WELL, HOBBES TOOK YOUR CHAIR. SORRY.

I LIKE MY CHAIRS PRE-WARMED.

YOU OWE ME.

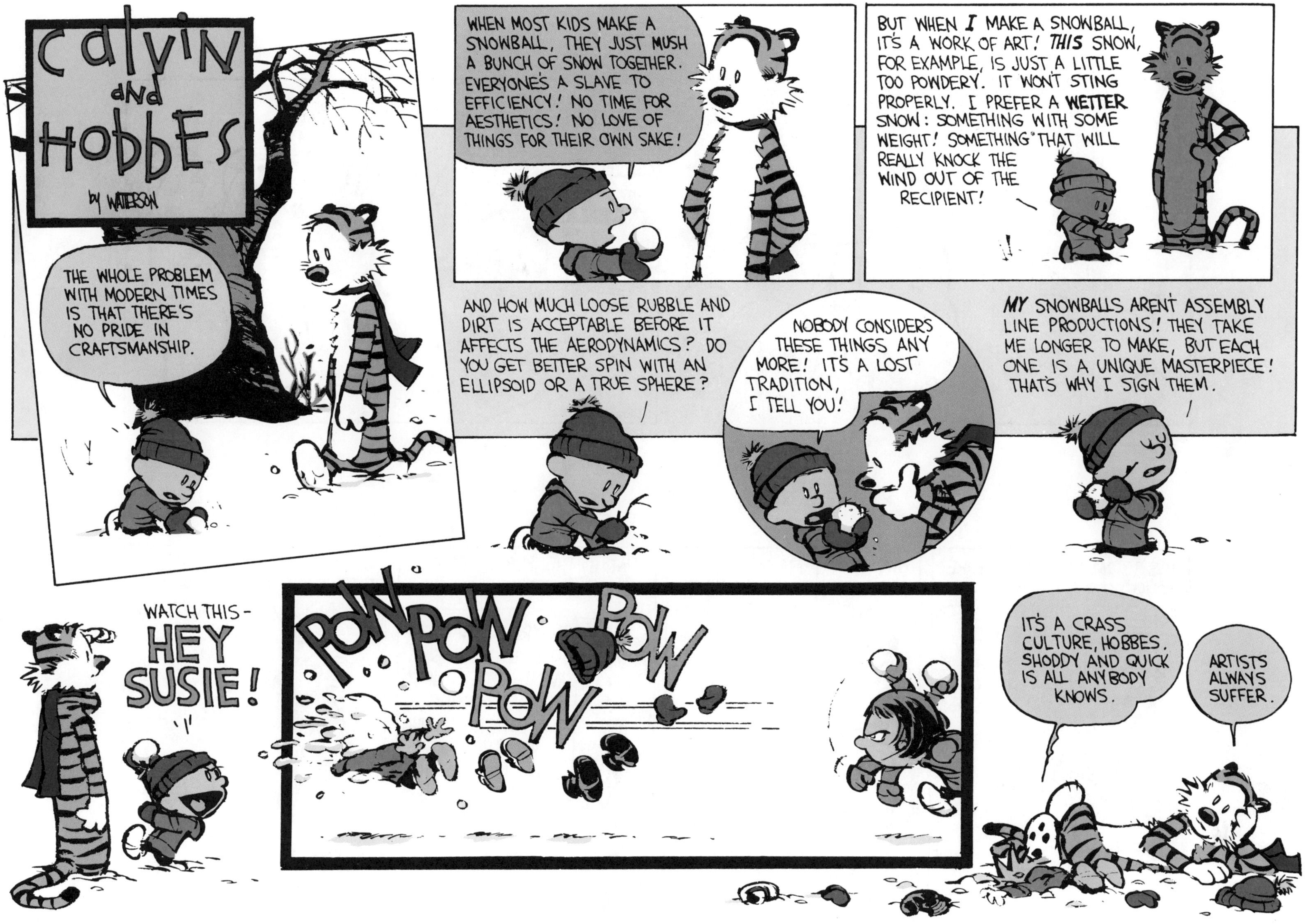
Calvin and Hobbes
by WATTERSON
THE WHOLE PROBLEM WITH MODERN TIMES IS THAT THERE'S NO PRIDE IN CRAFTSMANSHIP.
WHEN MOST KIDS MAKE A SNOWBALL, THEY JUST MUSH A BUNCH OF SNOW TOGETHER. EVERYONE'S A SLAVE TO EFFICIENCY! NO TIME FOR AESTHETICS! NO LOVE OF THINGS FOR THEIR OWN SAKE!
BUT WHEN I MAKE A SNOWBALL, IT'S A WORK OF ART! THIS SNOW, FOR EXAMPLE, IS JUST A LITTLE TOO POWDERY. IT WON'T STING PROPERLY. I PREFER A WETTER SNOW: SOMETHING WITH SOME WEIGHT! SOMETHING THAT WILL REALLY KNOCK THE WIND OUT OF THE RECIPIENT!
AND HOW MUCH LOOSE RUBBLE AND DIRT IS ACCEPTABLE BEFORE IT AFFECTS THE AERODYNAMICS? DO YOU GET BETTER SPIN WITH AN ELLIPSOID OR A TRUE SPHERE?
NOBODY CONSIDERS THESE THINGS ANY MORE! IT'S A LOST TRADITION, I TELL YOU!
MY SNOWBALLS AREN'T ASSEMBLY LINE PRODUCTIONS! THEY TAKE ME LONGER TO MAKE, BUT EACH ONE IS A UNIQUE MASTERPIECE! THAT'S WHY I SIGN THEM.
WATCH THIS - HEY SUSIE!
POW POW POW POW
IT'S A CRASS CULTURE, HOBBES. SHODDY AND QUICK IS ALL ANYBODY KNOWS.
ARTISTS ALWAYS SUFFER.

HE KNOWS I HATE THIS.

THIS IS MY SNOW SCULPTURE, "BOURGEOIS BUFFOON." CAN YOU BELIEVE MOM REJECTED MY GRANT APPLICATION TO CONTINUE MAKING THESE?
WHY DO YOU NEED A GRANT?
I'M ON THE CUTTING EDGE OF ART! MY WORK DESERVES PUBLIC SUPPORT!
WHAT IF THE PUBLIC DOESN'T LIKE YOUR WORK?
THEY'RE NOT SUPPOSED TO LIKE IT! THIS IS AVANT-GARDE STUFF! I'M CRITICIZING THE LOWBROWS WHO CAN'T APPRECIATE GREAT ART LIKE THIS!
BUT YOU'LL TAKE THEIR MONEY.
WHAT DO YOU WANT ME TO DO, SUFFER?!

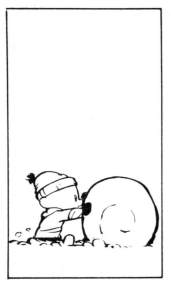

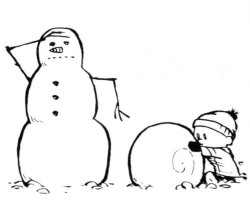

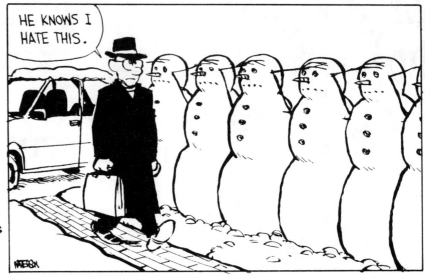

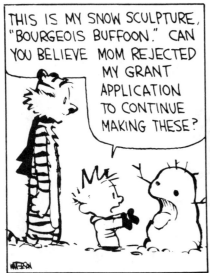

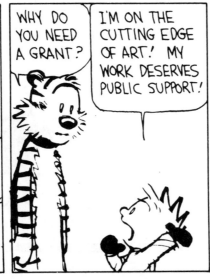

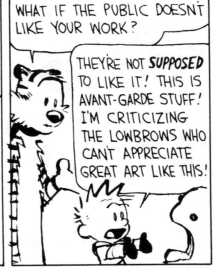

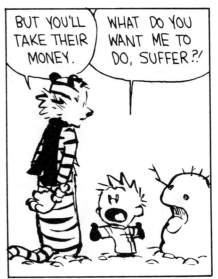

THIS SNOWMAN DOESN'T LOOK ESPECIALLY AVANT-GARDE.

ACTUALLY IT'S **VERY** AVANT-GARDE.

THIS IS MY NEW ART MOVEMENT, "NEO-REGIONALISM." I'M APPEALING TO POPULAR NOSTALGIA FOR THE SIMPLE VALUES OF RURAL AMERICA 50 YEARS AGO.

I FIGURE THE PUBLIC WILL EAT THIS UP AND I'LL MAKE A FORTUNE.

SO HOW IS THIS AVANT-GARDE?

IT'S SECRETLY IRONIC.

I'VE CONCLUDED THAT NOTHING BAD I DO IS MY FAULT.

OH?

RIGHT! BEING YOUNG AND IMPRESSIONABLE, I'M THE HELPLESS VICTIM OF COUNTLESS BAD INFLUENCES! AN UNWHOLESOME CULTURE PANDERS TO MY UNDEVELOPED VALUES AND PUSHES ME TO MALEFICENCE.

I TAKE NO RESPONSIBILITY FOR MY BEHAVIOR! I'M AN INNOCENT PAWN! IT'S SOCIETY'S FAULT!

THEN YOU NEED TO BUILD MORE CHARACTER. GO SHOVEL THE WALK.

THESE DISCUSSIONS NEVER GO WHERE THEY'RE SUPPOSED TO.

I SEE YOU WITH THAT SNOWBALL!
GO AHEAD AND THROW IT! I'M NOT SCARED! YOU COULDN'T HIT THE SIDE OF A BARN! C'MON, THROW IT! I DARE YOU!
POW!!
SERIOUSLY, YOU COULD NEVER HAVE DONE THAT IF MY TAUNTS HADN'T BOOSTED YOUR ADRENALIN.
I CAN ONLY FIND ONE OF YOUR SOCKS.

I READ THAT TEDDY ROOSEVELT ONCE SAID, "DO WHAT YOU CAN WITH WHAT YOU HAVE WHERE YOU ARE."
THAT'S GOOD ADVICE.
OF COURSE, I DOUBT HE WAS IN THE TUB WHEN HE SAID THAT.

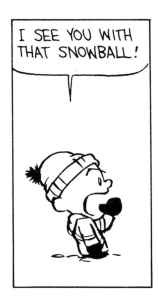

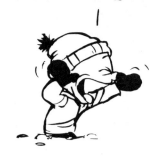

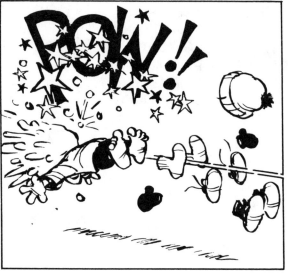

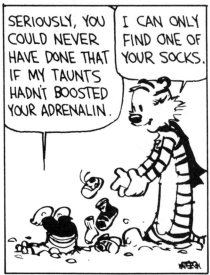

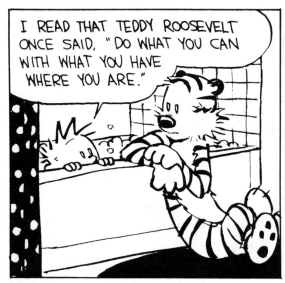

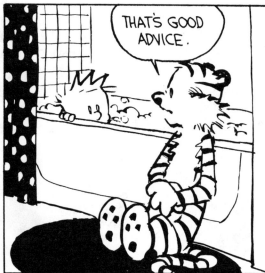

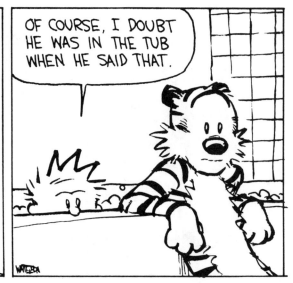

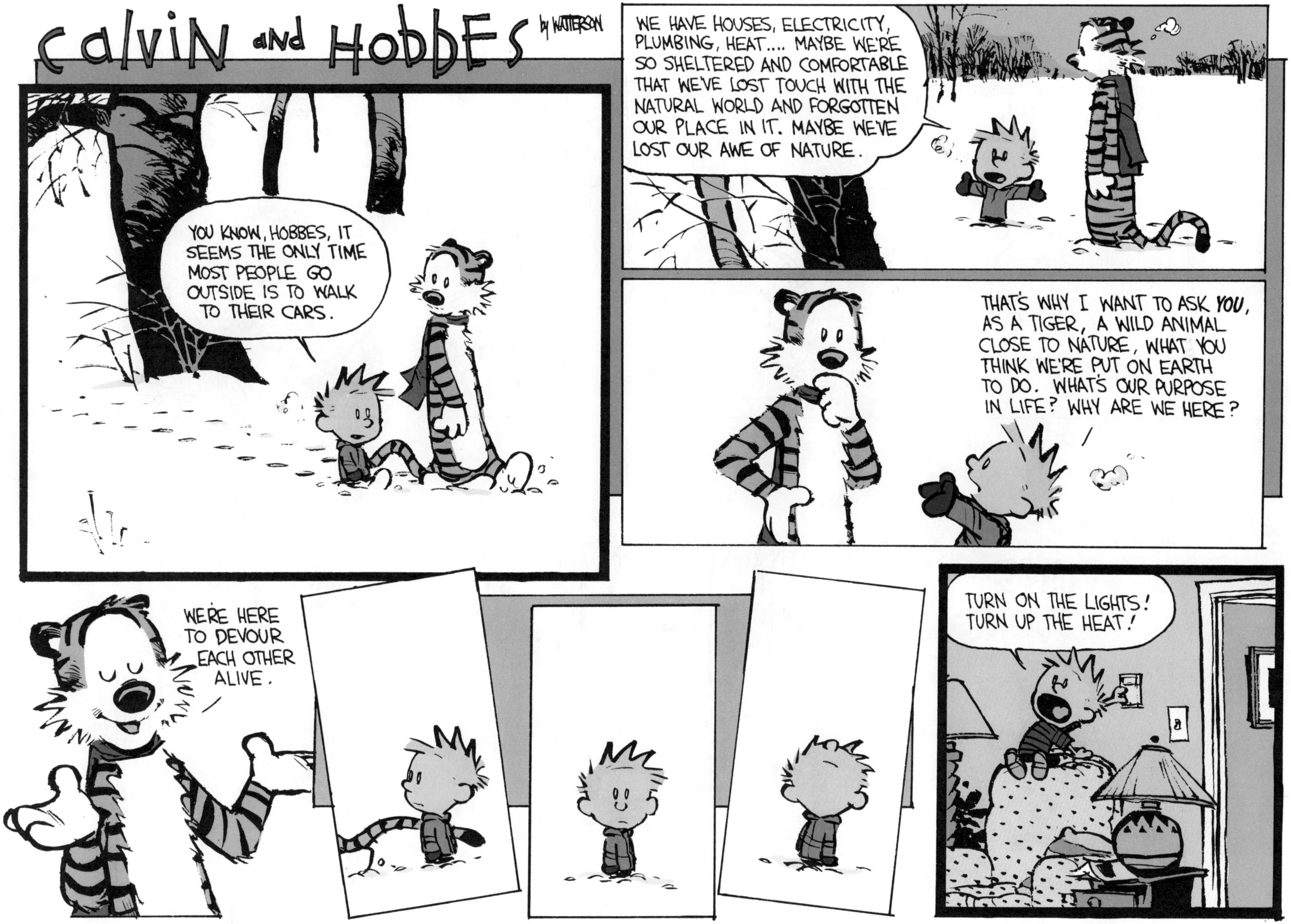
Calvin and Hobbes
by WATTERSON
YOU KNOW, HOBBES, IT SEEMS THE ONLY TIME MOST PEOPLE GO OUTSIDE IS TO WALK TO THEIR CARS.
WE HAVE HOUSES, ELECTRICITY, PLUMBING, HEAT.... MAYBE WE'RE SO SHELTERED AND COMFORTABLE THAT WE'VE LOST TOUCH WITH THE NATURAL WORLD AND FORGOTTEN OUR PLACE IN IT. MAYBE WE'VE LOST OUR AWE OF NATURE.
THAT'S WHY I WANT TO ASK YOU, AS A TIGER, A WILD ANIMAL CLOSE TO NATURE, WHAT YOU THINK WE'RE PUT ON EARTH TO DO. WHAT'S OUR PURPOSE IN LIFE? WHY ARE WE HERE?
WE'RE HERE TO DEVOUR EACH OTHER ALIVE.
TURN ON THE LIGHTS! TURN UP THE HEAT!

SHOVEL THE WALK! SHOVEL THE WALK! THAT'S ALL I'M GOOD FOR AROUND HERE.

WHAT ABOUT MY POWERFUL INTELLECT?! MY BUDDING GENIUS IS BEING SQUANDERED! I ASPIRE TO MORE THAN BRUTE SLAVE LABOR!

THESE HANDS! THESE AMAZING HANDS ARE DESTINED TO CREATE UNDREAMT-OF WONDERS, YET HERE THEY'RE WORN TO THE BONE IN UNFULFILLING DRUDGERY! WHAT A MONSTROUS INJUSTICE!

GEEZ, DON'T TELL ME LUNCH ISN'T READY!

DING DONG

YOU REALLY NEED PROFESSIONAL HELP.

WHAT MAKES YOU THINK *I* DID IT??

WHAT'S WRONG WITH EASTER ISLAND? I **LIKE** EASTER ISLAND.
WATERSON

HELLO, IS THIS THE HARDWARE STORE? YES, I'M WONDERING IF YOU SELL CATAPULTS.
NO?? WELL, I'M LOOKING FOR SOMETHING THAT CAN DELIVER A 50-POUND PAYLOAD OF SNOW ON A SMALL FEMININE TARGET. CAN YOU SUGGEST SOMETHING?
HELLO?
I DON'T UNDERSTAND HOW SOME OF THESE PLACES STAY IN BUSINESS.
WATERSON

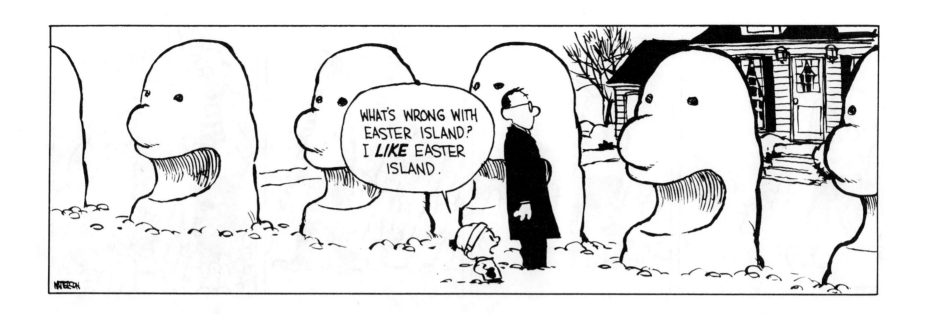

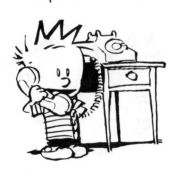

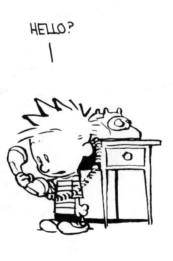

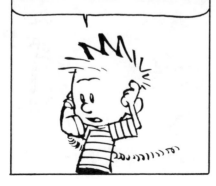

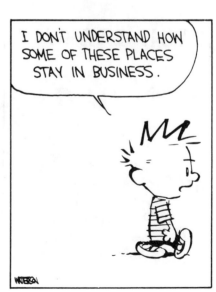

I DON'T THINK YOU HAVE ENOUGH TO DO.

I WON! I DID IT! I WON! I WON!
I'M THE CHAMPION! I'M THE BEST THERE IS! I'M THE TOP OF THE HEAP! HA HA HA!
IS THIS ALL THERE IS??

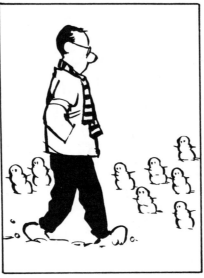

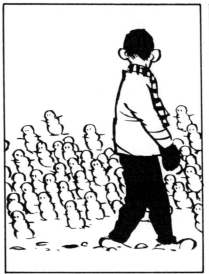

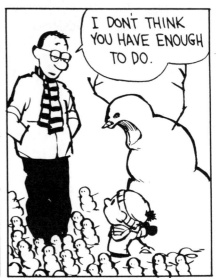

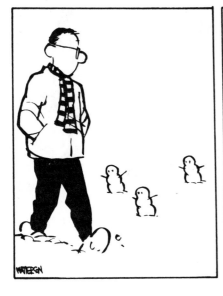

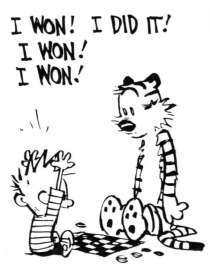

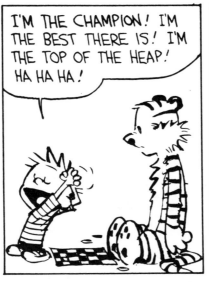

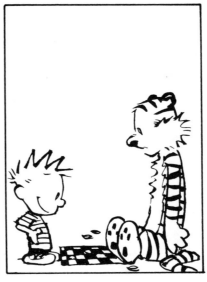

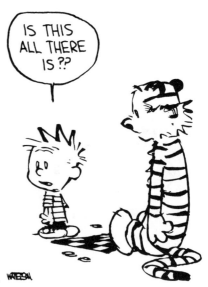

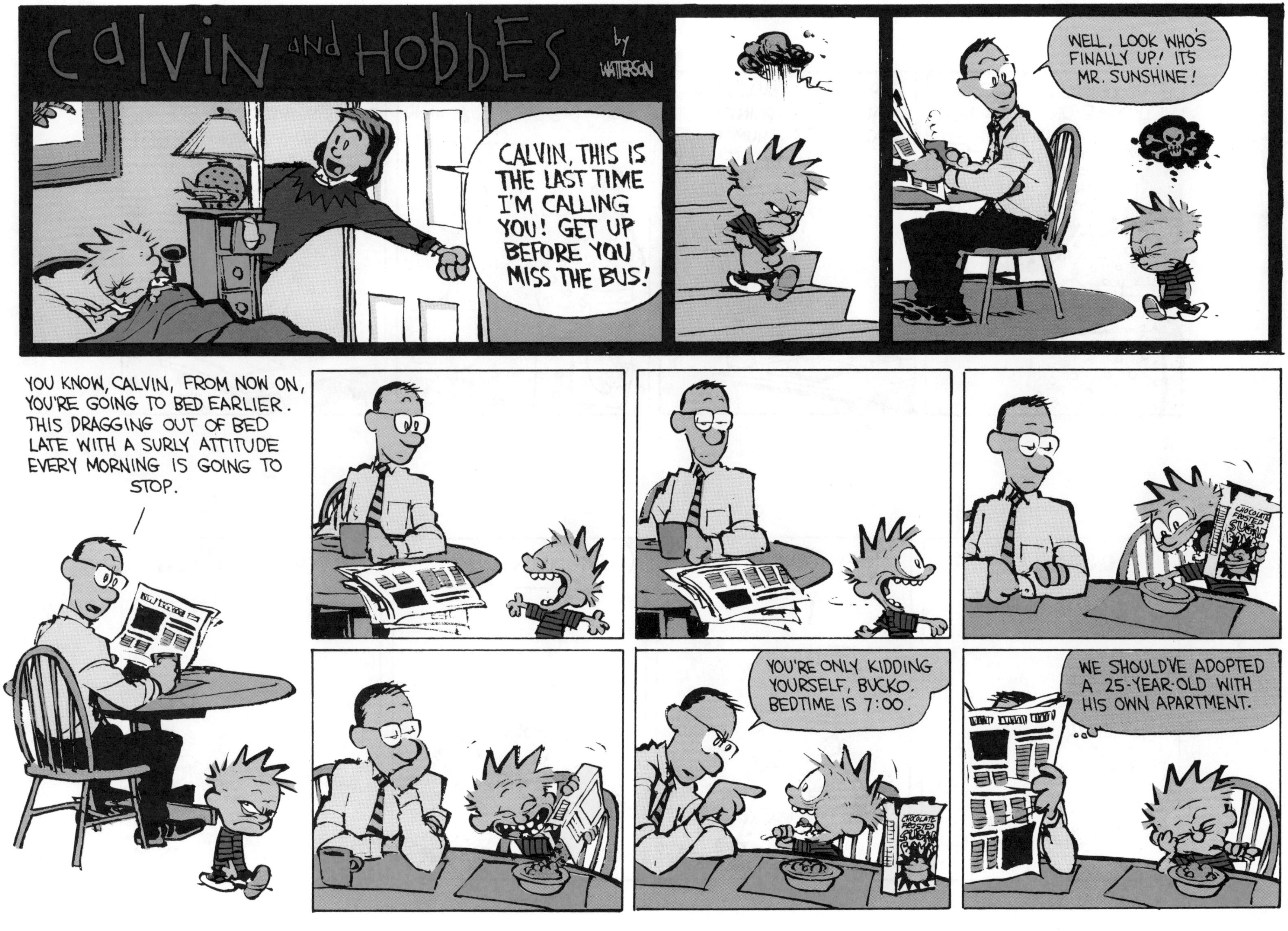
Calvin and Hobbes
by WATTERSON
CALVIN, THIS IS THE LAST TIME I'M CALLING YOU! GET UP BEFORE YOU MISS THE BUS!
WELL, LOOK WHO'S FINALLY UP! IT'S MR. SUNSHINE!
YOU KNOW, CALVIN, FROM NOW ON, YOU'RE GOING TO BED EARLIER. THIS DRAGGING OUT OF BED LATE WITH A SURLY ATTITUDE EVERY MORNING IS GOING TO STOP.
CHOCOLATE FROSTED SUGAR BOMBS
YOU'RE ONLY KIDDING YOURSELF, BUCKO. BEDTIME IS 7:00.
WE SHOULD'VE ADOPTED A 25-YEAR-OLD WITH HIS OWN APARTMENT.

IF THERE ARE NO QUESTIONS, WE'LL MOVE ON TO THE NEXT CHAPTER.
I HAVE A QUESTION.
CERTAINLY, CALVIN. WHAT IS IT?
WHAT'S THE POINT OF HUMAN EXISTENCE?
I MEANT ANY QUESTIONS ABOUT THE SUBJECT AT HAND.
OH.
FRANKLY, I'D LIKE TO HAVE THE ISSUE RESOLVED BEFORE I EXPEND ANY MORE ENERGY ON THIS.

EWWW.
EWWWW.
SCHLOOP
PLITCH
BLOP
EWWWWWW.
PLIP
PLOOP
PLOP
EWWWWWWW!
PLUBLIPTHH
THWIPP
PLUP

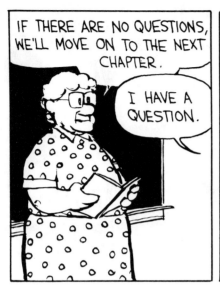

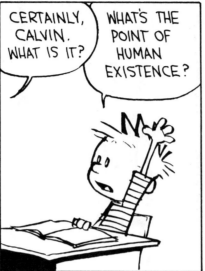

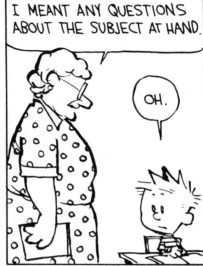

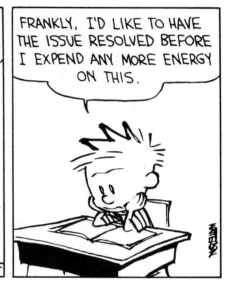

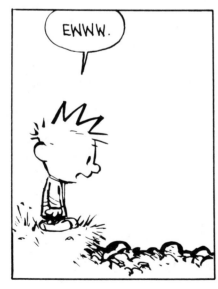

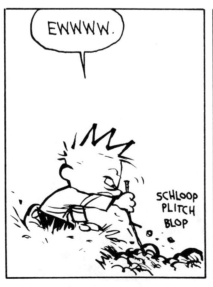

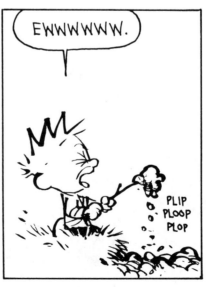

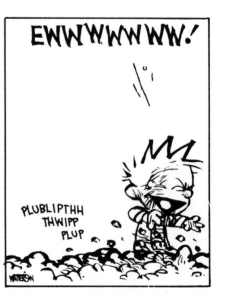

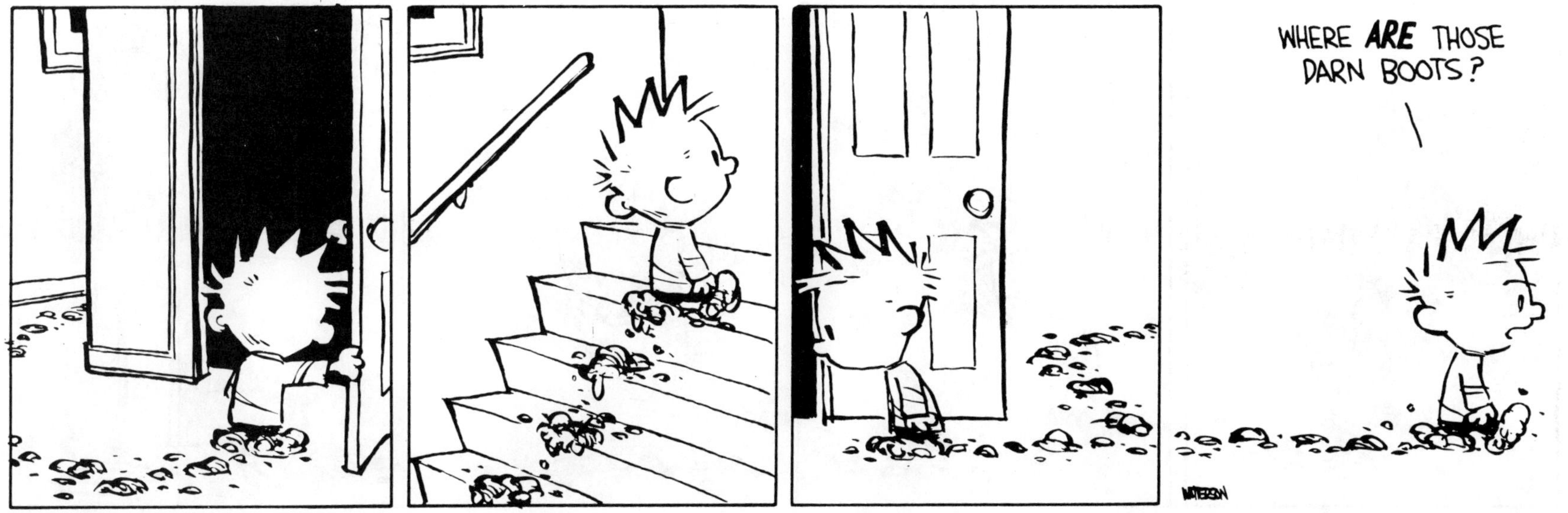
WHERE ARE THOSE DARN BOOTS?

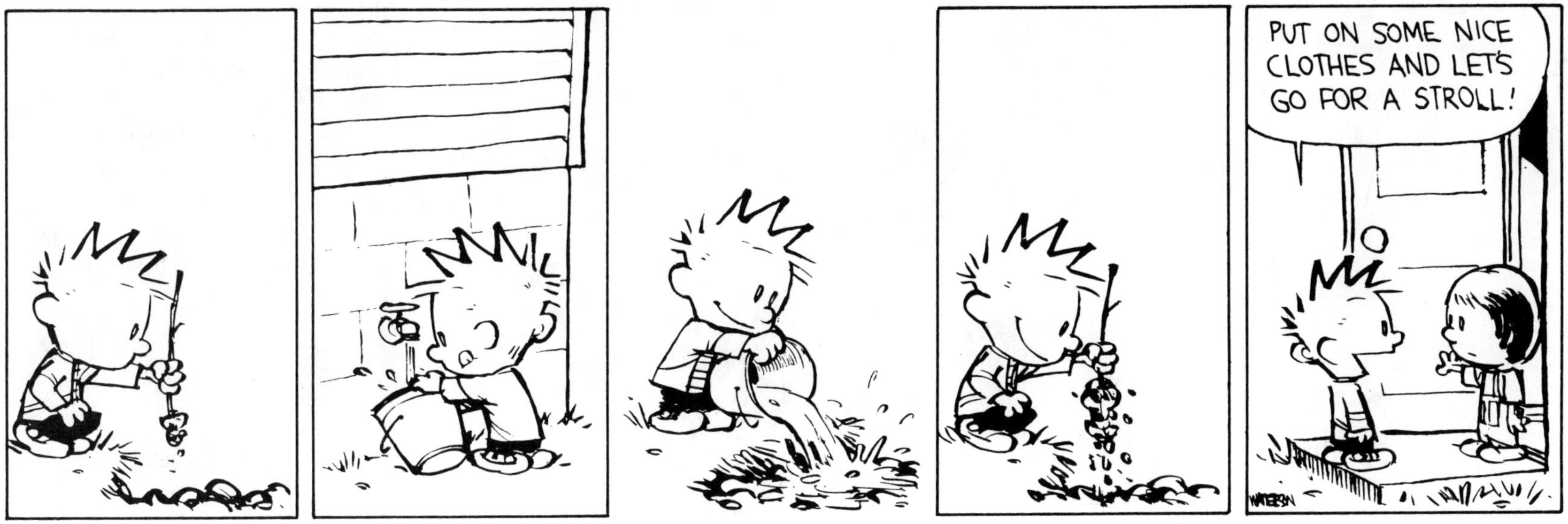
PUT ON SOME NICE CLOTHES AND LET'S GO FOR A STROLL!

IT COULDN'T BE AVOIDED.

RRRUMRUMM
BEEP BEEP
RRRRR RRUMMM
AUGHH!
I DON'T UNDERSTAND WHY YOU HAVE TO TAKE YOUR CLOTHES OFF TO PLAY CARS. IT'S VERY WEIRD.
JUST GIVE 'EM HERE, OK?

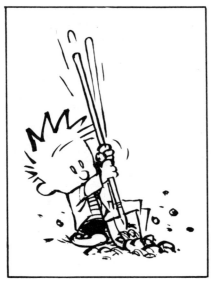

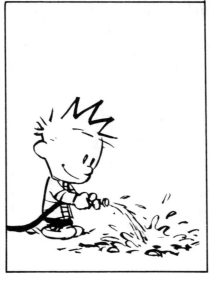

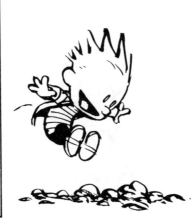

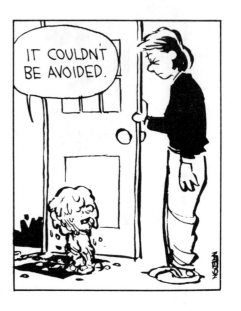

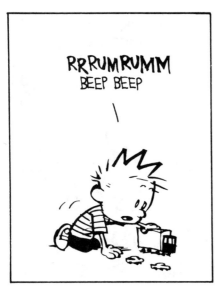

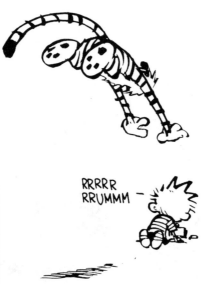

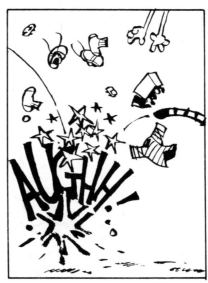

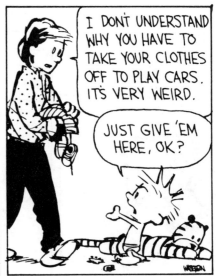

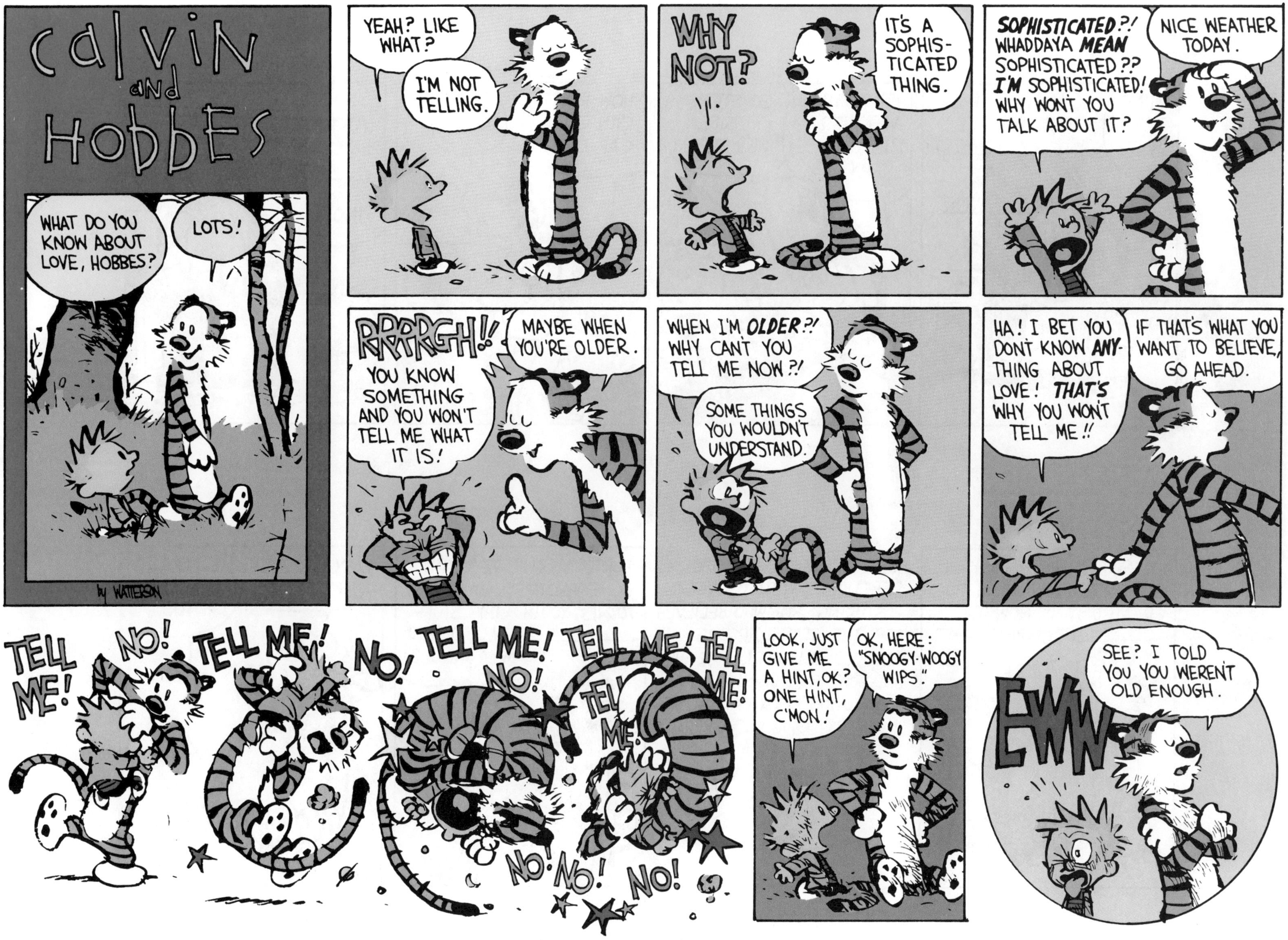
Calvin and Hobbes
WHAT DO YOU KNOW ABOUT LOVE, HOBBES?
LOTS!
by WATTERSON
YEAH? LIKE WHAT?
I'M NOT TELLING.
WHY NOT?
IT'S A SOPHISTICATED THING.
SOPHISTICATED?! WHADDAYA MEAN SOPHISTICATED?? I'M SOPHISTICATED! WHY WON'T YOU TALK ABOUT IT?
NICE WEATHER TODAY.
RRRRGH!!
YOU KNOW SOMETHING AND YOU WON'T TELL ME WHAT IT IS!
MAYBE WHEN YOU'RE OLDER.
WHEN I'M OLDER?! WHY CAN'T YOU TELL ME NOW?!
SOME THINGS YOU WOULDN'T UNDERSTAND.
HA! I BET YOU DON'T KNOW ANYTHING ABOUT LOVE! THAT'S WHY YOU WON'T TELL ME!!
IF THAT'S WHAT YOU WANT TO BELIEVE, GO AHEAD.
TELL ME!
NO!
TELL ME!
NO!
TELL ME!
NO!
TELL ME!
TELL ME!
TELL ME!
NO!
NO!
NO!
LOOK, JUST GIVE ME A HINT, OK? ONE HINT, C'MON!
OK, HERE: "SNOOGY-WOOGY WIPS."
EWWW
SEE? I TOLD YOU YOU WEREN'T OLD ENOUGH.

WHAT TIME IS IT?
GO LOOK AT THE CLOCK AND SEE.
WHAT'S THE WEATHER LIKE OUTSIDE TODAY?
GO STEP OUTSIDE AND SEE.
HOW FAST CAN OUR CAR GO?
GO....
....NICE TRY.
PHOOEY.

THE PROBLEM WITH ROCK'N'ROLL IS THAT THE GENERATION THAT CREATED IT IS NOW THE ESTABLISHMENT.
ROCK PRETENDS IT'S STILL REBELLIOUS WITH ITS VIDEO POSTURING, BUT WHO BELIEVES IT? THE STARS ARE 45-YEAR-OLD ZILLIONAIRES OR THEY ENDORSE SOFT DRINKS! THE "REVOLUTION" IS A CAPITALIST INDUSTRY! GIVE ME A BREAK!
FORTUNATELY, I'VE FOUND SOME PROTEST MUSIC FOR TODAY'S YOUTH! THIS STUFF REALLY OFFENDS MOM AND DAD!
EASY-LISTENING MUZAK?
I PLAY IT REAL QUIET, TOO.

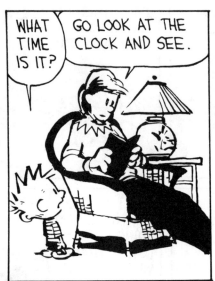

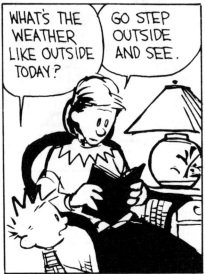

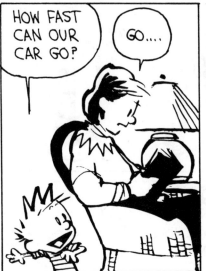

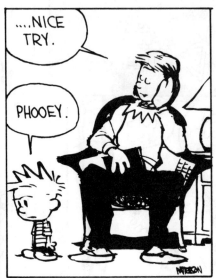

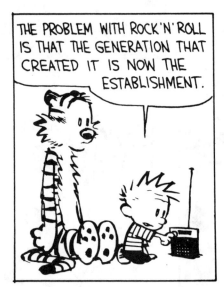

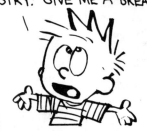

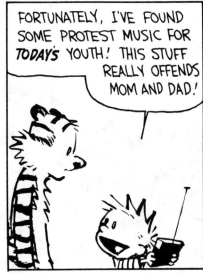

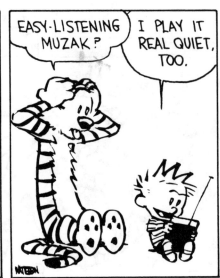

I DON'T WANT TO GO TO SCHOOL! I HATE SCHOOL! I'D RATHER DO *ANYTHING* THAN GO TO SCHOOL!

OK, HOW ABOUT IF *I* GO TO SCHOOL AND *YOU* GET A JOB?

YOU'LL LIKE WORKING TILL EVENING AND BEING RESPONSIBLE FOR THE SUBSISTENCE OF YOUR FAMILY, WITH A WHINY KID'S GRIPING FOR REWARD.

IT'S NICE TO KNOW THERE'S SO MUCH IN LIFE TO LOOK FORWARD TO.

I DON'T WANT TO PAY ANY DUES IN LIFE.

I WANT TO BE A ONE-IN-A-MILLION, OVERNIGHT SUCCESS! I WANT THE WORLD HANDED TO ME ON A SILVER PLATTER!

GOOD LUCK.

SURELY YOU CONCEDE I *DESERVE* IT!

* SNAP *

AAUGH!!

OOPS! INSTINCT KICKED IN BEFORE I KNEW THAT WAS YOU.

YOU KNEW DARN WELL THAT WAS ME!

I WISH I WAS STILL IN BED.

I'D HEAR THE WIND BLOWING THE RAIN AGAINST THE WINDOW PANES AND I'D PULL THE BLANKETS UP, GET ALL TOASTY AND COZY, AND FALL BACK ASLEEP.

INSTEAD, I'M OUT HERE, COLD AND WET, WAITING FOR THE SCHOOL BUS TO TAKE ME TO THE GULAG.

YEAH, I HOPE THE SHEETS ARE STILL WARM WHEN I GET BACK IN.

RUB IT IN, HOBBES.

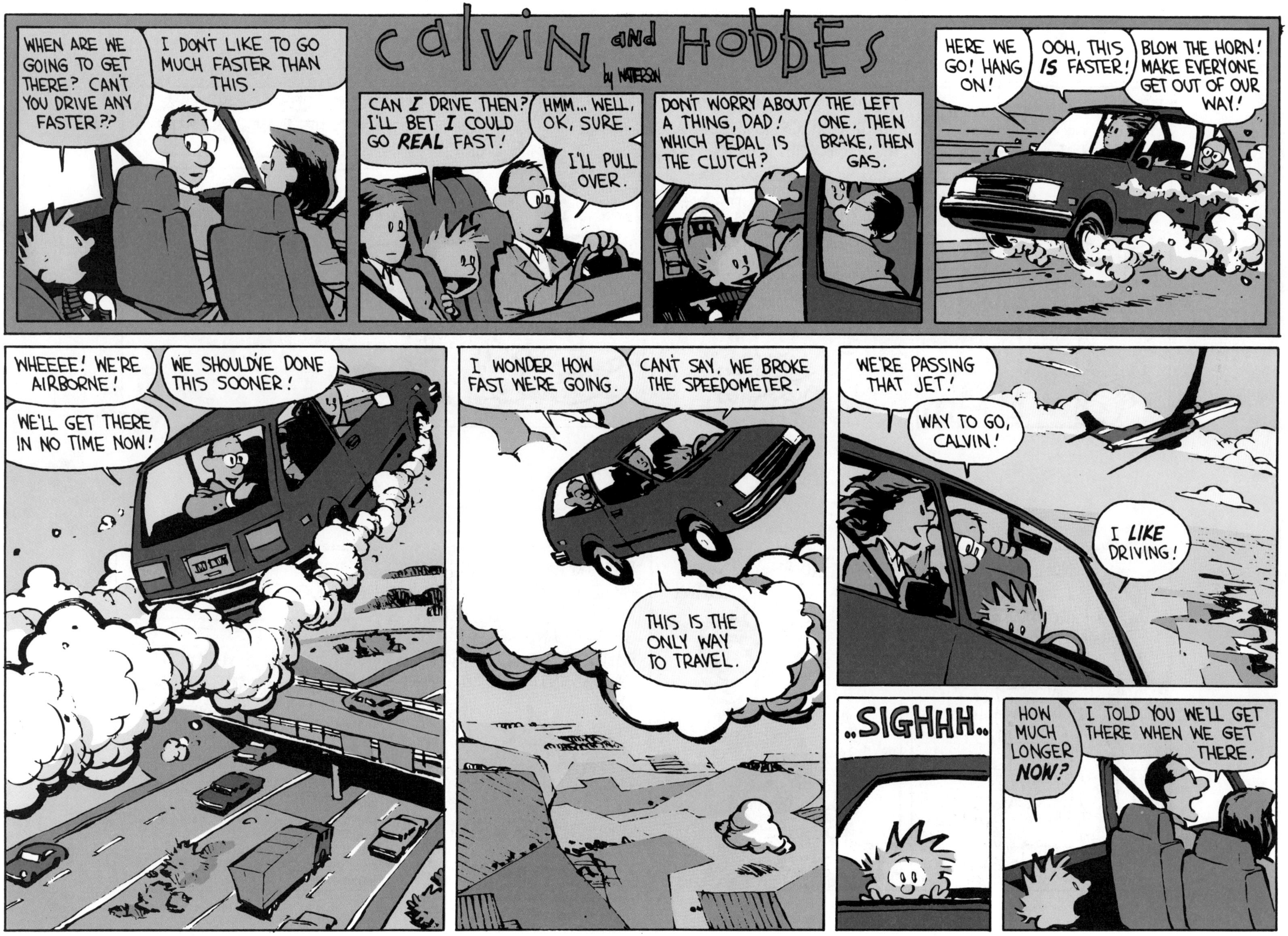

WHEN ARE WE GOING TO GET THERE? CAN'T YOU DRIVE ANY FASTER??
I DON'T LIKE TO GO MUCH FASTER THAN THIS.
Calvin and HobbEs
by WATTERSON
CAN I DRIVE THEN? I'LL BET I COULD GO REAL FAST!
HMM... WELL, OK, SURE.
I'LL PULL OVER.
DON'T WORRY ABOUT A THING, DAD! WHICH PEDAL IS THE CLUTCH?
THE LEFT ONE. THEN BRAKE, THEN GAS.
HERE WE GO! HANG ON!
OOH, THIS IS FASTER!
BLOW THE HORN! MAKE EVERYONE GET OUT OF OUR WAY!
WHEEEE! WE'RE AIRBORNE!
WE SHOULD'VE DONE THIS SOONER!
WE'LL GET THERE IN NO TIME NOW!
I WONDER HOW FAST WE'RE GOING.
CAN'T SAY. WE BROKE THE SPEEDOMETER.
THIS IS THE ONLY WAY TO TRAVEL.
WE'RE PASSING THAT JET!
WAY TO GO, CALVIN!
I LIKE DRIVING!
..SIGHHH..
HOW MUCH LONGER NOW?
I TOLD YOU WE'LL GET THERE WHEN WE GET THERE.

PEOPLE DON'T REALIZE WHAT A BURDEN IT IS BEING A GENIUS LIKE ME.

IT'S NOT EASY HAVING A MIND THAT OPERATES ON A HIGHER PLANE THAN EVERYONE ELSE'S! PEOPLE JUST REFUSE TO SEE THAT I'M THE CRUX OF ALL HISTORY, A BOY OF DESTINY!

I SUPPOSE ONE COULD RECOGNIZE A BOY OF DESTINY BY HIS PLANET-AND-STAR UNDERPANTS.

ANOTHER TRENCHANT COMMENT BY A JEALOUS LESSER INTELLECT.

MOM, FROM NOW ON, I DON'T WANT TO BE INTRODUCED TO PEOPLE AS PLAIN "CALVIN."

I WANT TO BE INTRODUCED AS "CALVIN, BOY OF DESTINY."

BOY OF DESTINY??

BUT YOU HAVE TO SAY IT RIGHT. PAUSE A LITTLE AFTER "BOY," AND SAY "DESTINY" A BIT SLOWER AND DEEPER FOR EMPHASIS. SAY IT, "BOY...... OF *DESSSTINY*," LIKE THAT!

I THINK I'M GOING TO STOP INTRODUCING YOU ALTOGETHER.

I WISH YOU HAD SOME CYMBALS TO CRASH AFTER YOU SAID IT.

HERE IS YOUR PAPER, SUSIE. VERY GOOD. HERE IS YOURS, CALVIN.

BY THE WAY, YOU CAN STOP SIGNING YOUR WORK "CALVIN, BOY OF DESTINY," AND I THINK YOUR TIME WOULD BE BETTER SPENT STUDYING THAN DRAWING "OFFICIAL NOTARY SEALS" AT THE BOTTOM.

BOY OF DESTINY?!

THAT'S RIGHT. BOY OF DESTINY!

EVERYONE *I* KNOW THINKS YOUR DESTINY IS A PRIVATE CAGE IN THE PRIMATE HOUSE.

YOUR DESTINY IS TO HAVE A SMILE THAT'S ALL GUMS.

SMASH

PING PING PING KRITCH KRUNCH

HE'S A TRICKY DEVIL, BUT I'LL GET HIM SOONER OR LATER!

APPARENTLY *I* RATE JUST BELOW *BUGS* WITH HER!

AND SHE COMPLAINS YOU DON'T HELP OUT AROUND THE HOUSE.

HEY DAD, LOOK AT THIS COMMERCIAL.
HOW COME YOU DON'T DRIVE A COOL SPORTS CAR LIKE THAT GUY?
THAT CAR COSTS $40,000.
AND LOOK AT THE BABE HE'S WITH. HOW COME MOM DOESN'T DRESS LIKE THAT?
YEAH, WHY DON'T YOU DRESS LIKE THAT?
BECAUSE YOUR ADOLESCENT FANTASIES REQUIRE AN ADOLESCENT MODEL WITH IMPLANTS, ...HONEY.
MAYBE YOU GUYS NEED TO DRINK MORE BEER.

MOM, CAN I HAVE SOME MONEY TO BUY A SATAN-WORSHIPING, SUICIDE-ADVOCATING HEAVY METAL ALBUM?
CALVIN, THE FACT THAT THESE BANDS HAVEN'T KILLED THEMSELVES IN RITUAL SELF-SACRIFICE SHOWS THAT THEY'RE JUST IN IT FOR THE MONEY LIKE EVERYONE ELSE. IT'S ALL FOR EFFECT. IF YOU WANT TO SHOCK AND PROVOKE, BE SINCERE ABOUT IT.
MAINSTREAM COMMERCIAL NIHILISM CAN'T BE TRUSTED?!
'FRAID NOT, KIDDO.
CHILDHOOD IS SO DISILLUSIONING.

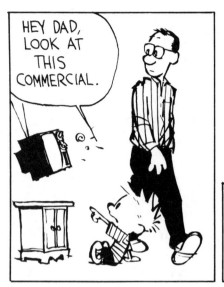

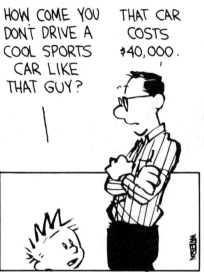

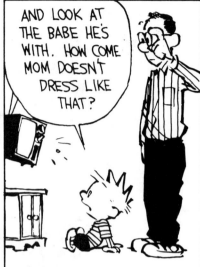

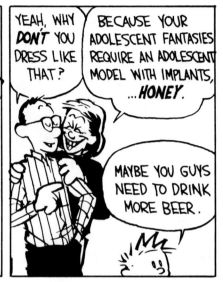

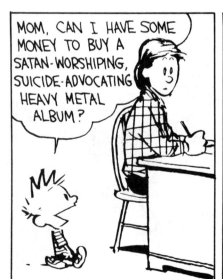

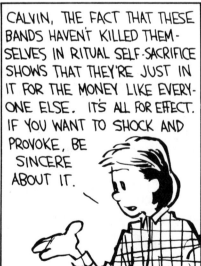

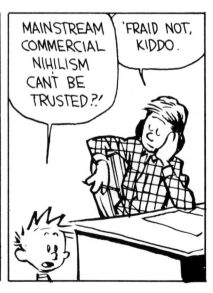

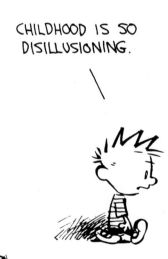

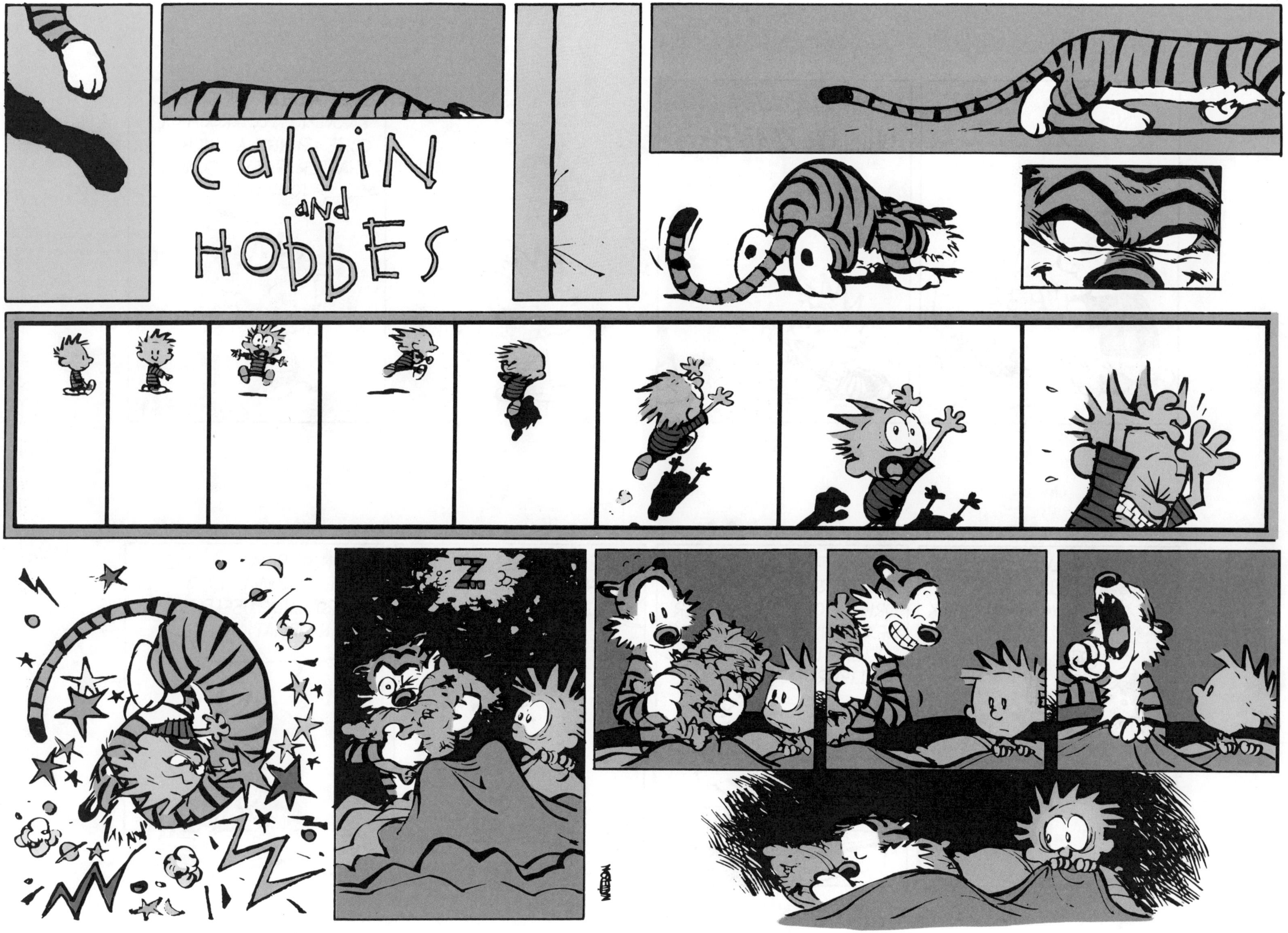
Calvin and Hobbes
Z

Wimp!
OH.... OH YEAH!??
WHAT REALLY BUGS ME IS KNOWING I'LL PROBABLY COME UP WITH A MUCH SHARPER RETORT SOMETIME TONIGHT.

CALVIN, CAN YOU TELL US WHAT LEWIS AND CLARK DID?
NO, BUT I CAN RECITE THE SECRET SUPERHERO ORIGIN OF EACH MEMBER OF CAPTAIN NAPALM'S THERMO-NUCLEAR LEAGUE OF LIBERTY.
SEE ME AFTER CLASS, CALVIN.
I'M NOT DUMB. I JUST HAVE A COMMAND OF THOROUGHLY USELESS INFORMATION.

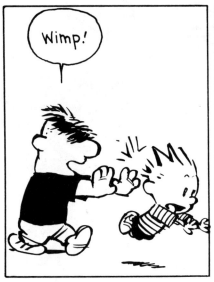

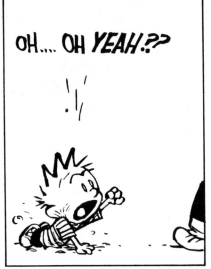

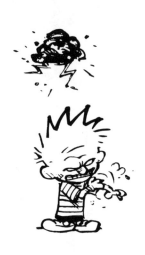

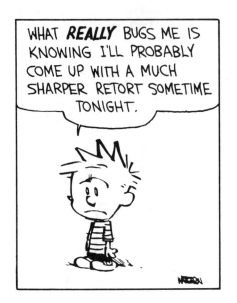

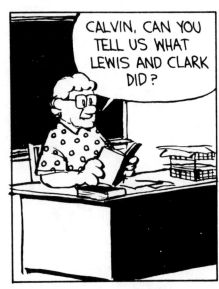

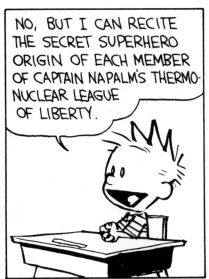

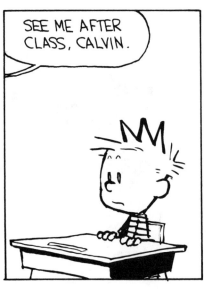

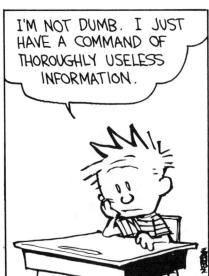

DID YOU EVEN READ THE HISTORY CHAPTER I ASSIGNED?

I TRIED TO, MISS WORMWOOD, BUT THE BOOK PUBLISHER DIDN'T USE THE PROPER PRINT FIXATIVE.

NEEDLESS TO SAY, WHEN I PICKED UP THE BOOK, ALL THE LETTERS SLID OFF THE PAGES AND FELL ON THE FLOOR IN A HEAP OF GIBBERISH.

I THINK MY EXCUSES NEED TO BE LESS EXTEMPORANEOUS.

COUNTY LIBRARY? REFERENCE DESK, PLEASE. HELLO? YES, I NEED A WORD DEFINITION.

WELL, THAT'S THE PROBLEM. I DON'T KNOW HOW TO SPELL IT AND I'M NOT ALLOWED TO SAY IT.

COULD YOU JUST RATTLE OFF ALL THE SWEAR WORDS YOU KNOW, AND I'LL STOP YOU WHEN... HELLO??

SEE IF *I* EVER VOTE FOR THEIR TAX LEVIES.

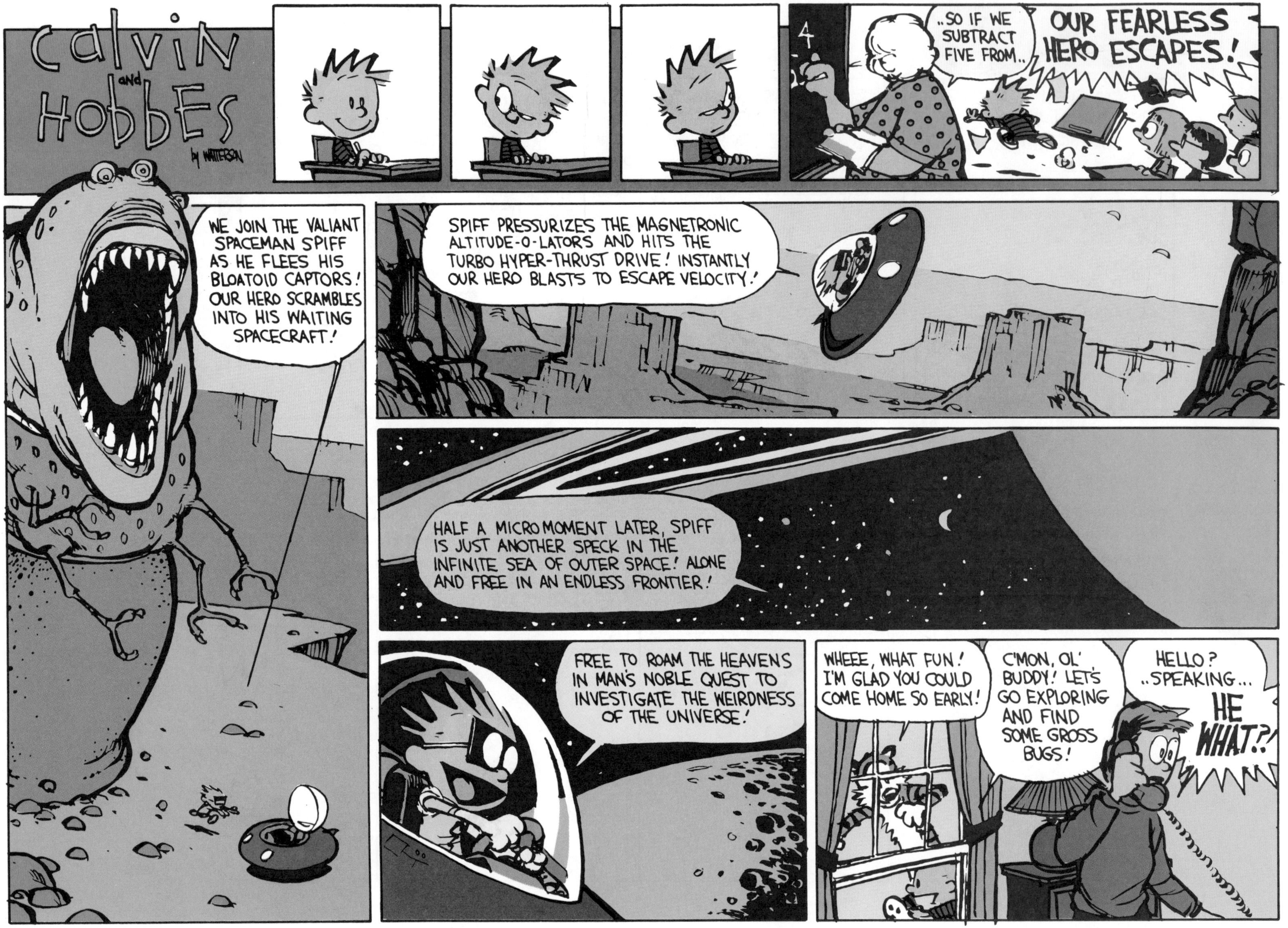
Calvin and Hobbes
by WATTERSON
..SO IF WE SUBTRACT FIVE FROM..
OUR FEARLESS HERO ESCAPES!
WE JOIN THE VALIANT SPACEMAN SPIFF AS HE FLEES HIS BLOATOID CAPTORS! OUR HERO SCRAMBLES INTO HIS WAITING SPACECRAFT!
SPIFF PRESSURIZES THE MAGNETRONIC ALTITUDE-O-LATORS AND HITS THE TURBO HYPER-THRUST DRIVE! INSTANTLY OUR HERO BLASTS TO ESCAPE VELOCITY!
HALF A MICROMOMENT LATER, SPIFF IS JUST ANOTHER SPECK IN THE INFINITE SEA OF OUTER SPACE! ALONE AND FREE IN AN ENDLESS FRONTIER!
FREE TO ROAM THE HEAVENS IN MAN'S NOBLE QUEST TO INVESTIGATE THE WEIRDNESS OF THE UNIVERSE!
WHEEE, WHAT FUN! I'M GLAD YOU COULD COME HOME SO EARLY!
C'MON, OL' BUDDY! LET'S GO EXPLORING AND FIND SOME GROSS BUGS!
HELLO? ..SPEAKING...
HE WHAT?!

I DON'T NEED A BATH! I CAN STAY CLEAN WITHOUT ONE!

LOOK, I'LL *LICK* MYSELF CLEAN! THAT'S WHAT HOBBES DOES! SEE, I'M GETTING CLEAN JUST LIKE HIM!

NICE GOING.

YOU HAVE A QUESTION, CALVIN?

YES! WHAT ASSURANCE DO I HAVE THAT THIS EDUCATION IS ADEQUATELY PREPARING ME FOR THE 21ST CENTURY?

AM I GETTING THE SKILLS I'LL NEED TO EFFECTIVELY COMPETE IN A TOUGH, GLOBAL ECONOMY? I WANT A HIGH-PAYING JOB WHEN I GET OUT OF HERE! I WANT OPPORTUNITY!

IN THAT CASE, YOUNG MAN, I SUGGEST YOU START WORKING HARDER. WHAT YOU GET OUT OF SCHOOL DEPENDS ON WHAT YOU PUT INTO IT.

OH.

THEN FORGET IT.

WHATCHA DOING?
DAD WANTS TO MOW THE LAWN, SO HE'S MAKING ME PICK UP STICKS.
HE SAID I MIGHT LEARN SOMETHING ABOUT THE SATISFACTION THAT COMES FROM A JOB WELL DONE.
AND DID YOU?
I SUPPOSE SO.
I THINK HE'S TRYING TO TELL ME THERE IS NONE.

MY TIGER IS DEEP IN SOMNOLENT SLEEP, DREAMING OF CHASES REMEMBERED!
Z
HIS KEEN EYES ARE GLINTING! HE DREAMS OF A SPRINTING SAMBAR WHO'LL SOON BE DISMEMBERED!
Z
Z
HMMMMMMM
Z

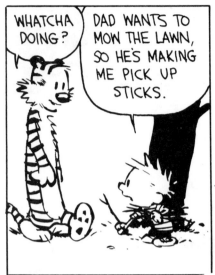

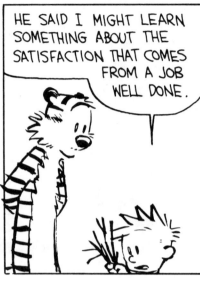

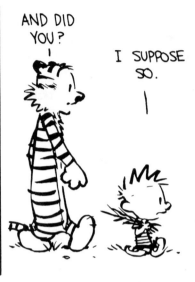

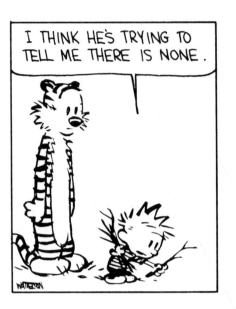

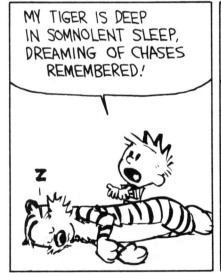

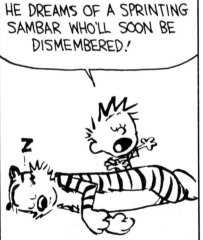

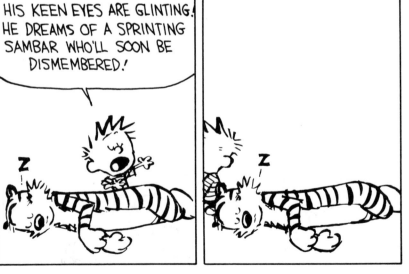

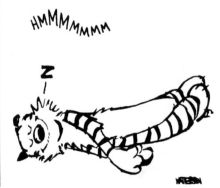

THIS ARTICLE SAYS THAT BY AGE SIX, MOST CHILDREN HAVE WATCHED 5,000 HOURS OF TV - A QUARTER OF THEIR WAKING LIVES!
I HAVEN'T WATCHED THAT MUCH! THINK OF ALL THE GREAT SHOWS I'VE MISSED! I'VE BEEN DEPRIVED OF CULTURAL REFERENCES! I'M IGNORANT OF COUNTLESS AMAZING PRODUCTS!
HURRY! IF I WATCH TV UNTIL BEDTIME, I CAN GET IN A FEW PRECIOUS EXTRA HOURS AND CATCH UP A BIT!
REMEDIAL VEGETATION.
HELP ME LEARN THIS THEME SONG, OK?

I THINK OUR NEWSPAPER NEEDS A NEW ADVICE COLUMNIST, SO I'M APPLYING FOR THE JOB.
SEE, I'VE WRITTEN SOME SAMPLE ANSWERS TO PEOPLE WHO WRITE IN.
"STOP WHINING AND GET A LIFE, BOZO."
"DON'T TELL ME YOUR STUPID PROBLEMS. I'VE GOT PLENTY OF MY OWN."
"GO SOAK YOUR HEAD, YOU BIG BABY."
"WANT SOME ADVICE? DROP DEAD."
I GUESS THAT COVERS ABOUT EVERYTHING.
CAN YOU IMAGINE DOING THIS FOR MONEY? WHAT A RACKET!

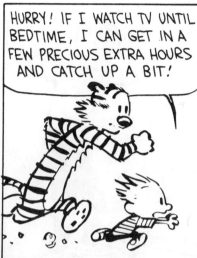

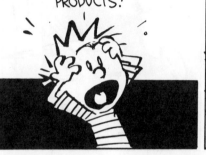

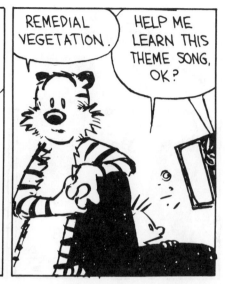

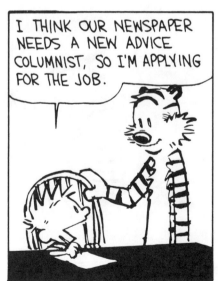

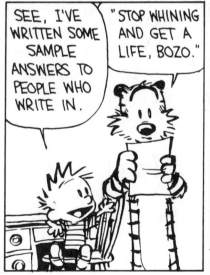

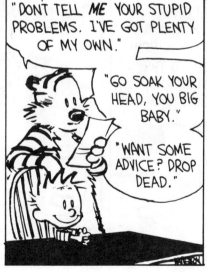

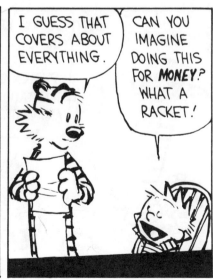

WHO EES THEES KÄHLYEEN?

DO YOU BELIEVE IN THE DEVIL? YOU KNOW, A SUPREME EVIL BEING DEDICATED TO THE TEMPTATION, CORRUPTION, AND DESTRUCTION OF MAN?
I'M NOT SURE MAN NEEDS THE HELP.
YOU JUST CAN'T TALK TO ANIMALS ABOUT THESE THINGS.

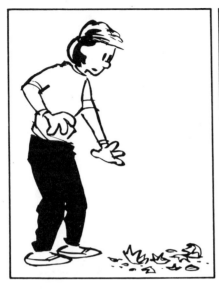

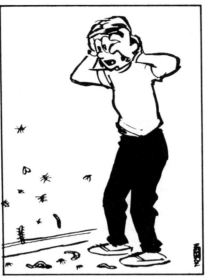

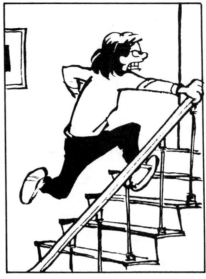

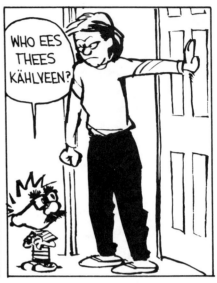

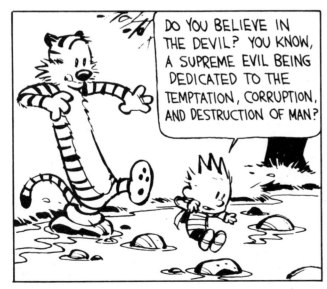

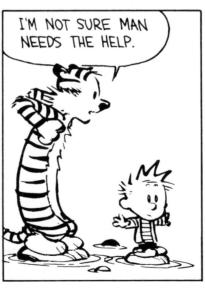

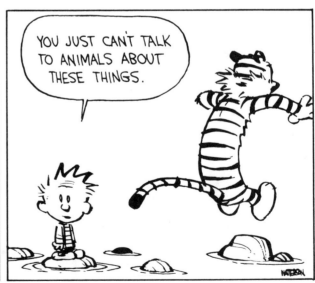

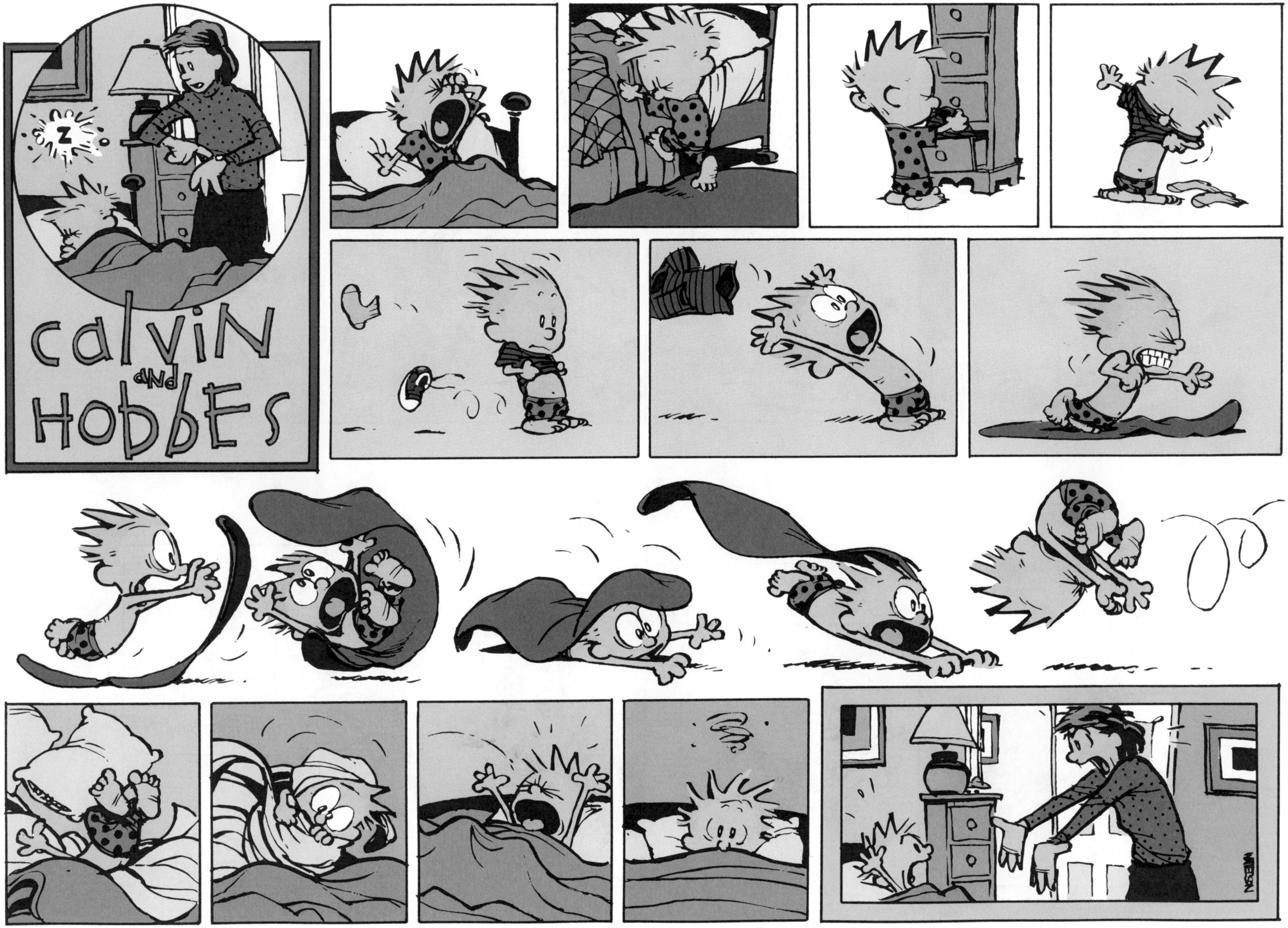
Z
calvin and HobbEs
WATTERSON

WHAT'S THIS?
TRY IT.
WHAT'S *IN* HERE? GRUBS??
TRY IT.
THAT MEANS I'M GOING TO HATE IT, RIGHT?
JUST TRY IT!
SHE'S MAD BECAUSE I BROKE HER CODE.

IF I'VE LEARNED ONE THING IN LIFE, IT'S THAT EVERYONE HAS HIS PRICE.
RAISE THE ANTE HIGH ENOUGH, AND THERE'S NO SUCH THING AS SCRUPLES! PEOPLE WILL DO *ANY*THING IF THE PRICE IS RIGHT!
WHAT'S *YOUR* PRICE?
TWO BUCKS COLD CASH UP FRONT.
I DON'T KNOW WHICH IS WORSE, ...THAT EVERYONE HAS HIS PRICE, OR THAT THE PRICE IS ALWAYS SO LOW.
I'D MAKE MINE HIGHER, BUT IT'S HARD TO FIND BUYERS AS IT IS.

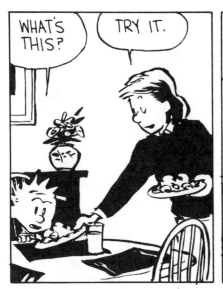

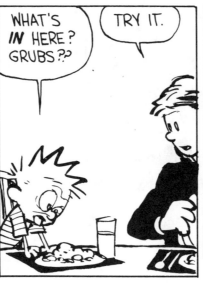

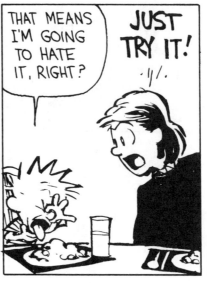

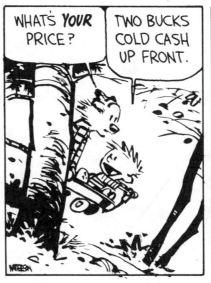

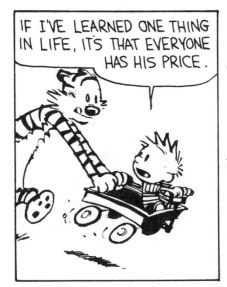

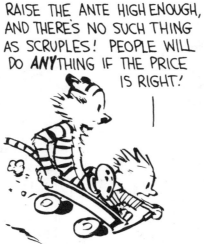

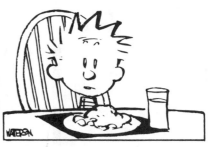

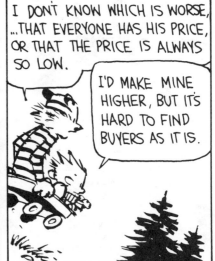

WHATCHA DOIN', DAD?

I'M BUSY TRYING TO FIX SOMETHING.

WHY BOTHER? ON THE RARE OCCASIONS WHEN YOU KNOW WHAT THE PROBLEM IS, YOU USUALLY MAKE IT WORSE AND HURT YOURSELF IN THE PROCESS!

I WISH I'D NOTICED THE BANDAGE ON HIS HAND BEFORE I SAID THAT.

I'M GOING ON A BIKE RIDE.

WHAT'S SO FUNNY?

NOTHING. HAVE A GOOD TIME.

LOOK, *I* DIDN'T DESIGN THIS OUTFIT! IT'S *PRACTICAL!*

HEY DAD, HOW'D YOU GET YOUR HEAD STUCK IN A BOWLING BALL? HA!

NEXT TIME, I'LL SQUIRT THEM BOTH WITH MY WATER BOTTLE.

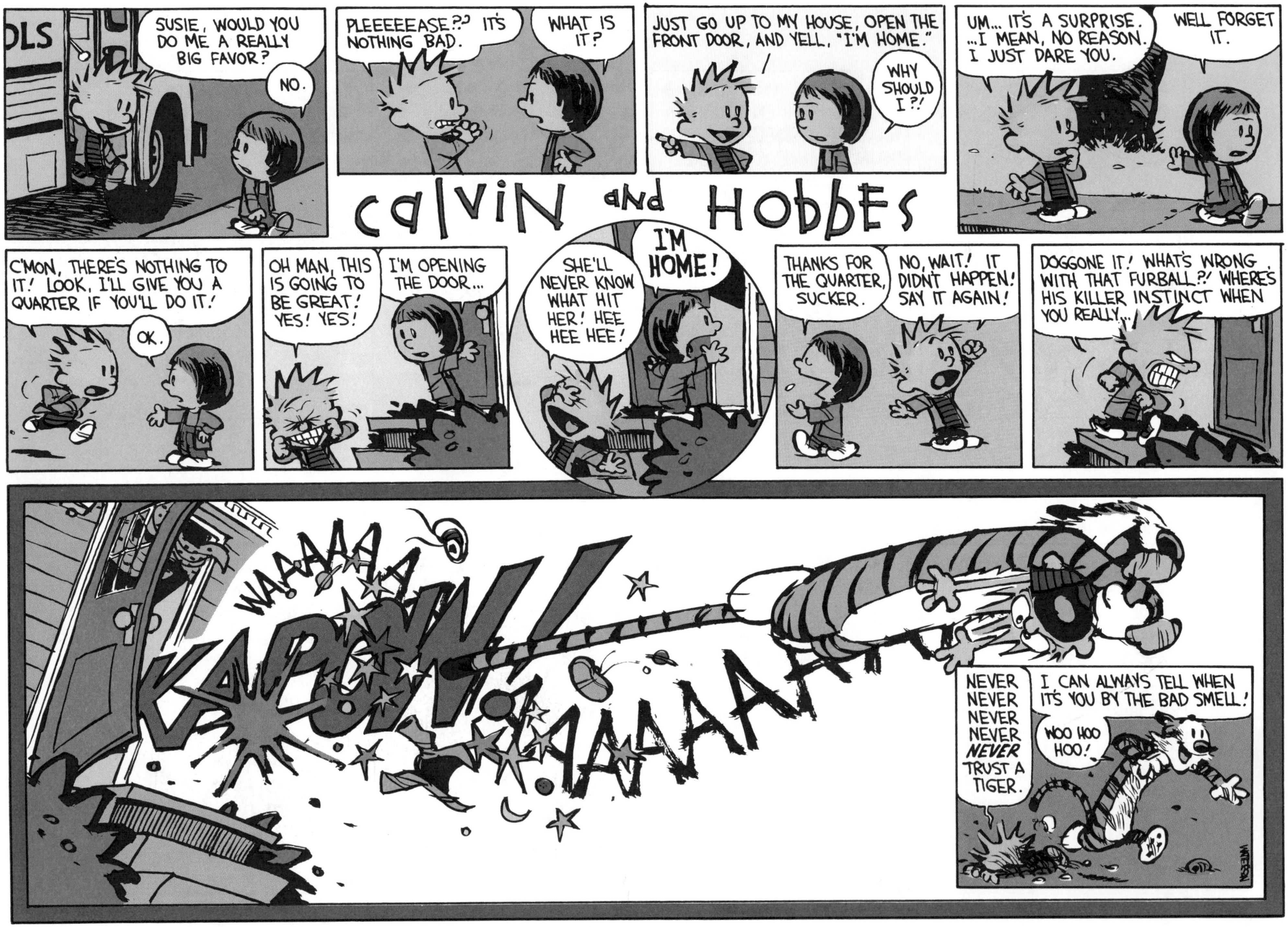
SUSIE, WOULD YOU DO ME A REALLY BIG FAVOR?
NO.
PLEEEEEASE?!? IT'S NOTHING BAD.
WHAT IS IT?
JUST GO UP TO MY HOUSE, OPEN THE FRONT DOOR, AND YELL, "I'M HOME."
WHY SHOULD I?!
UM... IT'S A SURPRISE. ...I MEAN, NO REASON. I JUST DARE YOU.
WELL FORGET IT.
calvin and HOBBES
C'MON, THERE'S NOTHING TO IT! LOOK, I'LL GIVE YOU A QUARTER IF YOU'LL DO IT!
OK.
OH MAN, THIS IS GOING TO BE GREAT! YES! YES!
I'M OPENING THE DOOR...
SHE'LL NEVER KNOW WHAT HIT HER! HEE HEE HEE!
I'M HOME!
THANKS FOR THE QUARTER, SUCKER.
NO, WAIT! IT DIDN'T HAPPEN! SAY IT AGAIN!
DOGGONE IT! WHAT'S WRONG WITH THAT FURBALL?! WHERE'S HIS KILLER INSTINCT WHEN YOU REALLY...
WAAAAAA
KAPOW!!
AAAAAAAAAHH
NEVER NEVER NEVER NEVER NEVER TRUST A TIGER.
I CAN ALWAYS TELL WHEN IT'S YOU BY THE BAD SMELL!
WOO HOO HOO!

TIGERS HAVE NO AMBITION, NO DRIVE! THEY DON'T ACCOMPLISH ANYTHING!
HOW DO YOU JUSTIFY YOURSELF?!

HEY MOM, CAN I GET SOME PLASTIC SURGERY? ALL THE CELEBRITIES DO IT!
HONEY, CELEBRITIES NEED THE FAT SUCKED OUT OF THEIR BRAINS, NOT THEIR BOTTOMS. WHAT ON EARTH DO YOU WANT CHANGED? YOU'RE FINE THE WAY YOU ARE!
I WANT ANOTHER EYE PUT IN MY FOREHEAD.

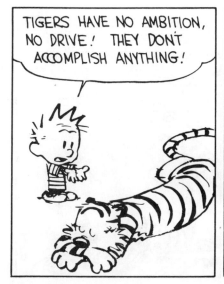

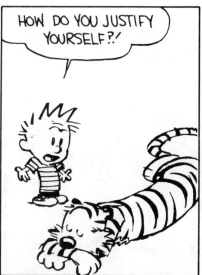

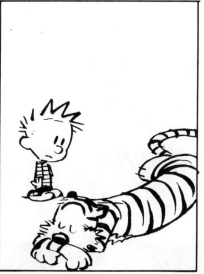

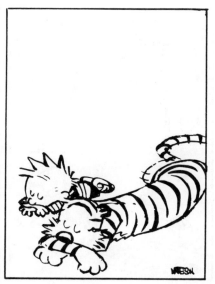

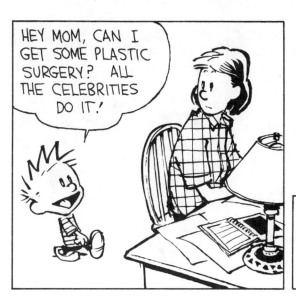

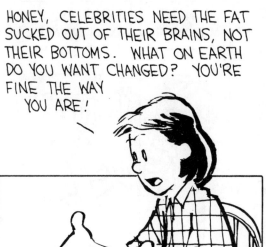

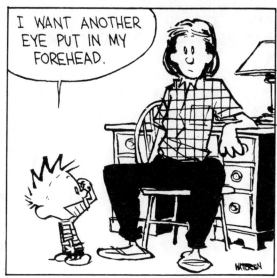

I'VE DECIDED I BELIEVE IN ASTROLOGY AND HOROSCOPES.
REALLY?
YOU BET. IT ONLY MAKES SENSE THAT EVERY FACET OF OUR DAILY LIVES SHOULD DEPEND UPON THE POSITION OF CELESTIAL BODIES HUNDREDS OF MILLIONS OF MILES AWAY.
LOOK HERE. TODAY I'LL HAVE "MANY KEY POLICIES IMPLEMENTED." I GET TO HAVE MY WAY!
OH THOSE MISCHIEVOUS PLANETS.
THE NEWSPAPER COULDN'T PRINT IT IF IT WEREN'T TRUE!
WATTERSON

MY HOROSCOPE SAYS, "TURN-ABOUT MEANS CIRCUMSTANCES IN YOUR FAVOR. ASSERT VIEWS IN CONFIDENT MANNER. LUNAR CYCLE HIGH, MANY OF YOUR KEY POLICIES WILL BE IMPLEMENTED."
ISN'T THAT GREAT? TODAY I'M FATED TO GET MY WAY! THE HEAVENS DECREE IT!
SO WHAT ARE YOUR "KEY POLICIES"?
WATTERSON
FIRST, OBVIOUSLY, IS "DON'T DO HOMEWORK." C'MON, LET'S GO OUT AND PLAY!
HERE COMES YOUR MOM AND IT LOOKS LIKE SHE HAS A BONE TO PICK WITH THE MOON.
HA! WATCH ME ASSERT MY VIEWS IN A CONFIDENT MANNER!

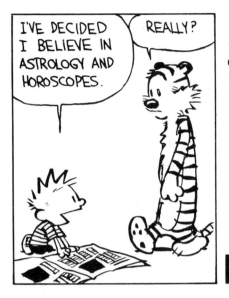

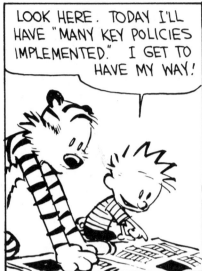

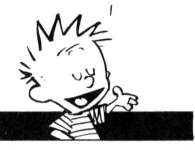

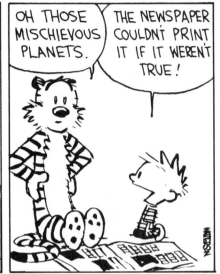

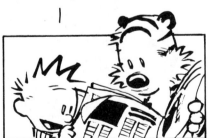

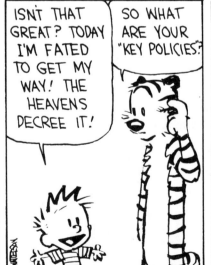

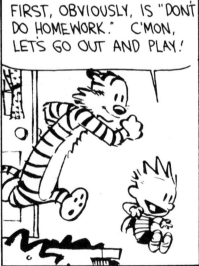

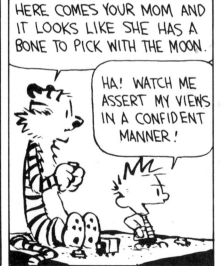

YOUR MOM DIDN'T CARE MUCH ABOUT THE LUNAR SANCTION OF YOUR NO-HOMEWORK POLICY, DID SHE?
HMPH.
WELL, MY HOROSCOPE SAID "*MANY* KEY POLICIES WILL BE IMPLEMENTED," NOT *ALL* OF THEM. BESIDES, IT SAYS TO EXPECT A TURNABOUT IN MY FAVOR. MOM WILL RELENT NEXT TIME FOR SURE.
WHAT ARE YOUR OTHER KEY POLICIES THEN?
NO BATHS, STAY UP LATE, DON'T GO TO SCHOOL... *THESE* ARE THE ONES THAT WILL BE IMPLEMENTED.
MAYBE THE ASTROLOGER WAS LOOKING THROUGH THE WRONG END OF THE TELESCOPE.
C'MON MOON, DO YOUR STUFF!

I THOUGHT I TOLD YOU TO TAKE YOUR BATH.
SORRY, MOM. YOU HAVE NO SAY IN THIS.
YOU'RE IN FOR A SURPRISE, BUSTER.
CIRCUMSTANCES ARE GOING TO TURN IN MY FAVOR! THAT'S WHAT MY HOROSCOPE SAYS!
ALL HUMAN AFFAIRS ARE DETERMINED BY STARS AND PLANETS, AND TODAY THEY SAY MY KEY POLICIES WILL BE IMPLEMENTED. THAT MEANS NO BATH AND NO BEDTIME!
BY GOLLY, IT'S NOT GOOD TO THWART THE INTENTIONS OF THE UNIVERSE!
FATE JUST ISN'T WHAT IT USED TO BE.

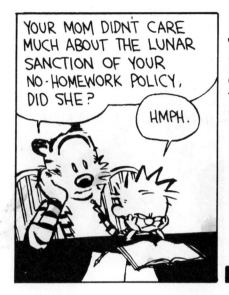

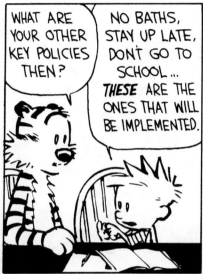

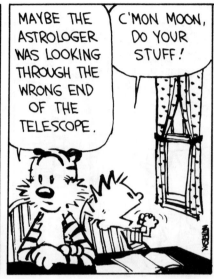

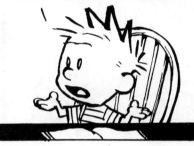

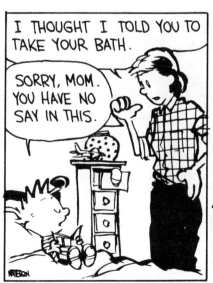

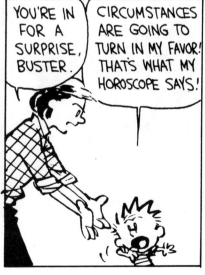

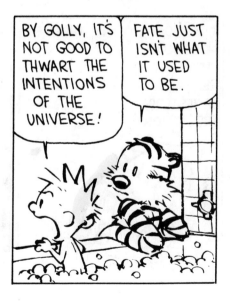

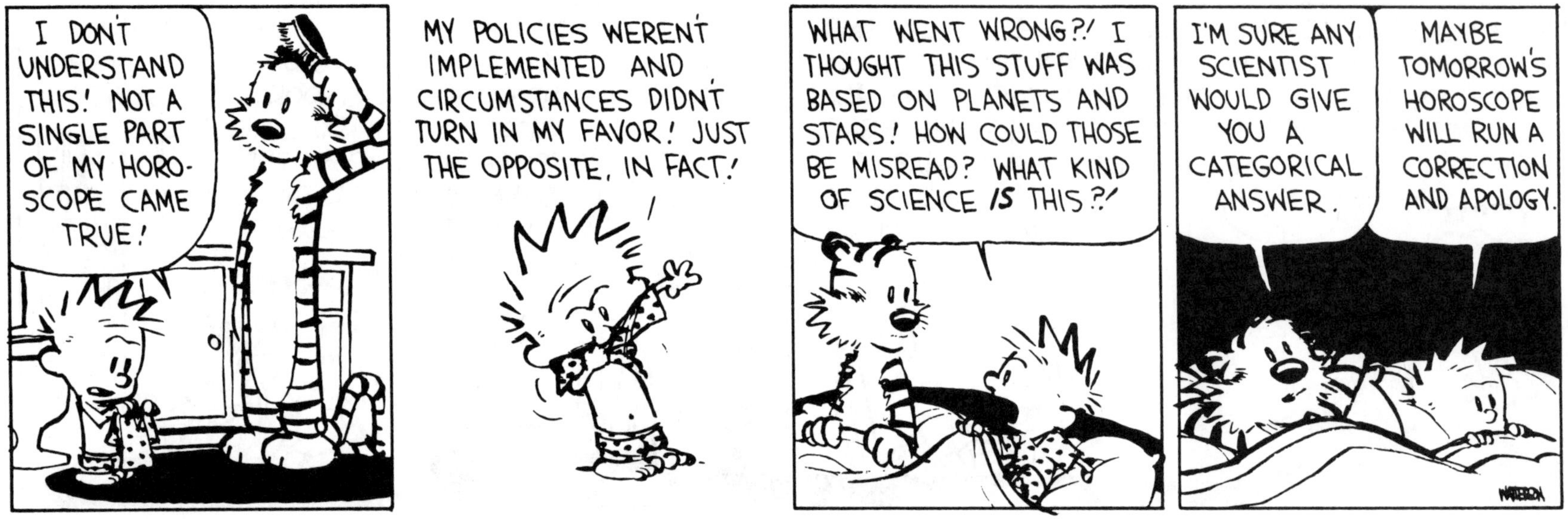
I DON'T UNDERSTAND THIS! NOT A SINGLE PART OF MY HORO-SCOPE CAME TRUE!
MY POLICIES WEREN'T IMPLEMENTED AND CIRCUMSTANCES DIDN'T TURN IN MY FAVOR! JUST THE OPPOSITE, IN FACT!
WHAT WENT WRONG?! I THOUGHT THIS STUFF WAS BASED ON PLANETS AND STARS! HOW COULD THOSE BE MISREAD? WHAT KIND OF SCIENCE IS THIS?!
I'M SURE ANY SCIENTIST WOULD GIVE YOU A CATEGORICAL ANSWER.
MAYBE TOMORROW'S HOROSCOPE WILL RUN A CORRECTION AND APOLOGY.

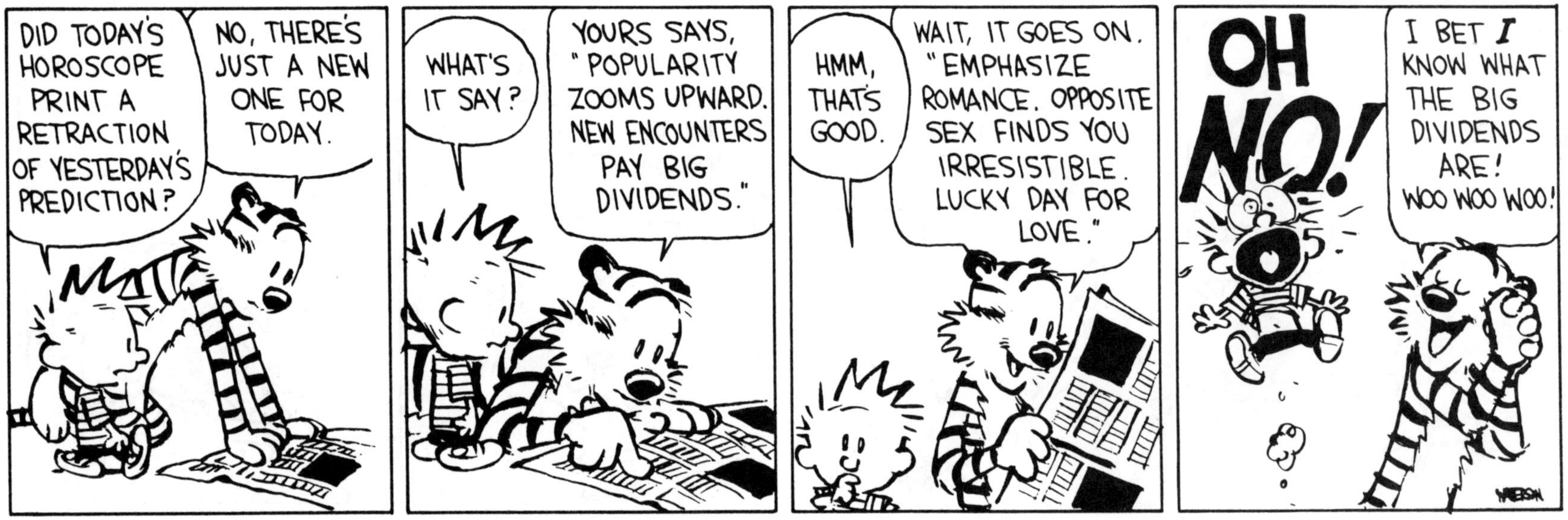
DID TODAY'S HOROSCOPE PRINT A RETRACTION OF YESTERDAY'S PREDICTION?
NO, THERE'S JUST A NEW ONE FOR TODAY.
WHAT'S IT SAY?
YOURS SAYS, "POPULARITY ZOOMS UPWARD. NEW ENCOUNTERS PAY BIG DIVIDENDS."
HMM, THAT'S GOOD.
WAIT, IT GOES ON. "EMPHASIZE ROMANCE. OPPOSITE SEX FINDS YOU IRRESISTIBLE. LUCKY DAY FOR LOVE."
OH NO!
I BET I KNOW WHAT THE BIG DIVIDENDS ARE! WOO WOO WOO!

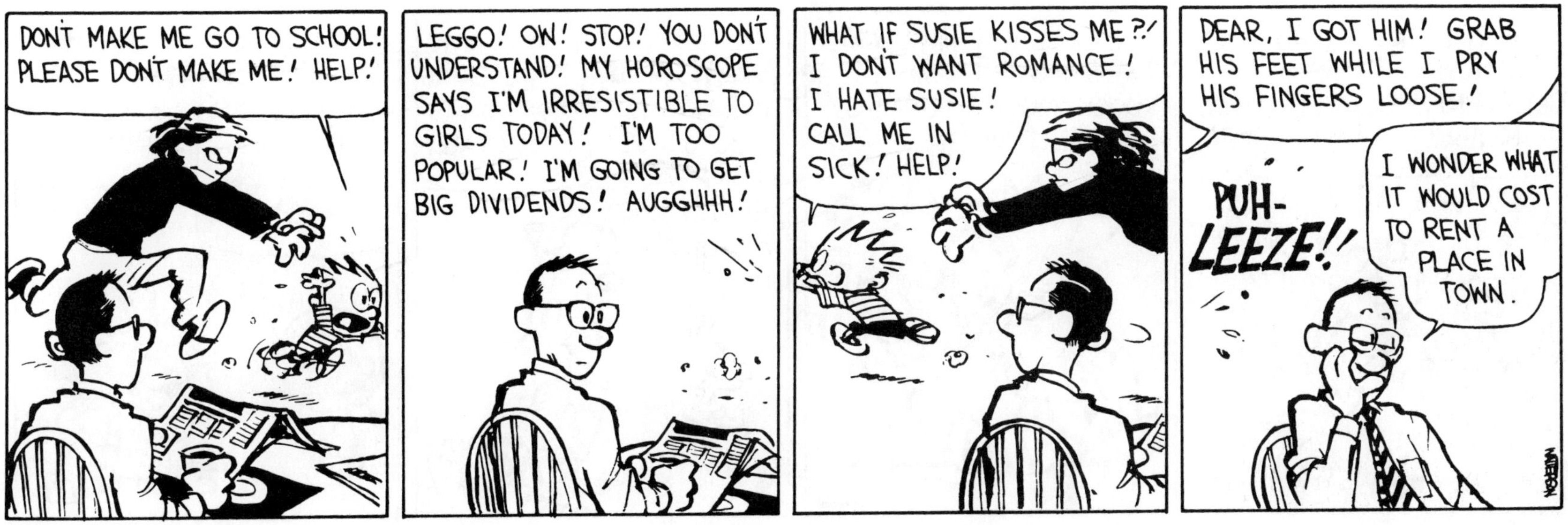
DON'T MAKE ME GO TO SCHOOL! PLEASE DON'T MAKE ME! HELP!
LEGGO! OW! STOP! YOU DON'T UNDERSTAND! MY HOROSCOPE SAYS I'M IRRESISTIBLE TO GIRLS TODAY! I'M TOO POPULAR! I'M GOING TO GET BIG DIVIDENDS! AUGGHHH!
WHAT IF SUSIE KISSES ME?! I DON'T WANT ROMANCE! I HATE SUSIE! CALL ME IN SICK! HELP!
DEAR, I GOT HIM! GRAB HIS FEET WHILE I PRY HIS FINGERS LOOSE!
PUH-LEEZE!!
I WONDER WHAT IT WOULD COST TO RENT A PLACE IN TOWN.

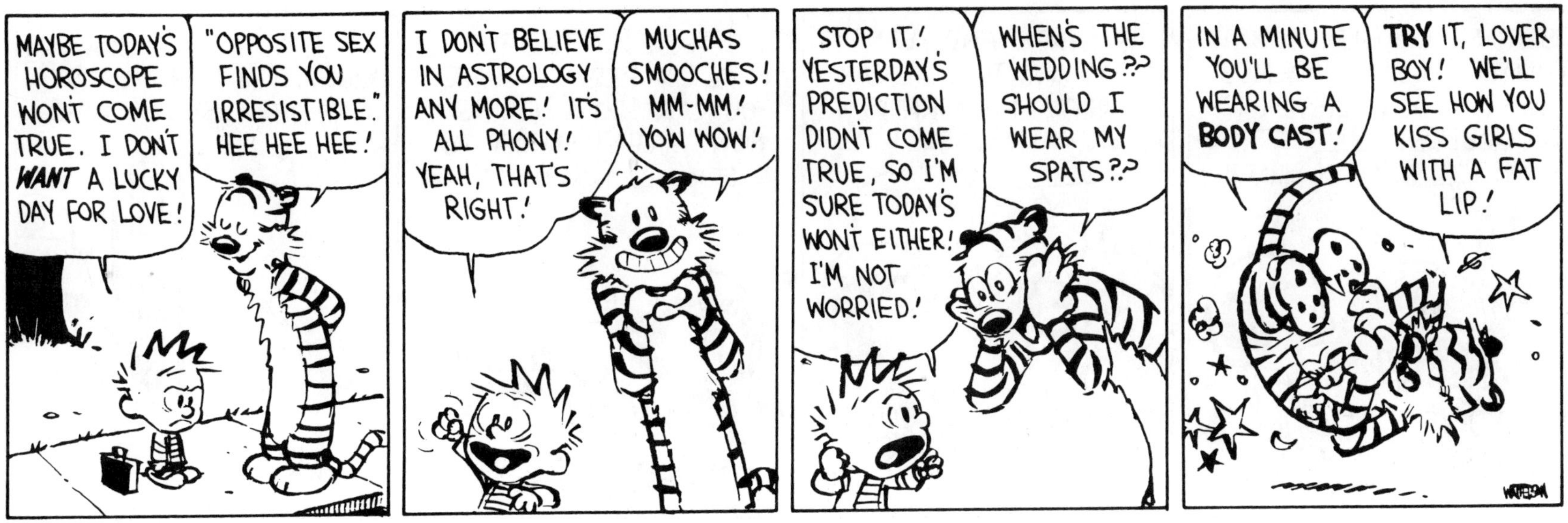
MAYBE TODAY'S HOROSCOPE WON'T COME TRUE. I DON'T *WANT* A LUCKY DAY FOR LOVE!
"OPPOSITE SEX FINDS YOU IRRESISTIBLE." HEE HEE HEE!
I DON'T BELIEVE IN ASTROLOGY ANY MORE! IT'S ALL PHONY! YEAH, THAT'S RIGHT!
MUCHAS SMOOCHES! MM-MM! YOW WOW!
STOP IT! YESTERDAY'S PREDICTION DIDN'T COME TRUE, SO I'M SURE TODAY'S WON'T EITHER! I'M NOT WORRIED!
WHEN'S THE WEDDING?? SHOULD I WEAR MY SPATS??
IN A MINUTE YOU'LL BE WEARING A **BODY CAST**!
TRY IT, LOVER BOY! WE'LL SEE HOW YOU KISS GIRLS WITH A FAT LIP!

TAKE IT BACK! I'M NEVER GETTING MARRIED! NEVER!
LOVE 'EM AND LEAVE 'EM, EH? YOU RAKE!
THAT DOES IT! I'M GONNA KNOCK YOU INTO NEXT WEEK!
WAIT! WAIT! SUSIE'S COMING!
WHAT? SHE IS? AUGH! SHE IS! I'VE GOT TO DISCOURAGE ROMANCE!
YOU CAN'T! SMOLDERING PASSION IS YOUR FATE!
GOSH, CALVIN, THE DIRT COVERING YOUR FEATURES IS A BIG IMPROVEMENT.
OH NO, IT'S TRUE! I'M A LOVE MAGNET!

STAY AWAY, SUSIE! I DON'T WANT ANY BIG DIVIDENDS, GOT IT? DON'T LISTEN TO HOBBES!
WHAT?
THE STARS AND PLANETS ARE DOING THIS! I CAN'T HELP IT! MY AURA IS UNCONTROLLABLE!
WHAT?
IT'S THE BUS! THE BUS IS HERE! WHEEE! I'M SAFE! YOU CAN'T DO ANYTHING NOW! HA HA! I'M OFF TO SCHOOL! HOORAYY!
WHAT?
THE WAY CALVIN'S BRAIN IS WIRED, YOU CAN ALMOST HEAR THE FUSES BLOWING.

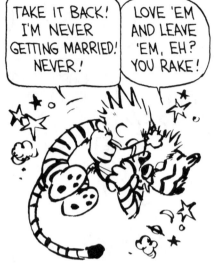

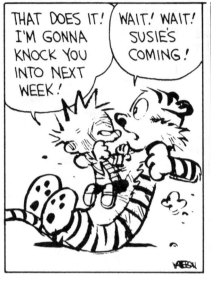

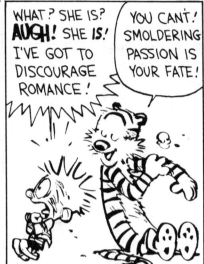

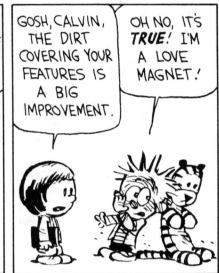

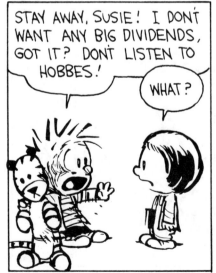

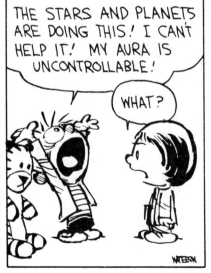

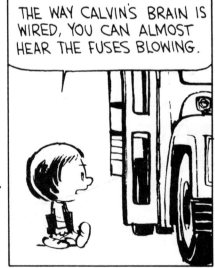

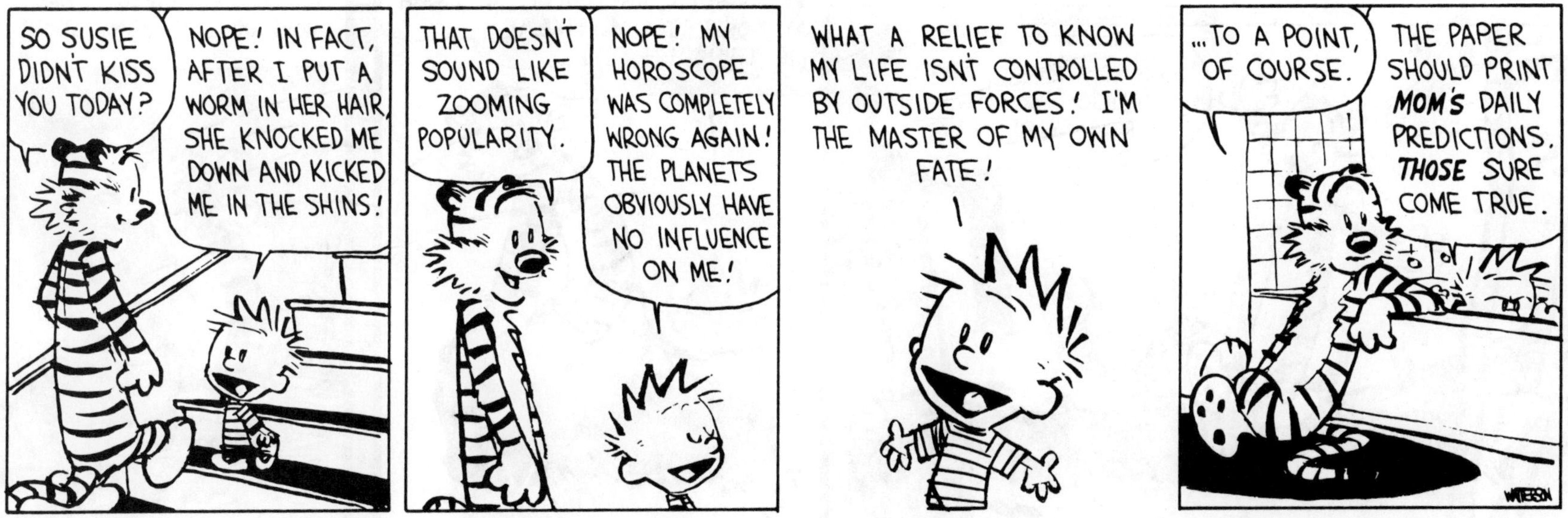
SO SUSIE DIDN'T KISS YOU TODAY?
NOPE! IN FACT, AFTER I PUT A WORM IN HER HAIR, SHE KNOCKED ME DOWN AND KICKED ME IN THE SHINS!
THAT DOESN'T SOUND LIKE ZOOMING POPULARITY.
NOPE! MY HOROSCOPE WAS COMPLETELY WRONG AGAIN! THE PLANETS OBVIOUSLY HAVE NO INFLUENCE ON ME!
WHAT A RELIEF TO KNOW MY LIFE ISN'T CONTROLLED BY OUTSIDE FORCES! I'M THE MASTER OF MY OWN FATE!
...TO A POINT, OF COURSE.
THE PAPER SHOULD PRINT MOM'S DAILY PREDICTIONS. THOSE SURE COME TRUE.

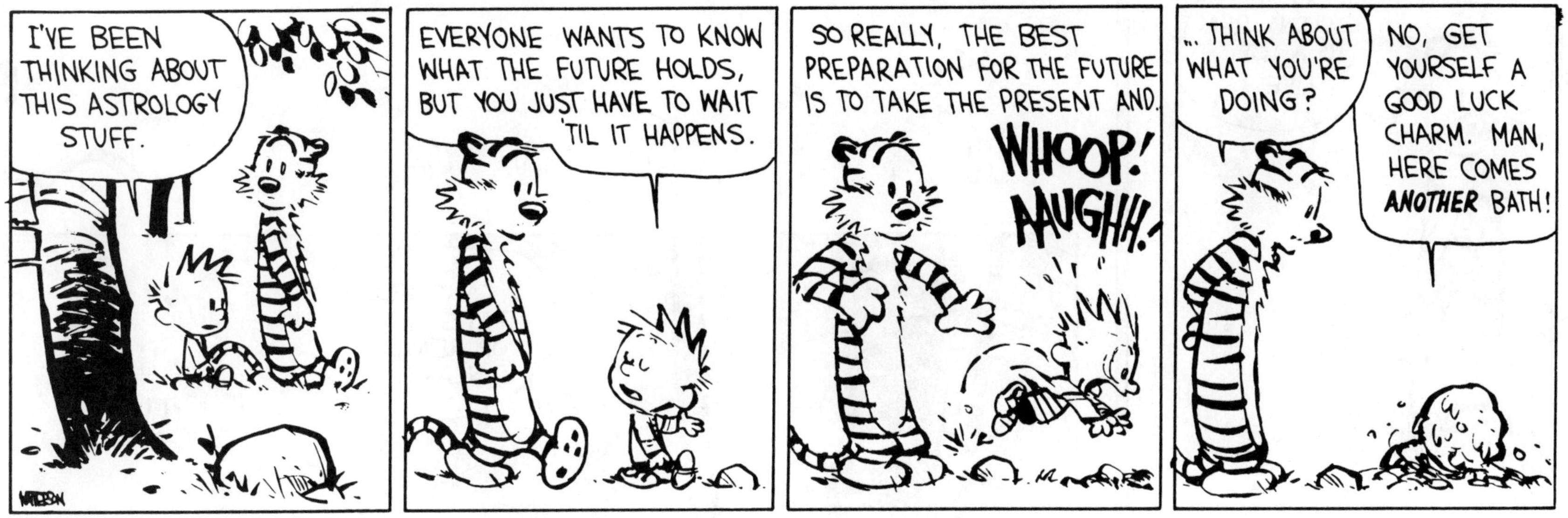
I'VE BEEN THINKING ABOUT THIS ASTROLOGY STUFF.
EVERYONE WANTS TO KNOW WHAT THE FUTURE HOLDS, BUT YOU JUST HAVE TO WAIT 'TIL IT HAPPENS.
SO REALLY, THE BEST PREPARATION FOR THE FUTURE IS TO TAKE THE PRESENT AND.
WHOOP!
AAUGHH!
.. THINK ABOUT WHAT YOU'RE DOING?
NO, GET YOURSELF A GOOD LUCK CHARM. MAN, HERE COMES ANOTHER BATH!

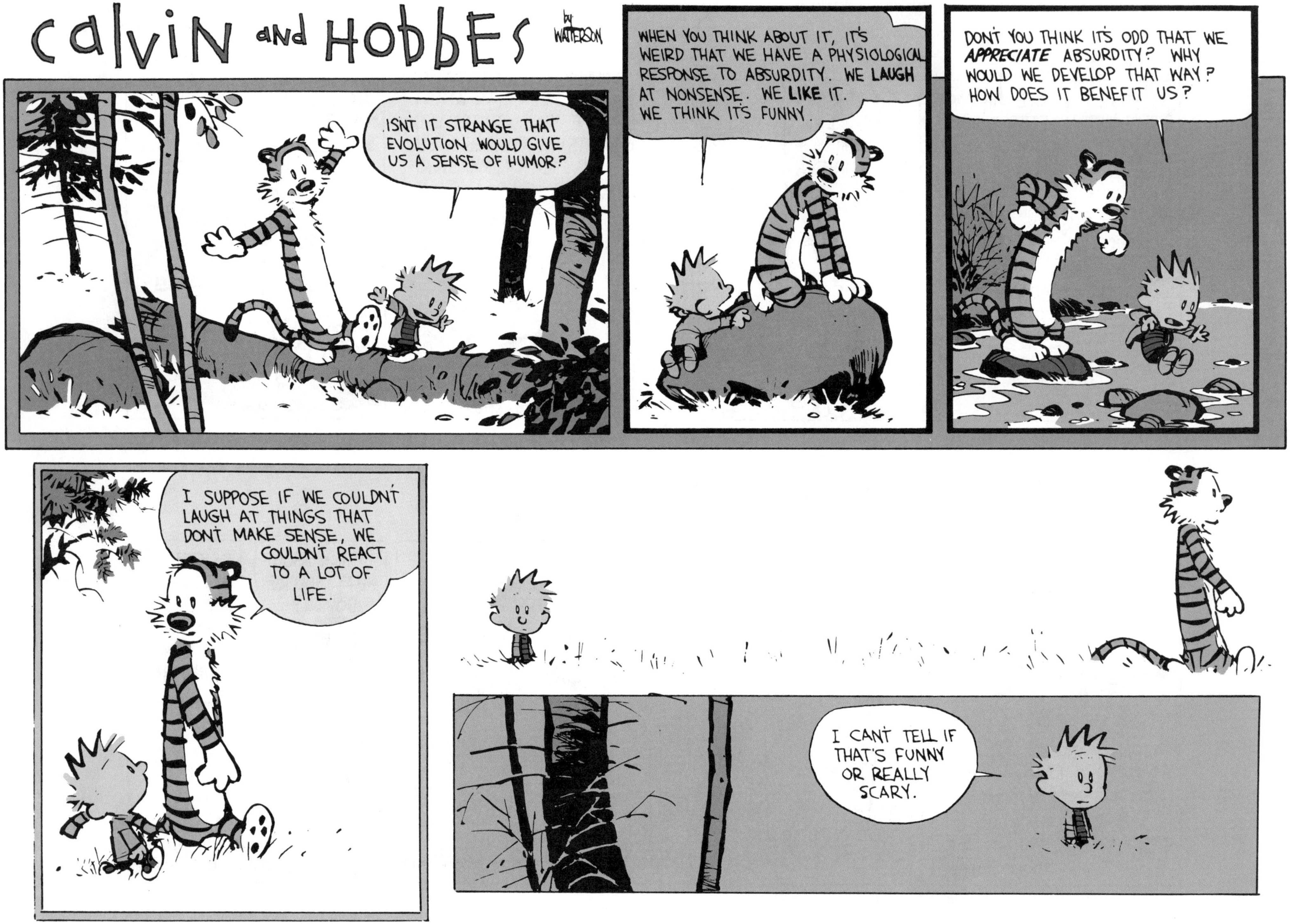
Calvin and HOBBES
by WATTERSON
ISN'T IT STRANGE THAT EVOLUTION WOULD GIVE US A SENSE OF HUMOR?
WHEN YOU THINK ABOUT IT, IT'S WEIRD THAT WE HAVE A PHYSIOLOGICAL RESPONSE TO ABSURDITY. WE **LAUGH** AT NONSENSE. WE **LIKE** IT. WE THINK IT'S FUNNY.
DON'T YOU THINK IT'S ODD THAT WE ***APPRECIATE*** ABSURDITY? WHY WOULD WE DEVELOP THAT WAY? HOW DOES IT BENEFIT US?
I SUPPOSE IF WE COULDN'T LAUGH AT THINGS THAT DON'T MAKE SENSE, WE COULDN'T REACT TO A LOT OF LIFE.
I CAN'T TELL IF THAT'S FUNNY OR REALLY SCARY.

I THINK WE NEED A NEW POLICY IN THIS HOUSE.

AND WHAT'S THAT?

FROM NOW ON, WHENEVER YOU TELL ME THINGS, I DON'T WANT TO HEAR ANY REASONS, EXPLANATIONS, SUBTLETY OR CONTEXT.

I JUST WANT TEN-SECOND SOUND BITES, OK?

SO MUCH FOR *THAT* POLICY.

FOR SCHOOL, WE'RE SUPPOSED TO WRITE A PARAGRAPH ABOUT WHAT OUR DADS DO.

"DAD: THE PARAGRAPH."

CATCHY TITLE, HUH?

"WHAT DOES MY DAD DO? MOSTLY, HE GETS ON MY NERVES. THE END."

YOU MAY GET A POINT FOR SUCCINCTNESS.

WELL WHAT ELSE IS THERE TO SAY?!

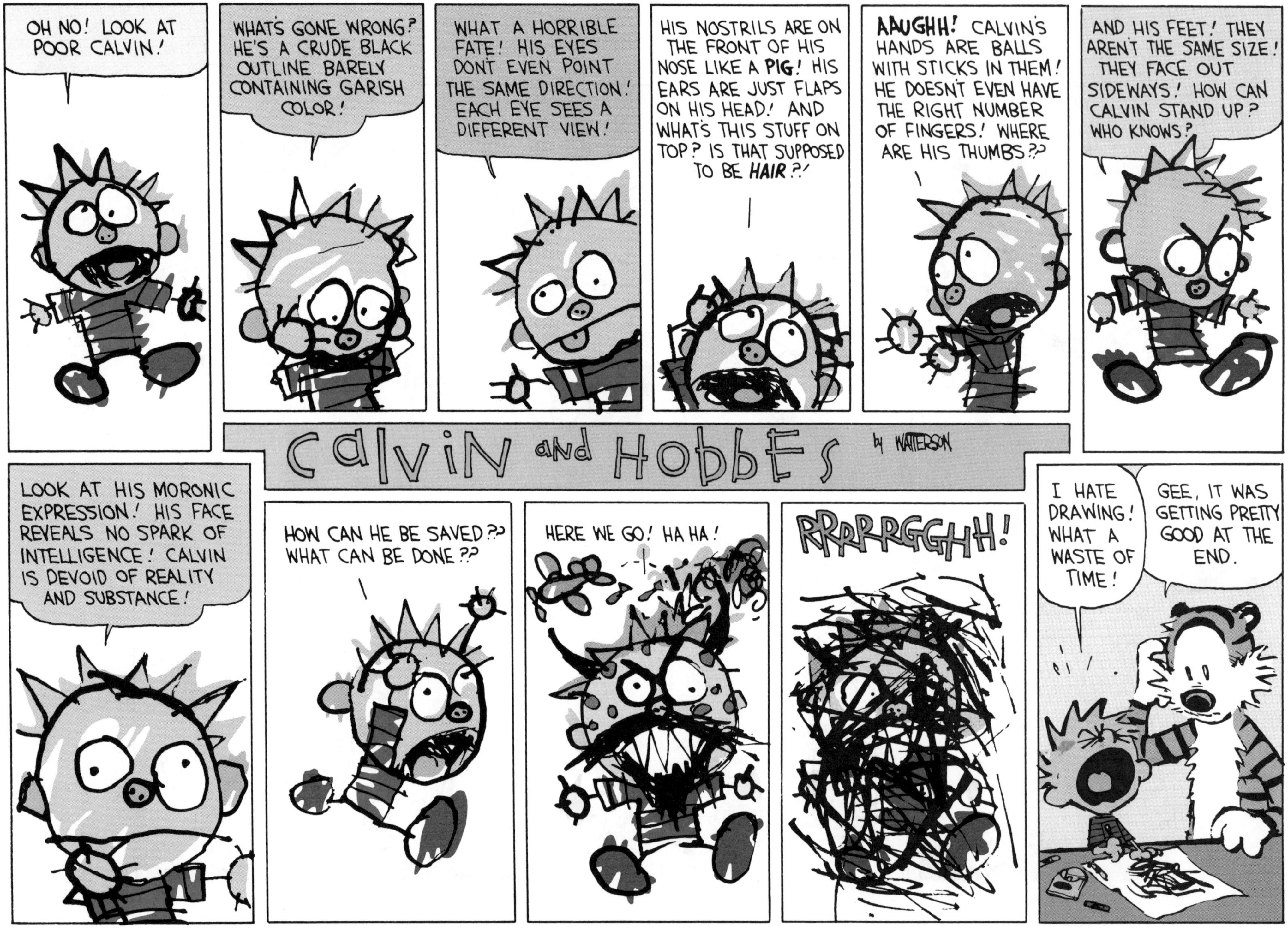
OH NO! LOOK AT POOR CALVIN!
WHAT'S GONE WRONG? HE'S A CRUDE BLACK OUTLINE BARELY CONTAINING GARISH COLOR!
WHAT A HORRIBLE FATE! HIS EYES DON'T EVEN POINT THE SAME DIRECTION! EACH EYE SEES A DIFFERENT VIEW!
HIS NOSTRILS ARE ON THE FRONT OF HIS NOSE LIKE A PIG! HIS EARS ARE JUST FLAPS ON HIS HEAD! AND WHAT'S THIS STUFF ON TOP? IS THAT SUPPOSED TO BE HAIR?!
AAUGHH! CALVIN'S HANDS ARE BALLS WITH STICKS IN THEM! HE DOESN'T EVEN HAVE THE RIGHT NUMBER OF FINGERS! WHERE ARE HIS THUMBS??
AND HIS FEET! THEY AREN'T THE SAME SIZE! THEY FACE OUT SIDEWAYS! HOW CAN CALVIN STAND UP? WHO KNOWS?
CALVIN AND HOBBES
by WATTERSON
LOOK AT HIS MORONIC EXPRESSION! HIS FACE REVEALS NO SPARK OF INTELLIGENCE! CALVIN IS DEVOID OF REALITY AND SUBSTANCE!
HOW CAN HE BE SAVED?? WHAT CAN BE DONE??
HERE WE GO! HA HA!
RRRRRGGHH!
I HATE DRAWING! WHAT A WASTE OF TIME!
GEE, IT WAS GETTING PRETTY GOOD AT THE END.

BAD NEWS, DAD. THE CHARACTER ISSUE IS KILLING YOU IN THE POLLS.
WHAT CHARACTER ISSUE?! I'VE GOT GREAT CHARACTER! I'VE GOT CHARACTER UP TO HERE!
THAT'S WHAT WE HATE.
MY ONLY FLAW IS A PRETERNATURAL INTOLERANCE OF PESKY KIDS.

PAUL GAUGUIN ASKED, "WHENCE DO WE COME? WHAT ARE WE? WHERE ARE WE GOING?"
WELL, I DON'T KNOW ABOUT ANYONE ELSE, BUT I CAME FROM MY ROOM, I'M A KID WITH BIG PLANS, AND I'M GOING OUTSIDE! SEE YA LATER!
SAY, WHO THE HECK IS PAUL GAUGUIN ANYWAY?

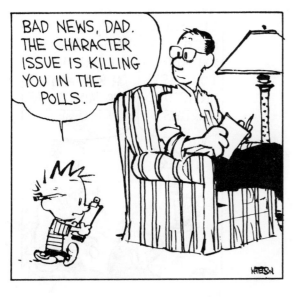

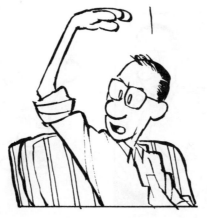

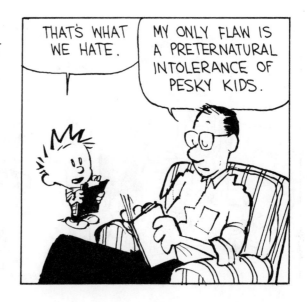

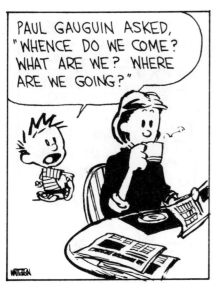

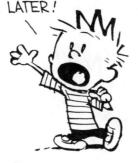

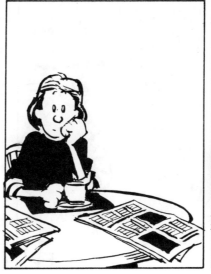

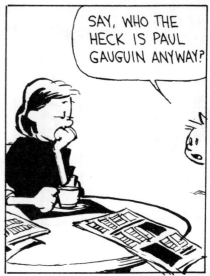

LOOK AT **THIS**, DAD! I'VE GOT FIVE DOLLARS IN HERE! I'M RICH!
I'VE BEEN SAVING MY CHANGE FOR WEEKS AND WEEKS, AND LOOK HOW MUCH I'VE GOT! GUESS WHAT I'M GOING TO DO WITH IT!
OPEN A SAVINGS ACCOUNT?
I'LL BET I KNOW WHY YOU GUYS DON'T GET INVITED TO PARTIES.
EVERY TIME YOU MAKE A DEPOSIT, YOU CAN THINK, "OH BOY, ANOTHER TWO MINUTES AT COLLEGE."
WATTERSON

MY GUM HAS LOST ITS FLAVOR.
WHEN THAT HAPPENS, I DON'T SPIT IT OUT. I JUST ADD A NEW PIECE.
AFTER A FEW PACKS, IT'S LIKE CHEWING A BIG, SOGGY SOCK! MY JAWS ACHE AND I CAN'T CLOSE MY LIPS, SO I WHEEZE THROUGH MY OPEN MOUTH AND DROOL!
AN ORIFICE IS AN AMUSING THING, ALL RIGHT.
ITH FUNNY HOW YOU NEFFA THEE GWOWN-UPTH DO THITH.
WATTERSON

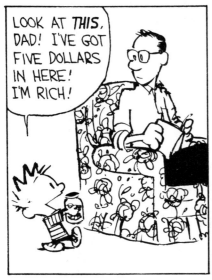

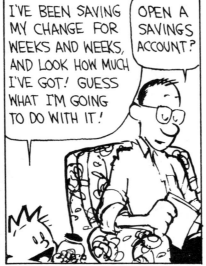

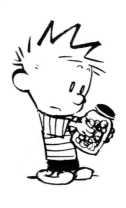

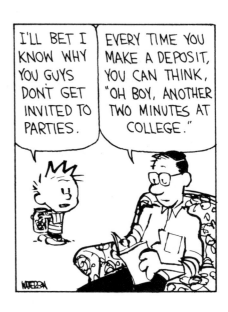

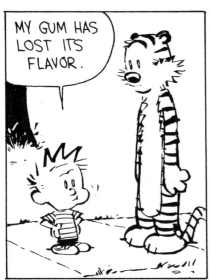

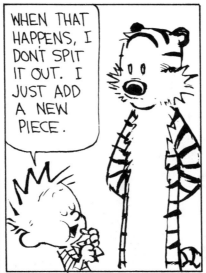

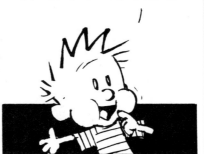

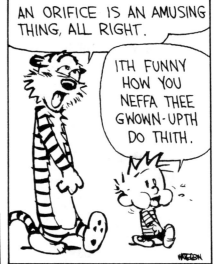

OH BOY, THE NEW ISSUE OF "CHEWING"!

YOU GET A MAGAZINE?

WOW, THIS LOOKS GREAT! "SPECIAL SUGARLESS GUM ISSUE - CHOOSING AN ARTIFICIAL SWEETENER THAT'S RIGHT FOR *YOU* .... TONGUE EXERCISES FOR BIGGER BUBBLES .... RAD FASHION KNEEPADS FOR WALKING AND CHEWING .... *PLUS* AN INTERVIEW WITH BAZOOKA JOE!"

SEE, IT'S ALL TARGET MARKETING! ADVERTISERS DON'T WASTE THEIR TIME ON MASS AUDIENCES ANY MORE. THEY FIND YOUR SPECIAL INTEREST AND THEY NAIL YOU!

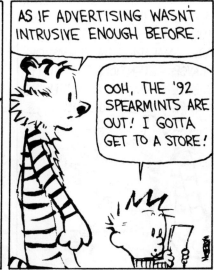

AS IF ADVERTISING WASN'T INTRUSIVE ENOUGH BEFORE.

OOH, THE '92 SPEARMINTS ARE OUT! I GOTTA GET TO A STORE!

I CAN'T BELIEVE THERE'S A MAGAZINE FOR GUM CHEWERS.

HECK, THERE MUST BE A *DOZEN* SUCH MAGAZINES.

EACH APPEALS TO A DIFFERENT FACTION. "CHEWING" IS HIGH-GLOSS, LITERATE AND SOPHISTICATED. "GUM ACTION" GOES FOR THE GONZO CHEWERS. "CHEWERS ILLUSTRATED" AIMS AT VINTAGE GUM COLLECTORS, AND SO ON!

EACH ONE ENCOURAGES YOU TO THINK YOU BELONG TO AN ELITE CLIQUE, SO ADVERTISERS CAN APPEAL TO YOUR EGO AND GET YOU TO CULTIVATE AN IMAGE THAT SETS YOU APART FROM THE CROWD. IT'S THE DIVIDE AND CONQUER TRICK.

I WONDER WHATEVER HAPPENED TO THE MELTING POT.

THERE'S NO MONEY IN IT.

HERE'S AN INTERESTING ARTICLE. THE TOP FIVE GUM BRANDS ARE COMPARED IN TERMS OF FLAVOR RETENTION, ELASTICITY, BUBBLE CAPACITY AND CHEWING REBOUND.
THE COMPUTER GRAPH SHOWS THE RESULTS, COMPENSATING FOR VARIOUS SALIVA ACIDITIES. IF YOU KNOW YOUR pH, THIS REALLY HELPS YOU CHOOSE THE PROPER GUM FOR YOUR CHEWING STYLE.
Chewing
WHAT KIND OF NUT WOULD **CARE** ABOUT ALL THIS?!
EVERYONE! THIS IS HARD DATA! IT LETS YOU QUANTIFY YOUR ENJOYMENT!
I THOUGHT FUN WAS SUPPOSED TO BE ***FUN***.
WELL ***I*** PREFER TO TRUST THE EXPERTS.
Chewing

HERE'S AN AD FOR A NEW GUM CALLED "HYPERBUBBLE," AND IT SAYS, "IF YOU'RE NOT CHEWING HYPERBUBBLE, YOU MIGHT AS WELL BE CHEWING YOUR CUD." OOH, GREAT COPY!
GOSH, AM I COOL ENOUGH TO CHEW HYPERBUBBLE? MAYBE I'M **NOT**! MAYBE IF YOU CHEW HYPERBUBBLE, YOU ***BECOME*** COOL!
OR MAYBE IF YOU CHEW IT, EVERYONE ***ASSUMES*** YOU'RE COOL, SO IT DOESN'T MATTER IF YOU ARE OR NOT! WHAT DO YOU THINK? SHOULD I BUY SOME?
IF YOUR EMOTIONAL SECURITY DEPENDS ON SATISFYING A NEED YOU DIDN'T HAVE UNTIL YOU READ THE AD, GO AHEAD.
I THINK I WILL! BOY, I'M GLAD I GET THIS MAGAZINE!

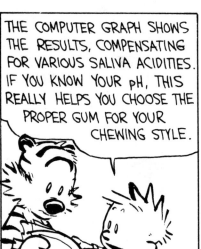

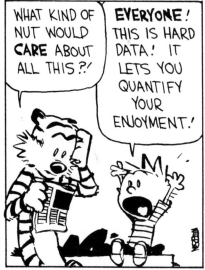

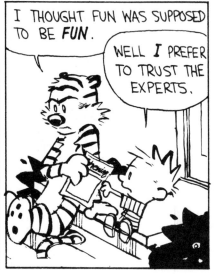

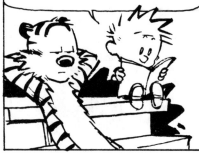

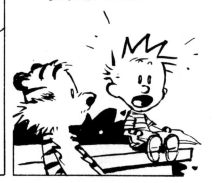

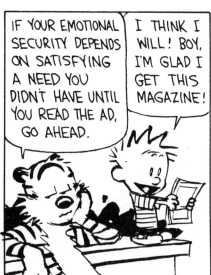

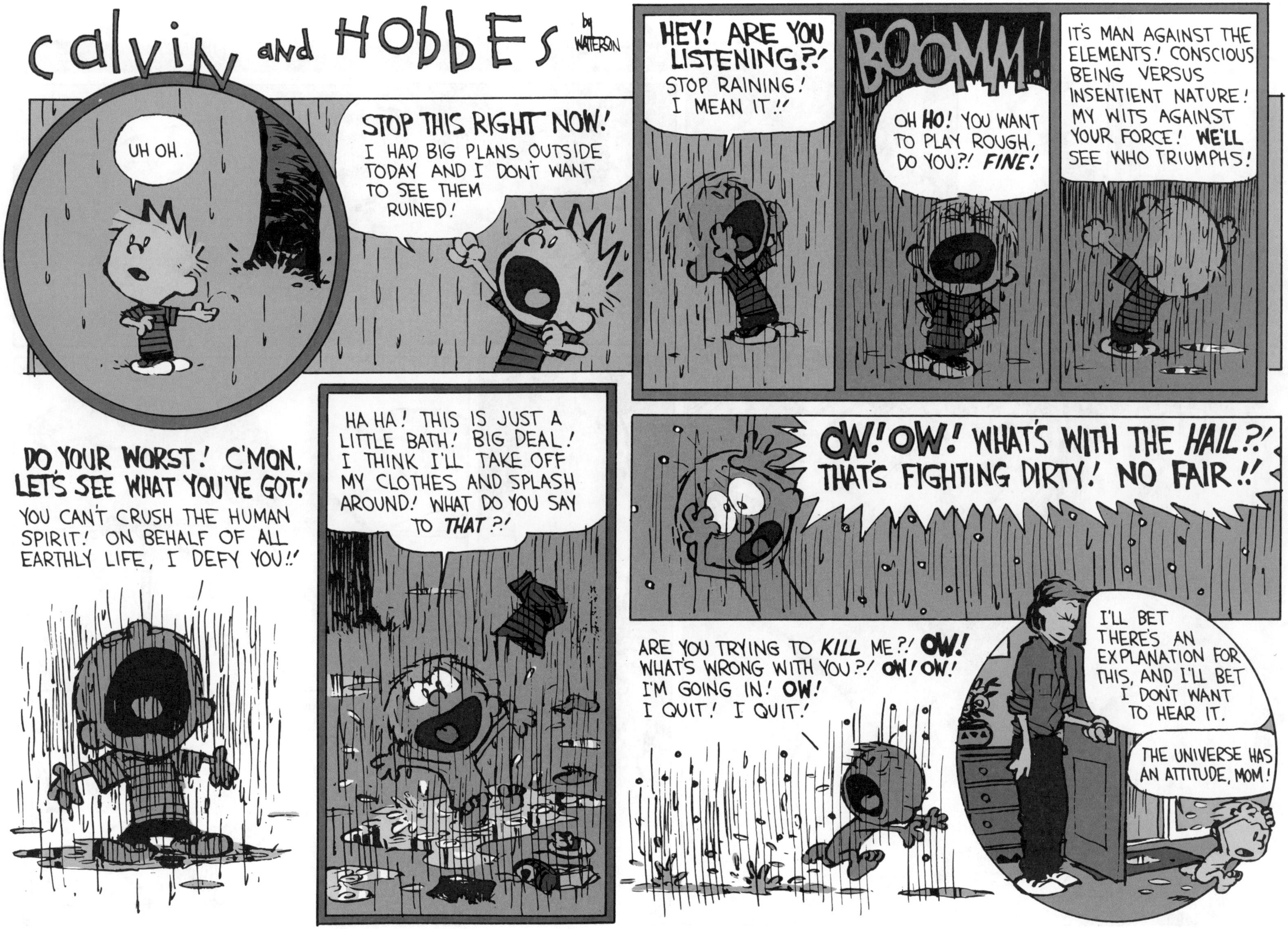
Calvin and HOBBES
by WATTERSON
UH OH.
STOP THIS RIGHT NOW! I HAD BIG PLANS OUTSIDE TODAY AND I DON'T WANT TO SEE THEM RUINED!
HEY! ARE YOU LISTENING?! STOP RAINING! I MEAN IT!!
BOOMM!
OH HO! YOU WANT TO PLAY ROUGH, DO YOU?! FINE!
IT'S MAN AGAINST THE ELEMENTS! CONSCIOUS BEING VERSUS INSENTIENT NATURE! MY WITS AGAINST YOUR FORCE! WE'LL SEE WHO TRIUMPHS!
DO YOUR WORST! C'MON, LET'S SEE WHAT YOU'VE GOT! YOU CAN'T CRUSH THE HUMAN SPIRIT! ON BEHALF OF ALL EARTHLY LIFE, I DEFY YOU!!
HA HA! THIS IS JUST A LITTLE BATH! BIG DEAL! I THINK I'LL TAKE OFF MY CLOTHES AND SPLASH AROUND! WHAT DO YOU SAY TO THAT?!
OW! OW! WHAT'S WITH THE HAIL?! THAT'S FIGHTING DIRTY! NO FAIR!!
ARE YOU TRYING TO KILL ME?! OW! WHAT'S WRONG WITH YOU?! OW! OW! I'M GOING IN! OW! I QUIT! I QUIT!
I'LL BET THERE'S AN EXPLANATION FOR THIS, AND I'LL BET I DON'T WANT TO HEAR IT.
THE UNIVERSE HAS AN ATTITUDE, MOM!

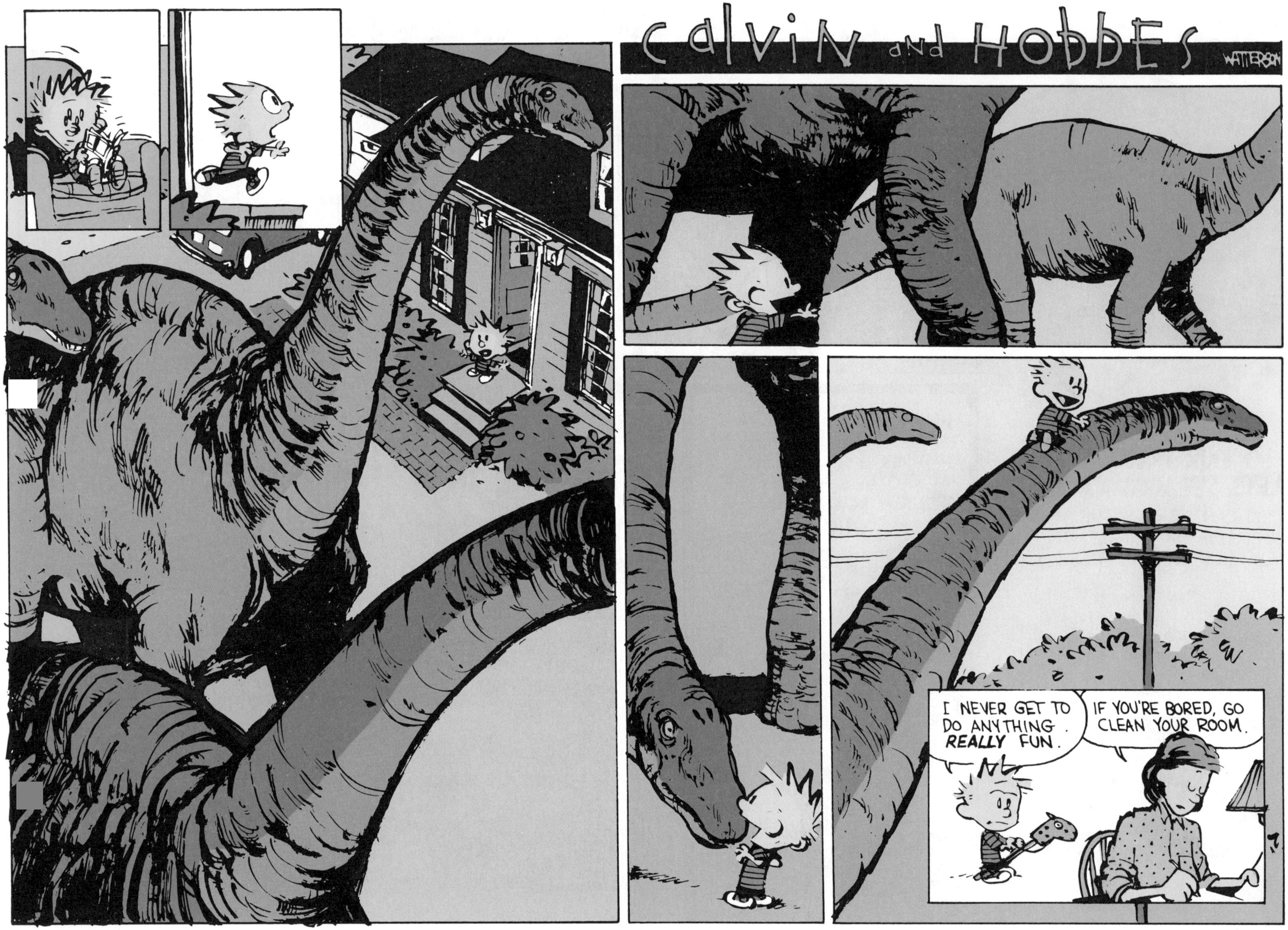
Calvin and HOBBES
WATTERSON
I NEVER GET TO DO ANYTHING REALLY FUN.
IF YOU'RE BORED, GO CLEAN YOUR ROOM.

YAHHH!
RRGGHH
MUNCH
MUNCH
MUNCH
YOU'RE RIGHT. FOOD **DOES** TASTE BETTER THIS WAY.

AS I, THE MANIACAL TYRANT, LOOK DOWN UPON MY PATHETIC SUBJECTS,...
..I REFLECT ON HOW THEIR PUNY LIVES MEAN NOTHING TO ME EXCEPT AS THE BRUTE LABOR NECESSARY TO EXECUTE MY MAD DESIGNS! MY LUNATIC WHIMS ARE THEIR LAWS! HA HA HA!
I THOUGHT I TOLD YOU TO GATHER THE TRASH.
BEING A PARENT MUST BE NICE.

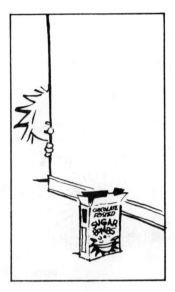

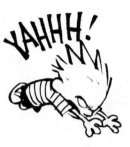

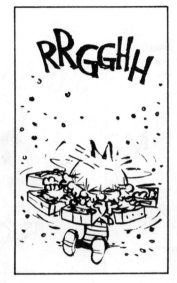

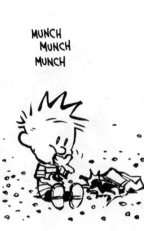

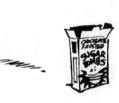

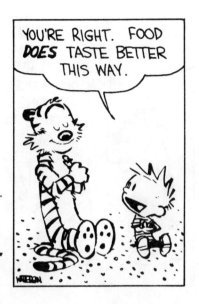

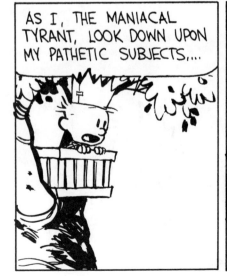

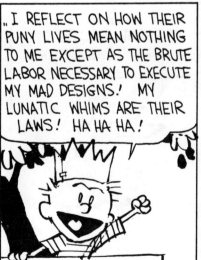

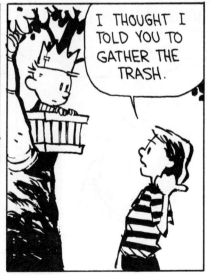

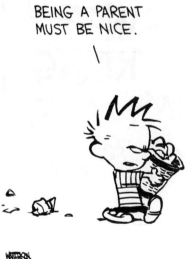

Outta my way, Twinky.

A PERSON CAN'T BE A DOORMAT UNLESS HE ALLOWS HIMSELF TO BE ONE! I REFUSE TO BUDGE!

SHOVE

ACK! OOF! UGH!

I'VE GOT TO STOP READING THOSE DUMB ADVICE COLUMNS.

RINGG, RINNG

HELLO, WE ARE UNABLE TO COME TO THE PHONE RIGHT NOW...

...SO PLEASE LEAVE A MESSAGE AT THE SOUND OF THE CLICK.

CLICK

MOST PEOPLE JUST MUDDLE THROUGH THEIR LIVES! THEY'RE PASSIVE AND UNMOTIVATED! THEY LACK AMBITION AND DRIVE!

NOT *ME*, THOUGH! I'M GOING TO HAVE AN *EPIC* LIFE! I'M GOING TO WRESTLE THE ISSUES OF THE AGE AND CHANGE THE COURSE OF HISTORY!

HOW ARE YOU GOING TO DO THAT?

I'M GOING TO SIT HERE AND WAIT, SO OPPORTUNITY WILL KNOW RIGHT WHERE TO FIND ME WHEN IT'S TIME TO CHANGE THE WORLD.

I WISH I'D BROUGHT A BOOK TO READ.

NAHH, IT'LL BE ANY MINUTE NOW.

OUT!

DARN!

OUR COUNTRY WAS FOUNDED A VERY LONG TIME AGO, ROUGHLY AROUND 200 B.C.

200 B.C. ?!

"BEFORE CALVIN."

THAT'S WHAT'S *IMPORTANT!*

WHEN I GROW UP, I'M NOT GOING TO READ THE NEWSPAPER AND I'M NOT GOING TO FOLLOW COMPLEX ISSUES AND I'M NOT GOING TO VOTE.

THAT WAY I CAN COMPLAIN THAT THE GOVERNMENT DOESN'T REPRESENT ME.

THEN, WHEN EVERYTHING GOES DOWN THE TUBES, I CAN SAY THE SYSTEM DOESN'T WORK AND JUSTIFY MY FURTHER LACK OF PARTICIPATION.

AN INGENIOUSLY SELF-FULFILLING PLAN.

IT'S A LOT MORE FUN TO BLAME THINGS THAN TO FIX THEM.

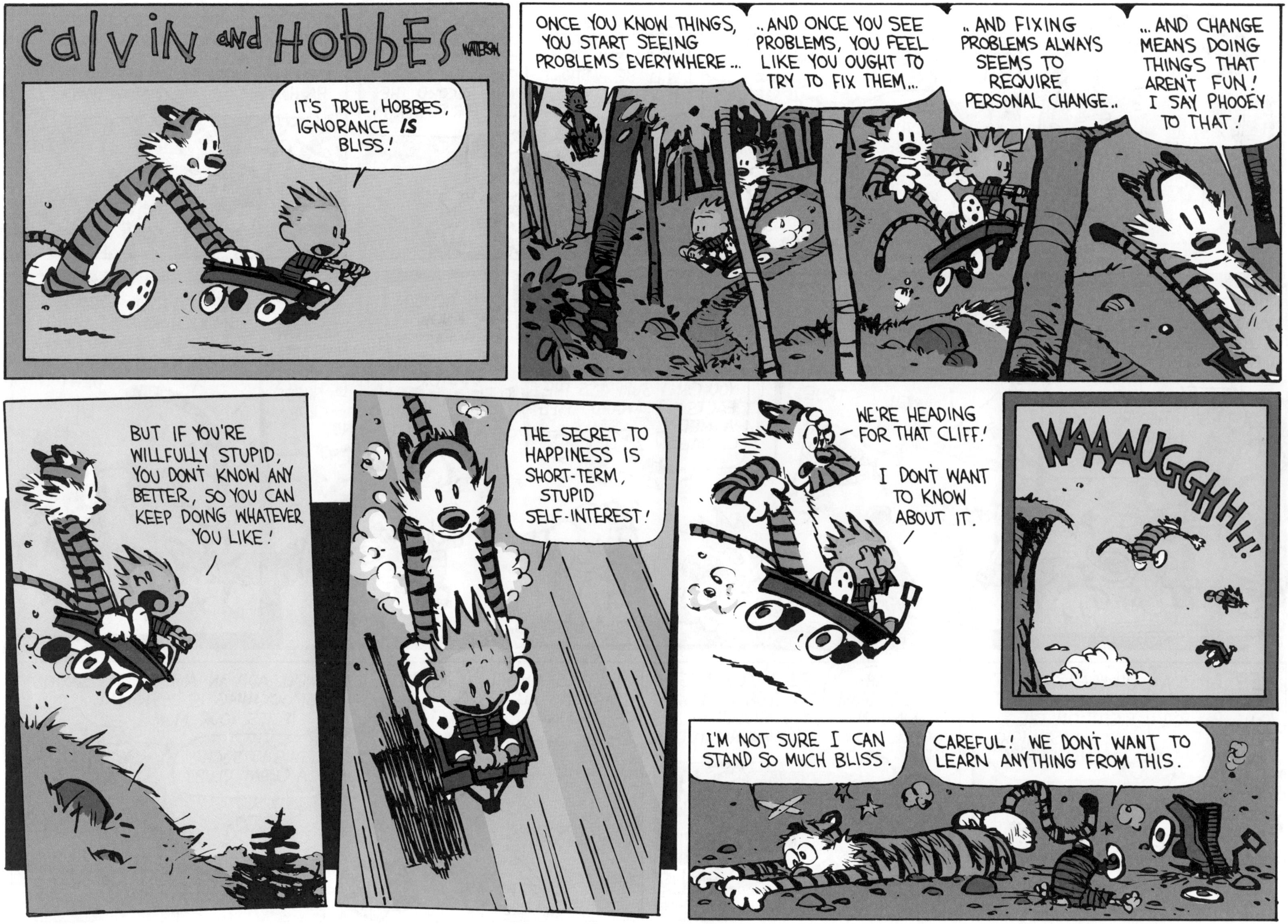
Calvin and HOBBES
WATTERSON
IT'S TRUE, HOBBES, IGNORANCE IS BLISS!
ONCE YOU KNOW THINGS, YOU START SEEING PROBLEMS EVERYWHERE...
..AND ONCE YOU SEE PROBLEMS, YOU FEEL LIKE YOU OUGHT TO TRY TO FIX THEM...
..AND FIXING PROBLEMS ALWAYS SEEMS TO REQUIRE PERSONAL CHANGE..
...AND CHANGE MEANS DOING THINGS THAT AREN'T FUN! I SAY PHOOEY TO THAT!
BUT IF YOU'RE WILLFULLY STUPID, YOU DON'T KNOW ANY BETTER, SO YOU CAN KEEP DOING WHATEVER YOU LIKE!
THE SECRET TO HAPPINESS IS SHORT-TERM, STUPID SELF-INTEREST!
WE'RE HEADING FOR THAT CLIFF!
I DON'T WANT TO KNOW ABOUT IT.
WAAAUGGHHH!
I'M NOT SURE I CAN STAND SO MUCH BLISS.
CAREFUL! WE DON'T WANT TO LEARN ANYTHING FROM THIS.

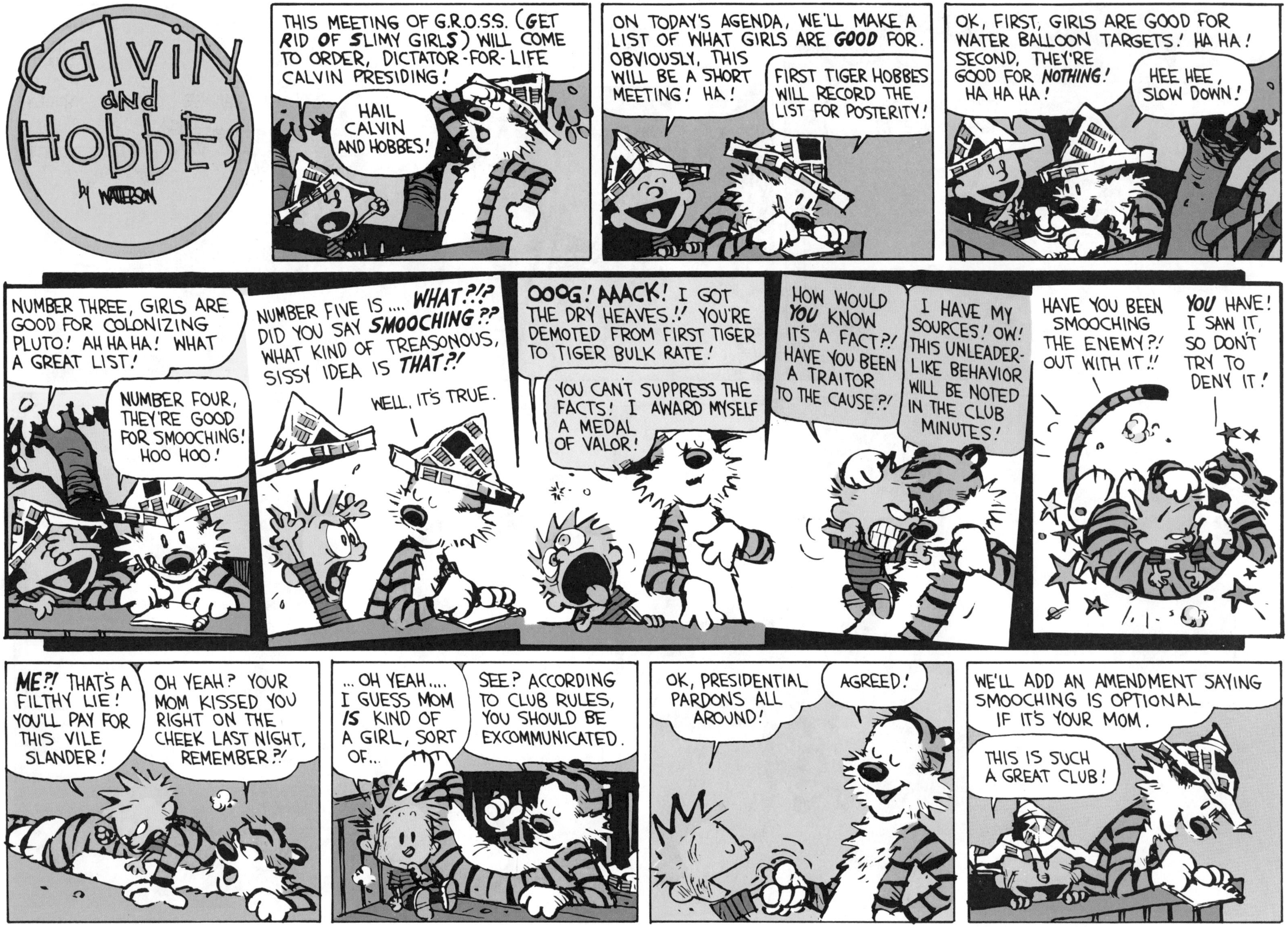
Calvin and Hobbes
by WATTERSON
THIS MEETING OF G.R.O.S.S. (GET RID OF SLIMY GIRLS) WILL COME TO ORDER, DICTATOR-FOR-LIFE CALVIN PRESIDING!
HAIL CALVIN AND HOBBES!
ON TODAY'S AGENDA, WE'LL MAKE A LIST OF WHAT GIRLS ARE GOOD FOR. OBVIOUSLY, THIS WILL BE A SHORT MEETING! HA!
FIRST TIGER HOBBES WILL RECORD THE LIST FOR POSTERITY!
OK, FIRST, GIRLS ARE GOOD FOR WATER BALLOON TARGETS! HA HA! SECOND, THEY'RE GOOD FOR NOTHING! HA HA HA!
HEE HEE, SLOW DOWN!
NUMBER THREE, GIRLS ARE GOOD FOR COLONIZING PLUTO! AH HA HA! WHAT A GREAT LIST!
NUMBER FOUR, THEY'RE GOOD FOR SMOOCHING! HOO HOO!
NUMBER FIVE IS .... WHAT?!? DID YOU SAY SMOOCHING?? WHAT KIND OF TREASONOUS, SISSY IDEA IS THAT?!
WELL, IT'S TRUE.
OOOG! AAACK! I GOT THE DRY HEAVES!! YOU'RE DEMOTED FROM FIRST TIGER TO TIGER BULK RATE!
YOU CAN'T SUPPRESS THE FACTS! I AWARD MYSELF A MEDAL OF VALOR!
HOW WOULD YOU KNOW IT'S A FACT?! HAVE YOU BEEN A TRAITOR TO THE CAUSE?!
I HAVE MY SOURCES! OW! THIS UNLEADER-LIKE BEHAVIOR WILL BE NOTED IN THE CLUB MINUTES!
HAVE YOU BEEN SMOOCHING THE ENEMY?! OUT WITH IT!!
YOU HAVE! I SAW IT, SO DON'T TRY TO DENY IT!
ME?! THAT'S A FILTHY LIE! YOU'LL PAY FOR THIS VILE SLANDER!
OH YEAH? YOUR MOM KISSED YOU RIGHT ON THE CHEEK LAST NIGHT, REMEMBER?!
... OH YEAH.... I GUESS MOM IS KIND OF A GIRL, SORT OF...
SEE? ACCORDING TO CLUB RULES, YOU SHOULD BE EXCOMMUNICATED.
OK, PRESIDENTIAL PARDONS ALL AROUND!
AGREED!
WE'LL ADD AN AMENDMENT SAYING SMOOCHING IS OPTIONAL IF IT'S YOUR MOM.
THIS IS SUCH A GREAT CLUB!

AW GEE, DID THE DARN OL' SUN MOVE SOME MORE ?!?
OH HUSH.

BASEBALL IS AN INTELLIGENT SPORT. THERE'S MORE TO IT THAN BRUTE FORCE.
IT MAY SEEM SLOW, BUT THAT'S BECAUSE IT'S A THINKING MAN'S GAME. THERE'S A LOT OF STRATEGY TO CONSIDER.
ESPECIALLY THE WAY WE PLAY!
RIGHT! NOW, THE FIRST PERSON TO DISCOVER TWELFTH BASE GETS A GHOST POINT AND ONE FREE "GET OUT OF JAIL"...

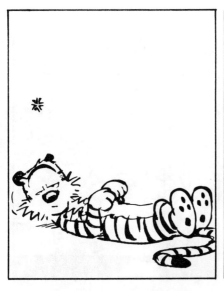

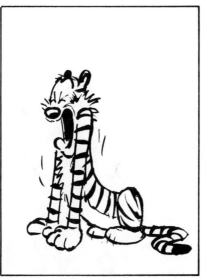

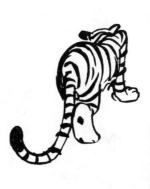

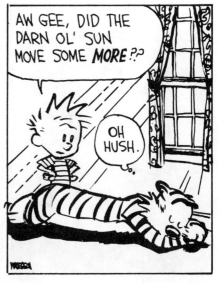

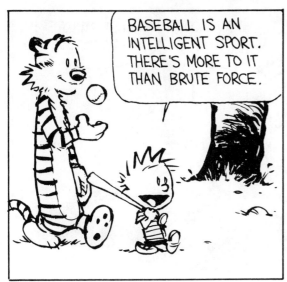

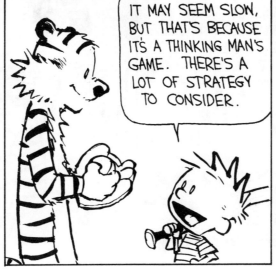

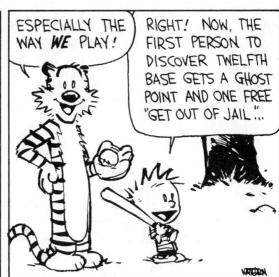

THIS IS THE WORST ASSIGNMENT EVER! I'M SUPPOSED TO THINK UP A STORY, WRITE IT, AND ILLUSTRATE IT BY TOMORROW!
DO I LOOK LIKE A NOVELIST?! THIS IS IMPOSSIBLE! I CAN'T TELL STORIES!
WHAT ABOUT YOUR EXPLANATION OF THE NOODLE INCIDENT?
THAT WASN'T A STORY! THAT WAS THE UNVARNISHED TRUTH!
OH, DON'T BE SO MODEST. YOU DESERVED A PULITZER.

DO YOU HAVE AN IDEA FOR YOUR STORY YET?
NO, I'M WAITING FOR INSPIRATION.
YOU CAN'T JUST TURN ON CREATIVITY LIKE A FAUCET. YOU HAVE TO BE IN THE RIGHT MOOD.
WHAT MOOD IS THAT?
LAST-MINUTE PANIC.

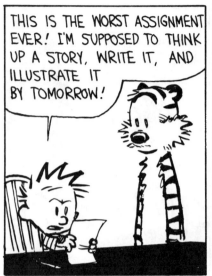

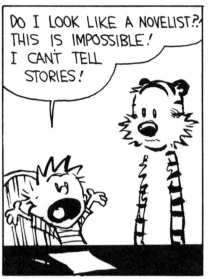

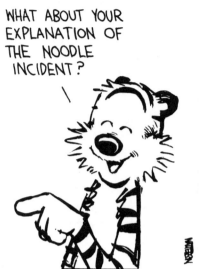

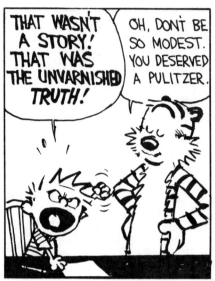

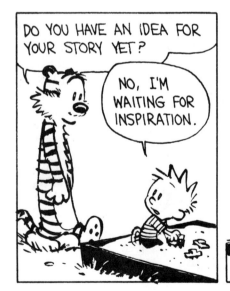

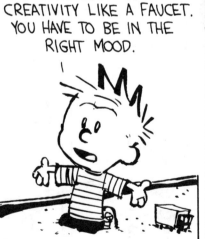

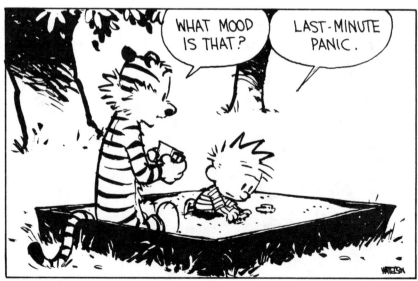

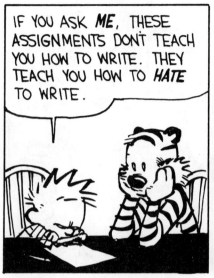

IF YOU ASK ME, THESE ASSIGNMENTS DON'T TEACH YOU HOW TO WRITE. THEY TEACH YOU HOW TO HATE TO WRITE.
DEADLINES, RULES HOW TO DO IT, GRADES... HOW CAN YOU BE CREATIVE WHEN SOMEONE'S BREATHING DOWN YOUR NECK?
I GUESS YOU SHOULD TRY NOT TO THINK ABOUT THE END RESULT TOO MUCH AND JUST HAVE FUN WITH THE PROCESS OF CREATING.
EVERY TIME I DO THAT, I END UP IN THE SCHOOL PSYCHOLOGIST'S OFFICE.
WELL, MAYBE NOT THAT MUCH FUN.
WATTERSON

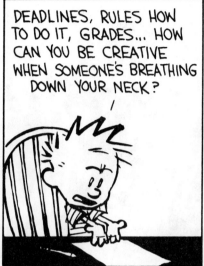

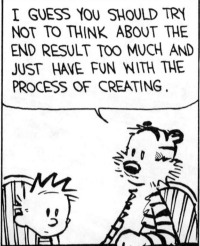

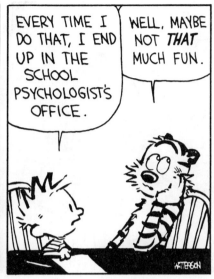

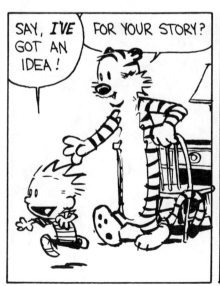

SAY, I'VE GOT AN IDEA!
FOR YOUR STORY?
NO, I THOUGHT OF A WAY I WON'T HAVE TO WRITE ONE!
OH NO.
HOP IN THE TIME MACHINE, HOBBES! WE'RE GOING A FEW HOURS INTO THE FUTURE! I'LL HAVE FINISHED MY STORY BY THEN, SO WE'LL JUST PICK IT UP AND BRING IT BACK TO THE PRESENT! THAT WAY, I WON'T HAVE TO WRITE IT!
SOMETHING DOESN'T MAKE SENSE HERE, AND I THINK IT'S ME SITTING IN THIS BOX.
RELAX! WE'LL BE BACK AS SOON AS WE GO.
TIME MACHINE

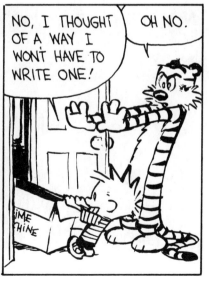

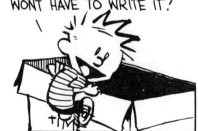

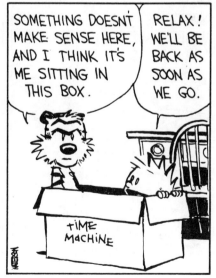

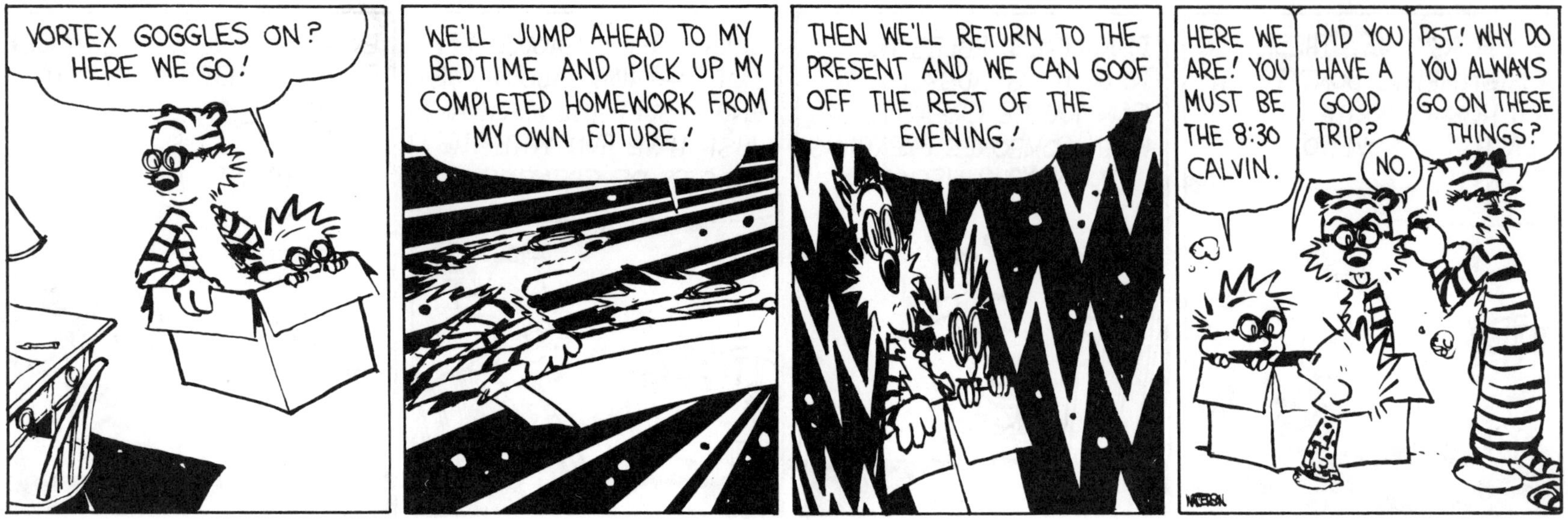
VORTEX GOGGLES ON? HERE WE GO!
WE'LL JUMP AHEAD TO MY BEDTIME AND PICK UP MY COMPLETED HOMEWORK FROM MY OWN FUTURE!
THEN WE'LL RETURN TO THE PRESENT AND WE CAN GOOF OFF THE REST OF THE EVENING!
HERE WE ARE! YOU MUST BE THE 8:30 CALVIN.
DID YOU HAVE A GOOD TRIP?
NO.
PST! WHY DO YOU ALWAYS GO ON THESE THINGS?

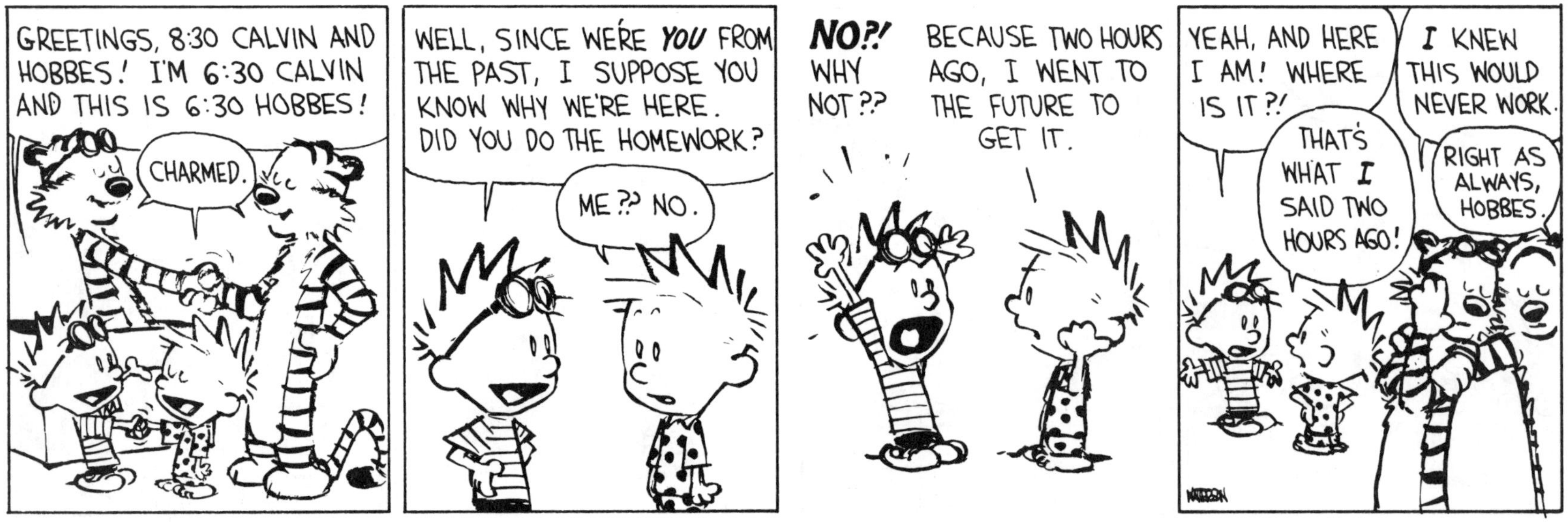
GREETINGS, 8:30 CALVIN AND HOBBES! I'M 6:30 CALVIN AND THIS IS 6:30 HOBBES!
CHARMED.
WELL, SINCE WE'RE *YOU* FROM THE PAST, I SUPPOSE YOU KNOW WHY WE'RE HERE. DID YOU DO THE HOMEWORK?
ME?? NO.
NO?! WHY NOT??
BECAUSE TWO HOURS AGO, I WENT TO THE FUTURE TO GET IT.
YEAH, AND HERE I AM! WHERE IS IT?!
THAT'S WHAT *I* SAID TWO HOURS AGO!
I KNEW THIS WOULD NEVER WORK.
RIGHT AS ALWAYS, HOBBES.

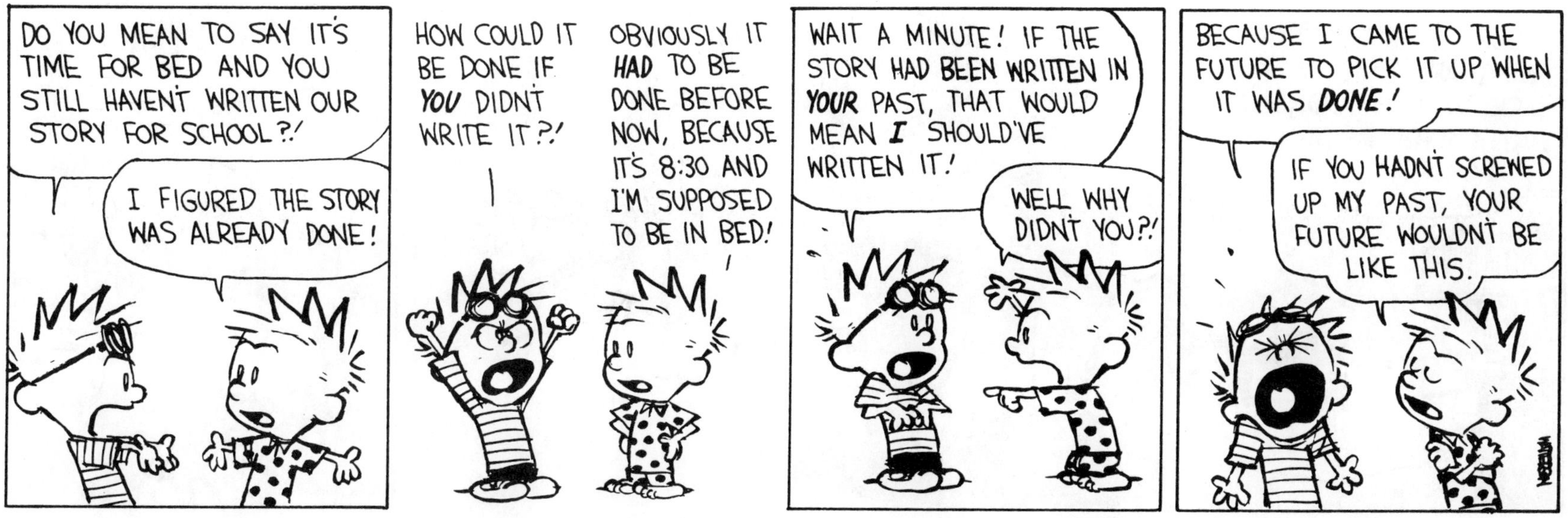
DO YOU MEAN TO SAY IT'S TIME FOR BED AND YOU STILL HAVEN'T WRITTEN OUR STORY FOR SCHOOL?!
I FIGURED THE STORY WAS ALREADY DONE!
HOW COULD IT BE DONE IF YOU DIDN'T WRITE IT?!
OBVIOUSLY IT HAD TO BE DONE BEFORE NOW, BECAUSE IT'S 8:30 AND I'M SUPPOSED TO BE IN BED!
WAIT A MINUTE! IF THE STORY HAD BEEN WRITTEN IN YOUR PAST, THAT WOULD MEAN I SHOULD'VE WRITTEN IT!
WELL WHY DIDN'T YOU?!
BECAUSE I CAME TO THE FUTURE TO PICK IT UP WHEN IT WAS DONE!
IF YOU HADN'T SCREWED UP MY PAST, YOUR FUTURE WOULDN'T BE LIKE THIS.

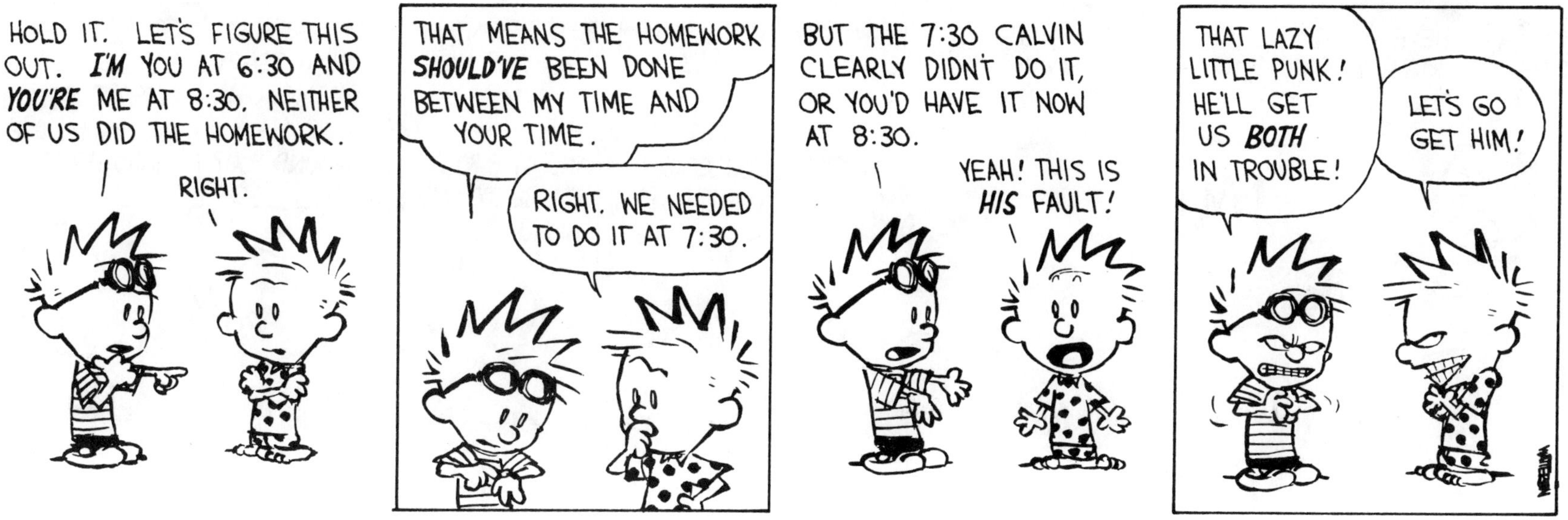
HOLD IT. LET'S FIGURE THIS OUT. I'M YOU AT 6:30 AND YOU'RE ME AT 8:30. NEITHER OF US DID THE HOMEWORK.
RIGHT.
THAT MEANS THE HOMEWORK SHOULD'VE BEEN DONE BETWEEN MY TIME AND YOUR TIME.
RIGHT. WE NEEDED TO DO IT AT 7:30.
BUT THE 7:30 CALVIN CLEARLY DIDN'T DO IT, OR YOU'D HAVE IT NOW AT 8:30.
YEAH! THIS IS HIS FAULT!
THAT LAZY LITTLE PUNK! HE'LL GET US BOTH IN TROUBLE!
LET'S GO GET HIM!

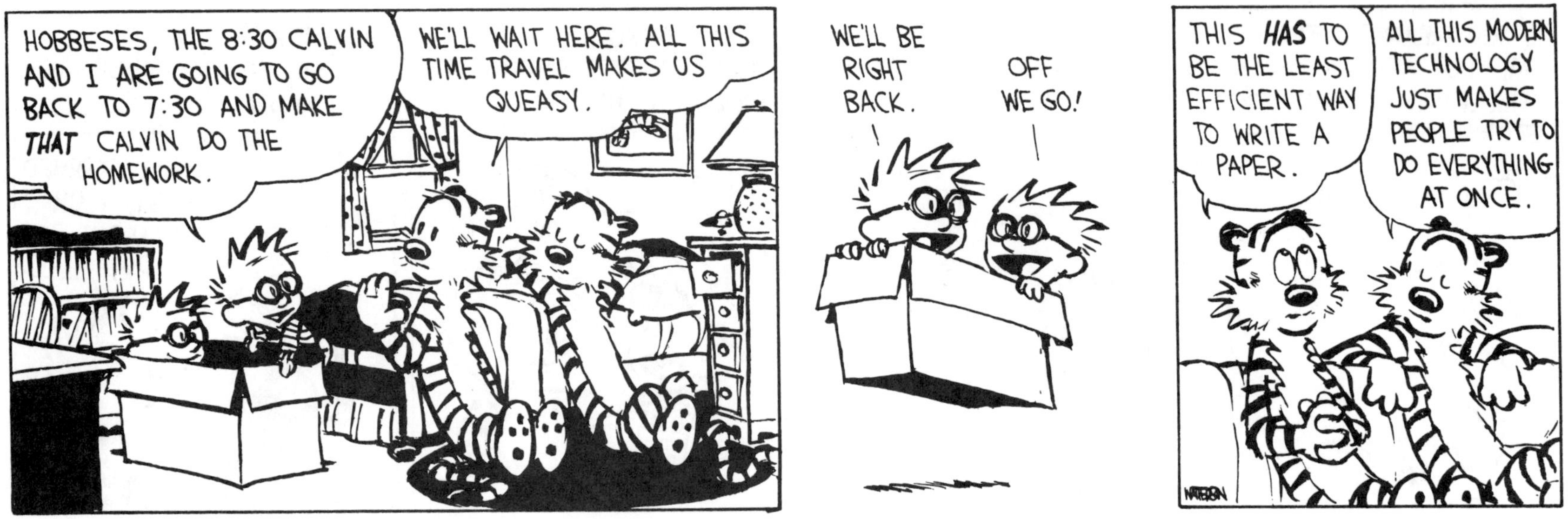
HOBBESES, THE 8:30 CALVIN AND I ARE GOING TO GO BACK TO 7:30 AND MAKE **THAT** CALVIN DO THE HOMEWORK.
WE'LL WAIT HERE. ALL THIS TIME TRAVEL MAKES US QUEASY.
WE'LL BE RIGHT BACK.
OFF WE GO!
THIS **HAS** TO BE THE LEAST EFFICIENT WAY TO WRITE A PAPER.
ALL THIS MODERN TECHNOLOGY JUST MAKES PEOPLE TRY TO DO EVERYTHING AT ONCE.

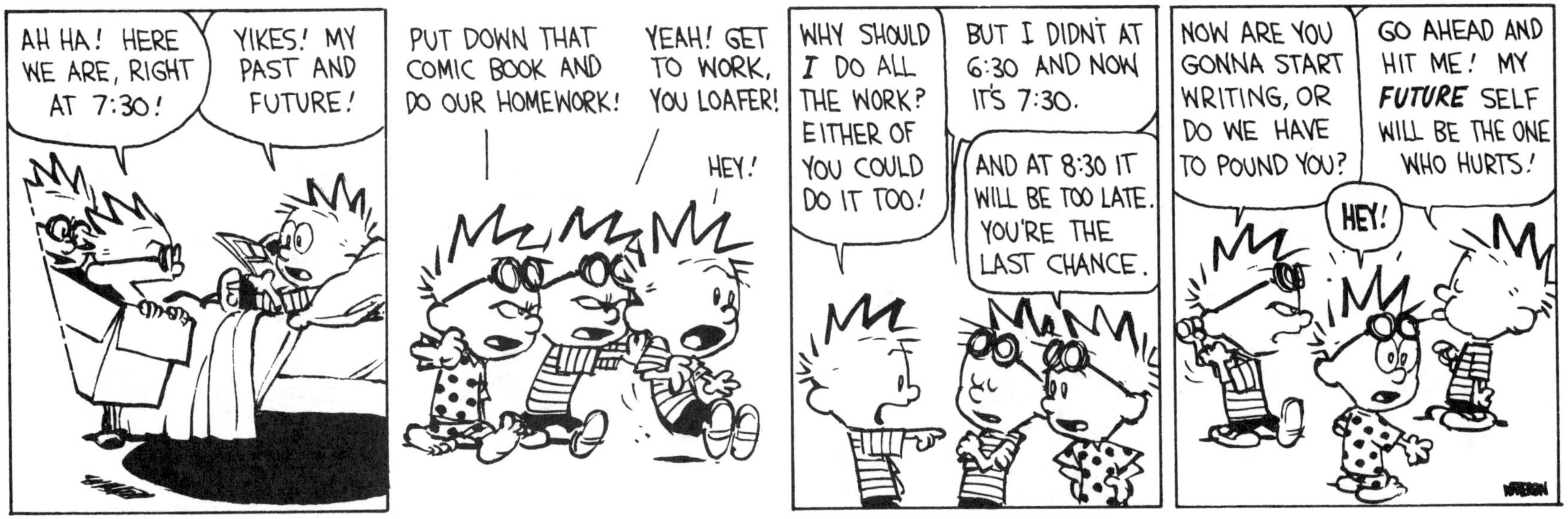
AH HA! HERE WE ARE, RIGHT AT 7:30!
YIKES! MY PAST AND FUTURE!
PUT DOWN THAT COMIC BOOK AND DO OUR HOMEWORK!
YEAH! GET TO WORK, YOU LOAFER!
HEY!
WHY SHOULD **I** DO ALL THE WORK? EITHER OF YOU COULD DO IT TOO!
BUT I DIDN'T AT 6:30 AND NOW IT'S 7:30.
AND AT 8:30 IT WILL BE TOO LATE. YOU'RE THE LAST CHANCE.
NOW ARE YOU GONNA START WRITING, OR DO WE HAVE TO POUND YOU?
HEY!
GO AHEAD AND HIT ME! MY **FUTURE** SELF WILL BE THE ONE WHO HURTS!

YOU KNOW, HOBBES, IF THE 7:30 CALVIN IS AT ALL LIKE THE 6:30 AND 8:30 CALVINS, I'LL BET HE ISN'T GOING TO WRITE THAT STORY.

YOU'RE RIGHT, HOBBES.

WHY DON'T *WE* WRITE A STORY WHILE WE'RE WAITING FOR THEM?

YEAH! CALVIN COULD USE IT FOR HIS CLASS THEN.

I'LL WRITE IT DOWN AND YOU CAN ILLUSTRATE IT!

OK, NOW WHAT SHOULD OUR STORY BE ABOUT?

CALVIN'S NOT HERE. LET'S WRITE ABOUT *HIM*! HEE HEE HEE!

HOO HOO! DRAWING CALVIN IS EASY! YOU JUST MAKE A BIG MOUTH AND ADD SOME HAIR!

LOOK, GUYS, YOU CAN'T GANG UP ON *ME*!

OH YEAH?

WHY NOT?

BECAUSE WE'RE ALL THE SAME CALVIN! IN ONE HOUR, THE 6:30 CALVIN WILL BE *ME*, AND IN ANOTHER HOUR, WE'LL *BOTH* BE THE 8:30 CALVIN!

THAT MEANS YOU GUYS WILL HAVE TO SUFFER WHATEVER YOU DO TO ME.

OH YEAH.

OOPS.

WHOSE DUMB IDEA WAS THIS ANYWAY? HIS?

HIS!

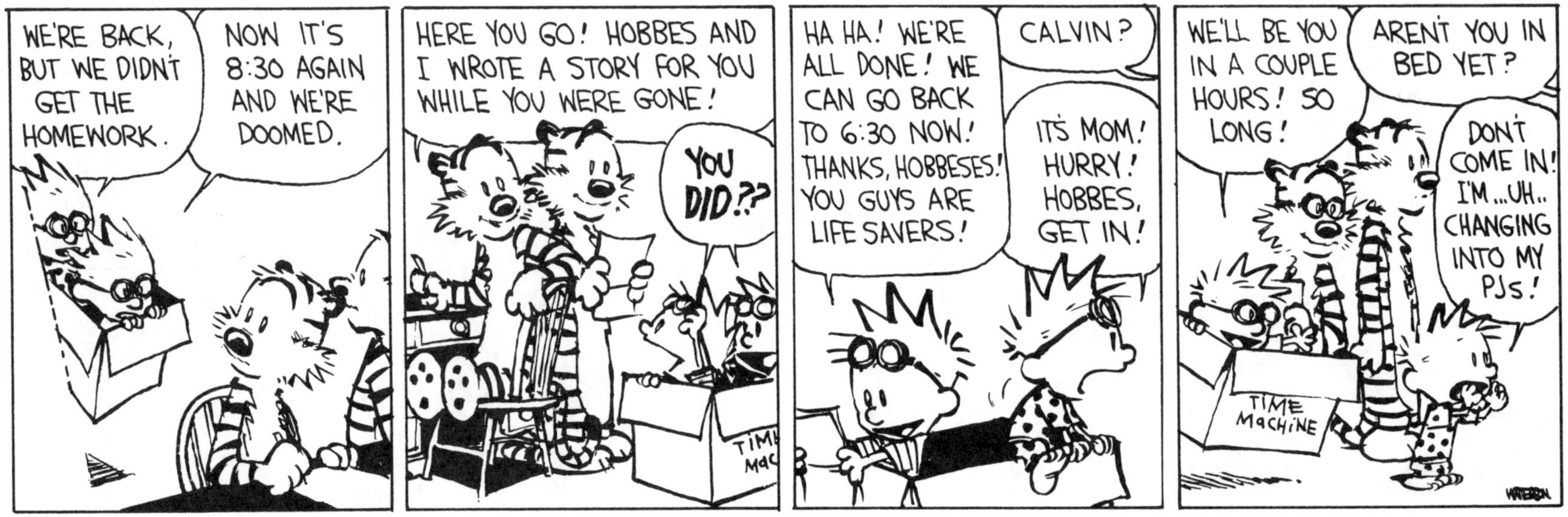
WE'RE BACK, BUT WE DIDN'T GET THE HOMEWORK.
NOW IT'S 8:30 AGAIN AND WE'RE DOOMED.
HERE YOU GO! HOBBES AND I WROTE A STORY FOR YOU WHILE YOU WERE GONE!
YOU DID?!?
HA HA! WE'RE ALL DONE! WE CAN GO BACK TO 6:30 NOW! THANKS, HOBBESES! YOU GUYS ARE LIFE SAVERS!
CALVIN?
IT'S MOM! HURRY! HOBBES, GET IN!
WE'LL BE YOU IN A COUPLE HOURS! SO LONG!
AREN'T YOU IN BED YET?
DON'T COME IN! I'M...UH.. CHANGING INTO MY PJs!
TIME MACHINE

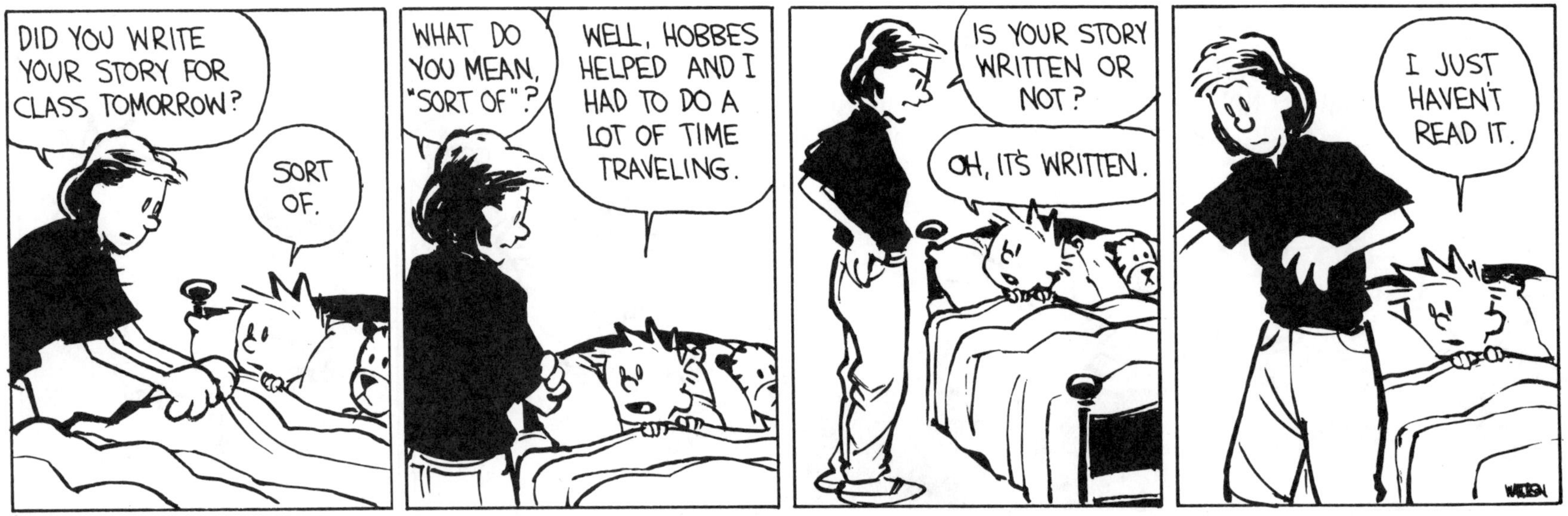
DID YOU WRITE YOUR STORY FOR CLASS TOMORROW?
SORT OF.
WHAT DO YOU MEAN, "SORT OF"?
WELL, HOBBES HELPED AND I HAD TO DO A LOT OF TIME TRAVELING.
IS YOUR STORY WRITTEN OR NOT?
OH, IT'S WRITTEN.
I JUST HAVEN'T READ IT.

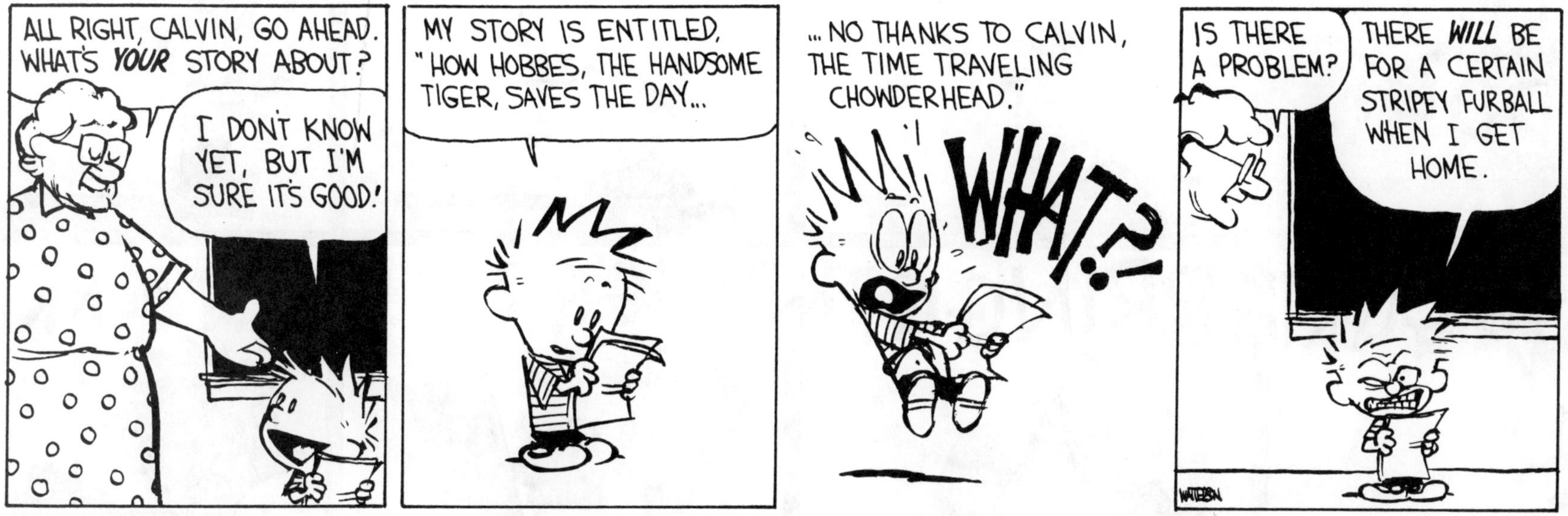
ALL RIGHT, CALVIN, GO AHEAD. WHAT'S YOUR STORY ABOUT?
I DON'T KNOW YET, BUT I'M SURE IT'S GOOD!
MY STORY IS ENTITLED, "HOW HOBBES, THE HANDSOME TIGER, SAVES THE DAY...
... NO THANKS TO CALVIN, THE TIME TRAVELING CHOWDERHEAD."
WHAT?!
IS THERE A PROBLEM?
THERE WILL BE FOR A CERTAIN STRIPEY FURBALL WHEN I GET HOME.
WATTERSON

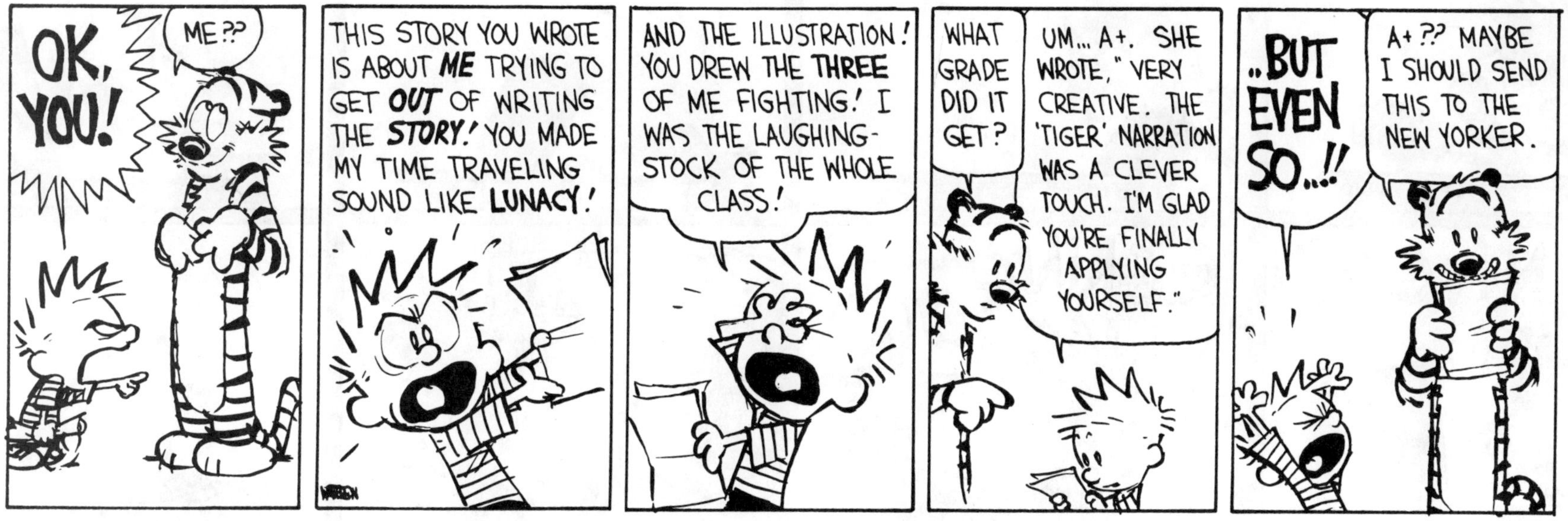
OK, YOU!
ME??
THIS STORY YOU WROTE IS ABOUT ME TRYING TO GET OUT OF WRITING THE STORY! YOU MADE MY TIME TRAVELING SOUND LIKE LUNACY!
WATTERSON
AND THE ILLUSTRATION! YOU DREW THE THREE OF ME FIGHTING! I WAS THE LAUGHING-STOCK OF THE WHOLE CLASS!
WHAT GRADE DID IT GET?
UM... A+. SHE WROTE, "VERY CREATIVE. THE 'TIGER' NARRATION WAS A CLEVER TOUCH. I'M GLAD YOU'RE FINALLY APPLYING YOURSELF."
..BUT EVEN SO..!!
A+?? MAYBE I SHOULD SEND THIS TO THE NEW YORKER.

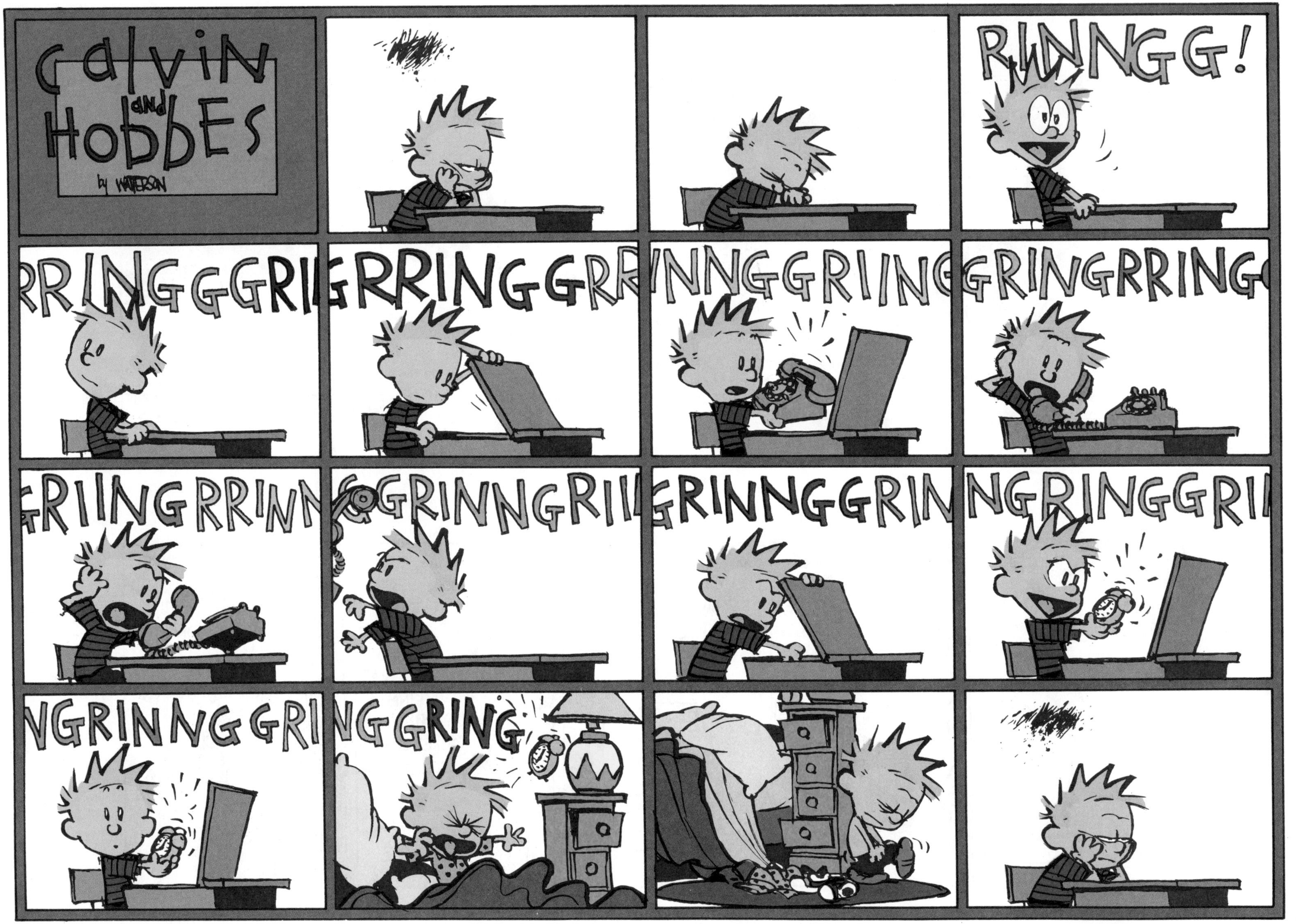
Calvin and Hobbes
by WATTERSON
RINNGG!
RRINGGGRI
GRRINGGRR
INNGGRIING
GRINGRRING
GRIINGRRINN
GRINNGRII
GRINNGGRIN
NGRINGGRI
NGRINNGGRI
NGGRING

YOU'LL BE PROUD TO KNOW I'M GOING TO DONATE ALL THE SNOT I SNEEZE TO HOSPITALS FOR MUCUS TRANS-FUSIONS.
OH STOP BEING DISGUSTING, CALVIN! NOBODY NEEDS THAT DONATED! WHAT AN IDEA!
OH.
I HAVE A JAR FOR YOU TO WASH.

DAD, WHERE DO BABIES COME FROM? IS IT TRUE A STORK LEAVES THEM SWADDLED IN A BUNDLE ON THE FRONT STEP?
IN MOST CASES, YES, BUT YOU WERE UNCEREMONIOUSLY DUMPED DOWN THE CHIMNEY BY A BIG, HAIRY PTERODACTYL.
COOL!
EXPLAINS A LOT, DOESN'T IT?

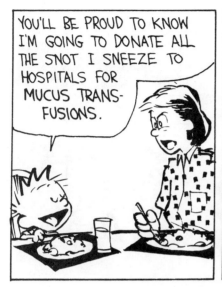

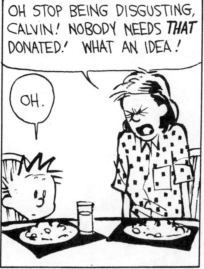

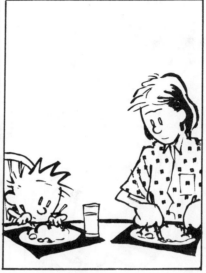

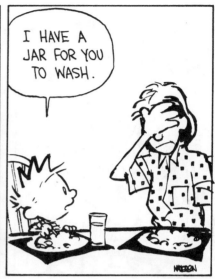

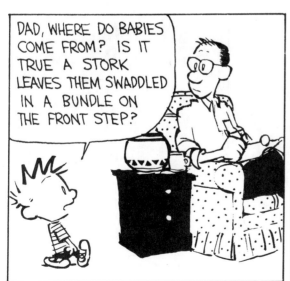

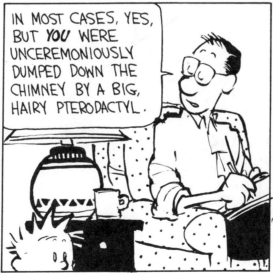

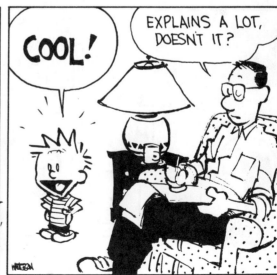

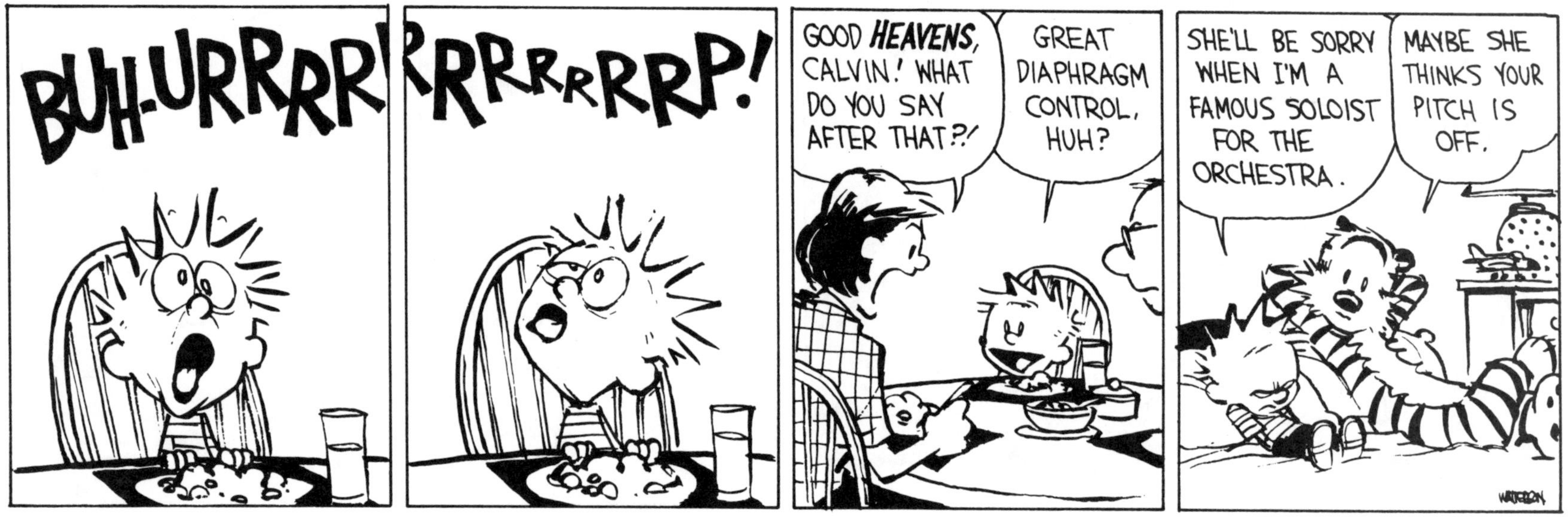
BUH-URRRRRRRRRRRRP!
GOOD HEAVENS, CALVIN! WHAT DO YOU SAY AFTER THAT?!
GREAT DIAPHRAGM CONTROL, HUH?
SHE'LL BE SORRY WHEN I'M A FAMOUS SOLOIST FOR THE ORCHESTRA.
MAYBE SHE THINKS YOUR PITCH IS OFF.
WATTERSON

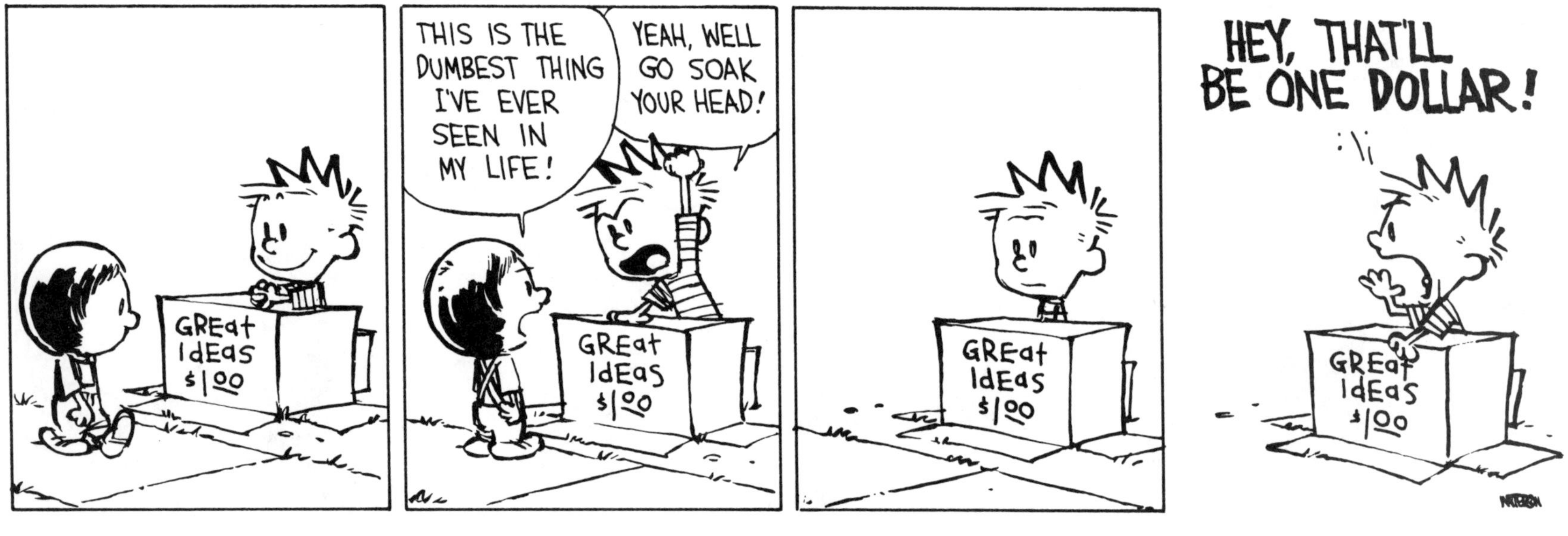
GREat IdEas $1.00
THIS IS THE DUMBEST THING I'VE EVER SEEN IN MY LIFE!
YEAH, WELL GO SOAK YOUR HEAD!
HEY, THAT'LL BE ONE DOLLAR!
WATTERSON

HOW DO I KNOW YOUR IDEAS ARE GREAT?
GREat IdEas $1.00
IT SAYS SO ON MY SIGN. WANT ONE?
I DON'T HAVE A DOLLAR.
GREat
NO PROBLEM! YOU CAN PUT 50 CENTS DOWN AND PAY 100% INTEREST IN DIME INSTALLMENTS OVER THE NEXT 10 DAYS!
PEOPLE JUST DON'T KNOW A GREAT IDEA WHEN THEY HEAR ONE.
GREat IdEas $1.00

I'M HAVING AN INVENTORY REDUCTION SALE! GREAT IDEAS ARE NOW JUST A QUARTER!
GREat IdEas NOW 25¢
OK, HERE. WHAT'S YOUR GREAT IDEA?
BUY SOME MORE!
GREat IdEas NOW 25¢
I'M GETTING ANOTHER GREAT IDEA RIGHT NOW.
ME TOO. SEE YA.
GREat

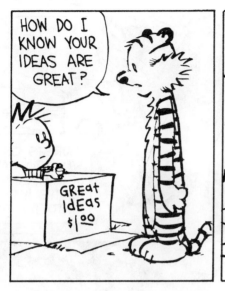

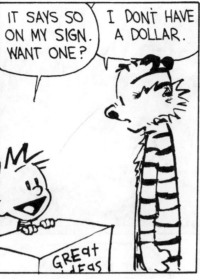

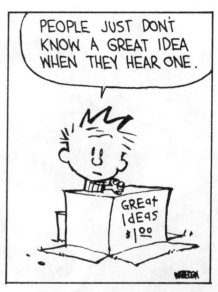

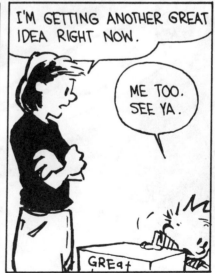

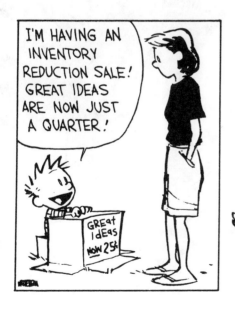

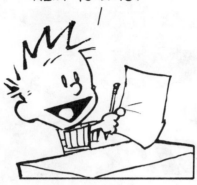

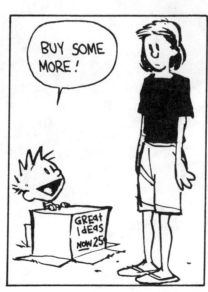

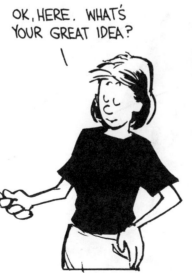

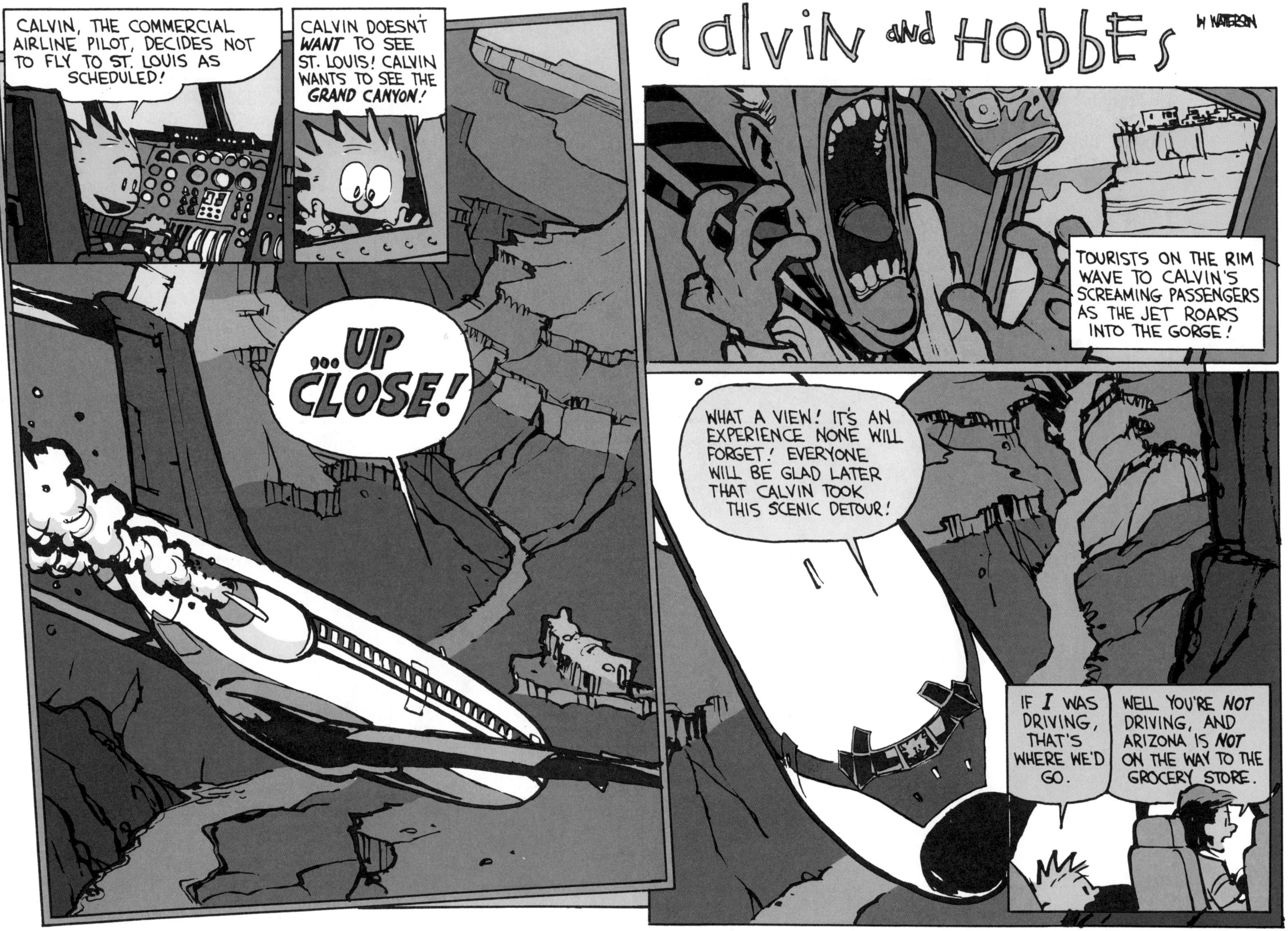
Calvin and Hobbes
by WATTERSON
CALVIN, THE COMMERCIAL AIRLINE PILOT, DECIDES NOT TO FLY TO ST. LOUIS AS SCHEDULED!
CALVIN DOESN'T WANT TO SEE ST. LOUIS! CALVIN WANTS TO SEE THE GRAND CANYON!
...UP CLOSE!
TOURISTS ON THE RIM WAVE TO CALVIN'S SCREAMING PASSENGERS AS THE JET ROARS INTO THE GORGE!
WHAT A VIEW! IT'S AN EXPERIENCE NONE WILL FORGET! EVERYONE WILL BE GLAD LATER THAT CALVIN TOOK THIS SCENIC DETOUR!
IF I WAS DRIVING, THAT'S WHERE WE'D GO.
WELL YOU'RE NOT DRIVING, AND ARIZONA IS NOT ON THE WAY TO THE GROCERY STORE.

ALLO? EEZ THEES DER POOBLIC LAHBRORRY? YAH?

I EM BEEG EEMPORTANT REZEARCHER OOND I REQUIRE EENGLISH VOOLGAR ZYNONYMS FOR DISGUSTINK BODY VUNKTIONS, YAH?

ALLO? ALLO?

NO LUCK?

THOSE LIBRARIANS ARE A SHARP BUNCH.

THIS TOWN JUST AIN'T BIG ENOUGH FER THE BOTH OF US!

YEP, I RECKON WE'LL HAVE TO ANNEX PART O' THE COUNTY!

MOM WON'T LET US PLAY WITH GUNS.

I GET TO BE THE ZONING BOARD!

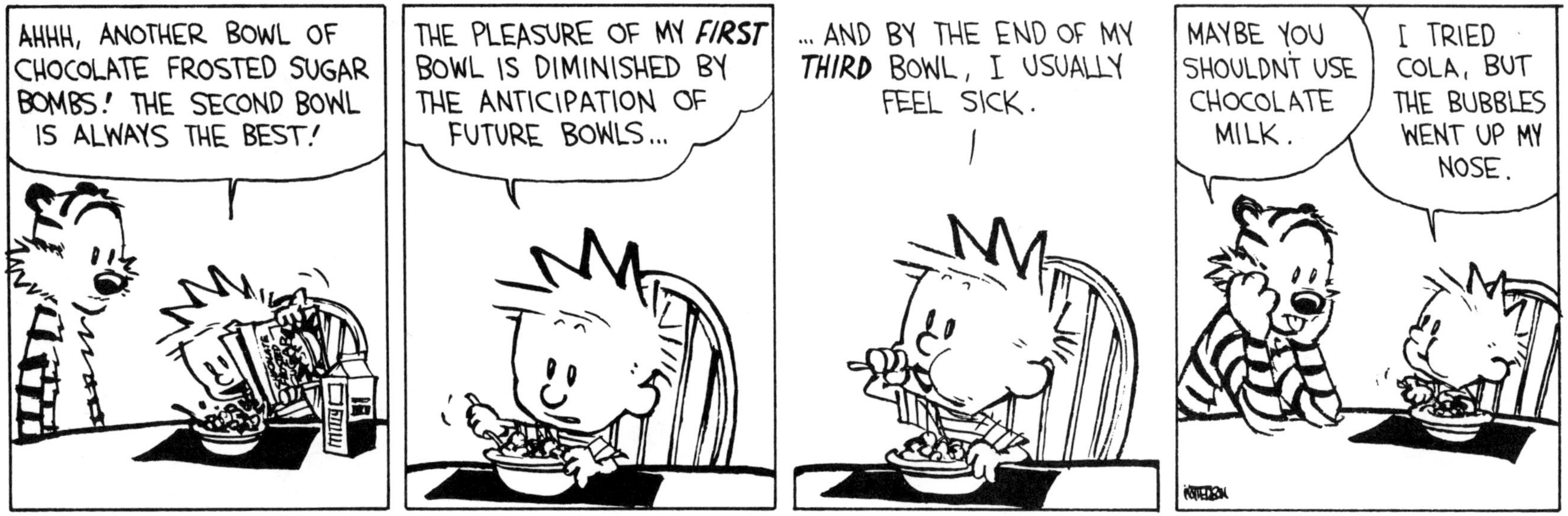
AHHH, ANOTHER BOWL OF CHOCOLATE FROSTED SUGAR BOMBS! THE SECOND BOWL IS ALWAYS THE BEST!
THE PLEASURE OF MY FIRST BOWL IS DIMINISHED BY THE ANTICIPATION OF FUTURE BOWLS...
... AND BY THE END OF MY THIRD BOWL, I USUALLY FEEL SICK.
MAYBE YOU SHOULDN'T USE CHOCOLATE MILK.
I TRIED COLA, BUT THE BUBBLES WENT UP MY NOSE.

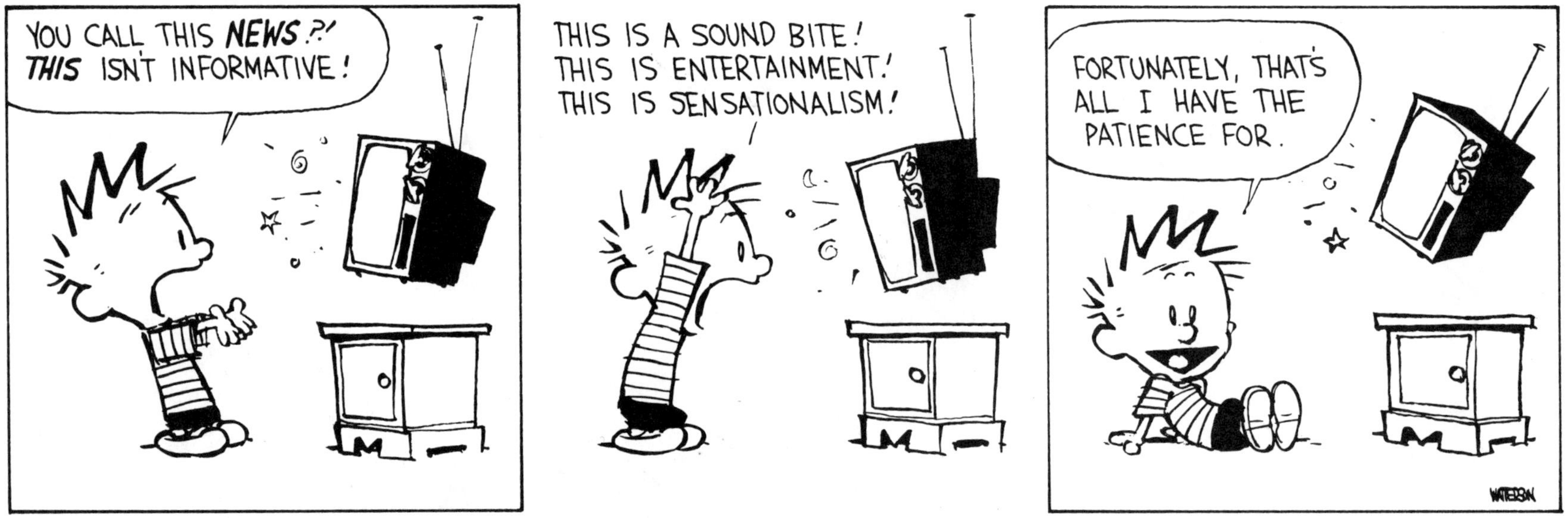
YOU CALL THIS NEWS?! THIS ISN'T INFORMATIVE!
THIS IS A SOUND BITE! THIS IS ENTERTAINMENT! THIS IS SENSATIONALISM!
FORTUNATELY, THAT'S ALL I HAVE THE PATIENCE FOR.

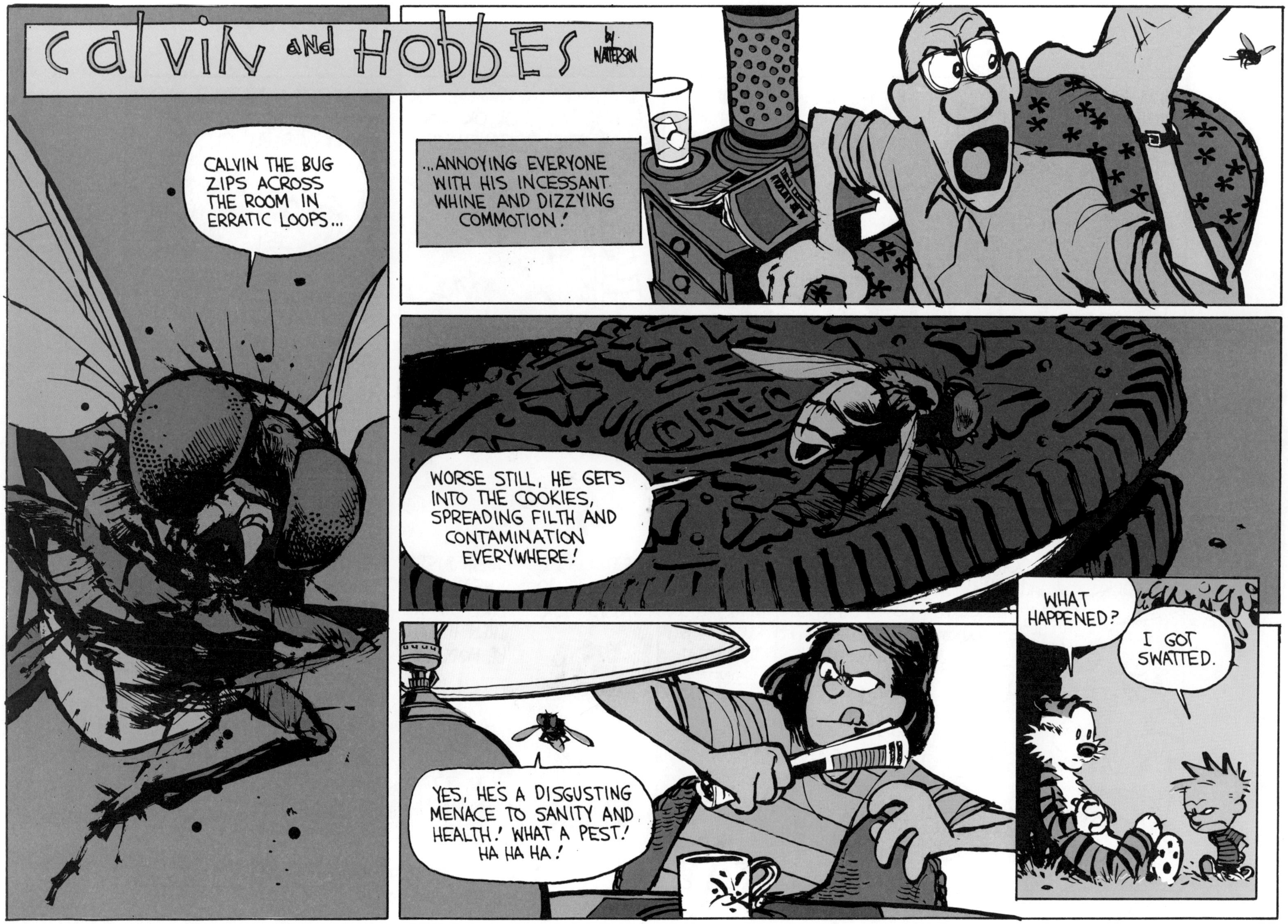
Calvin and Hobbes
by Watterson
CALVIN THE BUG ZIPS ACROSS THE ROOM IN ERRATIC LOOPS...
...ANNOYING EVERYONE WITH HIS INCESSANT WHINE AND DIZZYING COMMOTION!
WORSE STILL, HE GETS INTO THE COOKIES, SPREADING FILTH AND CONTAMINATION EVERYWHERE!
OREO
YES, HE'S A DISGUSTING MENACE TO SANITY AND HEALTH! WHAT A PEST! HA HA HA!
WHAT HAPPENED?
I GOT SWATTED.

MOM GOT ME SOME CLAY! WANT TO HELP ME MAKE SOMETHING?
DO WE GET SMOCKS? I WANT A SMOCK!
THIS KIND OF CLAY ISN'T THAT MESSY. YOU DON'T NEED A SMOCK.
I WANT A SMOCK!
OK, OK, YOU CAN HAVE A SMOCK!
LET'S GET A MARKER AND WRITE, "DON'T KNOCK MY SMOCK, OR I'LL CLEAN YOUR CLOCK."
I GUESS IT WOULDN'T SHOW IF DAD WORE HIS SUIT COAT.

I LIKE MY SMOCK.
GOOD. ...OK, I'LL DIVIDE UP THE CLAY. HERE'S YOURS.
YOU CAN TELL THE QUALITY OF THE ARTIST BY THE QUALITY OF HIS SMOCK.
UH HUH... YOU HAVE TO WORK THIS STUFF A BIT TO GET IT SOFT.
ACTUALLY, I JUST LIKE TO SAY SMOCK.
SEE, JUST KNEAD IT LIKE SO, AND THEN IT CAN BE MODELED.
SMOCK SMOCK SMOCK SMOCK SMOCK SMOCK!
WHAT ON EARTH IS WRONG WITH YOU?!

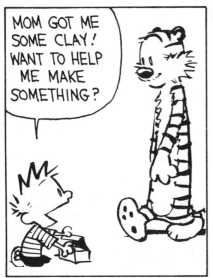

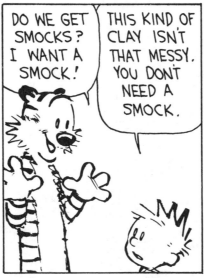

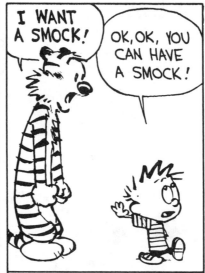

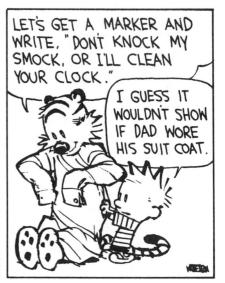

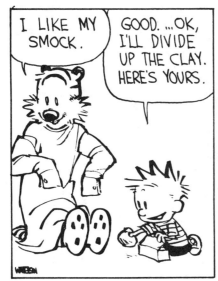

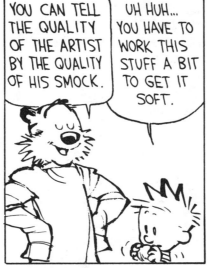

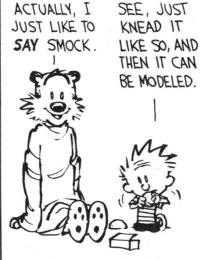

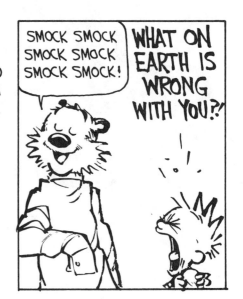

FINE ART IS DEAD, HOBBES. NOBODY UNDERSTANDS IT. NOBODY LIKES IT. NOBODY SEES IT. IT'S IRRELEVANT IN TODAY'S CULTURE.

IF YOU WANT TO INFLUENCE PEOPLE, *POPULAR* ART IS THE WAY TO GO. MASS MARKET COMMERCIAL ART IS THE FUTURE.

BESIDES, IT'S THE ONLY WAY TO MAKE SERIOUS MONEY AND THAT'S WHAT'S IMPORTANT ABOUT BEING AN ARTIST.

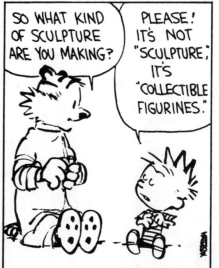

SO WHAT KIND OF SCULPTURE ARE YOU MAKING?

PLEASE! IT'S NOT "SCULPTURE," IT'S "COLLECTIBLE FIGURINES."

SEE, THE PROBLEM WITH FINE ART IS THAT IT'S SUPPOSED TO EXPRESS ORIGINAL TRUTHS.

BUT WHO LIKES ORIGINALITY AND TRUTH?! NOBODY! LIFE'S HARD ENOUGH WITHOUT IT! ONLY AN IDIOT WOULD *PAY* FOR IT!

BUT *POPULAR* ART KNOWS THE CUSTOMER IS ALWAYS RIGHT! PEOPLE WANT **MORE** OF WHAT THEY ALREADY **KNOW** THEY LIKE, SO POPULAR ART GIVES IT TO 'EM!

AND HOW *ARE* THE MOVIE SEQUELS THIS SUMMER?

GREAT! MAN, THERE'S NOTHING I HATE MORE THAN PAYING FIVE BUCKS AND HAVING TO DEAL WITH SOME NEW PLOT.

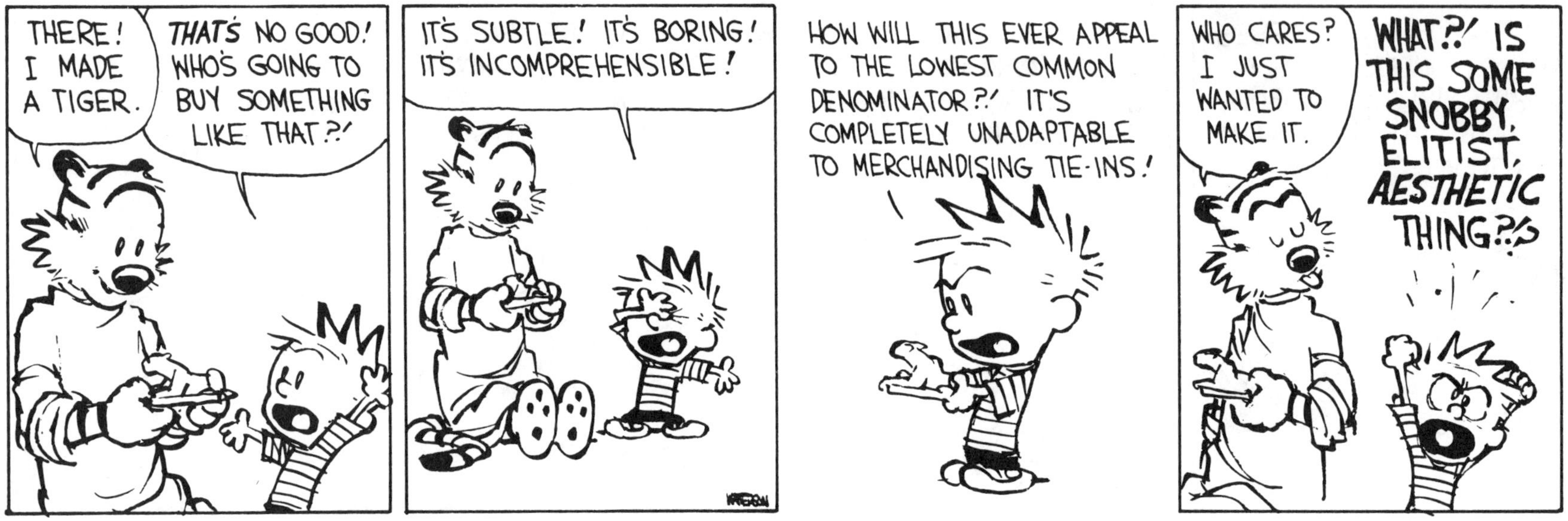
THERE! I MADE A TIGER.
THAT'S NO GOOD! WHO'S GOING TO BUY SOMETHING LIKE THAT?!
IT'S SUBTLE! IT'S BORING! IT'S INCOMPREHENSIBLE!
HOW WILL THIS EVER APPEAL TO THE LOWEST COMMON DENOMINATOR?! IT'S COMPLETELY UNADAPTABLE TO MERCHANDISING TIE-INS!
WHO CARES? I JUST WANTED TO MAKE IT.
WHAT?! IS THIS SOME SNOBBY, ELITIST, AESTHETIC THING?!

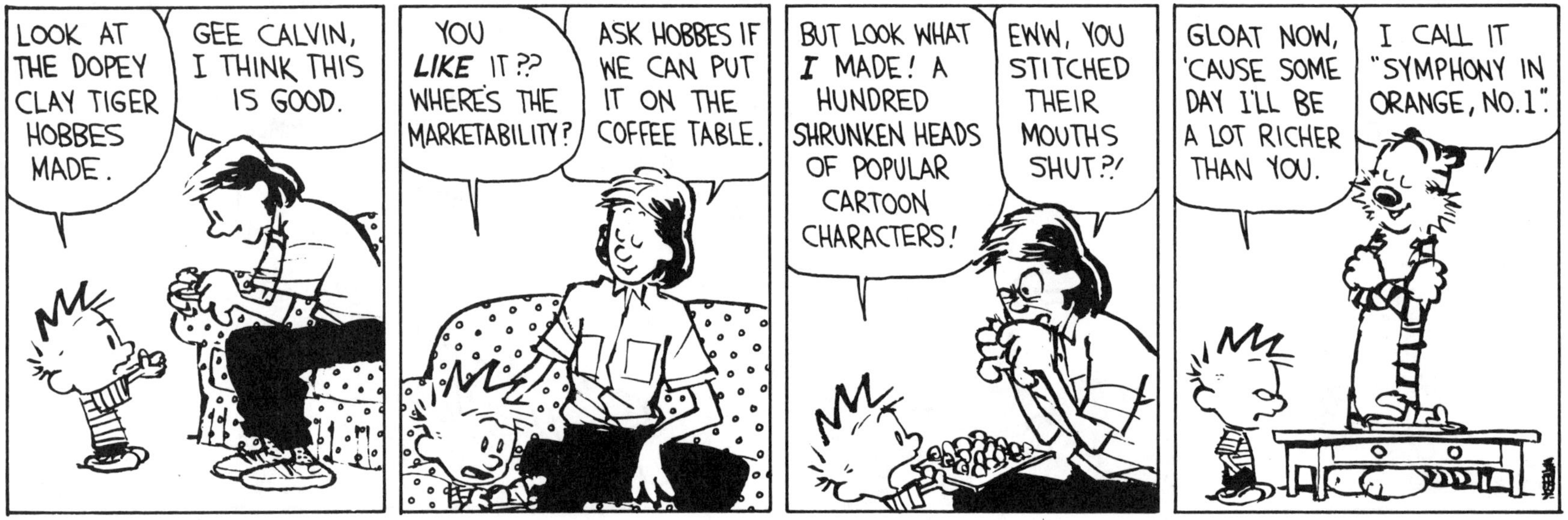
LOOK AT THE DOPEY CLAY TIGER HOBBES MADE.
GEE CALVIN, I THINK THIS IS GOOD.
YOU LIKE IT?? WHERE'S THE MARKETABILITY?
ASK HOBBES IF WE CAN PUT IT ON THE COFFEE TABLE.
BUT LOOK WHAT I MADE! A HUNDRED SHRUNKEN HEADS OF POPULAR CARTOON CHARACTERS!
EWW, YOU STITCHED THEIR MOUTHS SHUT?!
GLOAT NOW, 'CAUSE SOME DAY I'LL BE A LOT RICHER THAN YOU.
I CALL IT "SYMPHONY IN ORANGE, NO. 1".

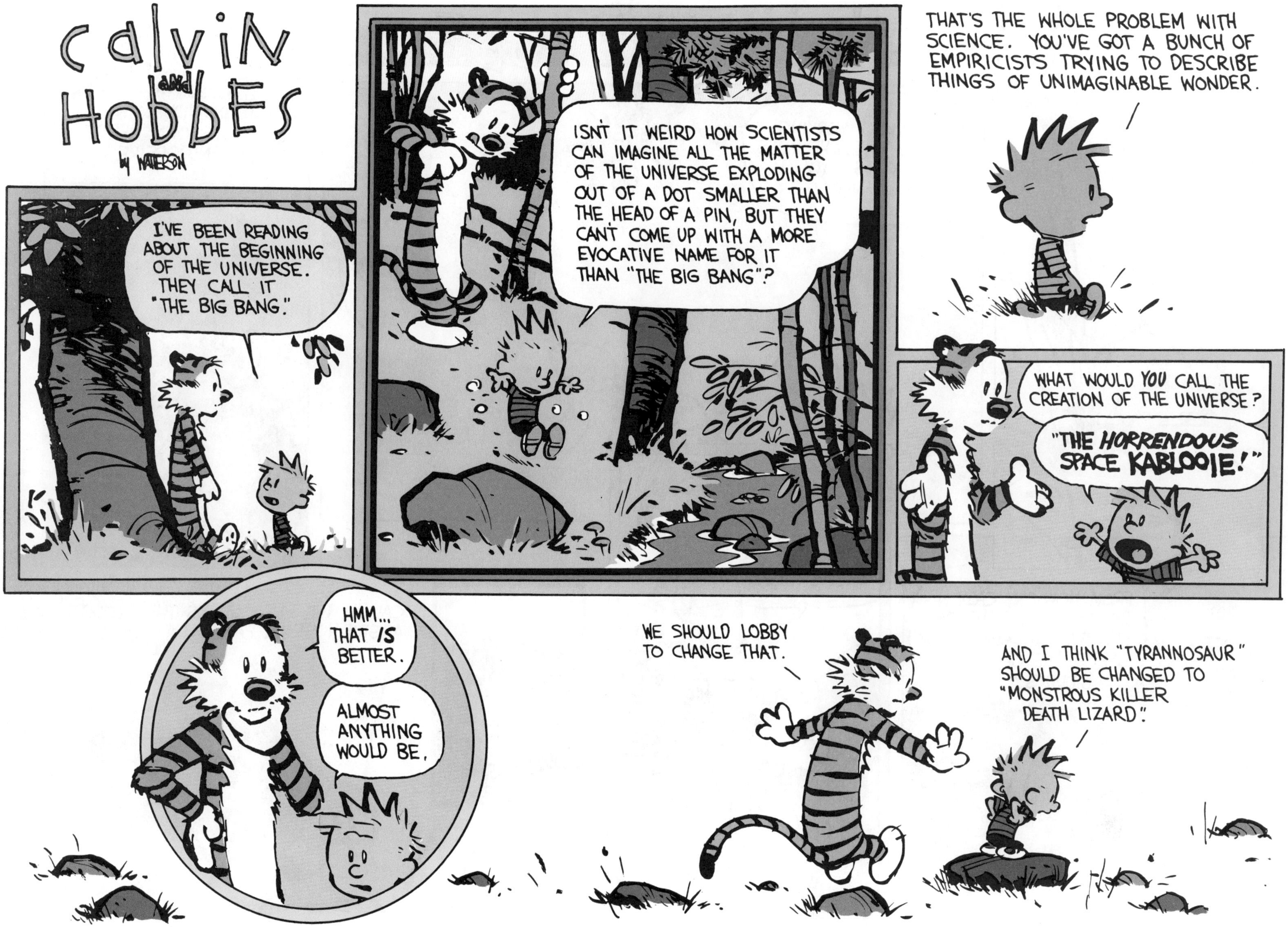
Calvin and Hobbes
by WATTERSON
I'VE BEEN READING ABOUT THE BEGINNING OF THE UNIVERSE. THEY CALL IT "THE BIG BANG."
ISN'T IT WEIRD HOW SCIENTISTS CAN IMAGINE ALL THE MATTER OF THE UNIVERSE EXPLODING OUT OF A DOT SMALLER THAN THE HEAD OF A PIN, BUT THEY CAN'T COME UP WITH A MORE EVOCATIVE NAME FOR IT THAN "THE BIG BANG"?
THAT'S THE WHOLE PROBLEM WITH SCIENCE. YOU'VE GOT A BUNCH OF EMPIRICISTS TRYING TO DESCRIBE THINGS OF UNIMAGINABLE WONDER.
WHAT WOULD *YOU* CALL THE CREATION OF THE UNIVERSE?
"THE ***HORRENDOUS*** SPACE **KABLOOIE!**"
HMM... THAT ***IS*** BETTER.
ALMOST ANYTHING WOULD BE.
WE SHOULD LOBBY TO CHANGE THAT.
AND I THINK "TYRANNOSAUR" SHOULD BE CHANGED TO "MONSTROUS KILLER DEATH LIZARD."

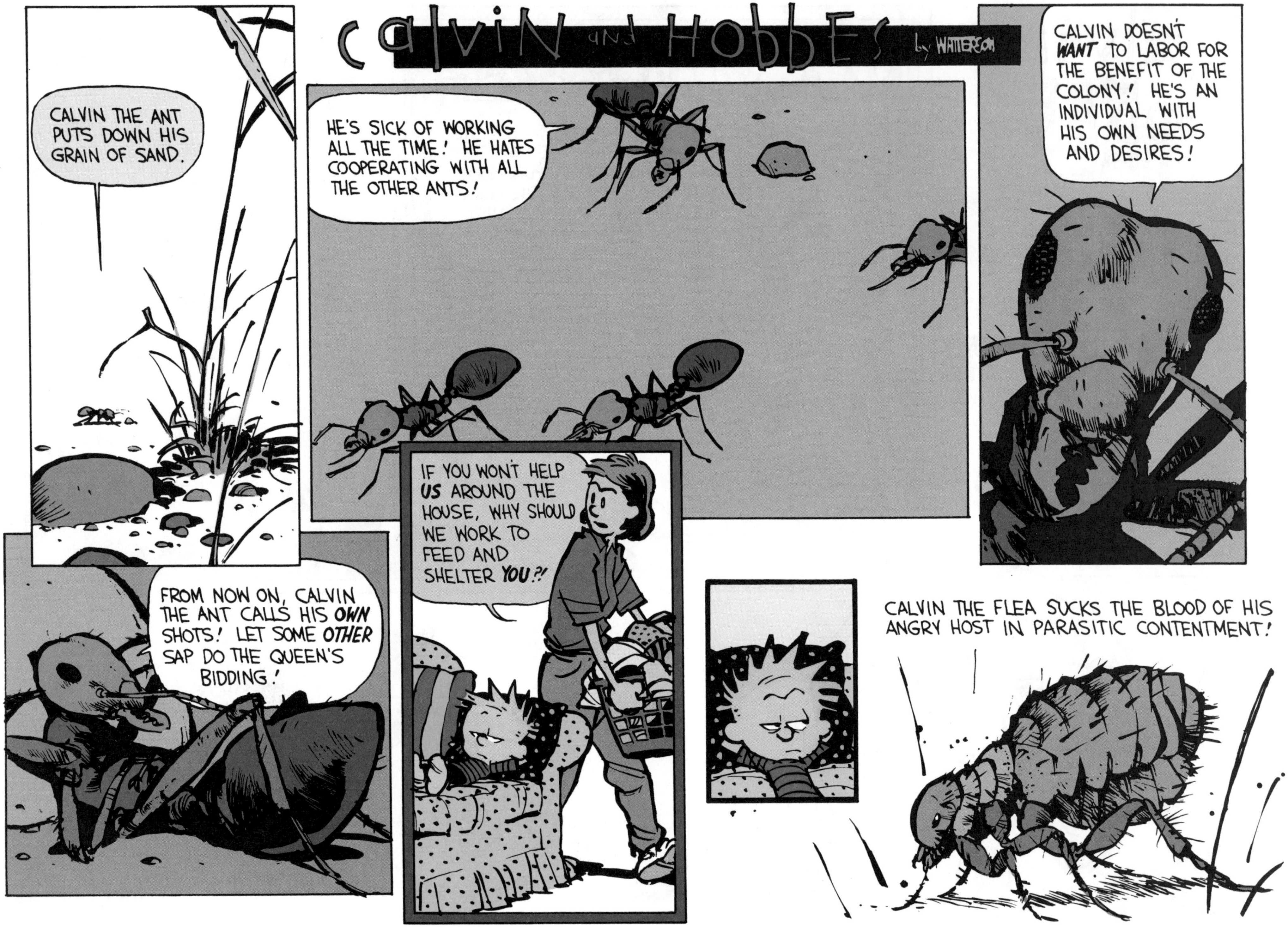

CALVIN AND HOBBES by WATTERSON
CALVIN THE ANT PUTS DOWN HIS GRAIN OF SAND.
HE'S SICK OF WORKING ALL THE TIME! HE HATES COOPERATING WITH ALL THE OTHER ANTS!
CALVIN DOESN'T WANT TO LABOR FOR THE BENEFIT OF THE COLONY! HE'S AN INDIVIDUAL WITH HIS OWN NEEDS AND DESIRES!
FROM NOW ON, CALVIN THE ANT CALLS HIS OWN SHOTS! LET SOME OTHER SAP DO THE QUEEN'S BIDDING!
IF YOU WON'T HELP US AROUND THE HOUSE, WHY SHOULD WE WORK TO FEED AND SHELTER YOU?!
CALVIN THE FLEA SUCKS THE BLOOD OF HIS ANGRY HOST IN PARASITIC CONTENTMENT!

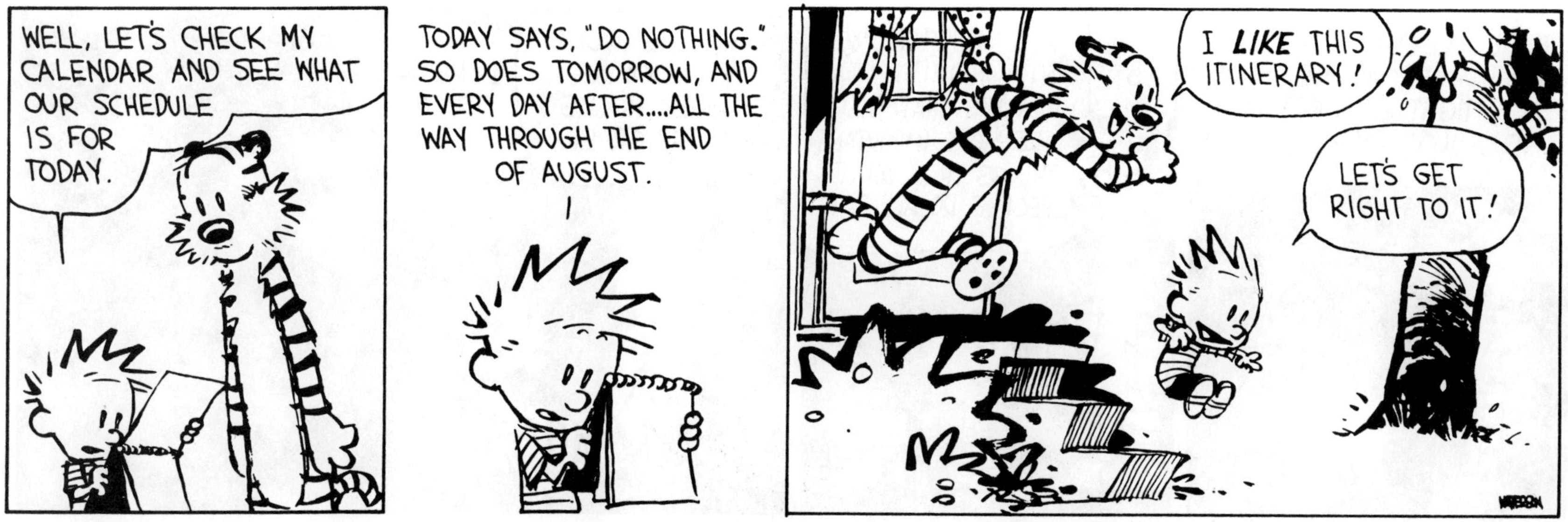
WELL, LET'S CHECK MY CALENDAR AND SEE WHAT OUR SCHEDULE IS FOR TODAY.
TODAY SAYS, "DO NOTHING." SO DOES TOMORROW, AND EVERY DAY AFTER....ALL THE WAY THROUGH THE END OF AUGUST.
I **LIKE** THIS ITINERARY!
LET'S GET RIGHT TO IT!

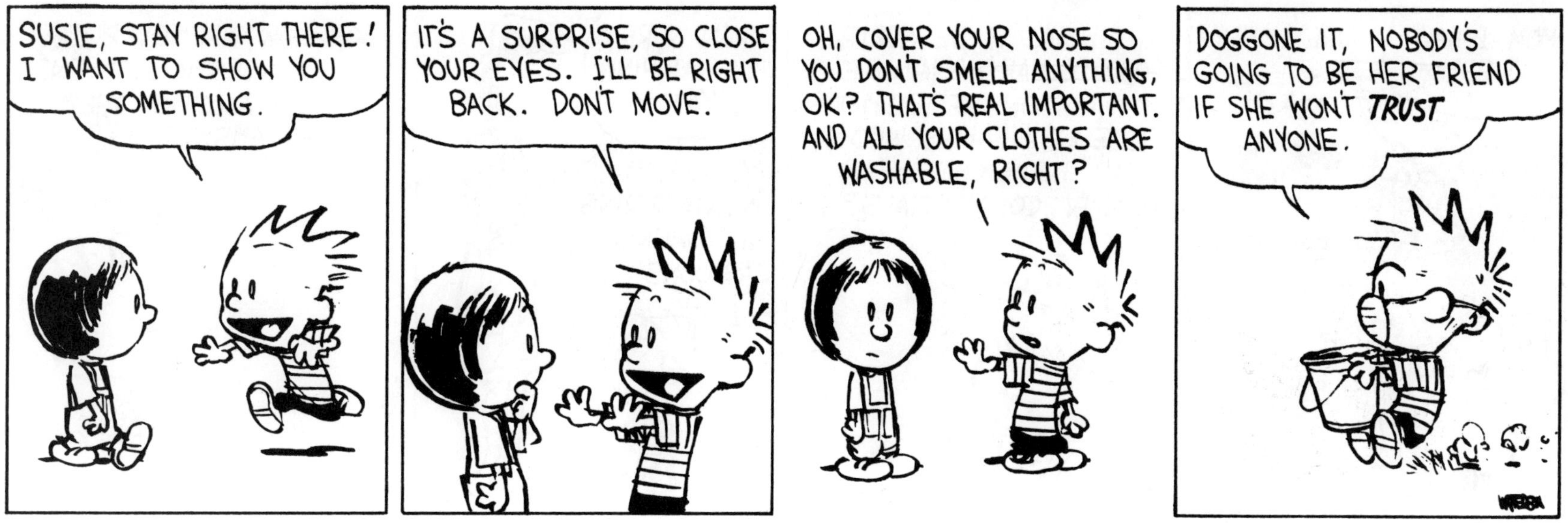
SUSIE, STAY RIGHT THERE! I WANT TO SHOW YOU SOMETHING.
IT'S A SURPRISE, SO CLOSE YOUR EYES. I'LL BE RIGHT BACK. DON'T MOVE.
OH, COVER YOUR NOSE SO YOU DON'T SMELL ANYTHING, OK? THAT'S REAL IMPORTANT. AND ALL YOUR CLOTHES ARE WASHABLE, RIGHT?
DOGGONE IT, NOBODY'S GOING TO BE HER FRIEND IF SHE WON'T **TRUST** ANYONE.

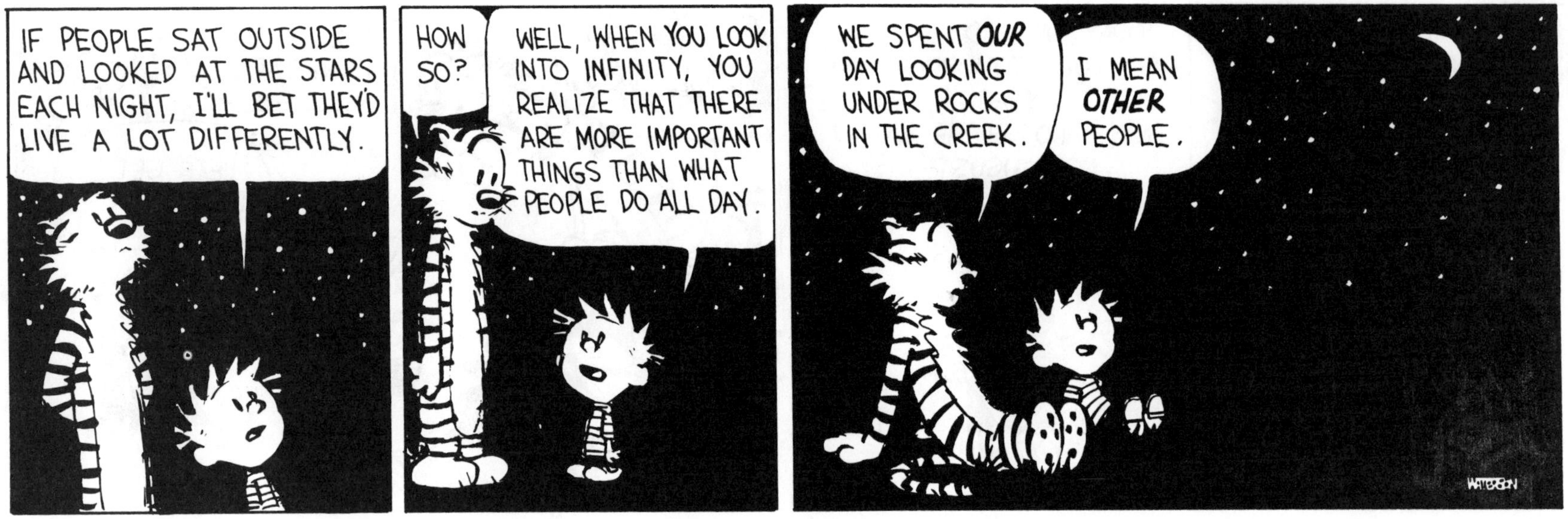
IF PEOPLE SAT OUTSIDE AND LOOKED AT THE STARS EACH NIGHT, I'LL BET THEY'D LIVE A LOT DIFFERENTLY.
HOW SO?
WELL, WHEN YOU LOOK INTO INFINITY, YOU REALIZE THAT THERE ARE MORE IMPORTANT THINGS THAN WHAT PEOPLE DO ALL DAY.
WE SPENT OUR DAY LOOKING UNDER ROCKS IN THE CREEK.
I MEAN OTHER PEOPLE.
WATERSON

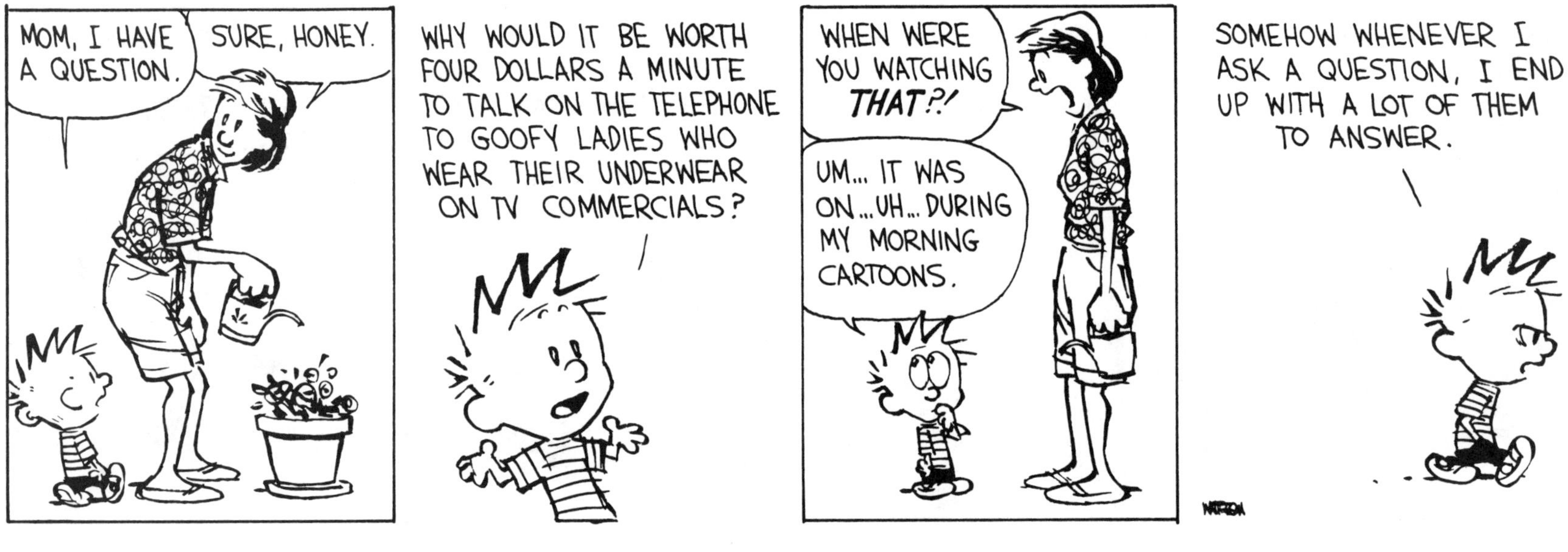
MOM, I HAVE A QUESTION.
SURE, HONEY.
WHY WOULD IT BE WORTH FOUR DOLLARS A MINUTE TO TALK ON THE TELEPHONE TO GOOFY LADIES WHO WEAR THEIR UNDERWEAR ON TV COMMERCIALS?
WHEN WERE YOU WATCHING THAT?!
UM... IT WAS ON... UH... DURING MY MORNING CARTOONS.
SOMEHOW WHENEVER I ASK A QUESTION, I END UP WITH A LOT OF THEM TO ANSWER.

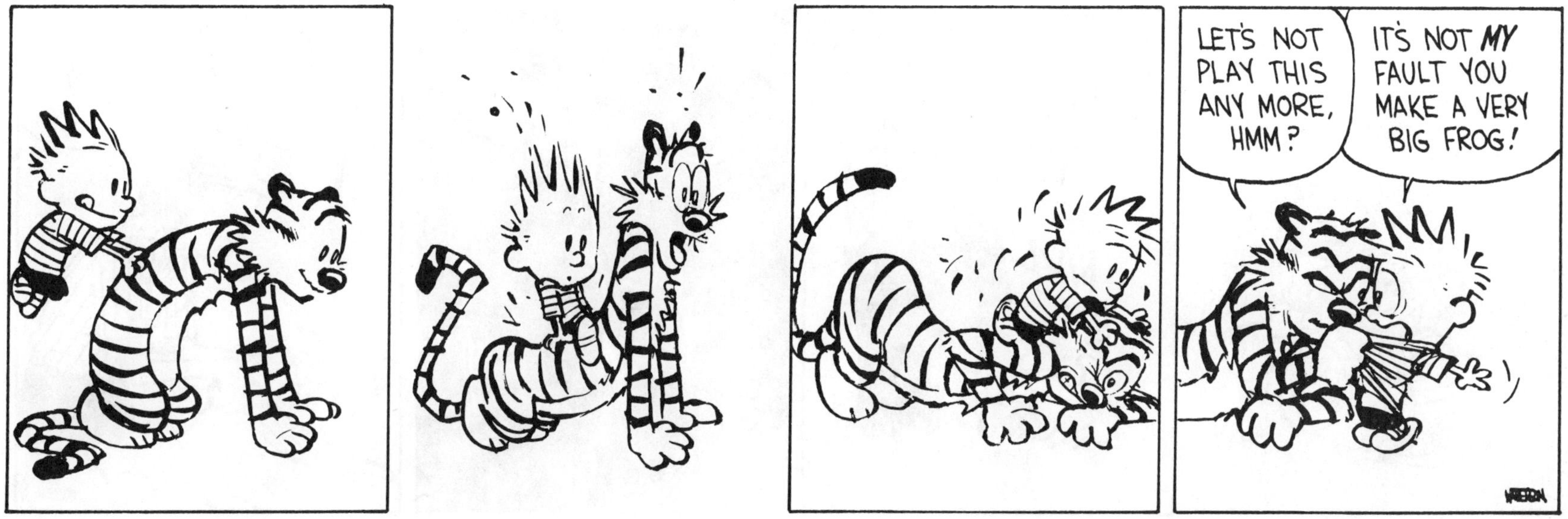
LET'S NOT PLAY THIS ANY MORE, HMM?
IT'S NOT *MY* FAULT YOU MAKE A VERY BIG FROG!

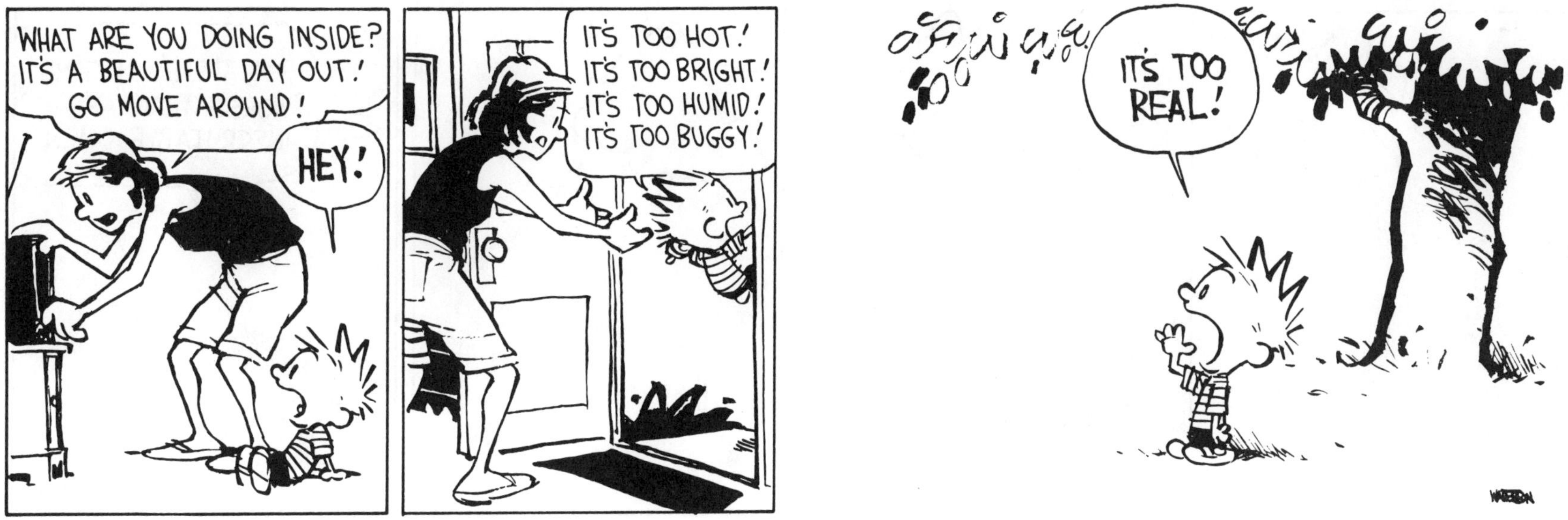
WHAT ARE YOU DOING INSIDE? IT'S A BEAUTIFUL DAY OUT! GO MOVE AROUND!
HEY!
IT'S TOO HOT! IT'S TOO BRIGHT! IT'S TOO HUMID! IT'S TOO BUGGY!
IT'S TOO REAL!

HEH HEH HEH!
HEH HEH HEH!
I WISH I HAD MORE ENEMIES.
I'M SURE YOU WILL SOMEDAY, HONEY.

BOY, THERE'S NOTHING WORSE THAN AN INSCRUTABLE OMEN.

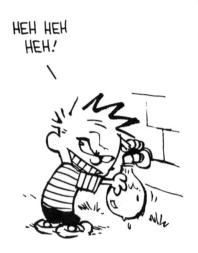

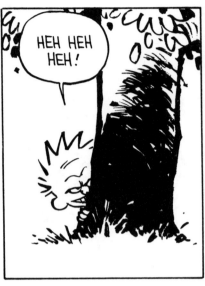

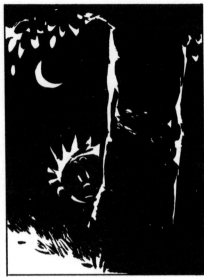

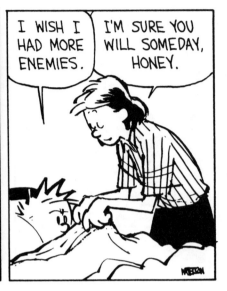

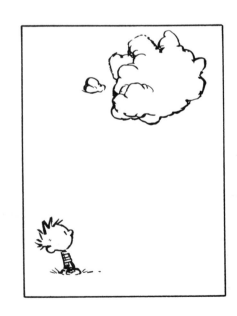

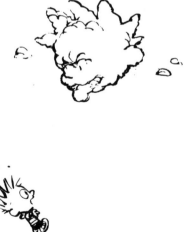

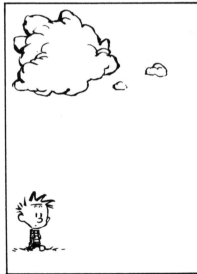

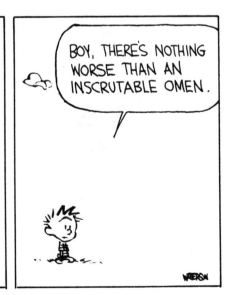

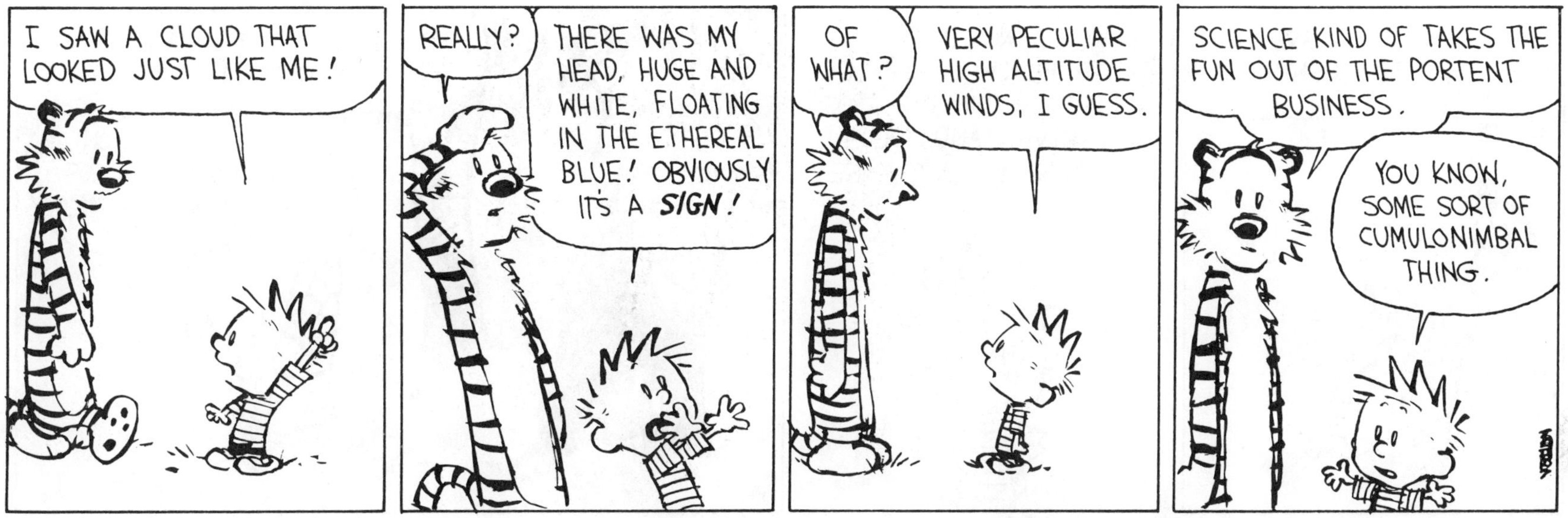
I SAW A CLOUD THAT LOOKED JUST LIKE ME!
REALLY?
THERE WAS MY HEAD, HUGE AND WHITE, FLOATING IN THE ETHEREAL BLUE! OBVIOUSLY IT'S A **SIGN**!
OF WHAT?
VERY PECULIAR HIGH ALTITUDE WINDS, I GUESS.
SCIENCE KIND OF TAKES THE FUN OUT OF THE PORTENT BUSINESS.
YOU KNOW, SOME SORT OF CUMULONIMBAL THING.

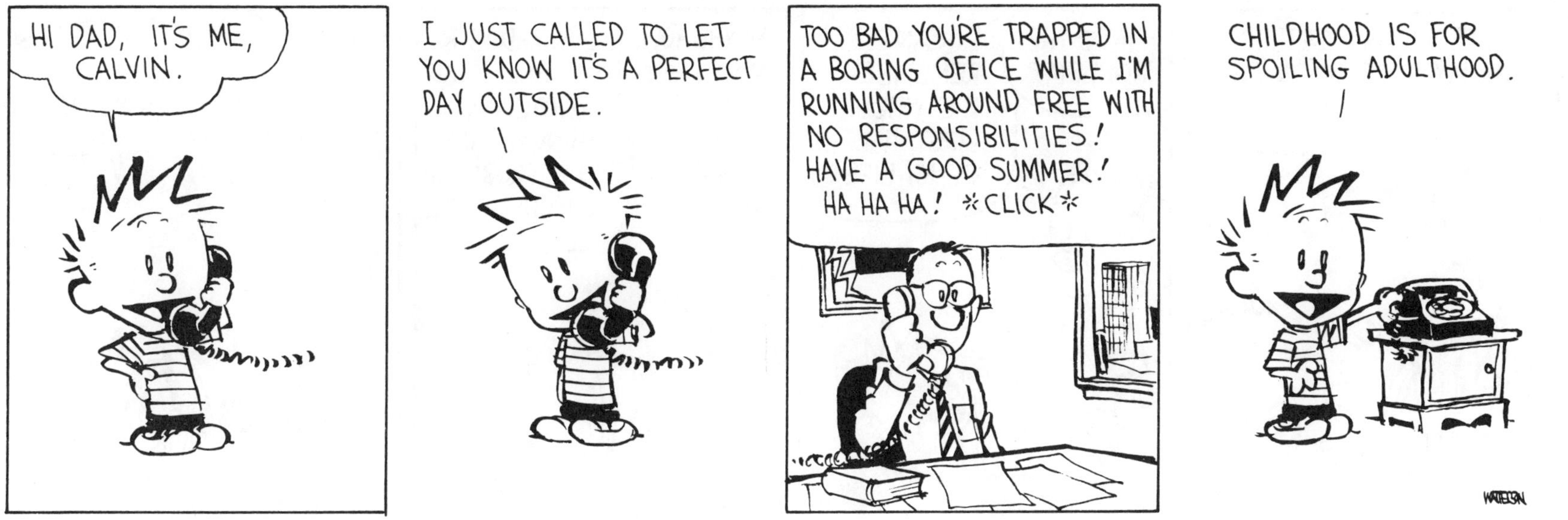
HI DAD, IT'S ME, CALVIN.
I JUST CALLED TO LET YOU KNOW IT'S A PERFECT DAY OUTSIDE.
TOO BAD YOU'RE TRAPPED IN A BORING OFFICE WHILE I'M RUNNING AROUND FREE WITH NO RESPONSIBILITIES! HAVE A GOOD SUMMER! HA HA HA! *CLICK*
CHILDHOOD IS FOR SPOILING ADULTHOOD.

PEOPLE ARE SO SELF-CENTERED.

THE WORLD WOULD BE A BETTER PLACE IF PEOPLE WOULD STOP THINKING ABOUT THEMSELVES AND FOCUS ON **OTHERS** FOR A CHANGE.

GEE, I WONDER WHO THAT MIGHT APPLY TO.

ME! EVERYONE SHOULD FOCUS MORE ON *ME!*

HERE I AM, ALL SET TO WRITE MY AUTOBIOGRAPHY, AND I'M STUCK!

WHAT'S THE PROBLEM?

I CAN'T REMEMBER THE WHOLE FIRST HALF OF MY LIFE!

MAYBE YOUR MOM KNOWS WHAT YOU DID.

I ASKED HER. SHE SAID I DID REVOLTING THINGS THAT ARE PROBABLY UNPUBLISHABLE.

WELL NO WONDER YOU SUPPRESSED THE MEMORIES.

MAYBE I WAS IN JAIL!

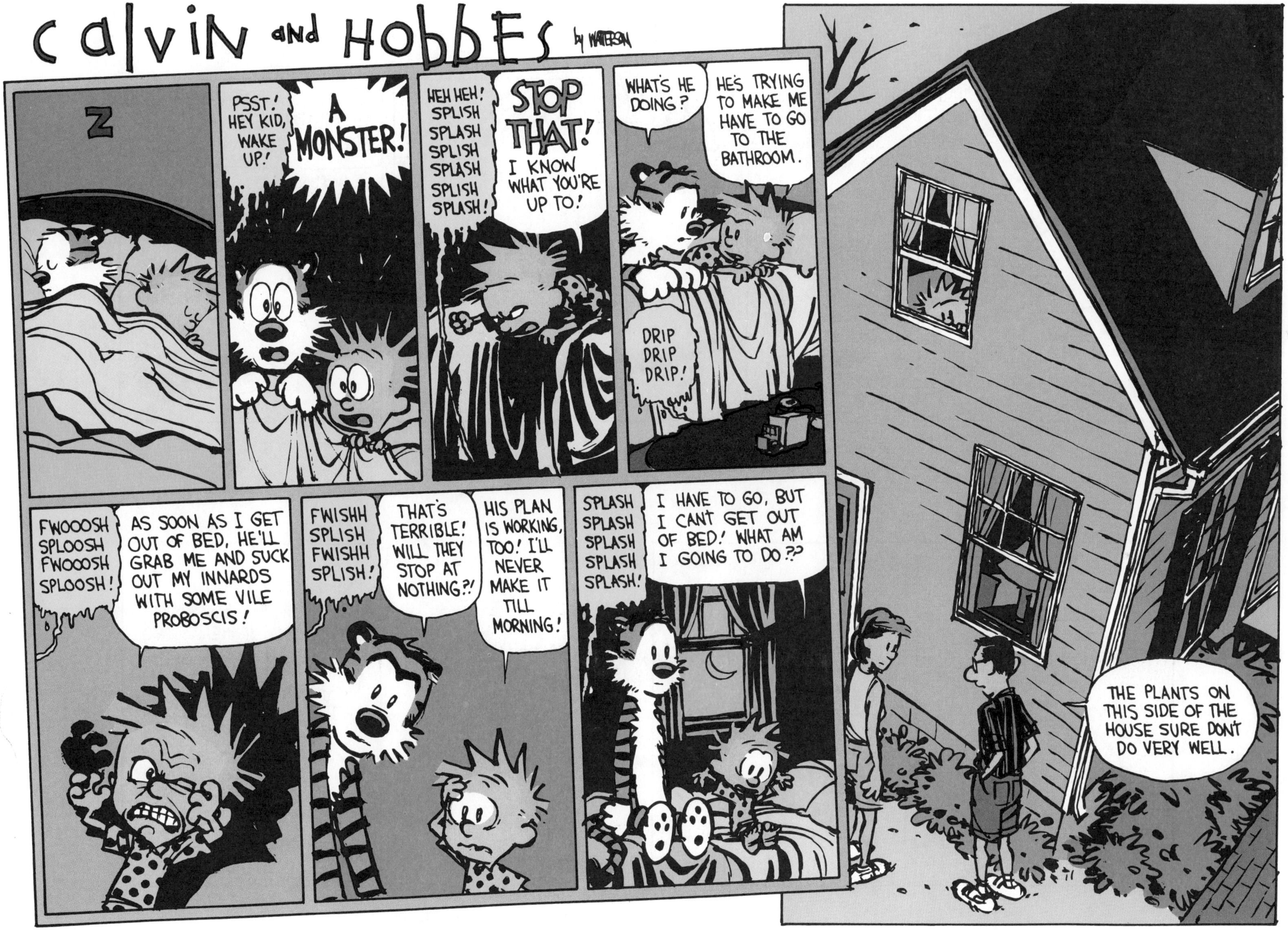
Calvin and HOBBES by WATTERSON
Z
PSST! HEY KID, WAKE UP!
A MONSTER!
HEH HEH! SPLISH SPLASH SPLISH SPLASH SPLISH SPLASH!
STOP THAT! I KNOW WHAT YOU'RE UP TO!
WHAT'S HE DOING?
HE'S TRYING TO MAKE ME HAVE TO GO TO THE BATHROOM.
DRIP DRIP DRIP!
FWOOOSH SPLOOSH FWOOOSH SPLOOSH!
AS SOON AS I GET OUT OF BED, HE'LL GRAB ME AND SUCK OUT MY INNARDS WITH SOME VILE PROBOSCIS!
FWISHH SPLISH FWISHH SPLISH!
THAT'S TERRIBLE! WILL THEY STOP AT NOTHING?!
HIS PLAN IS WORKING, TOO! I'LL NEVER MAKE IT TILL MORNING!
SPLASH SPLASH SPLASH SPLASH SPLASH!
I HAVE TO GO, BUT I CAN'T GET OUT OF BED! WHAT AM I GOING TO DO?!
THE PLANTS ON THIS SIDE OF THE HOUSE SURE DON'T DO VERY WELL.

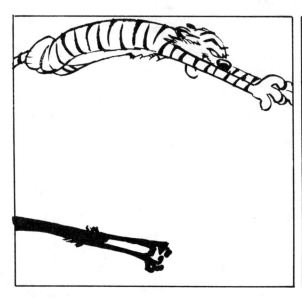

THE PROBLEM WITH TIGERS IS THEY HAVE NO SETTING BETWEEN "OFF" AND "HIGH."

HOO HOO HOO

I LET MY MIND WANDER AND IT DIDN'T COME BACK.

I FIGURED YOU'D LOST YOUR MIND YEARS AGO.

BUGS FLY IN SUCH CRAZY LOOPS AND ZIGZAGS. I WONDER WHY THEY DON'T GET DIZZY AND BARF.
MAYBE THEY DO!
EWW, GROSS! HA HA HA! BUT THEN WHY WOULD THEY KEEP FLYING THAT WAY?
MAYBE BUGS *LIKE* TO BARF!
EWWWW! THEY ***WOULD***!! HA HA HA HA! **BLAUGH**!
I TELL YOU, HOBBES, IT'S GREAT TO HAVE A FRIEND WHO APPRECIATES AN EARNEST DISCUSSION OF IDEAS.

WHAT IF WE DIE AND IT TURNS OUT GOD IS A BIG *CHICKEN*?? WHAT THEN?!
JUST EAT YOUR DINNER, OK?
ETERNAL CONSEQUENCES, THAT'S WHAT!

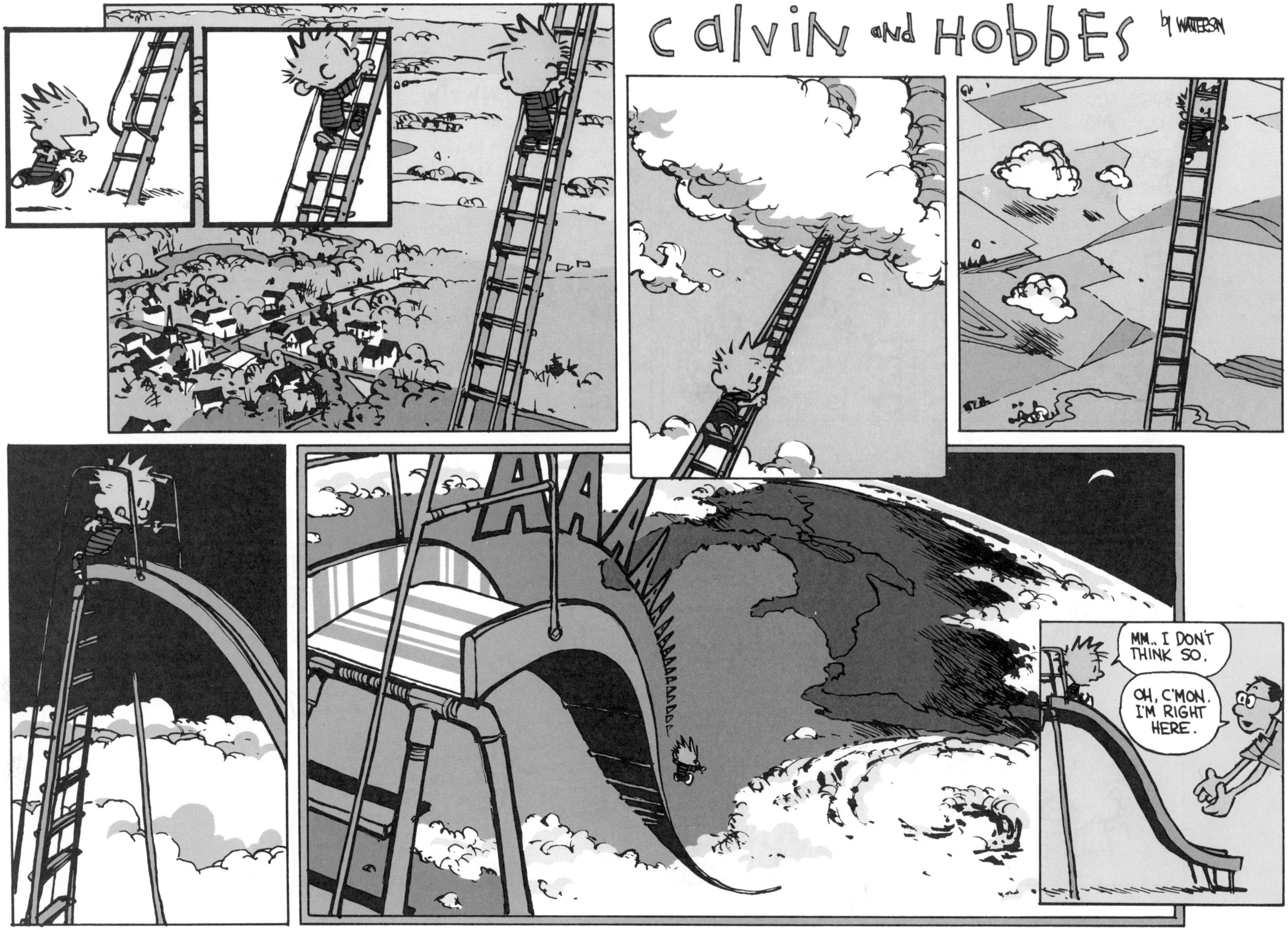
Calvin and HOBBES
by WATTERSON
MM.. I DON'T THINK SO.
OH, C'MON. I'M RIGHT HERE.

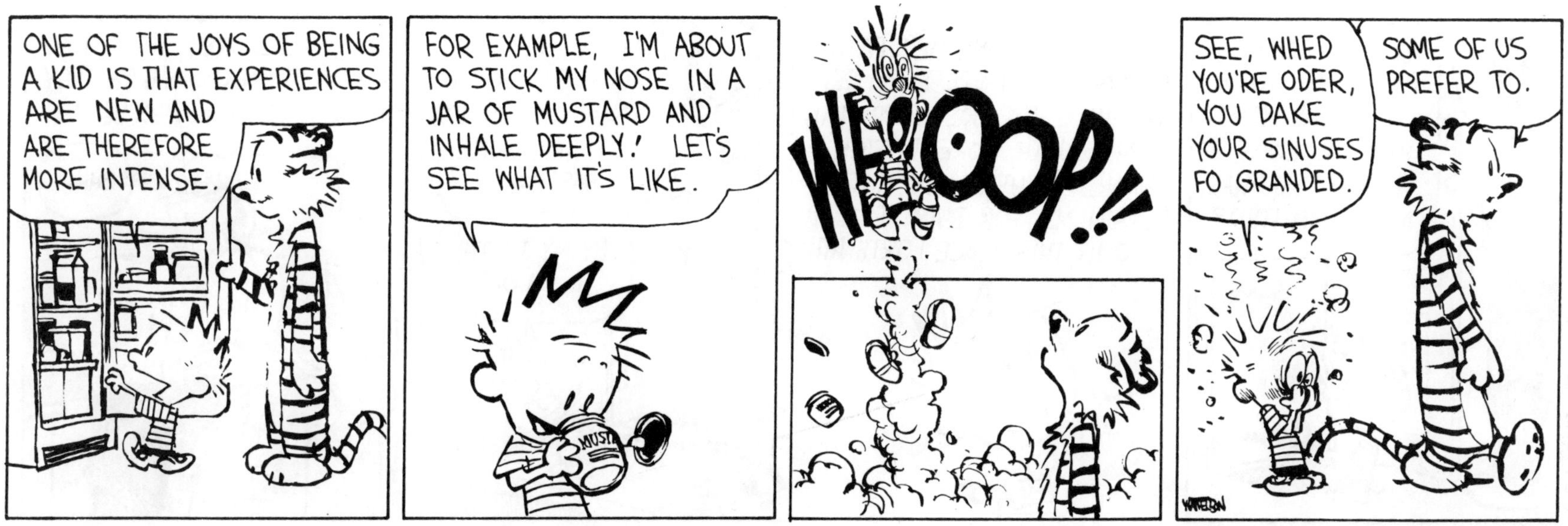
ONE OF THE JOYS OF BEING A KID IS THAT EXPERIENCES ARE NEW AND ARE THEREFORE MORE INTENSE.
FOR EXAMPLE, I'M ABOUT TO STICK MY NOSE IN A JAR OF MUSTARD AND INHALE DEEPLY! LET'S SEE WHAT IT'S LIKE.
WHOOOP!!
SEE, WHED YOU'RE ODER, YOU DAKE YOUR SINUSES FO GRANDED.
SOME OF US PREFER TO.

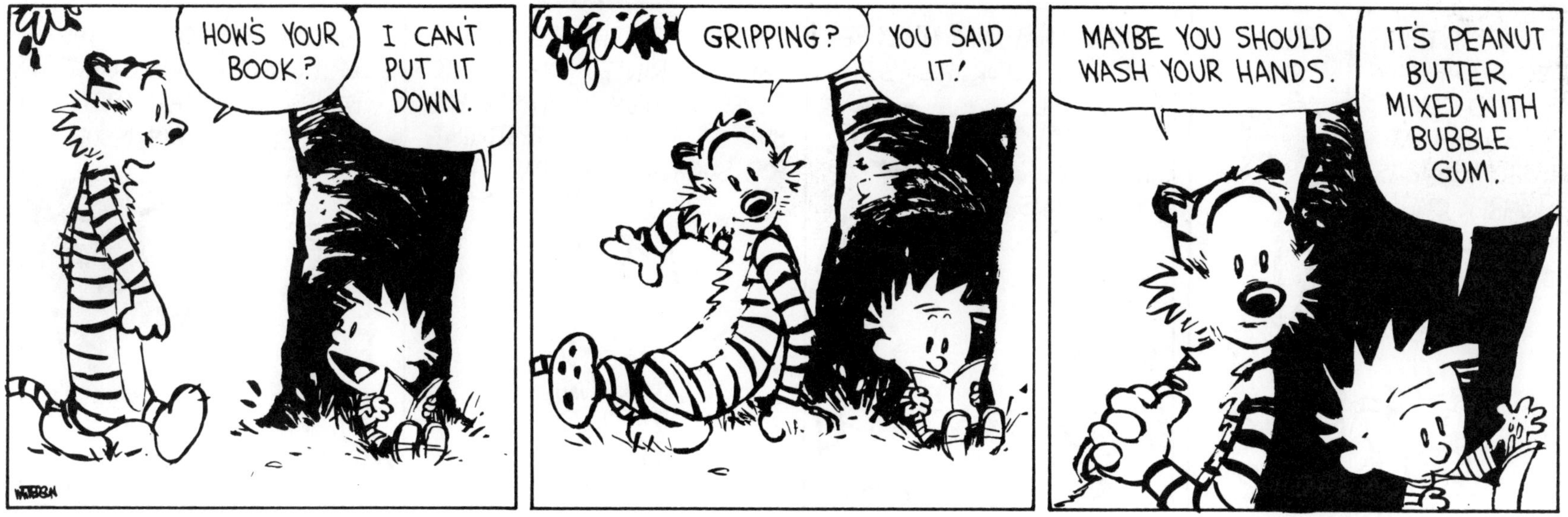
HOW'S YOUR BOOK?
I CAN'T PUT IT DOWN.
GRIPPING?
YOU SAID IT!
MAYBE YOU SHOULD WASH YOUR HANDS.
IT'S PEANUT BUTTER MIXED WITH BUBBLE GUM.

WHITHER GOEST THOU, YOUNG ROGUE? CAN THERE YET REMAIN SOME VILLANY THOU HAST NOT COMMITTED?

THOU DOST WRONG ME! FAITH, I KNOW NOT WHERE I WANDER. METHINKS THE MOST CAPRICIOUS ZEPHYR HATH MORE DESIGN THAN I. BUT LO: DO NOT DETAIN ME, FOR I AM RESOLV'D TO QUIT THIS PLACE FORTHWITH.

AY, BUT HEAR YOU THIS, I'LL SOON KNOW THY BUSINESS. GET THEE GONE, WASTREL!

BY MY TROTH, I AM OFF.

HOLY SCHLA*MOLY*, ISN'T THERE A COP SHOW ON WHERE THEY TALK LIKE REAL PEOPLE?

SHHH.

THE BEST THING ABOUT CAPTAIN STEROID COMIC BOOKS IS THAT EVERY ISSUE IS NUMBER ONE.

EVERY ISSUE??

SURE! THAT WAY THEY'RE *ALL* COLLECTOR ITEMS! THESE WILL BE WORTH BILLIONS OF DOLLARS SOME DAY!

OF COURSE, THEY'RE SO CHEAPLY PRINTED YOU HAVE TO PRESERVE THEM IN PLASTIC BAGS, BUT IT'S A SMALL INVESTMENT FOR SUCH A HUGE GUARANTEED RETURN.

GOSH, AND I KEEP BUYING BONDS.

LOOK AT THE GREAT COMMITTEE THAT DREW *THIS* ISSUE!

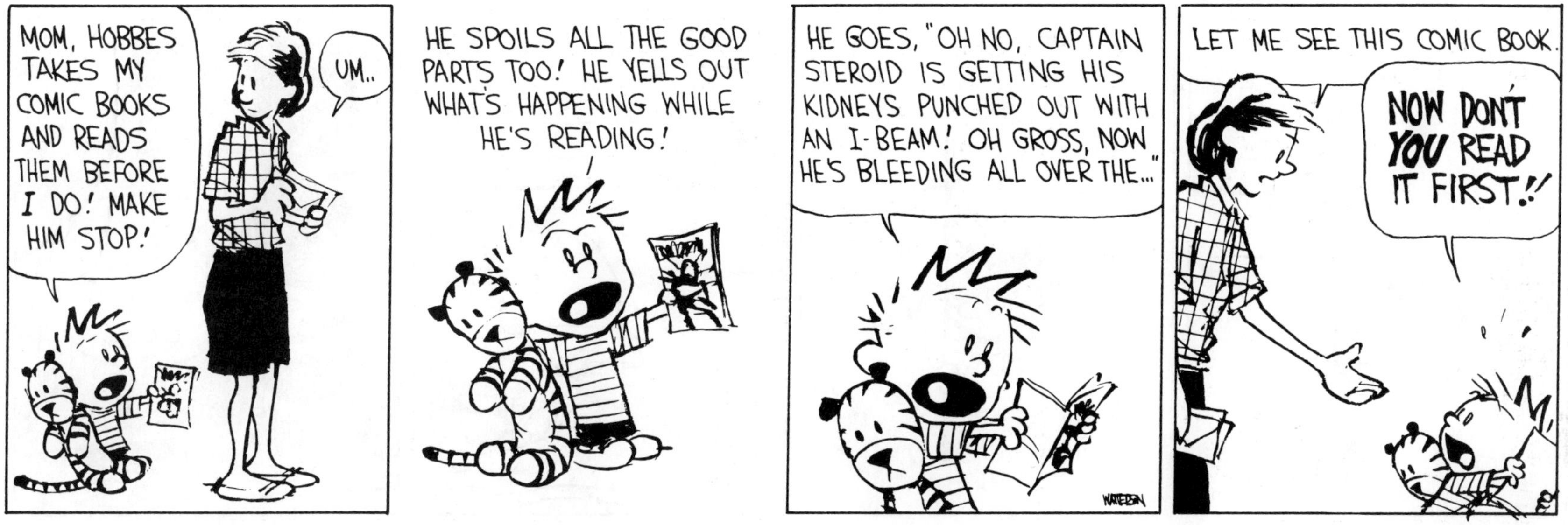
MOM, HOBBES TAKES MY COMIC BOOKS AND READS THEM BEFORE I DO! MAKE HIM STOP!
UM..
HE SPOILS ALL THE GOOD PARTS TOO! HE YELLS OUT WHAT'S HAPPENING WHILE HE'S READING!
HE GOES, "OH NO, CAPTAIN STEROID IS GETTING HIS KIDNEYS PUNCHED OUT WITH AN I-BEAM! OH GROSS, NOW HE'S BLEEDING ALL OVER THE..."
LET ME SEE THIS COMIC BOOK.
NOW DON'T YOU READ IT FIRST!!
WATTERSON

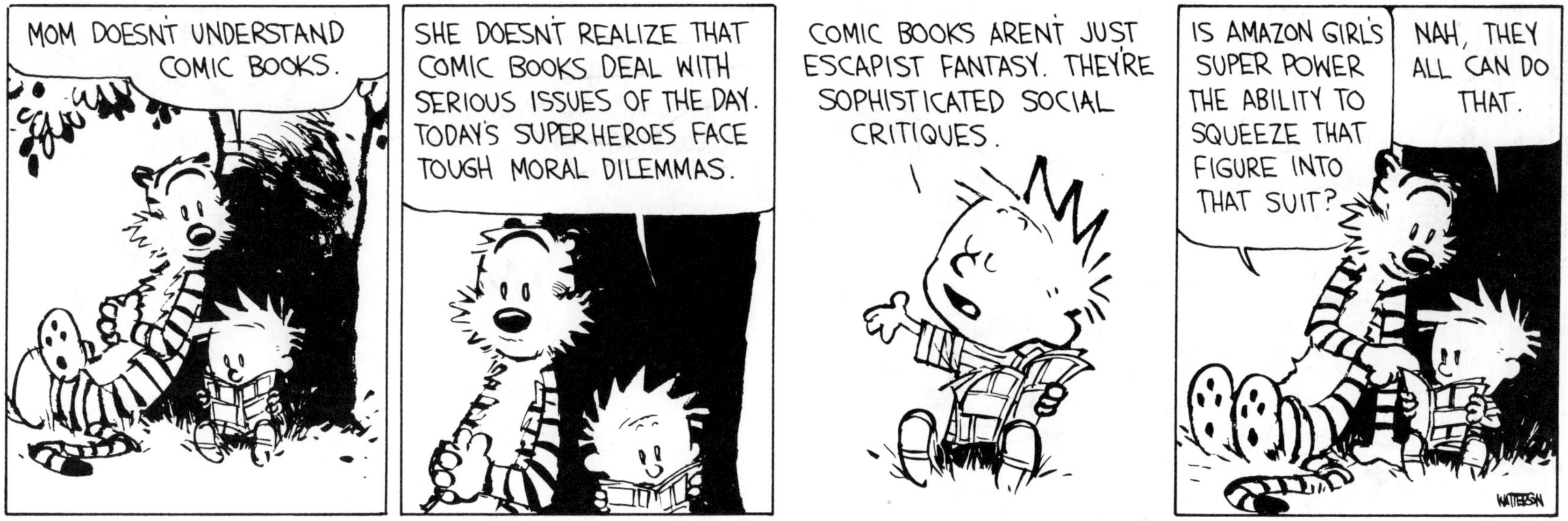
MOM DOESN'T UNDERSTAND COMIC BOOKS.
SHE DOESN'T REALIZE THAT COMIC BOOKS DEAL WITH SERIOUS ISSUES OF THE DAY. TODAY'S SUPERHEROES FACE TOUGH MORAL DILEMMAS.
COMIC BOOKS AREN'T JUST ESCAPIST FANTASY. THEY'RE SOPHISTICATED SOCIAL CRITIQUES.
IS AMAZON GIRL'S SUPER POWER THE ABILITY TO SQUEEZE THAT FIGURE INTO THAT SUIT?
NAH, THEY ALL CAN DO THAT.
WATTERSON

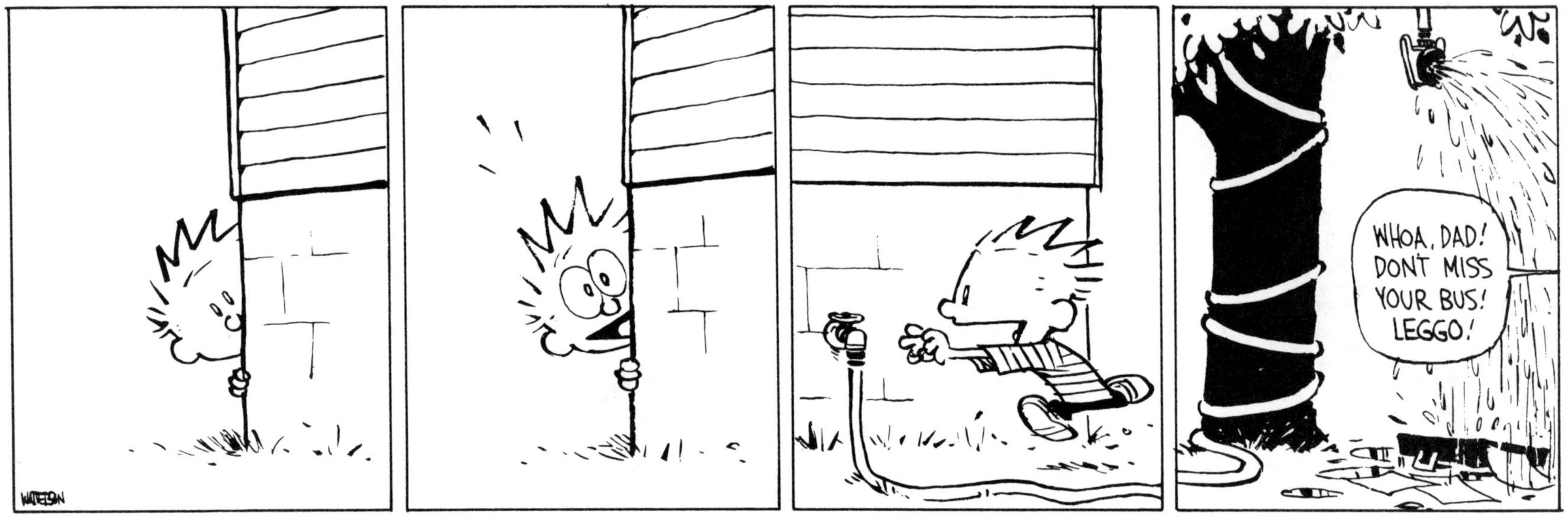
WATTERSON
WHOA, DAD! DON'T MISS YOUR BUS! LEGGO!

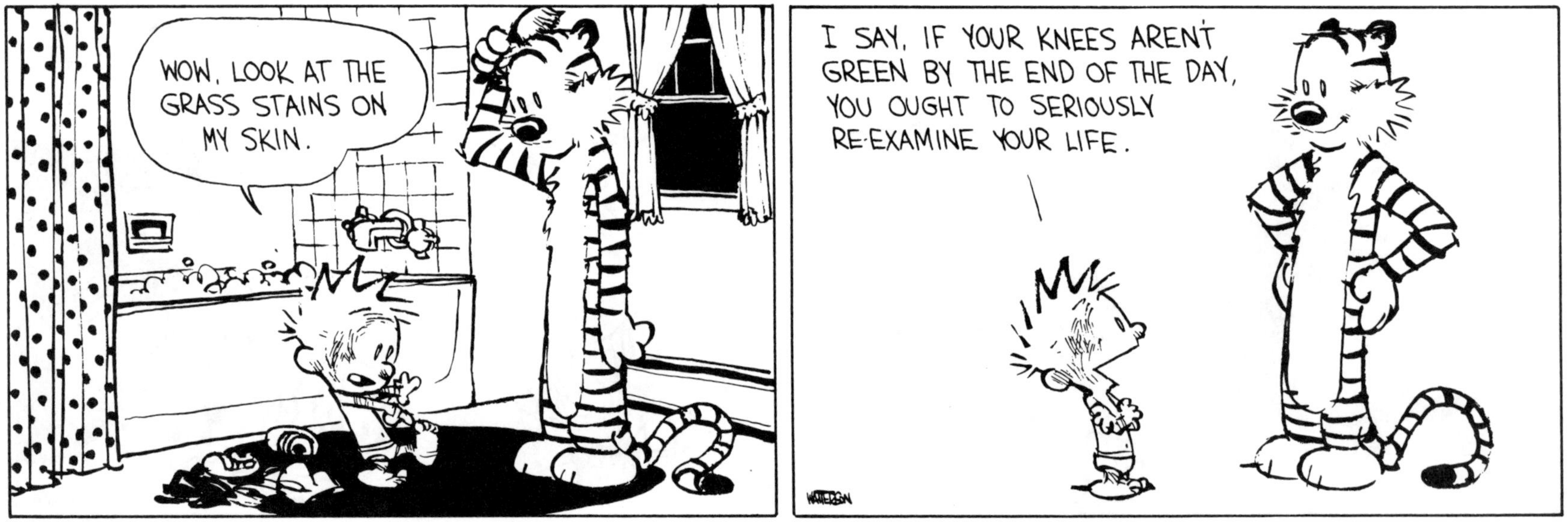
WOW, LOOK AT THE GRASS STAINS ON MY SKIN.
I SAY, IF YOUR KNEES AREN'T GREEN BY THE END OF THE DAY, YOU OUGHT TO SERIOUSLY RE-EXAMINE YOUR LIFE.
WATTERSON

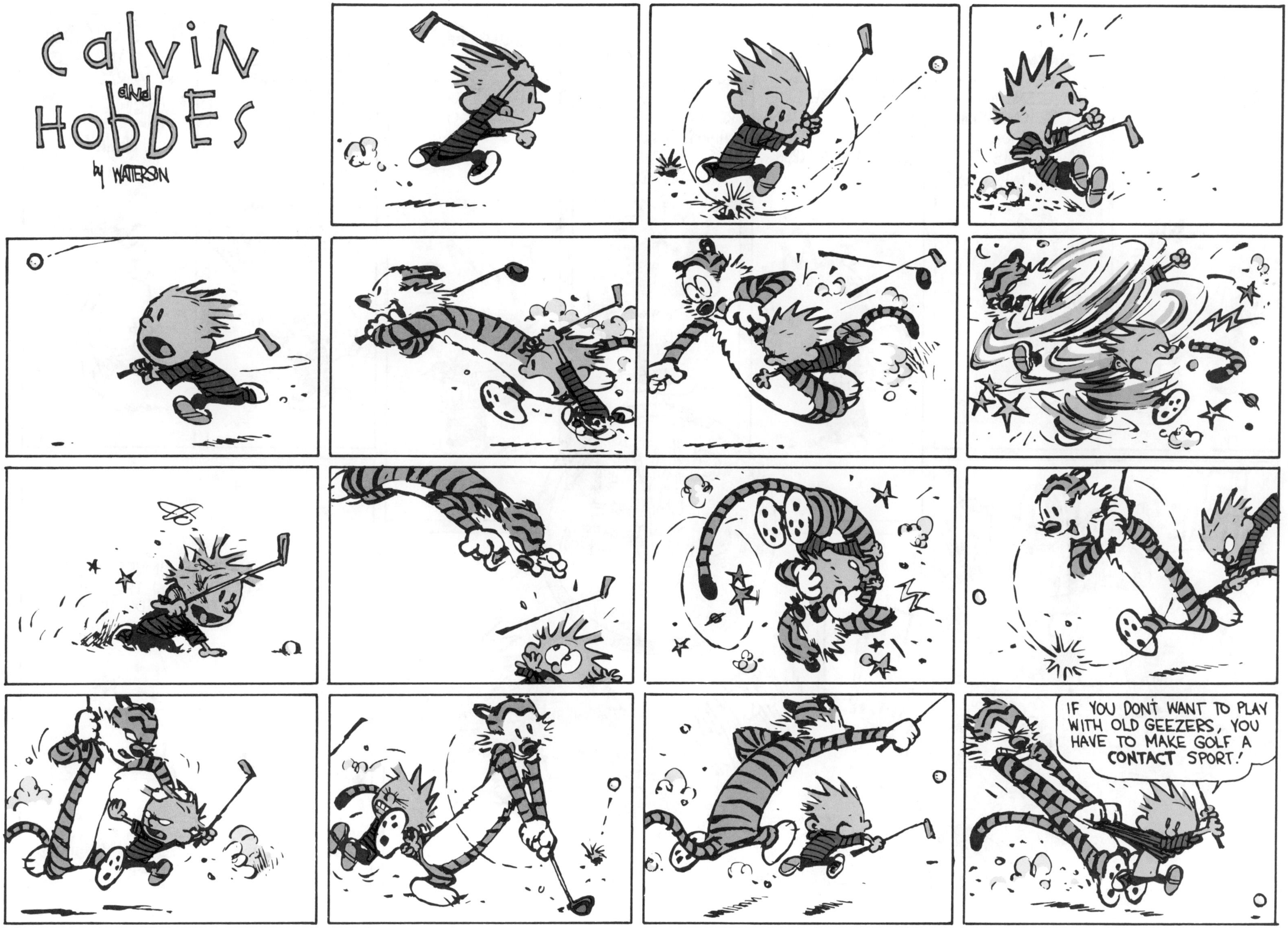
Calvin and Hobbes
by WATTERSON
IF YOU DON'T WANT TO PLAY WITH OLD GEEZERS, YOU HAVE TO MAKE GOLF A **CONTACT** SPORT!

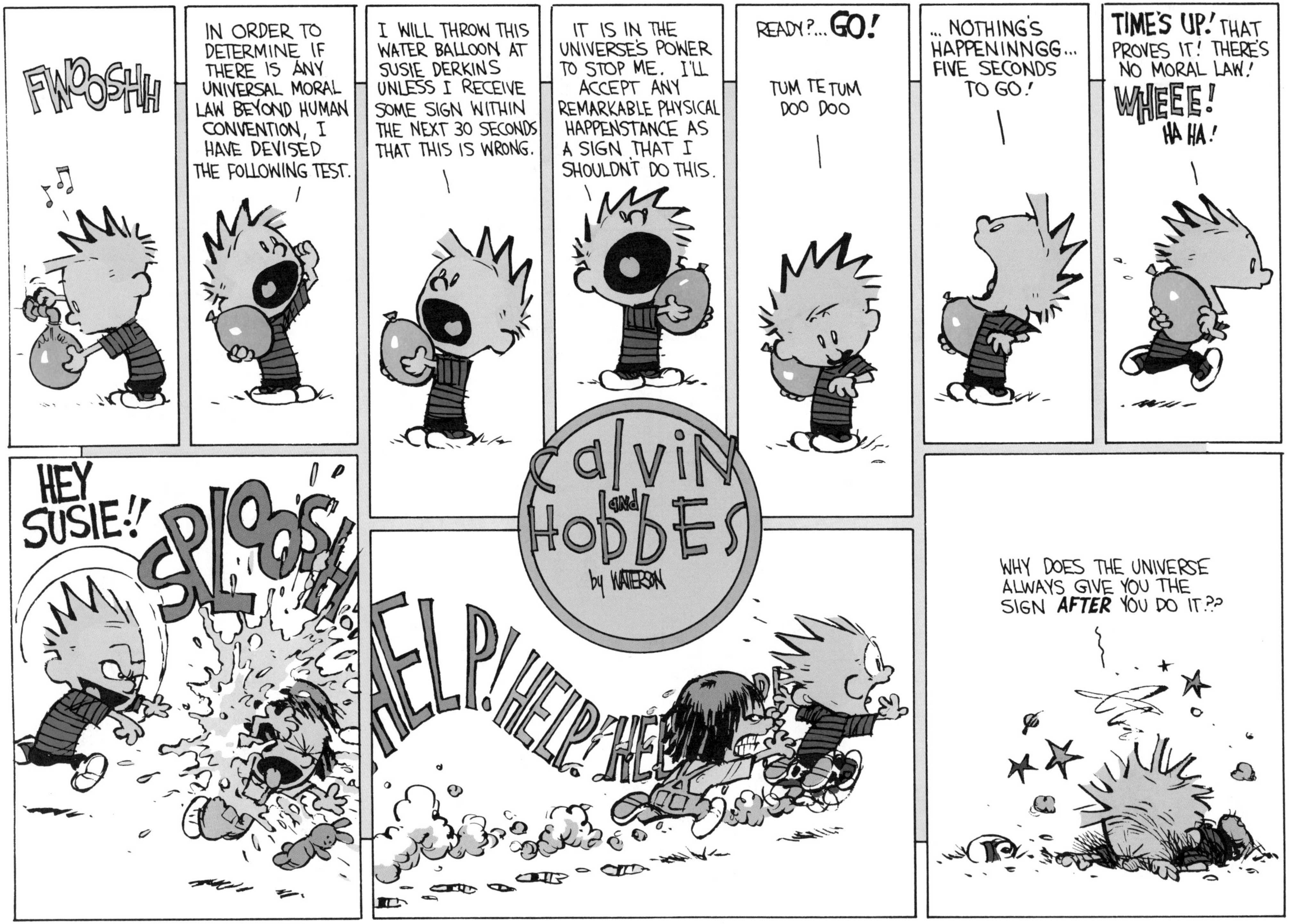
FWOOSHH
IN ORDER TO DETERMINE IF THERE IS ANY UNIVERSAL MORAL LAW BEYOND HUMAN CONVENTION, I HAVE DEVISED THE FOLLOWING TEST.
I WILL THROW THIS WATER BALLOON AT SUSIE DERKINS UNLESS I RECEIVE SOME SIGN WITHIN THE NEXT 30 SECONDS THAT THIS IS WRONG.
IT IS IN THE UNIVERSE'S POWER TO STOP ME. I'LL ACCEPT ANY REMARKABLE PHYSICAL HAPPENSTANCE AS A SIGN THAT I SHOULDN'T DO THIS.
READY?... GO!
TUM TE TUM DOO DOO
... NOTHING'S HAPPENINNGG... FIVE SECONDS TO GO!
TIME'S UP! THAT PROVES IT! THERE'S NO MORAL LAW!
WHEEE!
HA HA!
Calvin and Hobbes
by WATTERSON
HEY SUSIE!!
SPLOOSH
HELP! HELP! HEL
WHY DOES THE UNIVERSE ALWAYS GIVE YOU THE SIGN AFTER YOU DO IT??

IT'S TOO HOT TO SLEEP WITH YOU IN THE BED. YOU'RE BLOCKING THE BREEZE AND YOU TAKE UP TOO MUCH ROOM!
OPENING THE WINDOW MORE ISN'T GOING TO HELP! THE PROBLEM IS YOUR BIG, HOT, FURRY BODY!
HEY! LEGGO! I DIDN'T MEAN IT! NO! I'M COMFORTABLE! REALLY!
AND MOM CAN'T IMAGINE HOW MY PAJAMAS GET SO GRITTY.

I DON'T HAVE ANYTHING TO DO.
WELL THEN, WHY DON'T YOU GO CLEAN YOUR ROOM?
I WAS BRAGGING.

A Swift Kick in the Butt $1 00
HOW'S BUSINESS?
TERRIBLE.
THAT'S HARD TO BELIEVE.
I CAN'T UNDERSTAND IT.
EVERYBODY I KNOW NEEDS WHAT I'M SELLING!

WHEN YOU'RE AS LONG AS THE POOL, SWIMMING A LAP IN ZERO SECONDS ISN'T A RECORD!

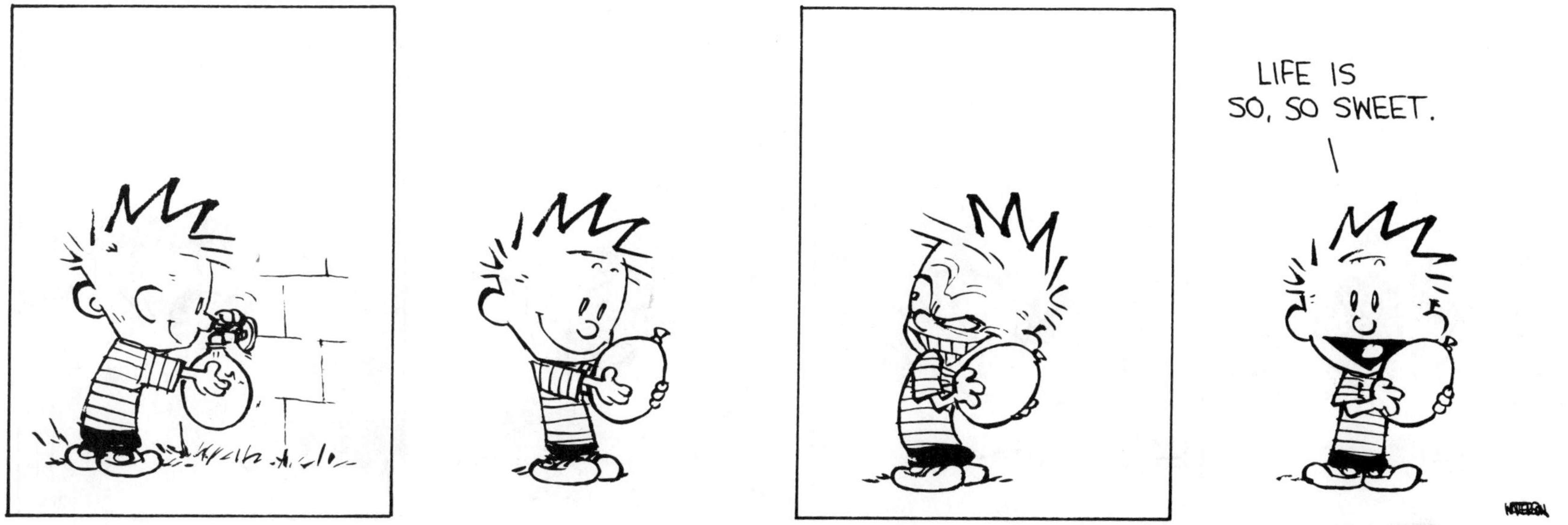
LIFE IS SO, SO SWEET.

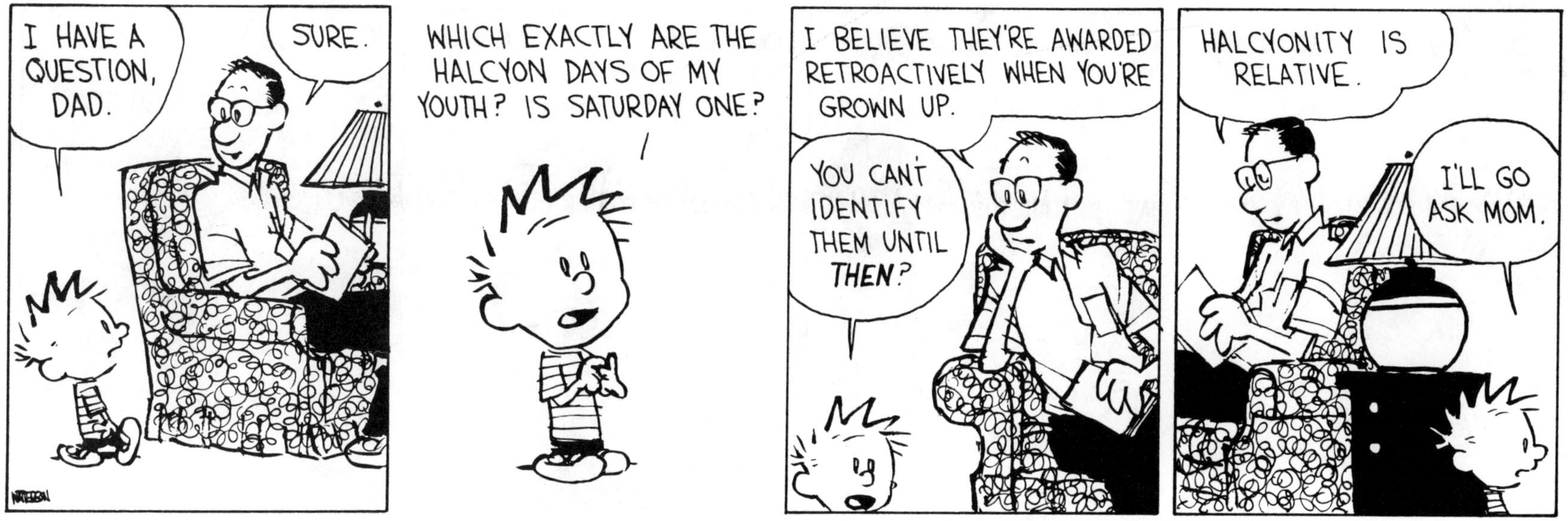
I HAVE A QUESTION, DAD.
SURE.
WHICH EXACTLY ARE THE HALCYON DAYS OF MY YOUTH? IS SATURDAY ONE?
I BELIEVE THEY'RE AWARDED RETROACTIVELY WHEN YOU'RE GROWN UP.
YOU CAN'T IDENTIFY THEM UNTIL *THEN*?
HALCYONITY IS RELATIVE.
I'LL GO ASK MOM.

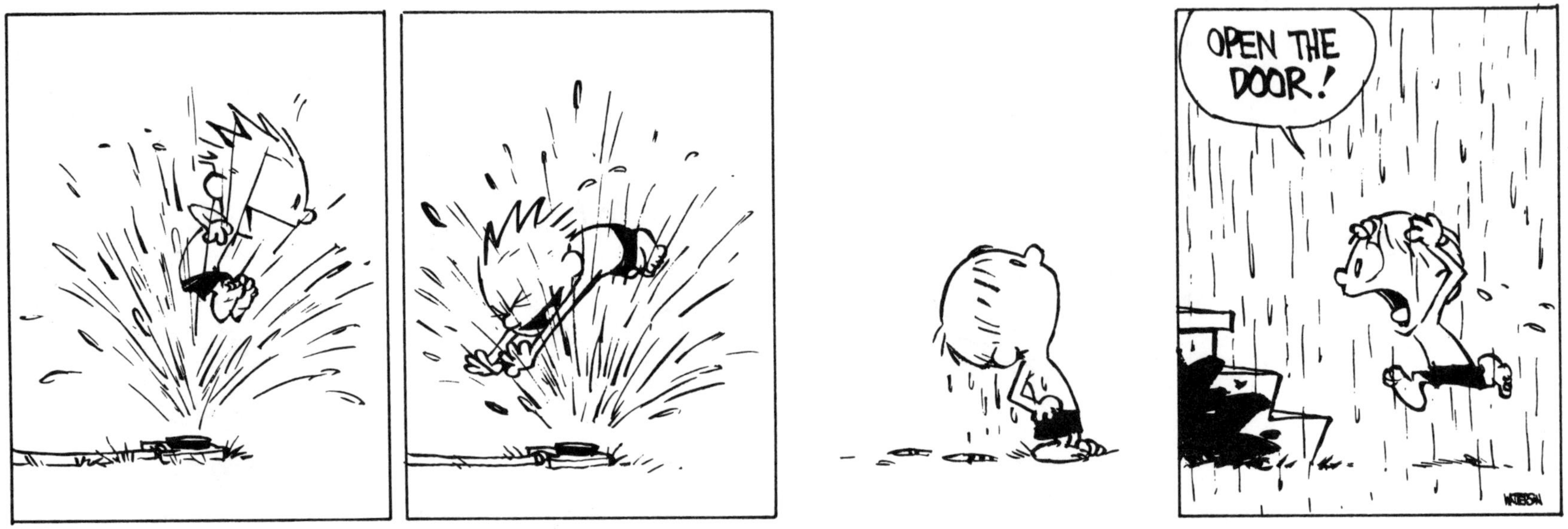
OPEN THE DOOR!

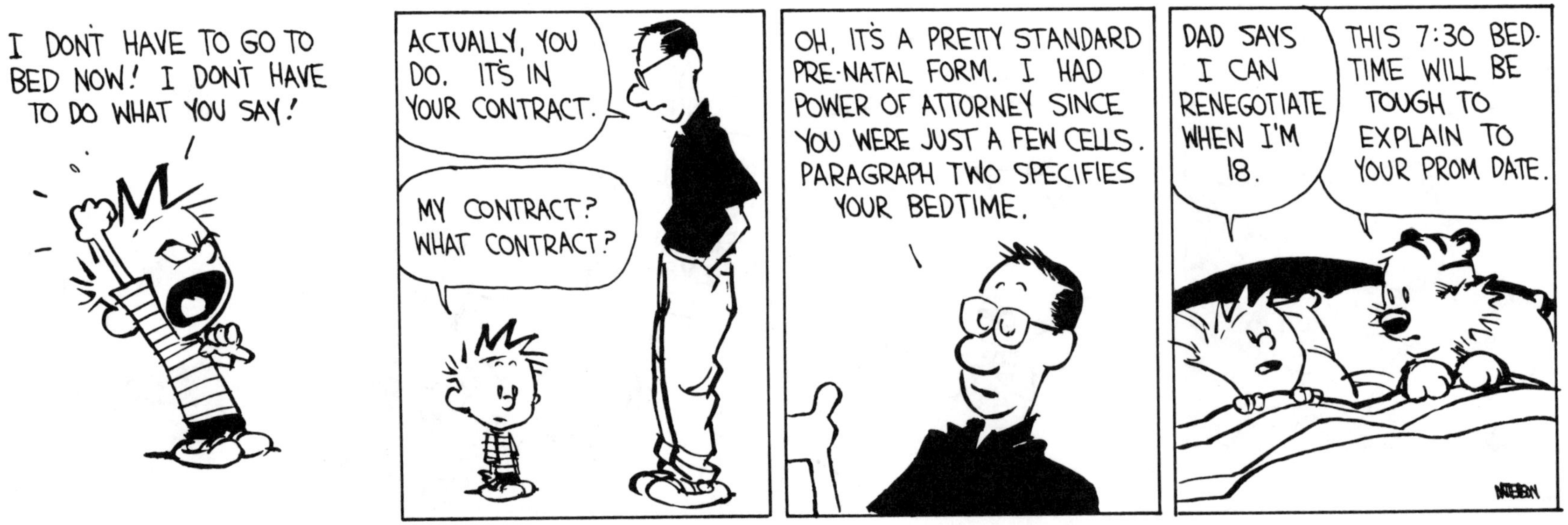
I DON'T HAVE TO GO TO BED NOW! I DON'T HAVE TO DO WHAT YOU SAY!
ACTUALLY, YOU DO. IT'S IN YOUR CONTRACT.
MY CONTRACT? WHAT CONTRACT?
OH, IT'S A PRETTY STANDARD PRE-NATAL FORM. I HAD POWER OF ATTORNEY SINCE YOU WERE JUST A FEW CELLS. PARAGRAPH TWO SPECIFIES YOUR BEDTIME.
DAD SAYS I CAN RENEGOTIATE WHEN I'M 18.
THIS 7:30 BEDTIME WILL BE TOUGH TO EXPLAIN TO YOUR PROM DATE.

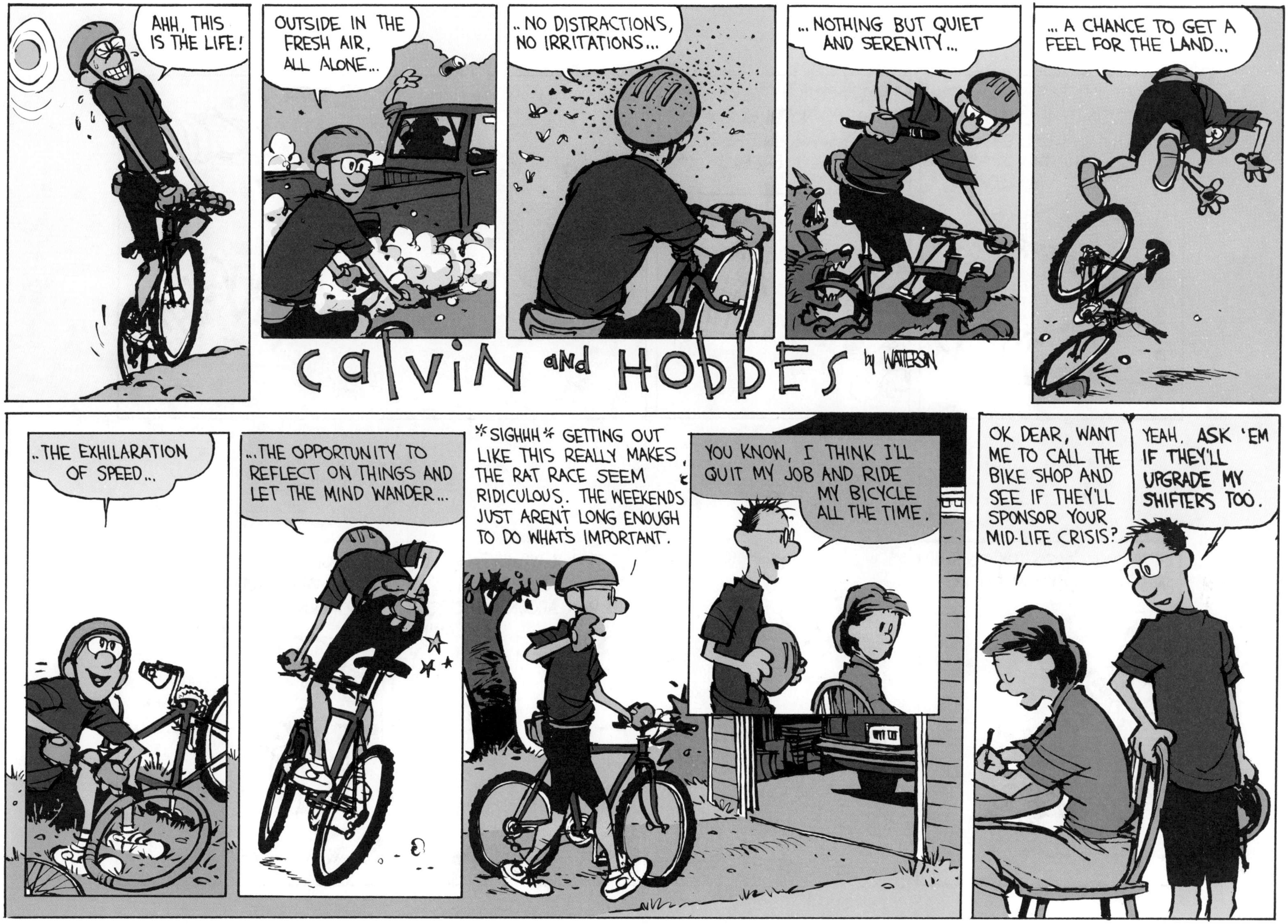
AHH, THIS IS THE LIFE!
OUTSIDE IN THE FRESH AIR, ALL ALONE...
.. NO DISTRACTIONS, NO IRRITATIONS...
... NOTHING BUT QUIET AND SERENITY...
... A CHANCE TO GET A FEEL FOR THE LAND...
CALVIN AND HOBBES
by WATTERSON
.. THE EXHILARATION OF SPEED...
... THE OPPORTUNITY TO REFLECT ON THINGS AND LET THE MIND WANDER...
SIGHHH GETTING OUT LIKE THIS REALLY MAKES THE RAT RACE SEEM RIDICULOUS. THE WEEKENDS JUST AREN'T LONG ENOUGH TO DO WHAT'S IMPORTANT.
YOU KNOW, I THINK I'LL QUIT MY JOB AND RIDE MY BICYCLE ALL THE TIME.
OK DEAR, WANT ME TO CALL THE BIKE SHOP AND SEE IF THEY'LL SPONSOR YOUR MID-LIFE CRISIS?
YEAH. ASK 'EM IF THEY'LL UPGRADE MY SHIFTERS TOO.

WHY DO YOU SLEEP SO MUCH?
I LIKE TO BE RESTED WHEN THINGS START TO HAPPEN.
WHAT ARE YOU TALKING ABOUT?!' NOTHING EVER HAPPENS AROUND HERE! GIVE ME A BREAK!
AAAUGHH!

C'MON, LET'S GO TRY TO FIND A BIG POISONOUS SNAKE!
WHAT WILL WE DO IF WE SEE ONE?
ARE YOU KIDDING? WE'LL SCARE OURSELVES SILLY AND RUN AROUND IN CIRCLES, SCREAMING LIKE A BUNCH OF LOONS!
I LOOK FORWARD TO WHEN WE'RE OLD ENOUGH TO GET OUR MORNING JOLT FROM COFFEE.
AHH, I'LL BET THAT WEARS OFF QUICKER.

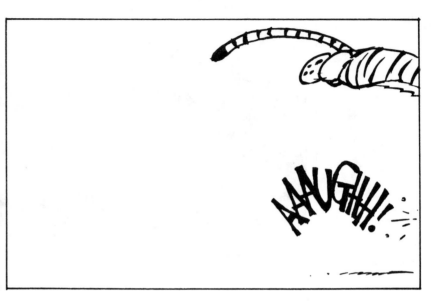

OH GREATEST OF THE MASS MEDIA, THANK YOU FOR ELEVATING EMOTION, REDUCING THOUGHT, AND STIFLING IMAGINATION.

THANK YOU FOR THE ARTIFICIALITY OF QUICK SOLUTIONS AND FOR THE INSIDIOUS MANIPULATION OF HUMAN DESIRES FOR COMMERCIAL PURPOSES.

THIS BOWL OF LUKEWARM TAPIOCA REPRESENTS MY BRAIN. I OFFER IT IN HUMBLE SACRIFICE. BESTOW THY FLICKERING LIGHT FOREVER.

YOU KNOW WHAT I'VE DISCOVERED?

WHAT?

A LITTLE RUDENESS AND DISRESPECT CAN ELEVATE A MEANINGLESS INTERACTION TO A BATTLE OF WILLS AND ADD DRAMA TO AN OTHERWISE DULL DAY.

OH, THAT'S GOOD TO KNOW.

IF YOU WEREN'T SUCH A MUTTONHEAD, YOU MIGHT HAVE THOUGHT OF IT YOURSELF!

SEE?? YOU PROVED MY POINT!

I SLEPT ON MY HAIR FUNNY.
I CAN TELL.
MAYBE IF I MOUSSE IT, IT WILL STAY LIKE THIS!
SEE IF YOUR MOM HAS ANY CURLERS FOR THE BACK!

HELLO, INFORMATION?
YES, WHAT EXACTLY IS THE DIFFERENCE BETWEEN A HOTDOG, A WIENER, AND A FRANKFURTER?
WHAT? WHADDAYA **MEAN**?! OK, **FINE**! THANKS FOR **NOTHING**, YOU FRAUD!!
AND I'VE HEARD THE "OPERATOR" ISN'T EVEN A SURGEON!
YOU CAN'T TRUST ANYONE.

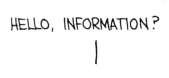

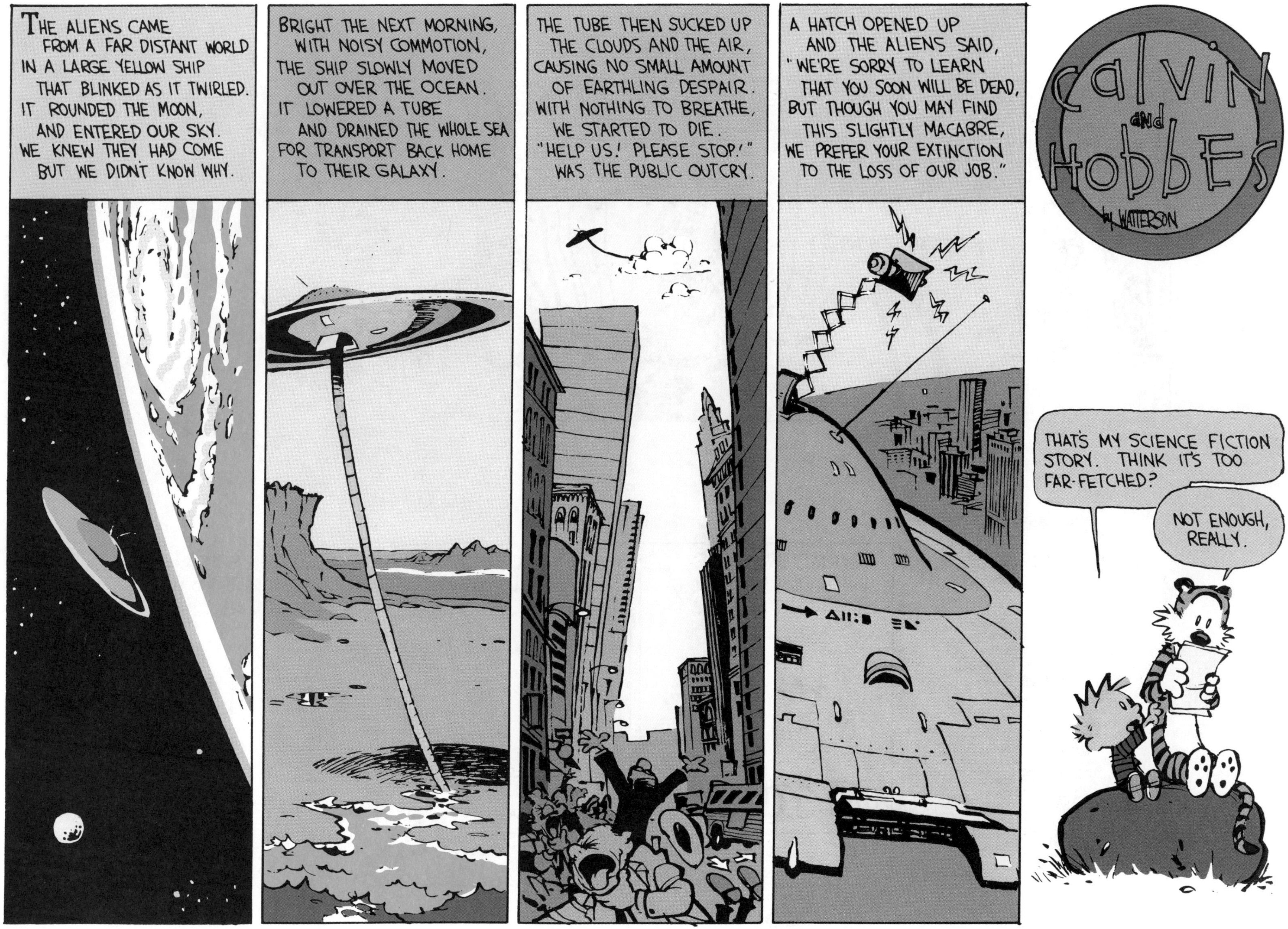
THE ALIENS CAME FROM A FAR DISTANT WORLD IN A LARGE YELLOW SHIP THAT BLINKED AS IT TWIRLED. IT ROUNDED THE MOON, AND ENTERED OUR SKY. WE KNEW THEY HAD COME BUT WE DIDN'T KNOW WHY.
BRIGHT THE NEXT MORNING, WITH NOISY COMMOTION, THE SHIP SLOWLY MOVED OUT OVER THE OCEAN. IT LOWERED A TUBE AND DRAINED THE WHOLE SEA FOR TRANSPORT BACK HOME TO THEIR GALAXY.
THE TUBE THEN SUCKED UP THE CLOUDS AND THE AIR, CAUSING NO SMALL AMOUNT OF EARTHLING DESPAIR. WITH NOTHING TO BREATHE, WE STARTED TO DIE. "HELP US! PLEASE STOP!" WAS THE PUBLIC OUTCRY.
A HATCH OPENED UP AND THE ALIENS SAID, "WE'RE SORRY TO LEARN THAT YOU SOON WILL BE DEAD, BUT THOUGH YOU MAY FIND THIS SLIGHTLY MACABRE, WE PREFER YOUR EXTINCTION TO THE LOSS OF OUR JOB."
Calvin and Hobbes
by WATTERSON
THAT'S MY SCIENCE FICTION STORY. THINK IT'S TOO FAR-FETCHED?
NOT ENOUGH, REALLY.

I'M SICK OF HEARING ABOUT PERSONAL RESPONSIBILITY! I'VE ALREADY **DONE** MY PART TO MAKE THE WORLD A BETTER PLACE TO LIVE.

REALLY?

SURE! I WAS **BORN**!

OH YES, I FORGOT TO THANK YOU.

JOIN THE CLUB!

MAN, IT MUST BE 100 DEGREES TODAY!

ANIMALS SURE ARE DUMB TO HAVE ALL THAT FUR.

PEOPLE SURE ARE UGLY WITHOUT IT.

!

I'LL BET HE'S CRANKY BECAUSE HE'S SO HOT.

RUN FOR YOUR LIFE! THERE'S A MILLION ANGRY HORNETS COMING!
THEY'RE INSANE WITH RAGE! THEY'LL STING ANYONE IN THEIR PATH! LOUSY BUGS!
WHAT ARE THEY MAD ABOUT?
I'VE BEEN THROWING ROCKS AT THEIR NEST ALL MORNING.
A REAL FRIEND WOULDN'T TAKE THEIR SIDE!!

WHEE HEE HEE
SPLOOSHH
OH, WHAT AN AWFUL THING I DID! HOW I REGRET IT NOW! I HEREBY RESOLVE TO CHANGE MY EVIL WAYS! OH REMORSE, REMORSE!
MY PENITENT SINNER SHTICK NEEDS WORK.

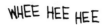

Calvin and Hobbes
by WATTERSON
SOMETHING'S WRONG! WE SHOULD'VE TOUCHED DOWN BY NOW!
OH NO! WE MISCALCULATED! REDUCE FORWARD MOMENTUM!
LANDING LEG IS OUT OF ALIGNMENT!
COMMUNICATION LINES ARE BROKEN!
VIEW PORTS OPEN! FOCUS! FOCUS!
ROTATE UPPER APPENDAGES!
AAUGH! RED ALERT! WE'RE GOING DOWN!
CRASH POSITIONS!
RETRACT LEFT LANDING LEG! REDISTRIBUTE ALL WEIGHT!
CIRCUIT OVERLOAD! ESSENTIAL FUNCTIONS ONLY!
IT'S TOO LATE!
ADRENALIN AT MAXIMUM!
PREPARE FOR IMPACT!
AAAAAAAA
KABOOM
GOODNESS! ARE YOU ALL RIGHT?!
DAMAGE ASSESSMENT IS UNDER WAY.

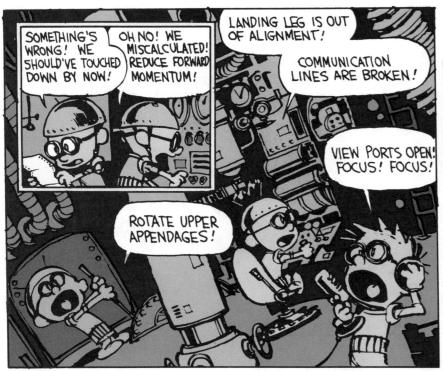

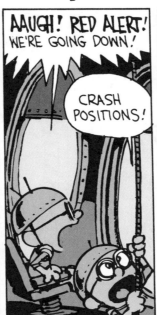

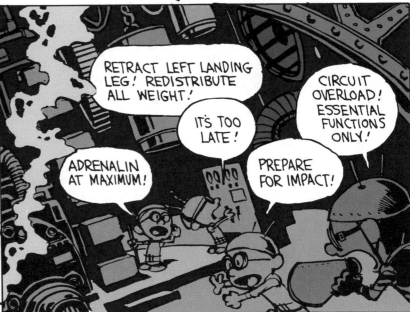

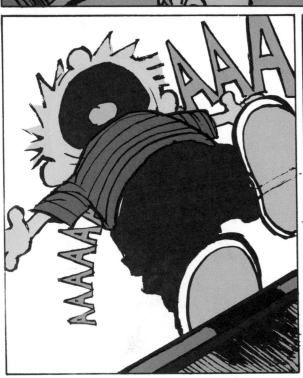

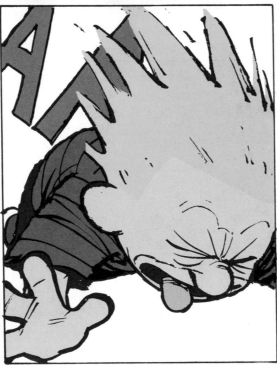

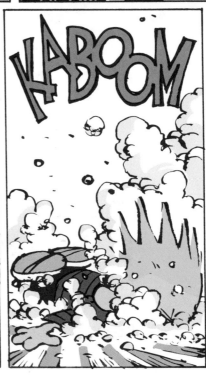

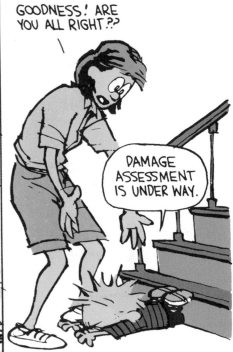

TA DA DA DAAAAA! I'M *STUPENDOUS MAN!*

KAPWINNNGGG!

VIRTUAL REALITY HAS NOTHING ON CALVIN.

I FEEL I HAVE AN OBLIGATION TO KEEP A JOURNAL OF MY THOUGHTS.

OH?

BEING A GENIUS, MY IDEAS ARE NATURALLY MORE IMPORTANT AND INTERESTING THAN OTHER PEOPLE'S, SO I FIGURE THE WORLD WOULD BENEFIT FROM A RECORD OF MY MENTAL ACTIVITIES.

HOW PHILANTHROPIC OF YOU.

WELL, THE WORLD ISN'T GOING TO GET IT CHEAP.

SO WHAT ARE YOU WRITING TODAY?

I COULDN'T REALLY THINK OF ANYTHING, SO I'M DRAWING SOME MARTIANS ATTACKING INDIANAPOLIS.

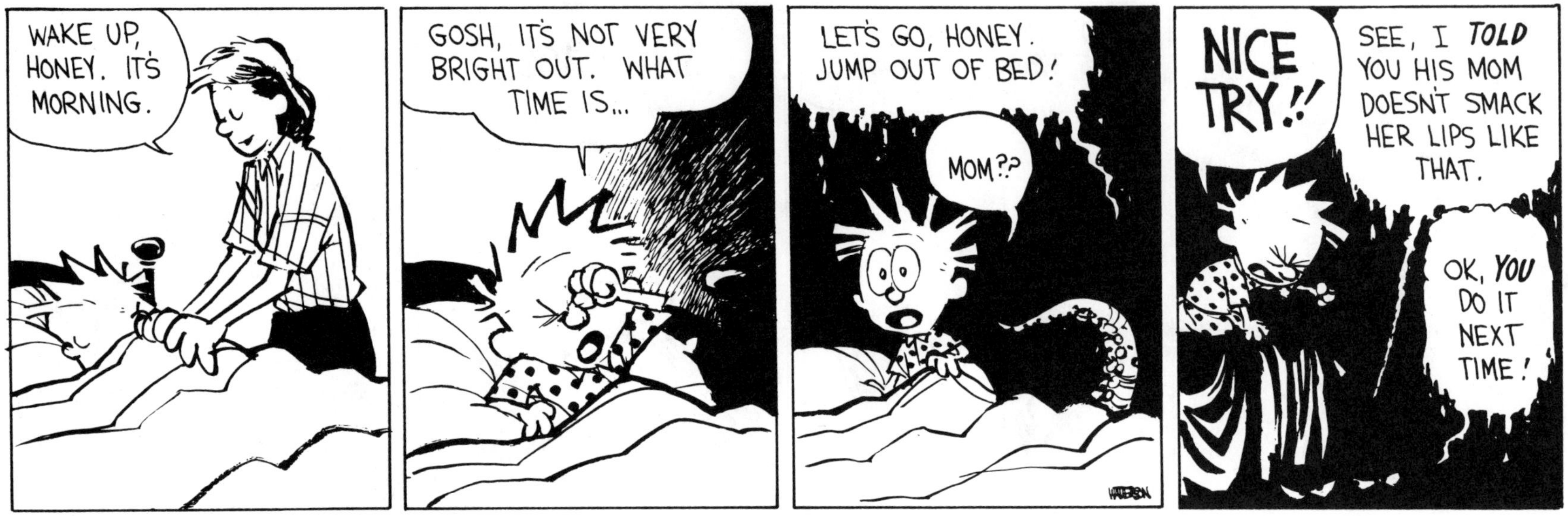
WAKE UP, HONEY. IT'S MORNING.
GOSH, IT'S NOT VERY BRIGHT OUT. WHAT TIME IS...
LET'S GO, HONEY. JUMP OUT OF BED!
MOM?!?
NICE TRY!!
SEE, I TOLD YOU HIS MOM DOESN'T SMACK HER LIPS LIKE THAT.
OK, YOU DO IT NEXT TIME!

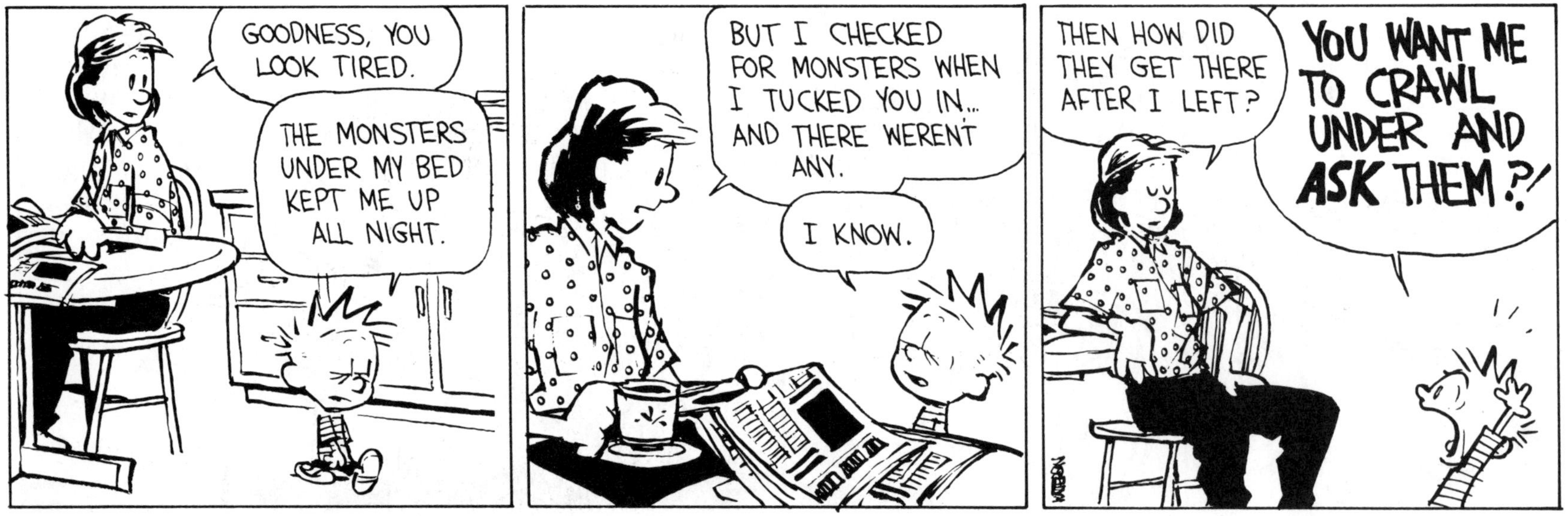
GOODNESS, YOU LOOK TIRED.
THE MONSTERS UNDER MY BED KEPT ME UP ALL NIGHT.
BUT I CHECKED FOR MONSTERS WHEN I TUCKED YOU IN... AND THERE WEREN'T ANY.
I KNOW.
THEN HOW DID THEY GET THERE AFTER I LEFT?
YOU WANT ME TO CRAWL UNDER AND ASK THEM?!

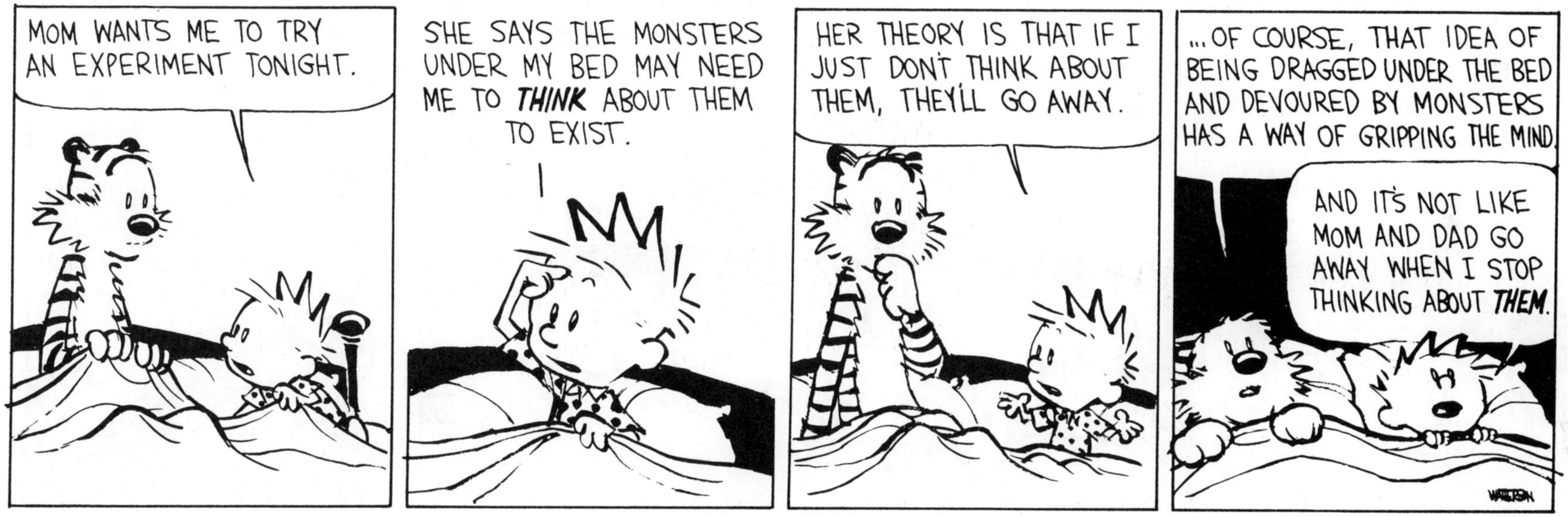
MOM WANTS ME TO TRY AN EXPERIMENT TONIGHT.
SHE SAYS THE MONSTERS UNDER MY BED MAY NEED ME TO **THINK** ABOUT THEM TO EXIST.
HER THEORY IS THAT IF I JUST DON'T THINK ABOUT THEM, THEY'LL GO AWAY.
...OF COURSE, THAT IDEA OF BEING DRAGGED UNDER THE BED AND DEVOURED BY MONSTERS HAS A WAY OF GRIPPING THE MIND.
AND IT'S NOT LIKE MOM AND DAD GO AWAY WHEN I STOP THINKING ABOUT **THEM**.
WATTERSON

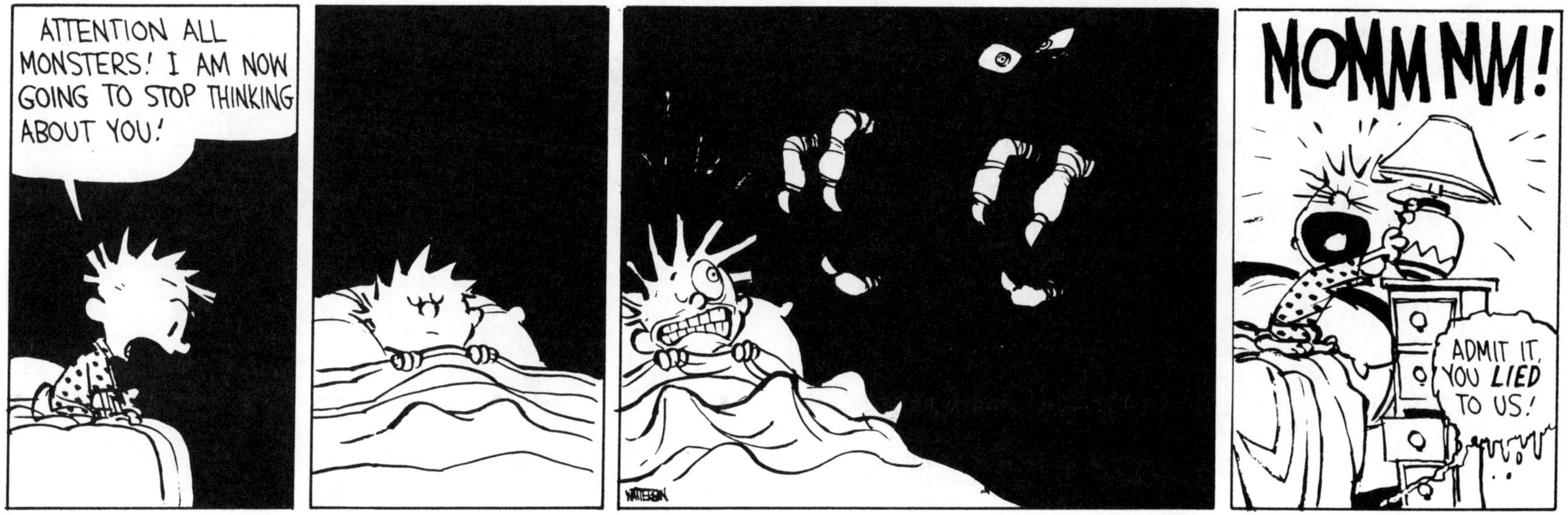
ATTENTION ALL MONSTERS! I AM NOW GOING TO STOP THINKING ABOUT YOU!
WATTERSON
MOMMMM!
ADMIT IT, YOU **LIED** TO US!

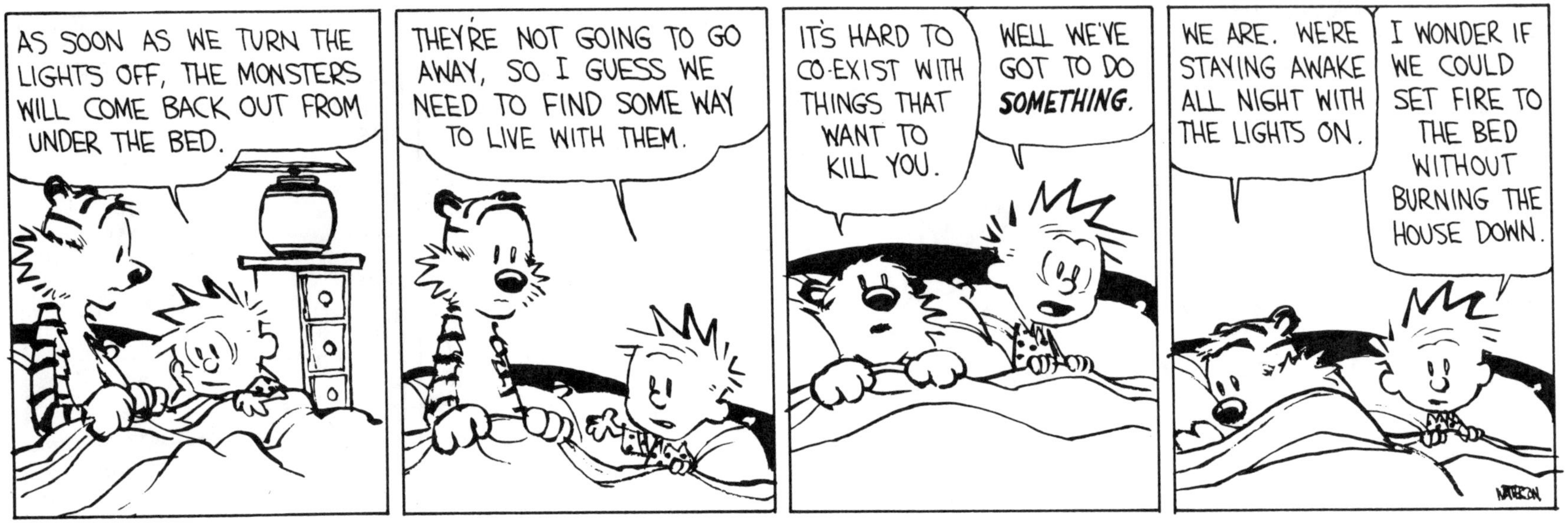
AS SOON AS WE TURN THE LIGHTS OFF, THE MONSTERS WILL COME BACK OUT FROM UNDER THE BED.
THEY'RE NOT GOING TO GO AWAY, SO I GUESS WE NEED TO FIND SOME WAY TO LIVE WITH THEM.
IT'S HARD TO CO-EXIST WITH THINGS THAT WANT TO KILL YOU.
WELL WE'VE GOT TO DO **SOMETHING**.
WE ARE. WE'RE STAYING AWAKE ALL NIGHT WITH THE LIGHTS ON.
I WONDER IF WE COULD SET FIRE TO THE BED WITHOUT BURNING THE HOUSE DOWN.

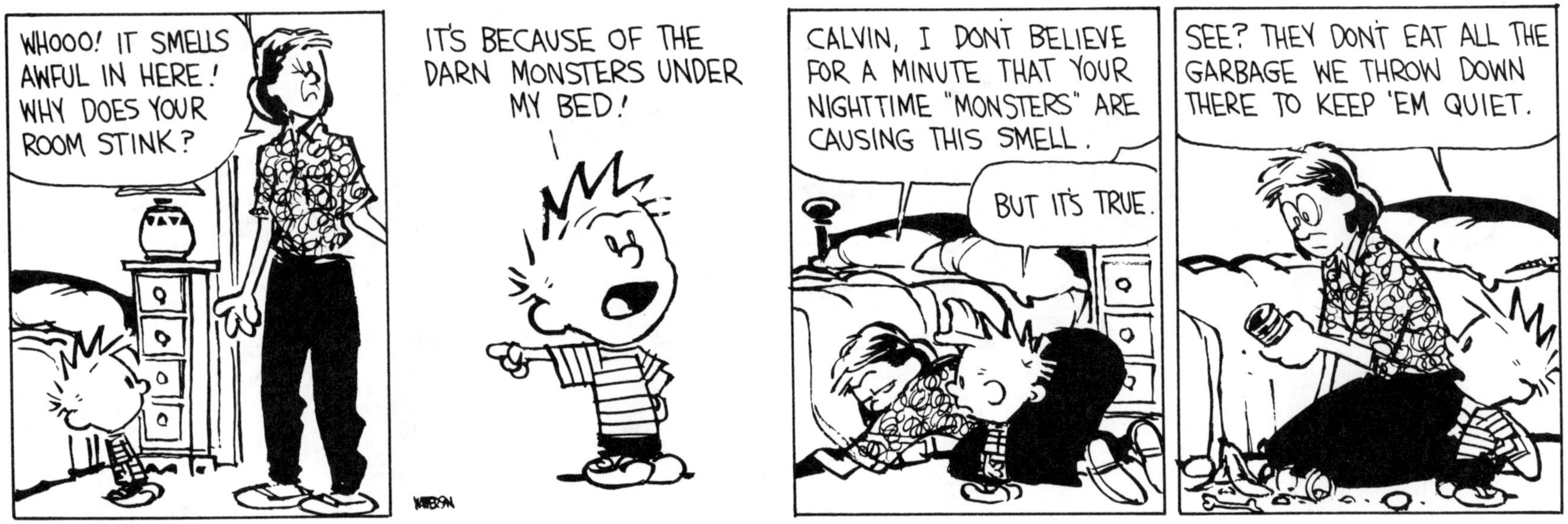
WHOOO! IT SMELLS AWFUL IN HERE! WHY DOES YOUR ROOM STINK?
IT'S BECAUSE OF THE DARN MONSTERS UNDER MY BED!
CALVIN, I DON'T BELIEVE FOR A MINUTE THAT YOUR NIGHTTIME "MONSTERS" ARE CAUSING THIS SMELL.
BUT IT'S TRUE.
SEE? THEY DON'T EAT ALL THE GARBAGE WE THROW DOWN THERE TO KEEP 'EM QUIET.

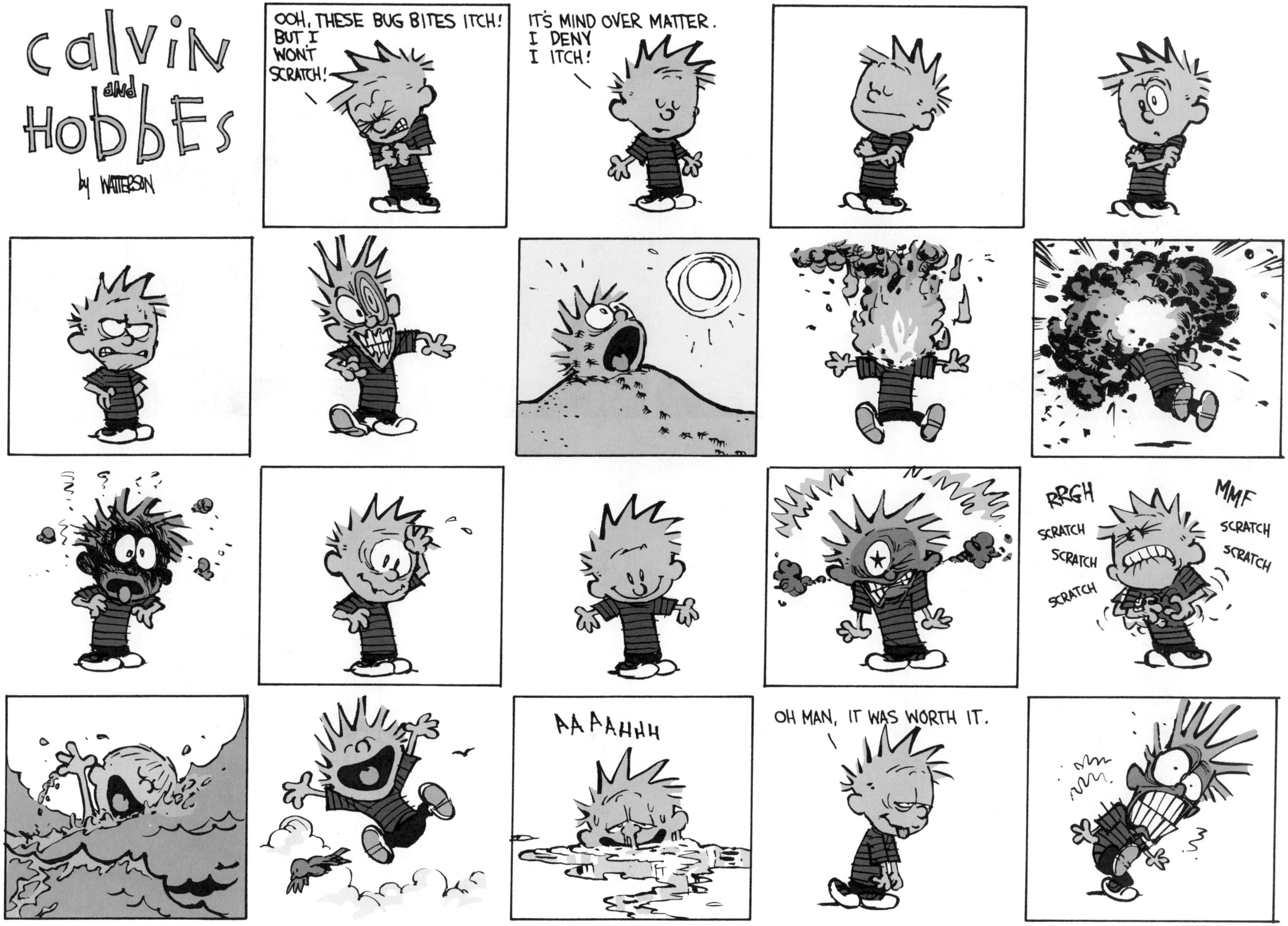

Calvin and Hobbes
by WATTERSON
OOH, THESE BUG BITES ITCH! BUT I WON'T SCRATCH!
IT'S MIND OVER MATTER. I DENY I ITCH!
RRGH
MMF
SCRATCH
SCRATCH
SCRATCH
SCRATCH
SCRATCH
AAAAHHH
OH MAN, IT WAS WORTH IT.

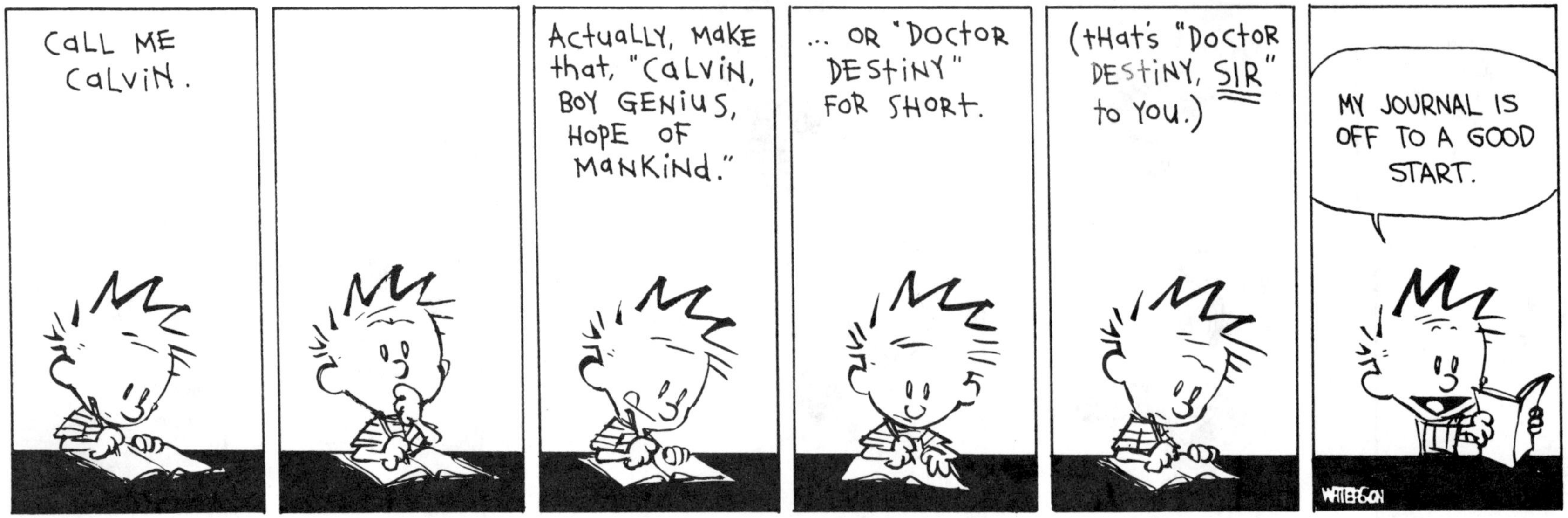
CALL ME CALVIN.
ACTUALLY, MAKE THAT, "CALVIN, BOY GENIUS, HOPE OF MANKIND."
... OR "DOCTOR DESTINY" FOR SHORT.
(THAT'S "DOCTOR DESTINY, SIR" TO YOU.)
MY JOURNAL IS OFF TO A GOOD START.
WATTERSON

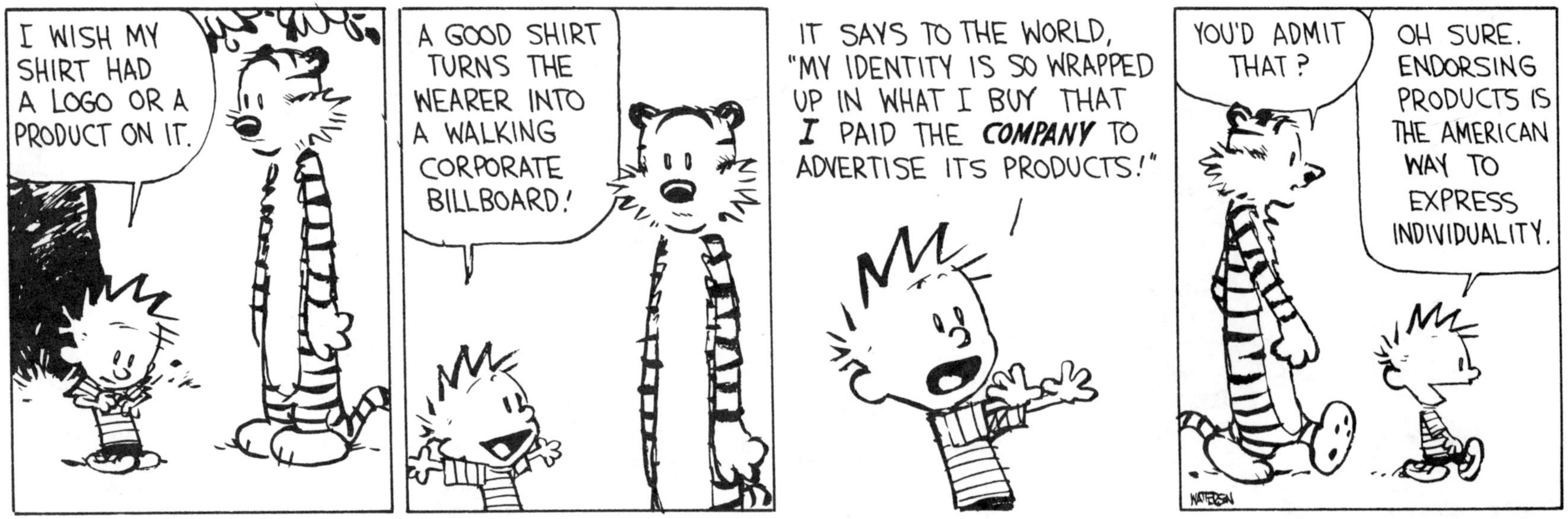
I WISH MY SHIRT HAD A LOGO OR A PRODUCT ON IT.
A GOOD SHIRT TURNS THE WEARER INTO A WALKING CORPORATE BILLBOARD!
IT SAYS TO THE WORLD, "MY IDENTITY IS SO WRAPPED UP IN WHAT I BUY THAT I PAID THE COMPANY TO ADVERTISE ITS PRODUCTS!"
YOU'D ADMIT THAT?
OH SURE. ENDORSING PRODUCTS IS THE AMERICAN WAY TO EXPRESS INDIVIDUALITY.
WATTERSON

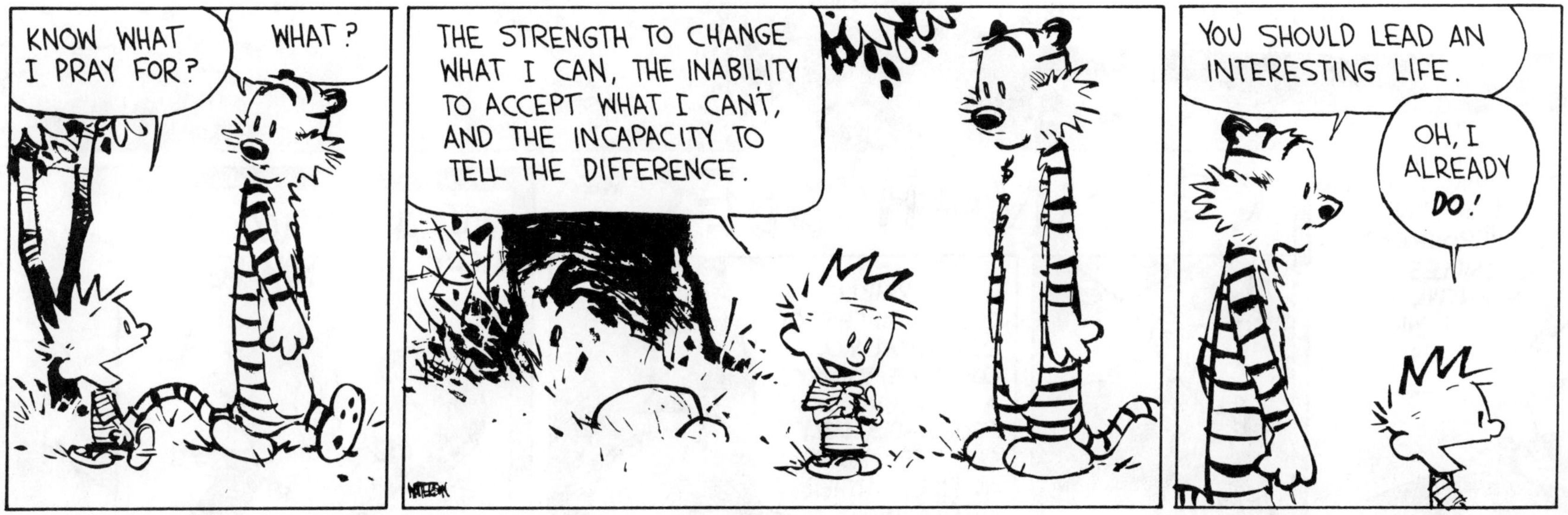
KNOW WHAT I PRAY FOR?
WHAT?
THE STRENGTH TO CHANGE WHAT I CAN, THE INABILITY TO ACCEPT WHAT I CAN'T, AND THE INCAPACITY TO TELL THE DIFFERENCE.
YOU SHOULD LEAD AN INTERESTING LIFE.
OH, I ALREADY **DO**!

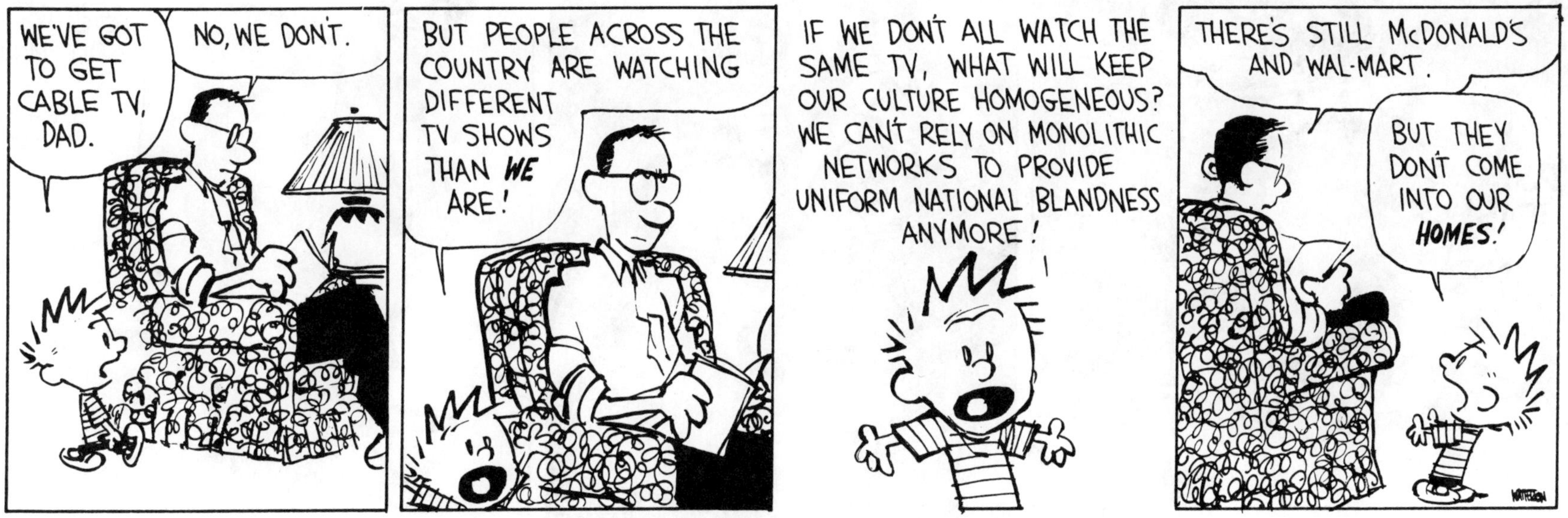
WE'VE GOT TO GET CABLE TV, DAD.
NO, WE DON'T.
BUT PEOPLE ACROSS THE COUNTRY ARE WATCHING DIFFERENT TV SHOWS THAN **WE** ARE!
IF WE DON'T ALL WATCH THE SAME TV, WHAT WILL KEEP OUR CULTURE HOMOGENEOUS? WE CAN'T RELY ON MONOLITHIC NETWORKS TO PROVIDE UNIFORM NATIONAL BLANDNESS ANYMORE!
THERE'S STILL McDONALD'S AND WAL-MART.
BUT THEY DON'T COME INTO OUR **HOMES**!

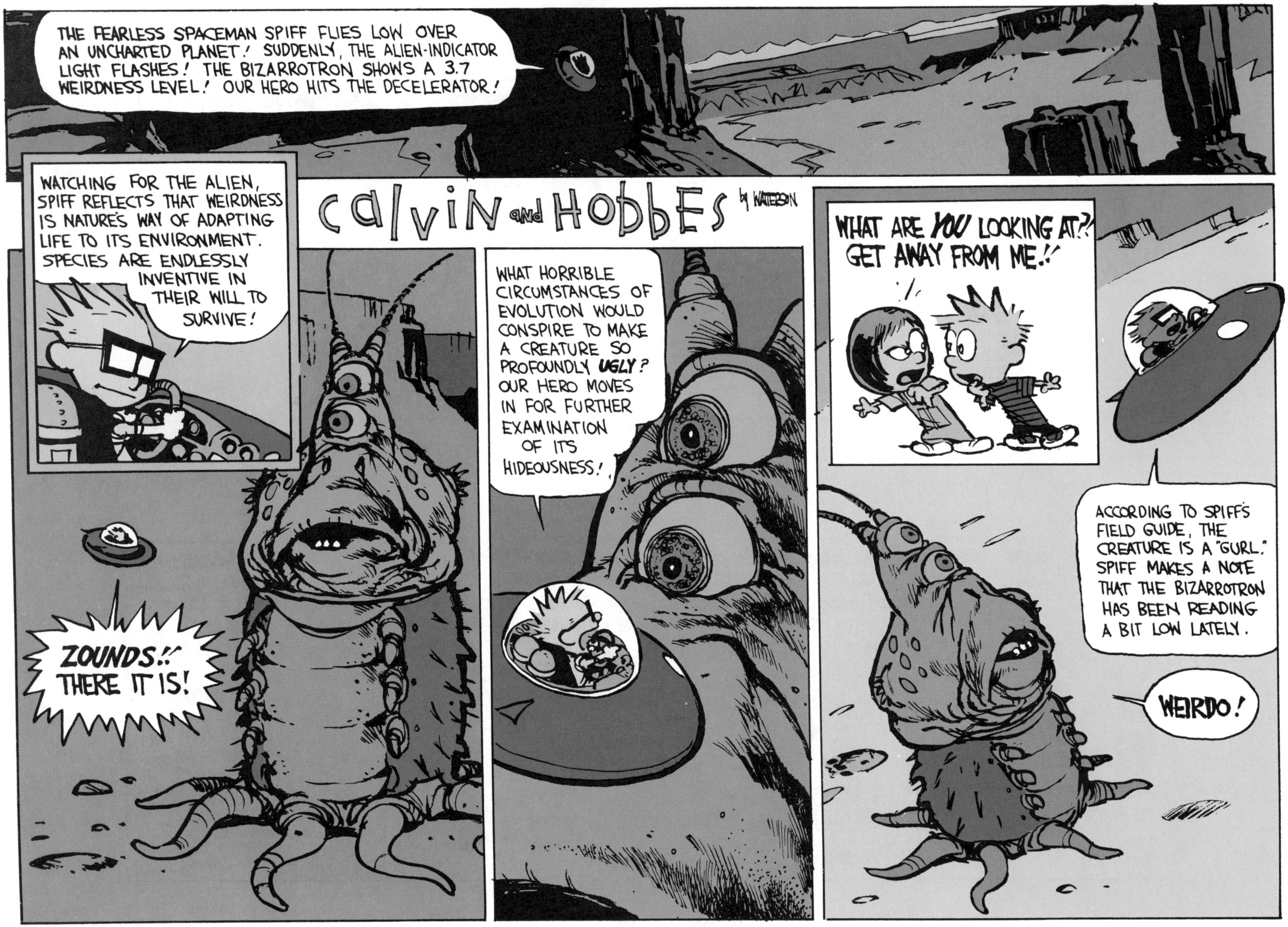
THE FEARLESS SPACEMAN SPIFF FLIES LOW OVER AN UNCHARTED PLANET! SUDDENLY, THE ALIEN-INDICATOR LIGHT FLASHES! THE BIZARROTRON SHOWS A 3.7 WEIRDNESS LEVEL! OUR HERO HITS THE DECELERATOR!
WATCHING FOR THE ALIEN, SPIFF REFLECTS THAT WEIRDNESS IS NATURE'S WAY OF ADAPTING LIFE TO ITS ENVIRONMENT. SPECIES ARE ENDLESSLY INVENTIVE IN THEIR WILL TO SURVIVE!
Calvin and HOBBES by WATTERSON
ZOUNDS!! THERE IT IS!
WHAT HORRIBLE CIRCUMSTANCES OF EVOLUTION WOULD CONSPIRE TO MAKE A CREATURE SO PROFOUNDLY UGLY? OUR HERO MOVES IN FOR FURTHER EXAMINATION OF ITS HIDEOUSNESS!
WHAT ARE YOU LOOKING AT?! GET AWAY FROM ME!!
ACCORDING TO SPIFF'S FIELD GUIDE, THE CREATURE IS A "GURL." SPIFF MAKES A NOTE THAT THE BIZARROTRON HAS BEEN READING A BIT LOW LATELY.
WEIRDO!

WHERE DO THE CANDIDATES STAND ON DINOSAUR RESEARCH?! THAT'S WHAT *I* WANT TO KNOW!

WHICH PARTY HAS THE PRO-PALEONTOLOGY PLATFORM PLANK? THEY CAN'T IGNORE THE DINOSAUR VOTE!

IF NOBODY PANDERS TO US, WE'LL THROW THE ELECTION! WE'LL STAY HOME! WE'RE DISAFFECTED, DISENFRANCHISED AND DISCOMBOBULATED!

WE SINGLE-ISSUE ACTIVISTS LIKE TO HAVE OUR "HOT BUTTONS" PUSHED.

HEY DAD, KNOW WHAT I FIGURED OUT? THE MEANING OF WORDS ISN'T A FIXED THING! ANY WORD CAN MEAN ANYTHING!

BY GIVING WORDS NEW MEANINGS, ORDINARY ENGLISH CAN BECOME AN EXCLUSIONARY CODE! TWO GENERATIONS CAN BE DIVIDED BY THE SAME LANGUAGE!

TO THAT END, I'LL BE INVENTING NEW DEFINITIONS FOR COMMON WORDS, SO WE'LL BE UNABLE TO COMMUNICATE.

DON'T YOU THINK THAT'S TOTALLY SPAM? IT'S LUBRICATED! WELL, I'M PHASING.

MARVY. FAB. FAR OUT.

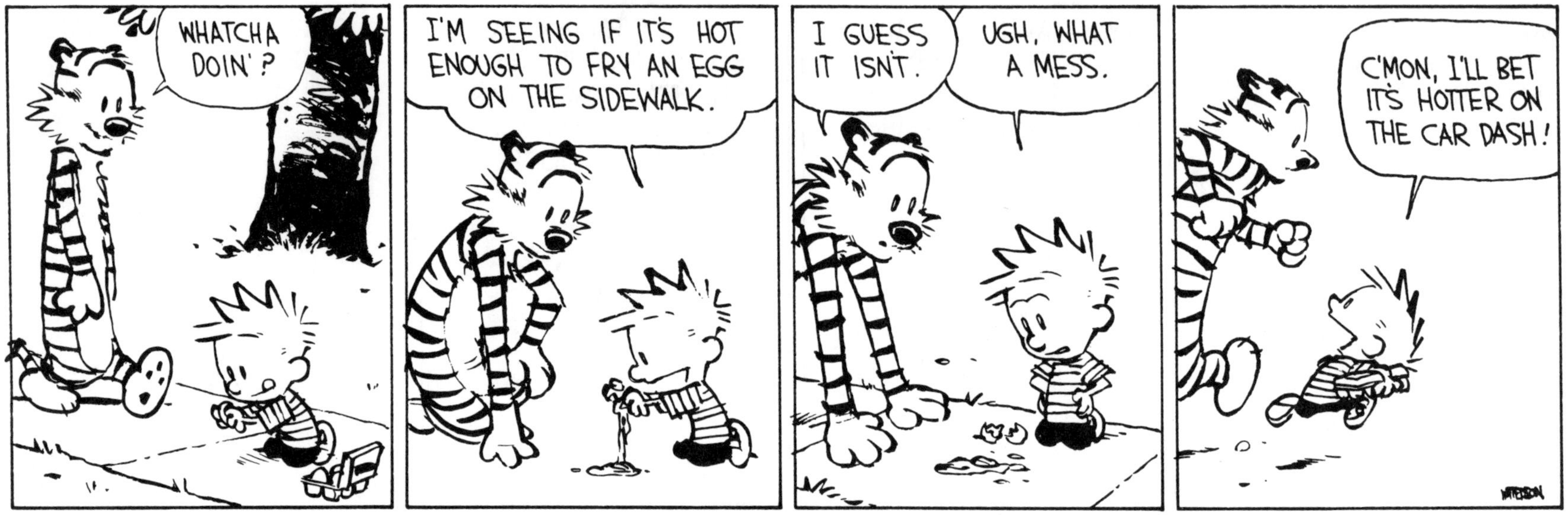
WHATCHA DOIN'?
I'M SEEING IF IT'S HOT ENOUGH TO FRY AN EGG ON THE SIDEWALK.
I GUESS IT ISN'T.
UGH, WHAT A MESS.
C'MON, I'LL BET IT'S HOTTER ON THE CAR DASH!

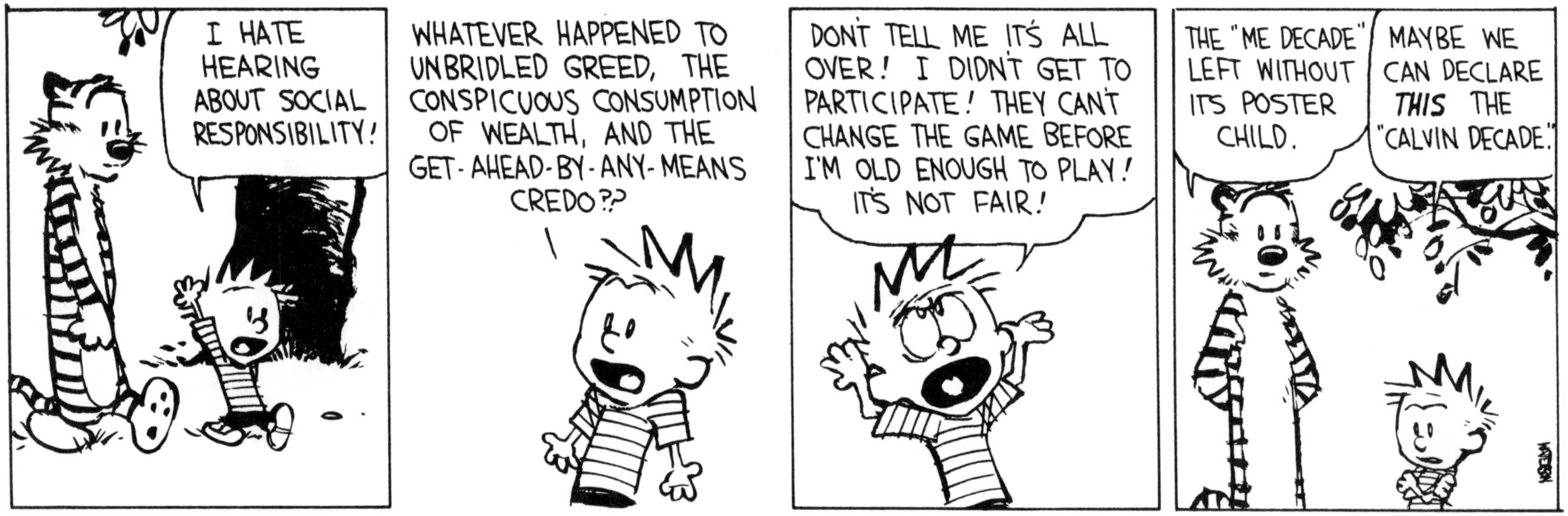
I HATE HEARING ABOUT SOCIAL RESPONSIBILITY!
WHATEVER HAPPENED TO UNBRIDLED GREED, THE CONSPICUOUS CONSUMPTION OF WEALTH, AND THE GET-AHEAD-BY-ANY-MEANS CREDO??
DON'T TELL ME IT'S ALL OVER! I DIDN'T GET TO PARTICIPATE! THEY CAN'T CHANGE THE GAME BEFORE I'M OLD ENOUGH TO PLAY! IT'S NOT FAIR!
THE "ME DECADE" LEFT WITHOUT ITS POSTER CHILD.
MAYBE WE CAN DECLARE ***THIS*** THE "CALVIN DECADE."

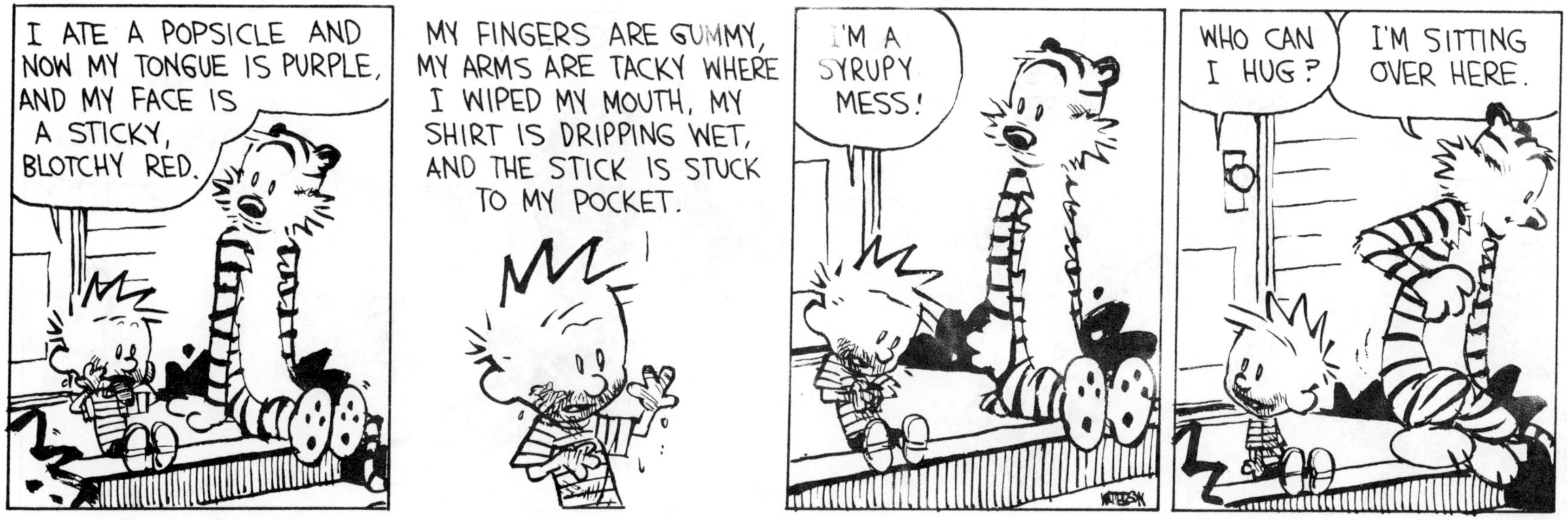
I ATE A POPSICLE AND NOW MY TONGUE IS PURPLE, AND MY FACE IS A STICKY, BLOTCHY RED.
MY FINGERS ARE GUMMY, MY ARMS ARE TACKY WHERE I WIPED MY MOUTH, MY SHIRT IS DRIPPING WET, AND THE STICK IS STUCK TO MY POCKET.
I'M A SYRUPY MESS!
WHO CAN I HUG?
I'M SITTING OVER HERE.

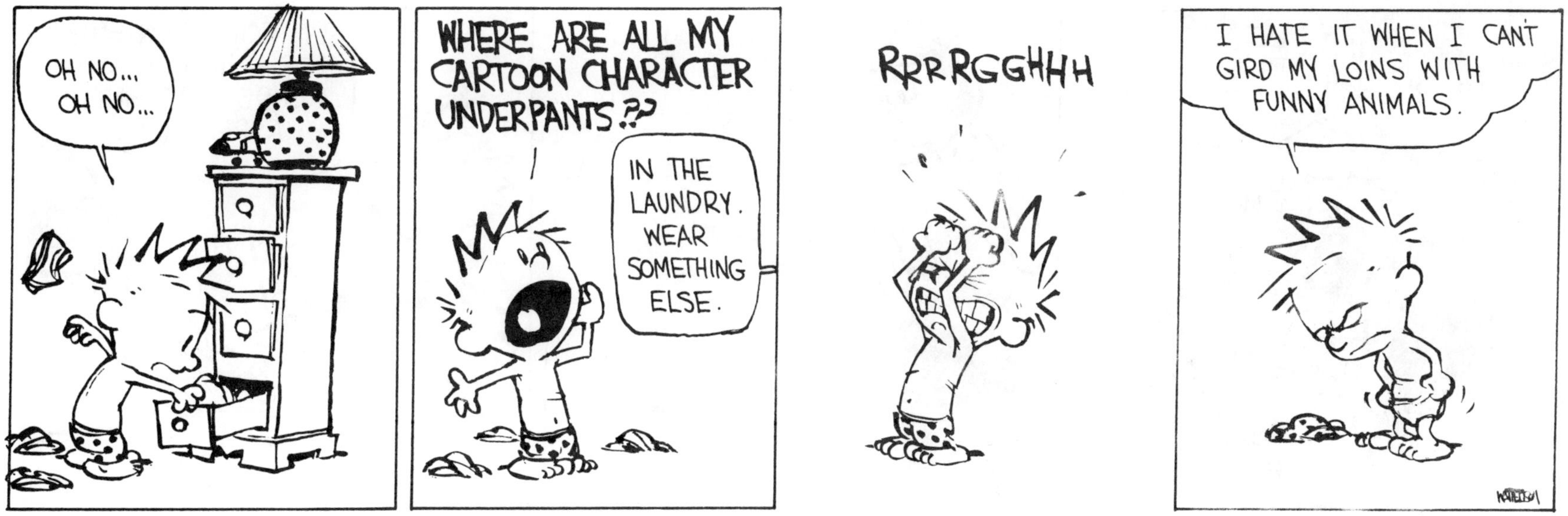
OH NO... OH NO...
WHERE ARE ALL MY CARTOON CHARACTER UNDERPANTS ?!?
IN THE LAUNDRY. WEAR SOMETHING ELSE.
RRRRGGHHH
I HATE IT WHEN I CAN'T GIRD MY LOINS WITH FUNNY ANIMALS.

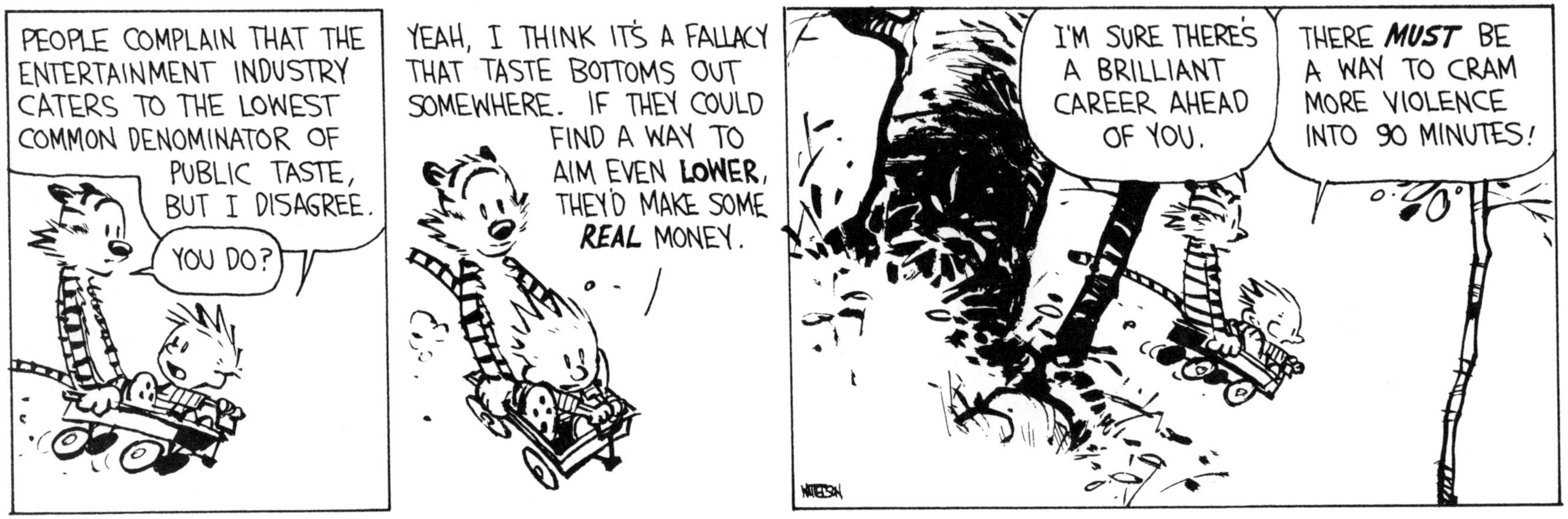
PEOPLE COMPLAIN THAT THE ENTERTAINMENT INDUSTRY CATERS TO THE LOWEST COMMON DENOMINATOR OF PUBLIC TASTE, BUT I DISAGREE.
YOU DO?
YEAH, I THINK IT'S A FALLACY THAT TASTE BOTTOMS OUT SOMEWHERE. IF THEY COULD FIND A WAY TO AIM EVEN LOWER, THEY'D MAKE SOME REAL MONEY.
I'M SURE THERE'S A BRILLIANT CAREER AHEAD OF YOU.
THERE MUST BE A WAY TO CRAM MORE VIOLENCE INTO 90 MINUTES!

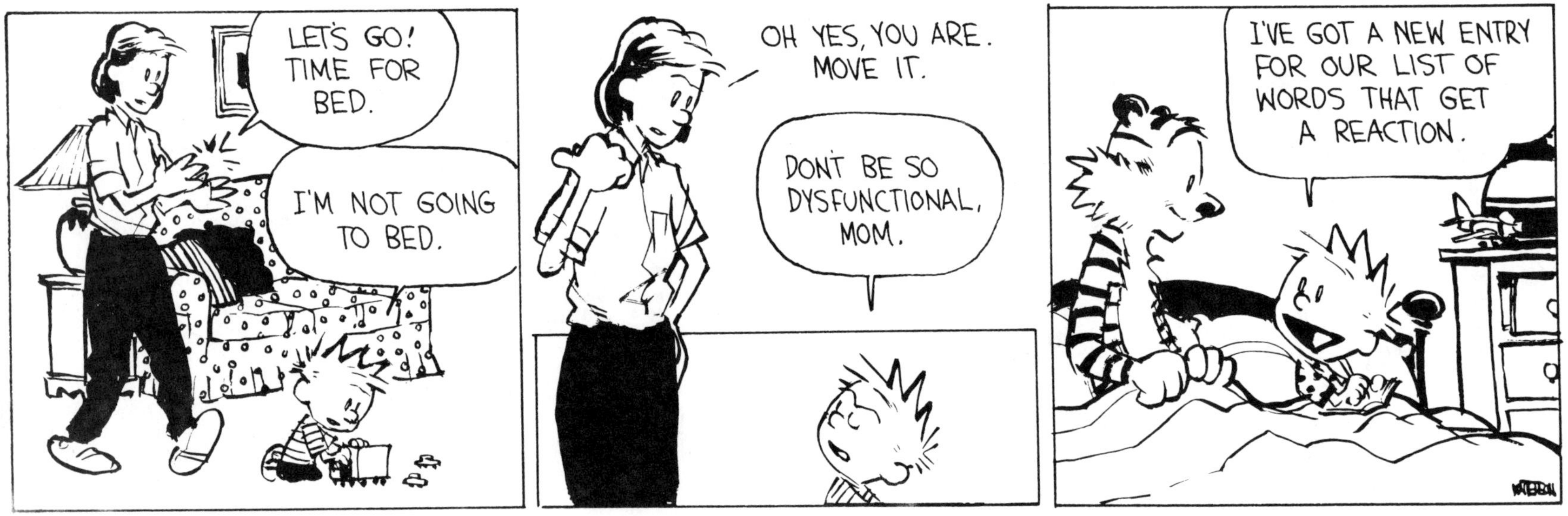
LET'S GO! TIME FOR BED.
I'M NOT GOING TO BED.
OH YES, YOU ARE. MOVE IT.
DON'T BE SO DYSFUNCTIONAL, MOM.
I'VE GOT A NEW ENTRY FOR OUR LIST OF WORDS THAT GET A REACTION.

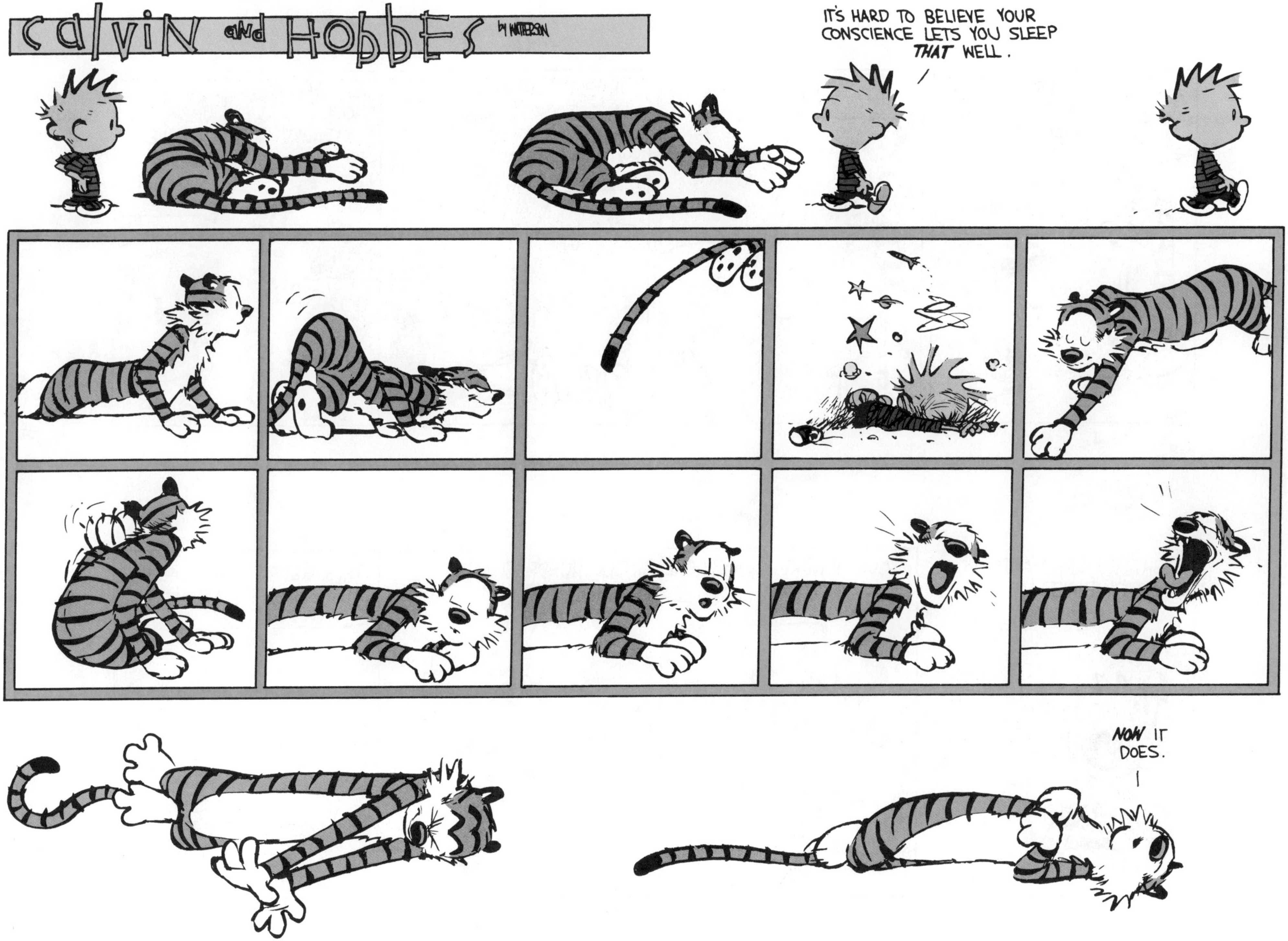
Calvin and HOBBES by WATTERSON
IT'S HARD TO BELIEVE YOUR CONSCIENCE LETS YOU SLEEP *THAT* WELL.
NOW IT DOES.

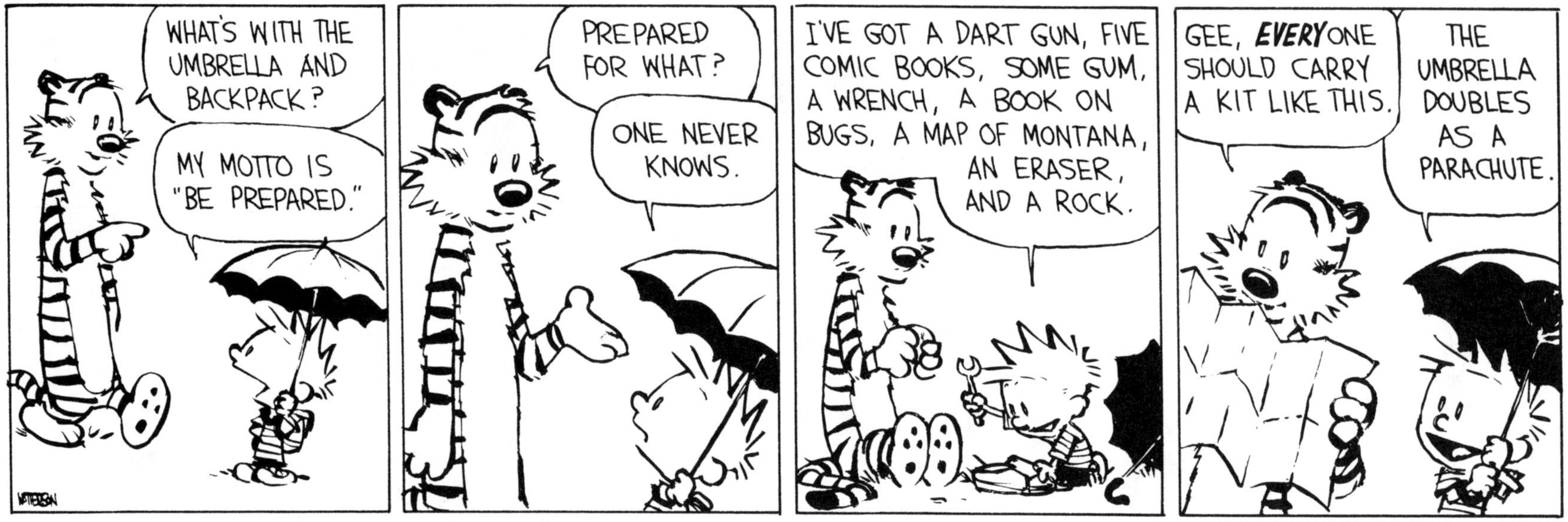
WHAT'S WITH THE UMBRELLA AND BACKPACK?
MY MOTTO IS "BE PREPARED."
PREPARED FOR WHAT?
ONE NEVER KNOWS.
I'VE GOT A DART GUN, FIVE COMIC BOOKS, SOME GUM, A WRENCH, A BOOK ON BUGS, A MAP OF MONTANA, AN ERASER, AND A ROCK.
GEE, **EVERY**ONE SHOULD CARRY A KIT LIKE THIS.
THE UMBRELLA DOUBLES AS A PARACHUTE.

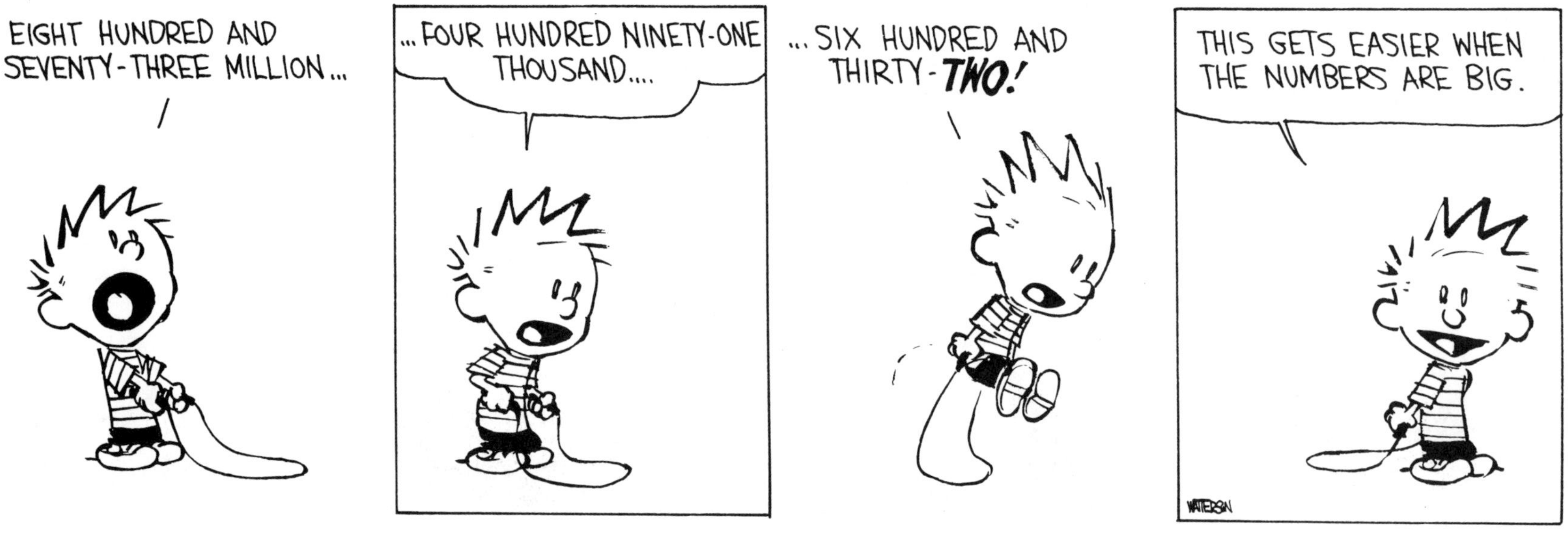
EIGHT HUNDRED AND SEVENTY-THREE MILLION...
...FOUR HUNDRED NINETY-ONE THOUSAND....
...SIX HUNDRED AND THIRTY-***TWO!***
THIS GETS EASIER WHEN THE NUMBERS ARE BIG.

YES, CALVIN?
MISS WORMWOOD, I'M A FIERCE ADVOCATE OF THE SEPARATION OF CHURCH AND STATE.
NEVERTHELESS, I FEEL THE NEED FOR SPIRITUAL GUIDANCE AND COMFORT AS I FACE THE DAY'S STRUGGLES.
SO I WAS WONDERING IF I COULD STRIP DOWN, SMEAR MYSELF WITH PASTE, AND SET FIRE TO THIS LITTLE EFFIGY OF YOU IN A NON-DENOMINATIONAL SORT OF WAY.
BOY, WHAT A TOUCHY SUBJECT!
PRINCIPAL

I DON'T WANNA TAKE A BATH! I DON'T WANNA TAKE A BATH! YOU CAN'T MAKE ME!
AGHH! LEGGO! LEGGO! NO NO NO NO NO NO NO! PUT ME DOWN!
I WISH I WAS DEAD! I HATE YOU ALL! I HATE EVERYTHING! AARRGGHHH!
WHENEVER I HEAR ABOUT PEOPLE TRYING TO REDISCOVER THE "CHILD WITHIN," I WANT TO SCREAM.

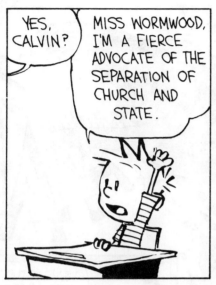

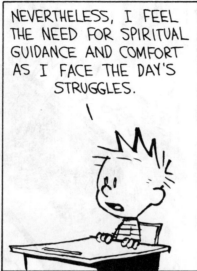

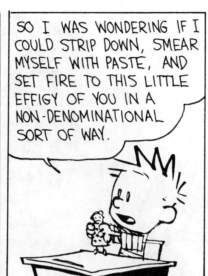

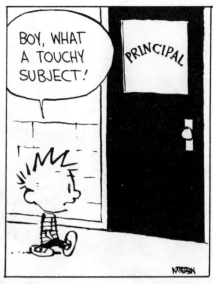

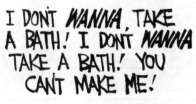

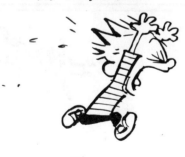

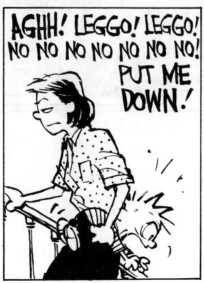

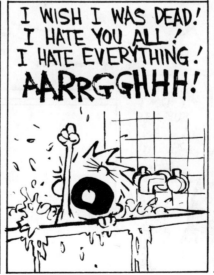

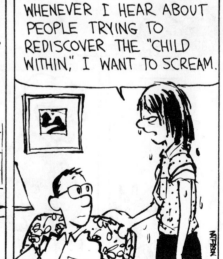

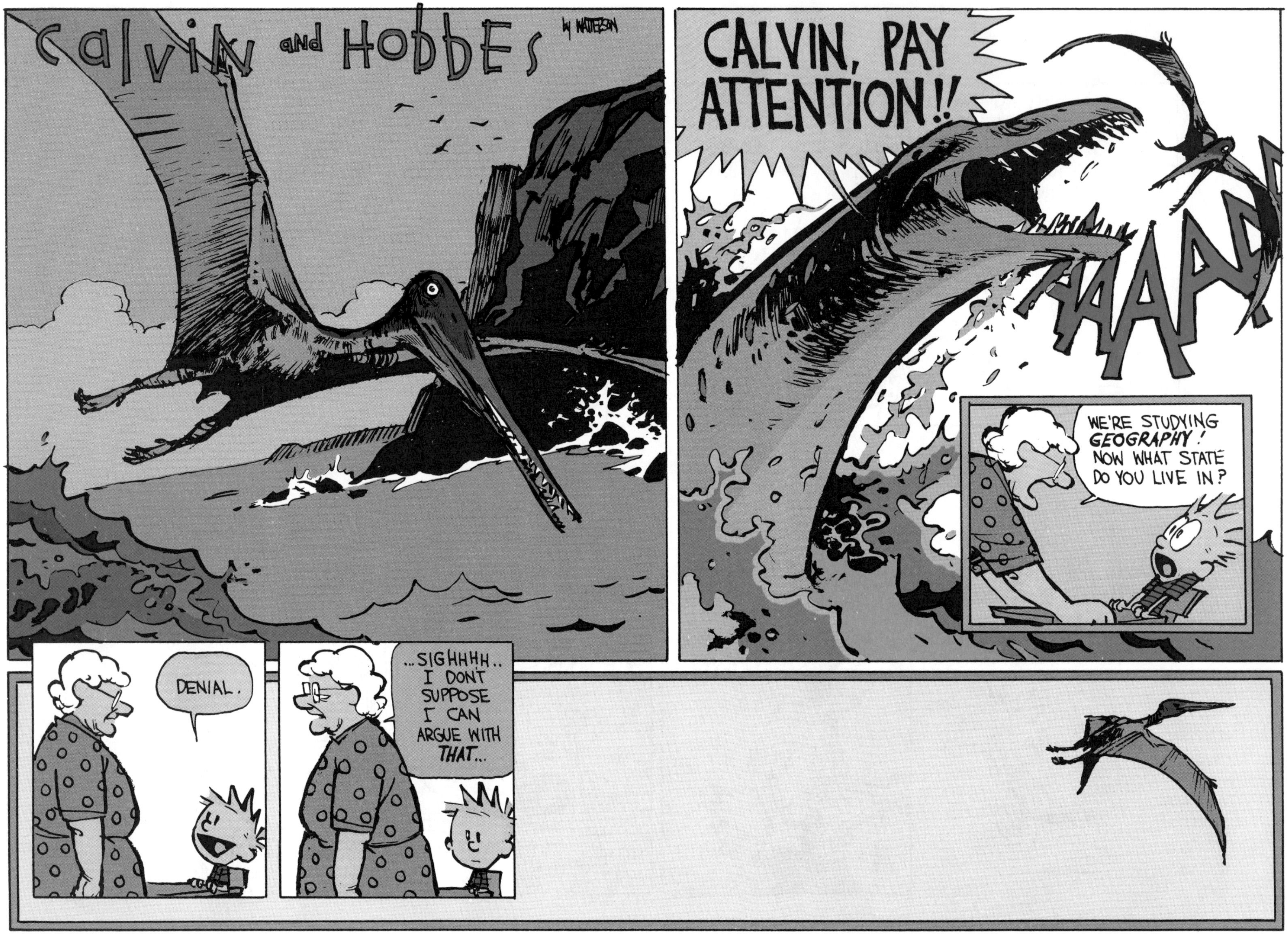
Calvin and Hobbes
by WATTERSON
CALVIN, PAY ATTENTION!!
WE'RE STUDYING GEOGRAPHY! NOW WHAT STATE DO YOU LIVE IN?
DENIAL.
..SIGHHHH.. I DON'T SUPPOSE I CAN ARGUE WITH THAT...

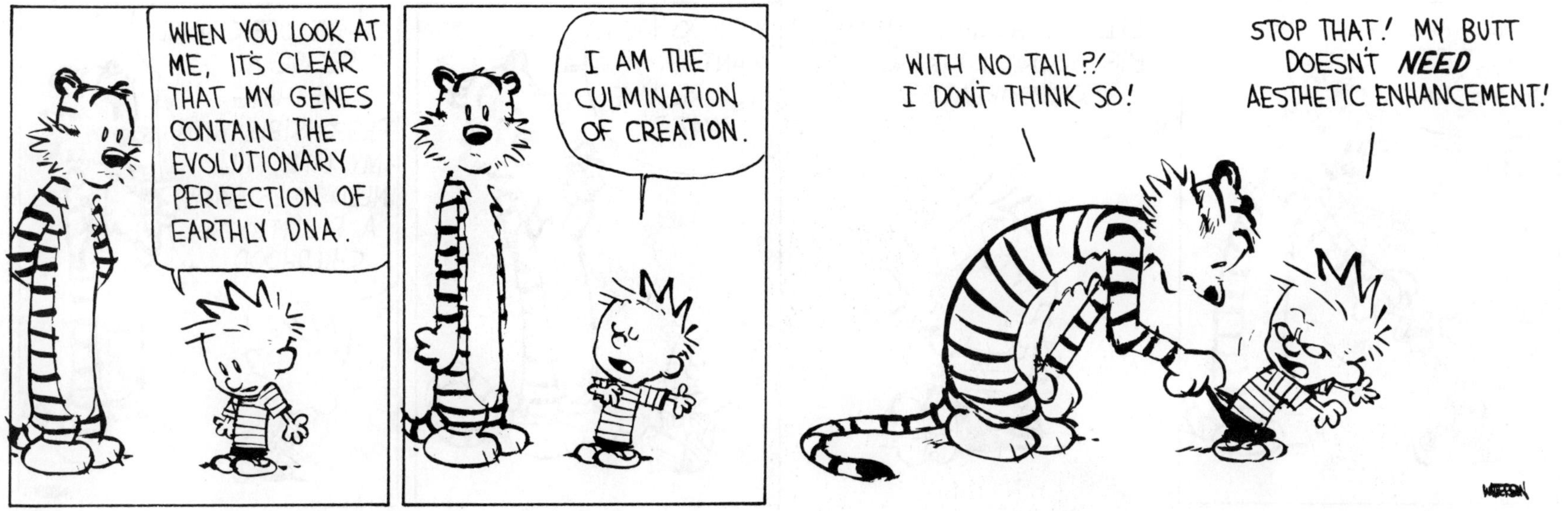
WHEN YOU LOOK AT ME, IT'S CLEAR THAT MY GENES CONTAIN THE EVOLUTIONARY PERFECTION OF EARTHLY DNA.
I AM THE CULMINATION OF CREATION.
WITH NO TAIL?! I DON'T THINK SO!
STOP THAT! MY BUTT DOESN'T NEED AESTHETIC ENHANCEMENT!

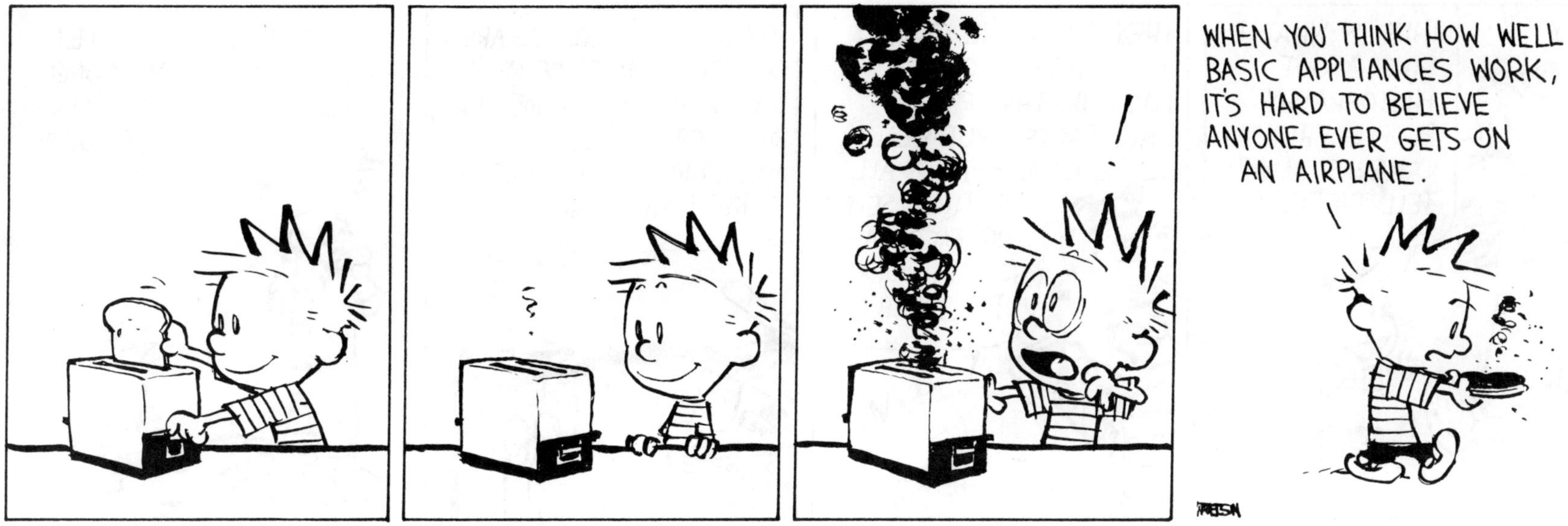
!
WHEN YOU THINK HOW WELL BASIC APPLIANCES WORK, IT'S HARD TO BELIEVE ANYONE EVER GETS ON AN AIRPLANE.

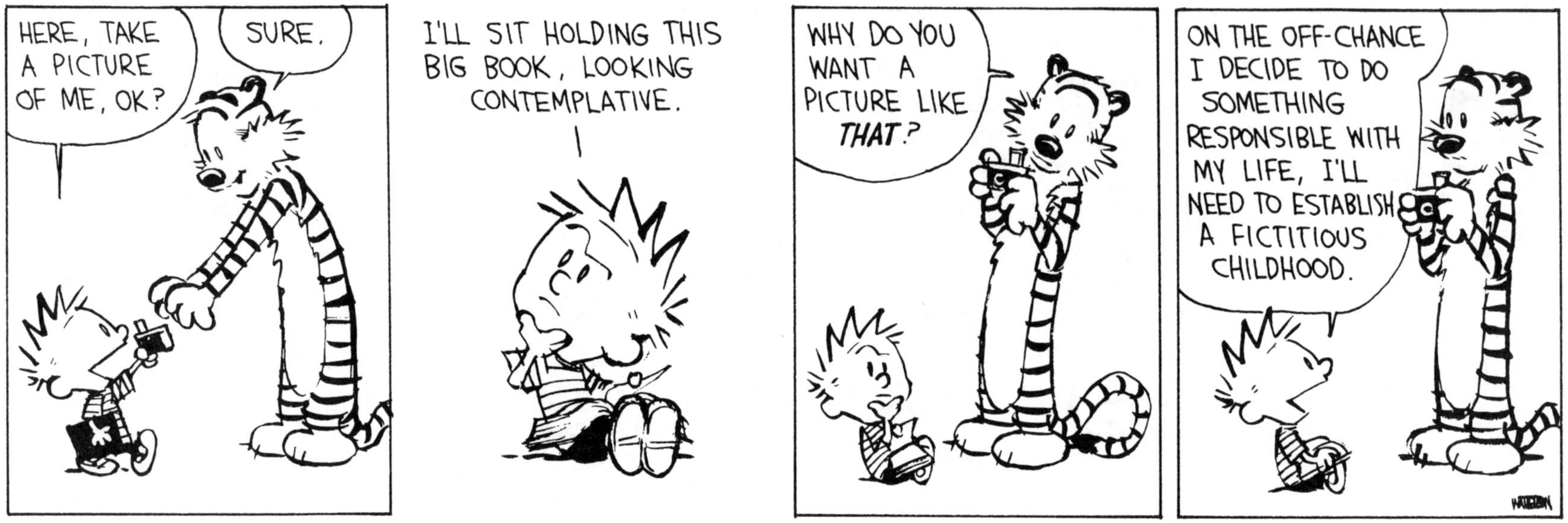
HERE, TAKE A PICTURE OF ME, OK?
SURE.
I'LL SIT HOLDING THIS BIG BOOK, LOOKING CONTEMPLATIVE.
WHY DO YOU WANT A PICTURE LIKE *THAT*?
ON THE OFF-CHANCE I DECIDE TO DO SOMETHING RESPONSIBLE WITH MY LIFE, I'LL NEED TO ESTABLISH A FICTITIOUS CHILDHOOD.

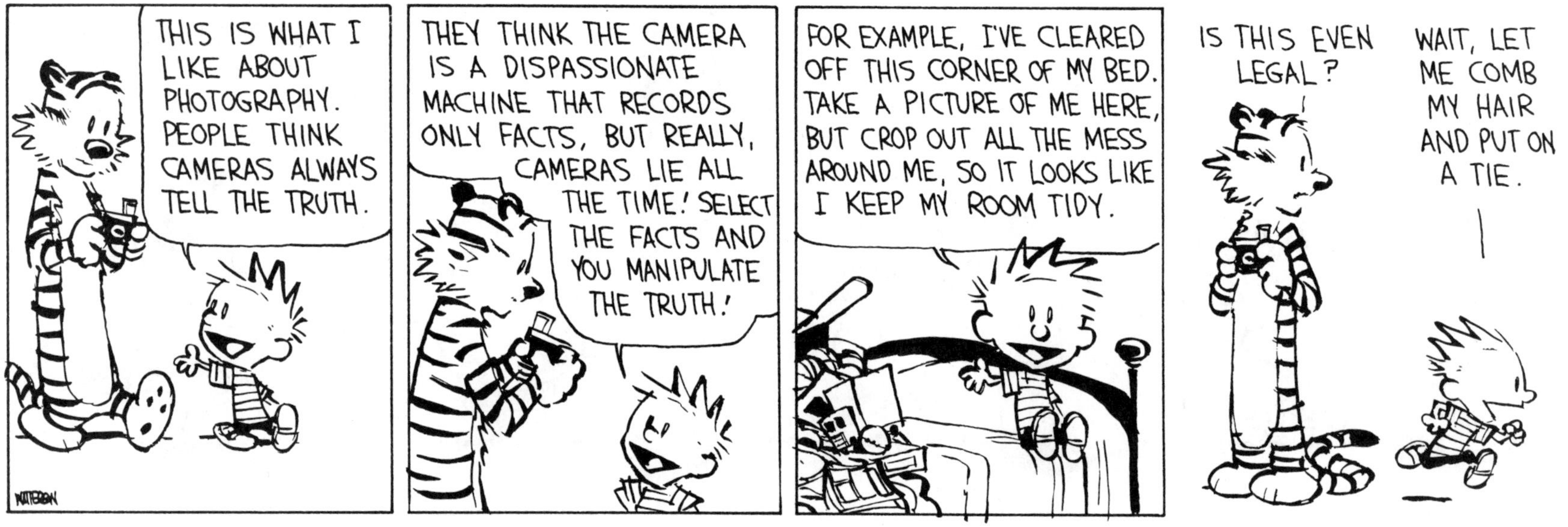
THIS IS WHAT I LIKE ABOUT PHOTOGRAPHY. PEOPLE THINK CAMERAS ALWAYS TELL THE TRUTH.
THEY THINK THE CAMERA IS A DISPASSIONATE MACHINE THAT RECORDS ONLY FACTS, BUT REALLY, CAMERAS LIE ALL THE TIME! SELECT THE FACTS AND YOU MANIPULATE THE TRUTH!
FOR EXAMPLE, I'VE CLEARED OFF THIS CORNER OF MY BED. TAKE A PICTURE OF ME HERE, BUT CROP OUT ALL THE MESS AROUND ME, SO IT LOOKS LIKE I KEEP MY ROOM TIDY.
IS THIS EVEN LEGAL?
WAIT, LET ME COMB MY HAIR AND PUT ON A TIE.

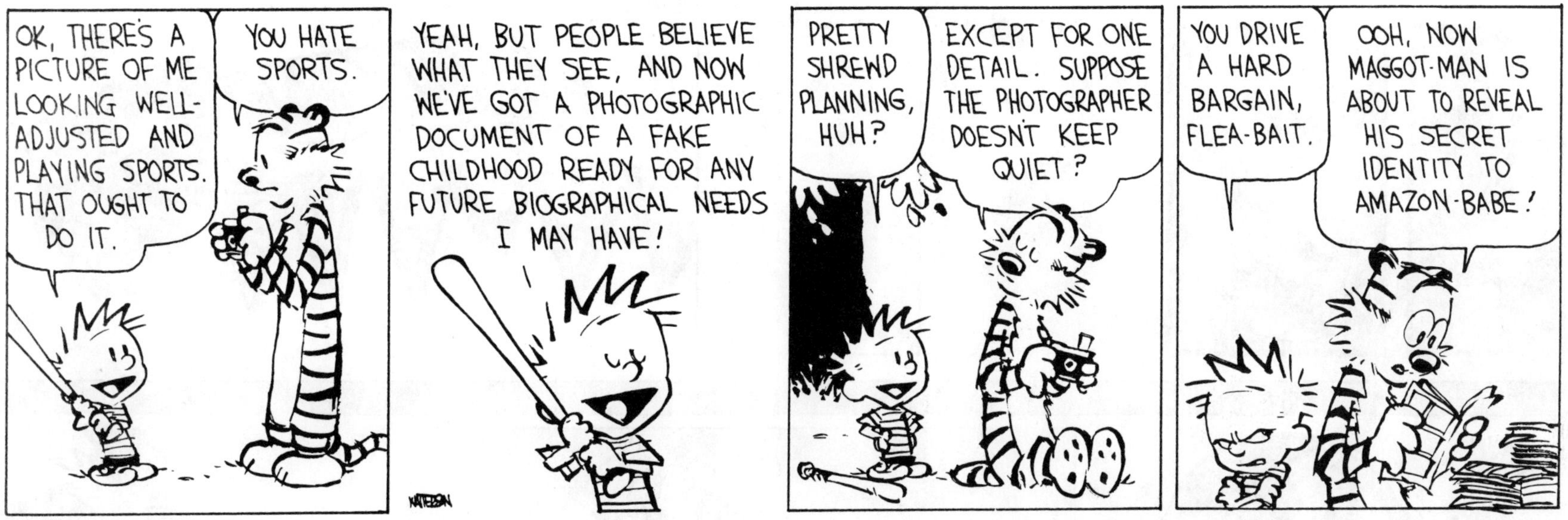
OK, THERE'S A PICTURE OF ME LOOKING WELL-ADJUSTED AND PLAYING SPORTS. THAT OUGHT TO DO IT.
YOU HATE SPORTS.
YEAH, BUT PEOPLE BELIEVE WHAT THEY SEE, AND NOW WE'VE GOT A PHOTOGRAPHIC DOCUMENT OF A FAKE CHILDHOOD READY FOR ANY FUTURE BIOGRAPHICAL NEEDS I MAY HAVE!
PRETTY SHREWD PLANNING, HUH?
EXCEPT FOR ONE DETAIL. SUPPOSE THE PHOTOGRAPHER DOESN'T KEEP QUIET?
YOU DRIVE A HARD BARGAIN, FLEA-BAIT.
OOH, NOW MAGGOT-MAN IS ABOUT TO REVEAL HIS SECRET IDENTITY TO AMAZON-BABE!

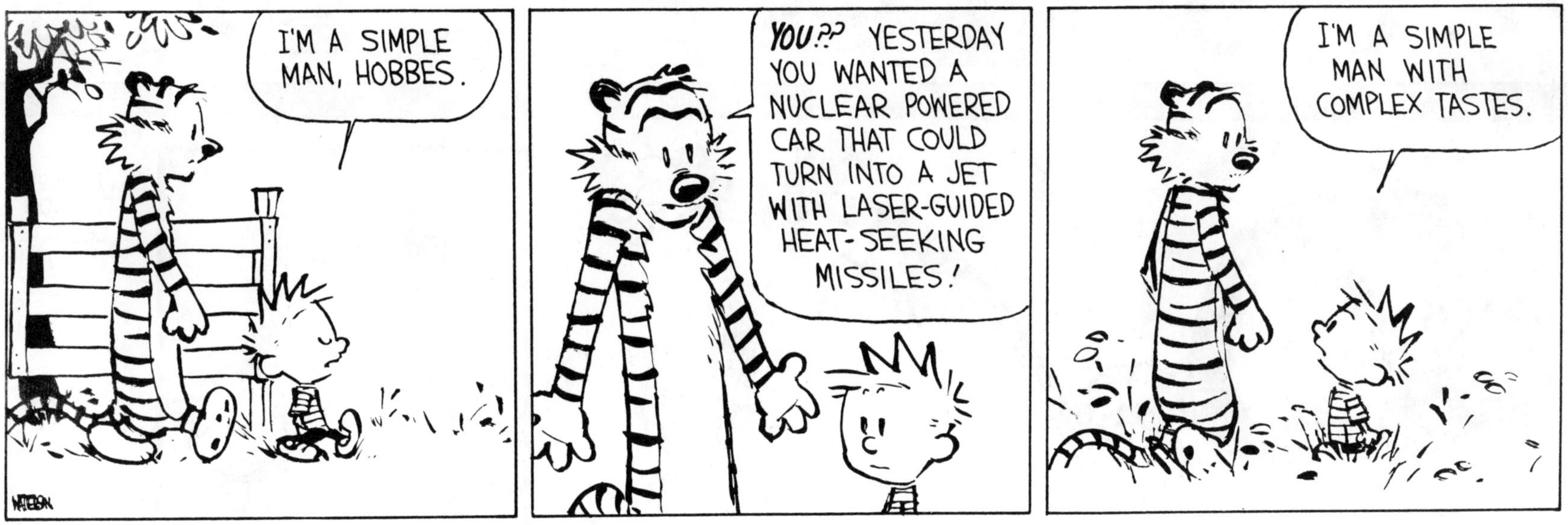
I'M A SIMPLE MAN, HOBBES.
YOU?? YESTERDAY YOU WANTED A NUCLEAR POWERED CAR THAT COULD TURN INTO A JET WITH LASER-GUIDED HEAT-SEEKING MISSILES!
I'M A SIMPLE MAN WITH COMPLEX TASTES.

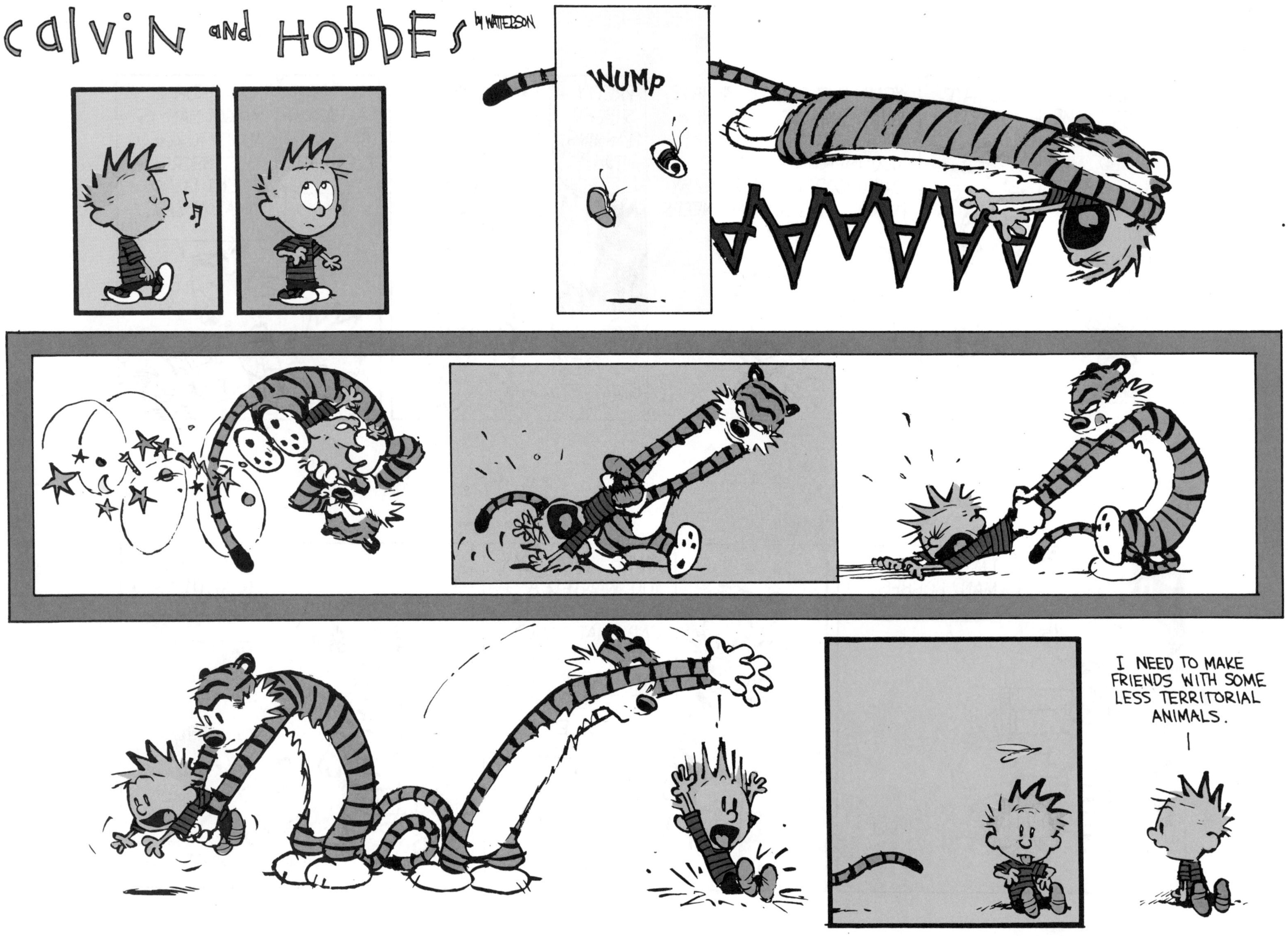
Calvin and Hobbes
by WATTERSON
WUMP
I NEED TO MAKE FRIENDS WITH SOME LESS TERRITORIAL ANIMALS.

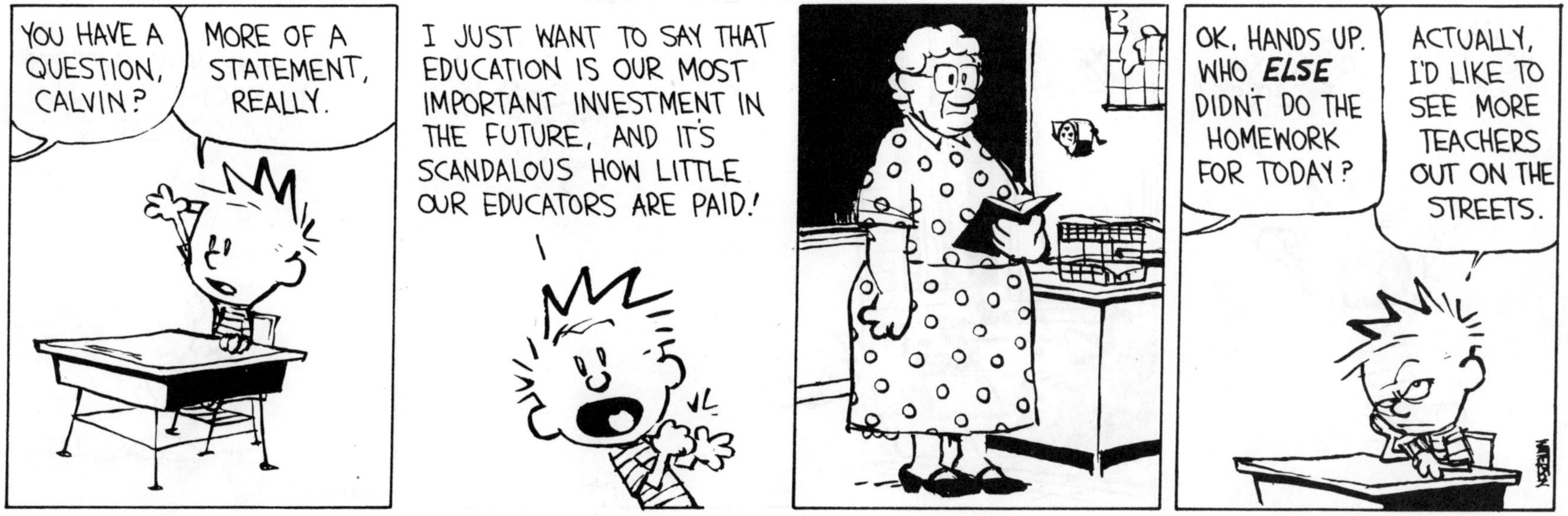
YOU HAVE A QUESTION, CALVIN?
MORE OF A STATEMENT, REALLY.
I JUST WANT TO SAY THAT EDUCATION IS OUR MOST IMPORTANT INVESTMENT IN THE FUTURE, AND IT'S SCANDALOUS HOW LITTLE OUR EDUCATORS ARE PAID!
OK, HANDS UP. WHO ELSE DIDN'T DO THE HOMEWORK FOR TODAY?
ACTUALLY, I'D LIKE TO SEE MORE TEACHERS OUT ON THE STREETS.

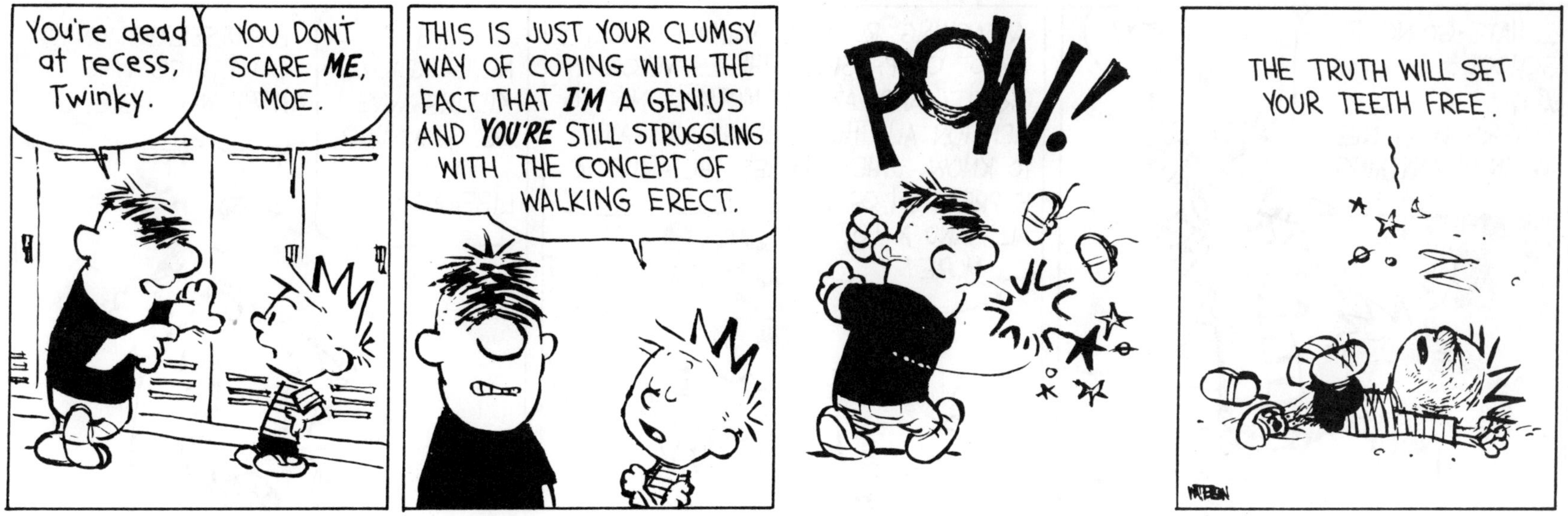
You're dead at recess, Twinky.
YOU DON'T SCARE ME, MOE.
THIS IS JUST YOUR CLUMSY WAY OF COPING WITH THE FACT THAT I'M A GENIUS AND YOU'RE STILL STRUGGLING WITH THE CONCEPT OF WALKING ERECT.
POW!
THE TRUTH WILL SET YOUR TEETH FREE.

I HATE SCHOOL! I'M NOT GOING TO SCHOOL EVER AGAIN! I REFUSE!

I THINK MOM LETTERED IN SHOT PUT HER JUNIOR YEAR.

I HATE GOING TO SCHOOL. I WISH *I* WAS A TIGER. TIGERS DON'T NEED TO KNOW ANYTHING.

HEY!

ATTACKING RUNNING ANIMALS INVOLVES A LOT OF PHYSICS. THERE'S VELOCITY, GRAVITY AND LAWS OF MOTION, NOT TO MENTION ALL THE BIOLOGY WE HAVE TO KNOW. THEN THERE'S THE ARTISTIC EXPRESSION OF IT ALL, AND A LOT MORE!

GOSH, I NEVER REALIZED KILLING WAS SO GROUNDED IN THE LIBERAL ARTS.

MY DISSERTATION ON ETHICS WAS *VERY* WELL RECEIVED.

I FIGURED OUT HOW I CAN ACHIEVE SUCCESS WITHOUT HARD WORK.
HOW?
I'LL FIND A PROFESSION WHERE EVERYONE IN IT IS WORSE THAN ME!
THAT MIGHT TAKE HARD WORK.

ACT CASUAL.

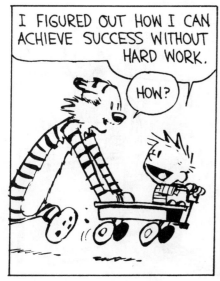

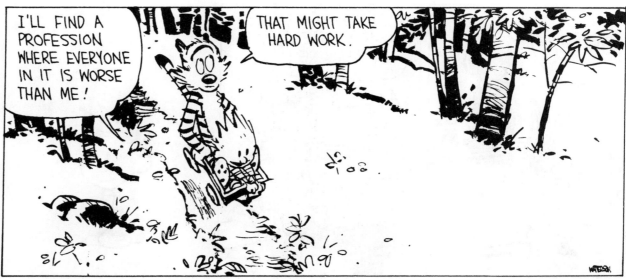

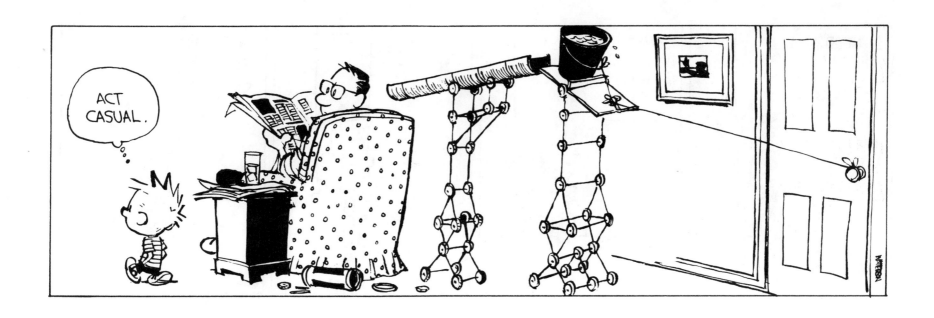

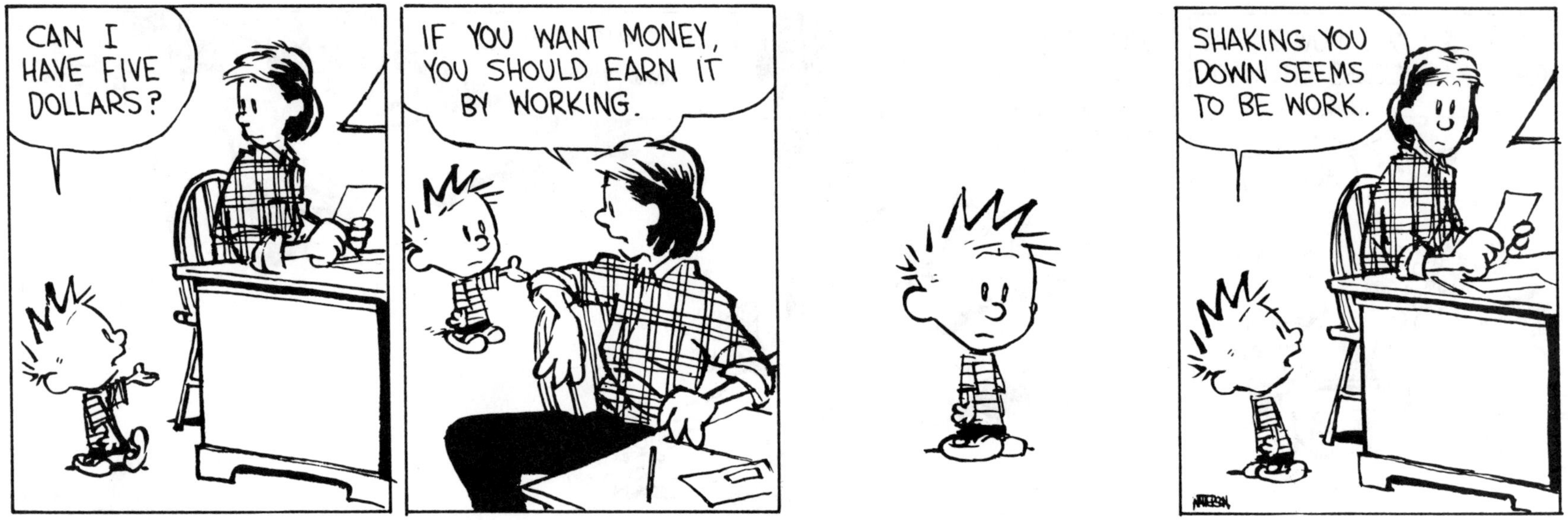
CAN I HAVE FIVE DOLLARS?
IF YOU WANT MONEY, YOU SHOULD EARN IT BY WORKING.
SHAKING YOU DOWN SEEMS TO BE WORK.

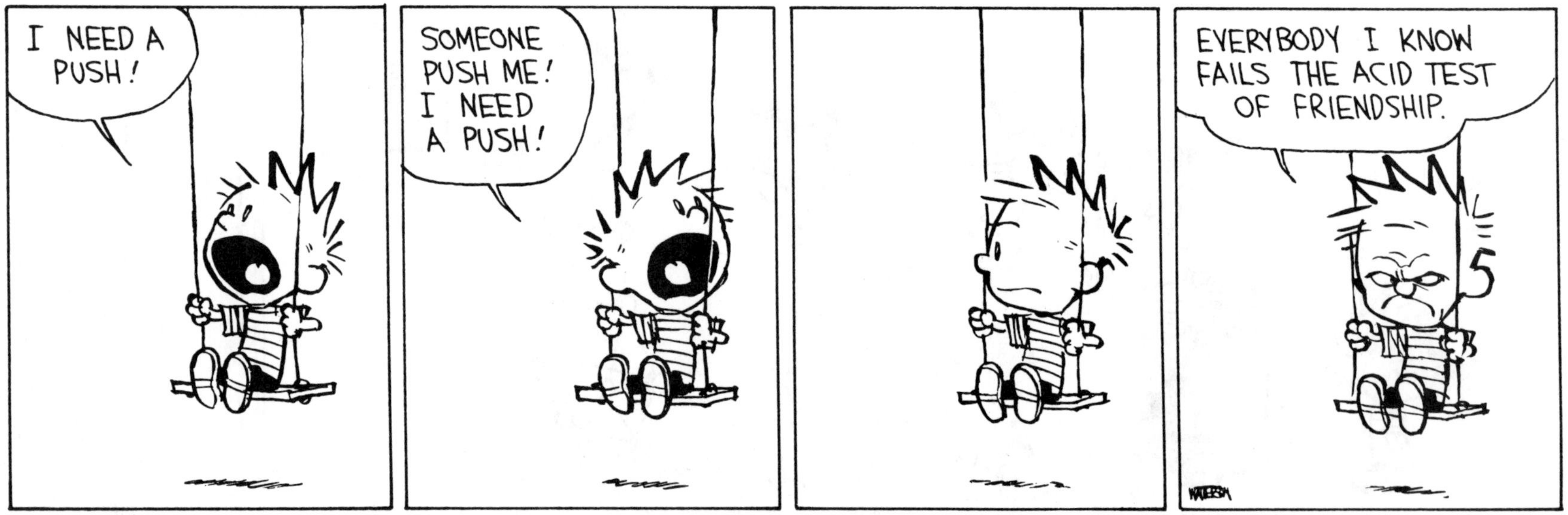
I NEED A PUSH!
SOMEONE PUSH ME! I NEED A PUSH!
EVERYBODY I KNOW FAILS THE ACID TEST OF FRIENDSHIP.

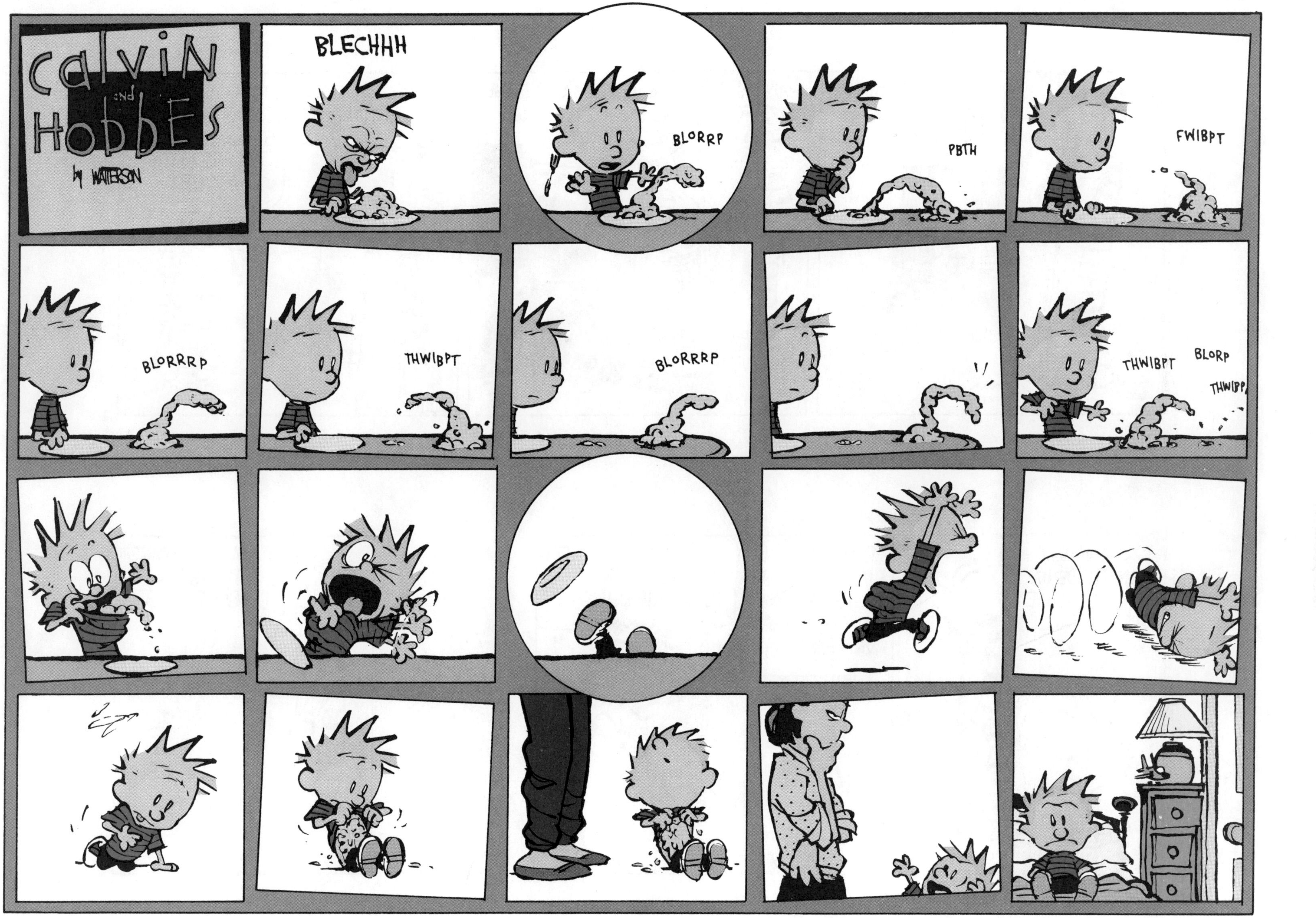
Calvin and Hobbes
by WATTERSON
BLECHHH
BLORRP
PBTH
FWIBPT
BLORRRP
THWIBPT
BLORRRP
THWIBPT
BLORP
THWIBP

AREN'T YOU SUPPOSED TO BE DOING YOUR HOMEWORK?
I'M PRETTY SURE THE ASSIGNMENT WAS OPTIONAL.
DENIAL SPRINGS ETERNAL.
IT'S NOT DENIAL. I'M JUST VERY SELECTIVE ABOUT THE REALITY I ACCEPT.

I SAY A DAY WITHOUT DENIAL IS A DAY YOU'VE GOT TO FACE.
FROM NOW ON, I'M NOT GOING TO THINK ABOUT ANYTHING THAT'S UNPLEASANT.
ISN'T THAT A PRETTY SELF-DECEIVING WAY TO GO THROUGH LIFE?
I'M NOT GOING TO THINK ABOUT THAT.

TIME FOR YOUR BATH. LET'S GO.
SORRY, I'M IN DENIAL ABOUT BATHS.
FINE. GO AHEAD AND DENY IT.
!
NOBODY RESPECTS MY DENIAL.

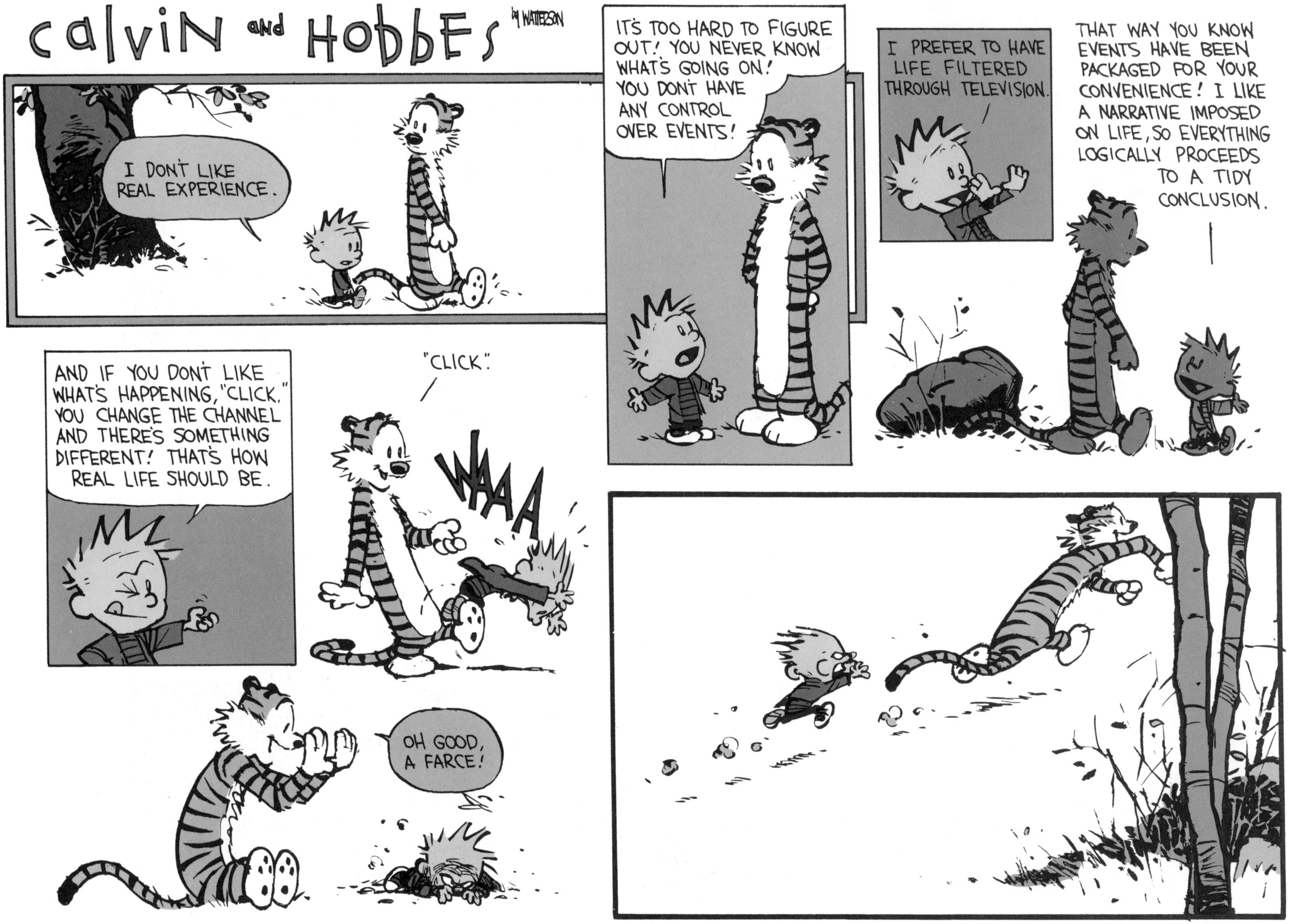
Calvin and Hobbes
by WATTERSON
I DON'T LIKE REAL EXPERIENCE.
IT'S TOO HARD TO FIGURE OUT! YOU NEVER KNOW WHAT'S GOING ON! YOU DON'T HAVE ANY CONTROL OVER EVENTS!
I PREFER TO HAVE LIFE FILTERED THROUGH TELEVISION.
THAT WAY YOU KNOW EVENTS HAVE BEEN PACKAGED FOR YOUR CONVENIENCE! I LIKE A NARRATIVE IMPOSED ON LIFE, SO EVERYTHING LOGICALLY PROCEEDS TO A TIDY CONCLUSION.
AND IF YOU DON'T LIKE WHAT'S HAPPENING, "CLICK," YOU CHANGE THE CHANNEL AND THERE'S SOMETHING DIFFERENT! THAT'S HOW REAL LIFE SHOULD BE.
"CLICK."
WAAA
OH GOOD, A FARCE!

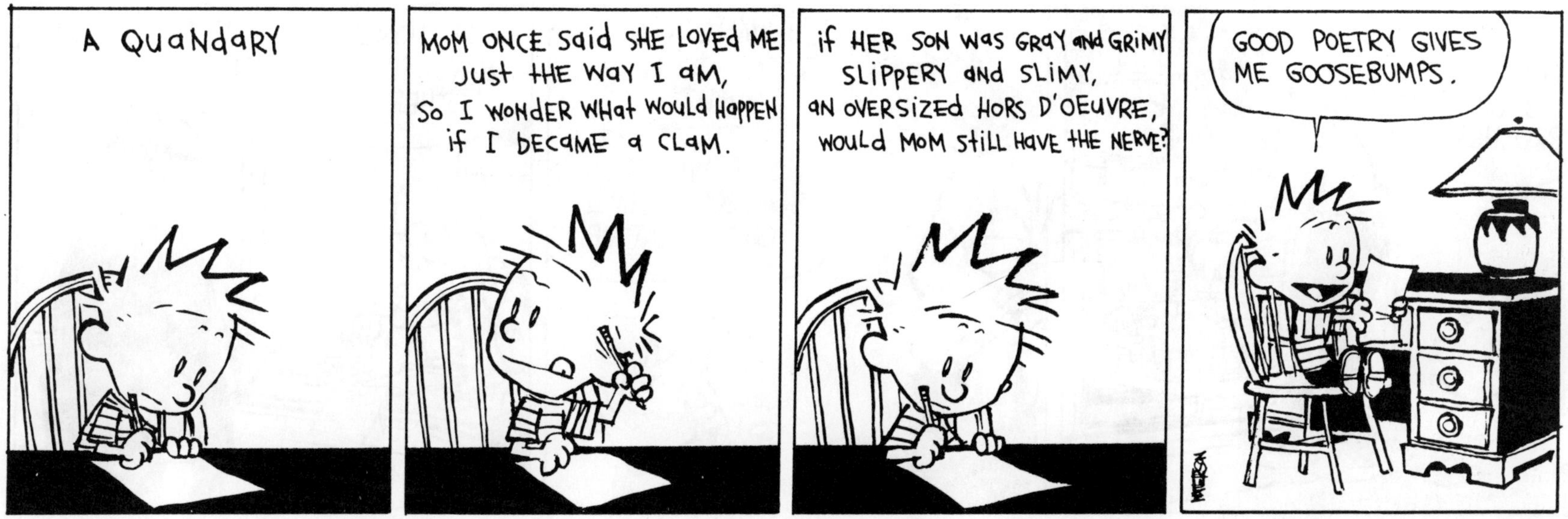
A QUANDARY
MOM ONCE SAID SHE LOVED ME JUST THE WAY I AM, SO I WONDER WHAT WOULD HAPPEN IF I BECAME A CLAM.
IF HER SON WAS GRAY AND GRIMY SLIPPERY AND SLIMY, AN OVERSIZED HORS D'OEUVRE, WOULD MOM STILL HAVE THE NERVE?
GOOD POETRY GIVES ME GOOSEBUMPS.

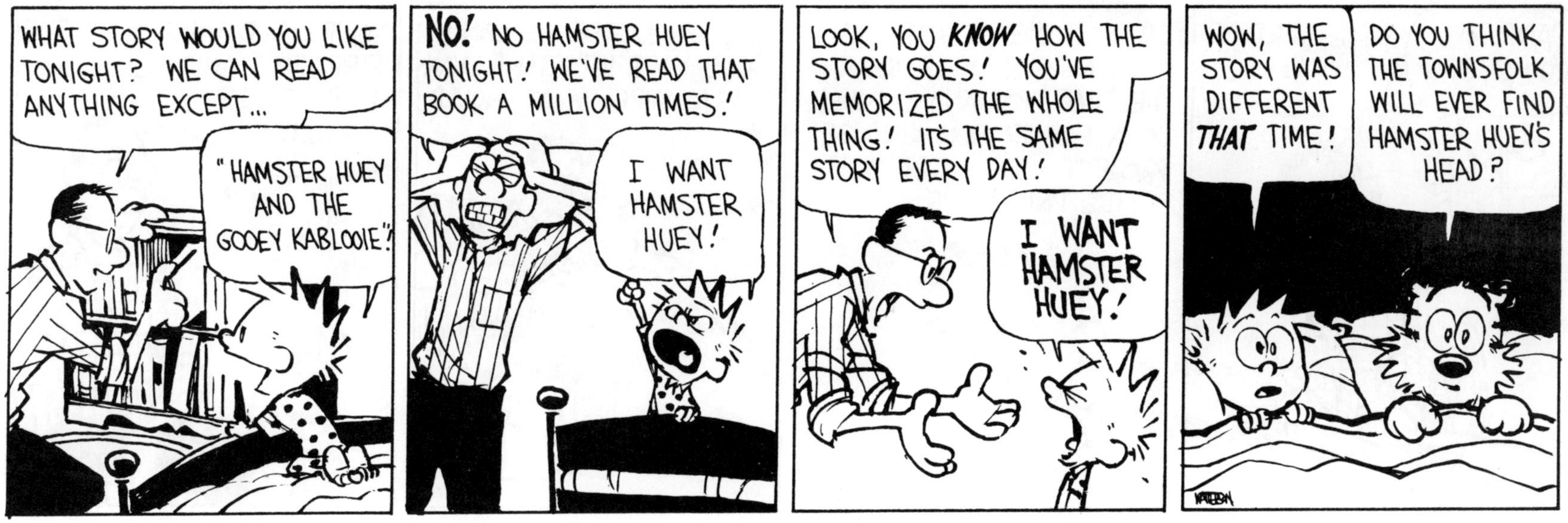
WHAT STORY WOULD YOU LIKE TONIGHT? WE CAN READ ANYTHING EXCEPT...
"HAMSTER HUEY AND THE GOOEY KABLOOIE"!
NO! NO HAMSTER HUEY TONIGHT! WE'VE READ THAT BOOK A MILLION TIMES!
I WANT HAMSTER HUEY!
LOOK, YOU KNOW HOW THE STORY GOES! YOU'VE MEMORIZED THE WHOLE THING! IT'S THE SAME STORY EVERY DAY!
I WANT HAMSTER HUEY!
WOW, THE STORY WAS DIFFERENT THAT TIME!
DO YOU THINK THE TOWNSFOLK WILL EVER FIND HAMSTER HUEY'S HEAD?

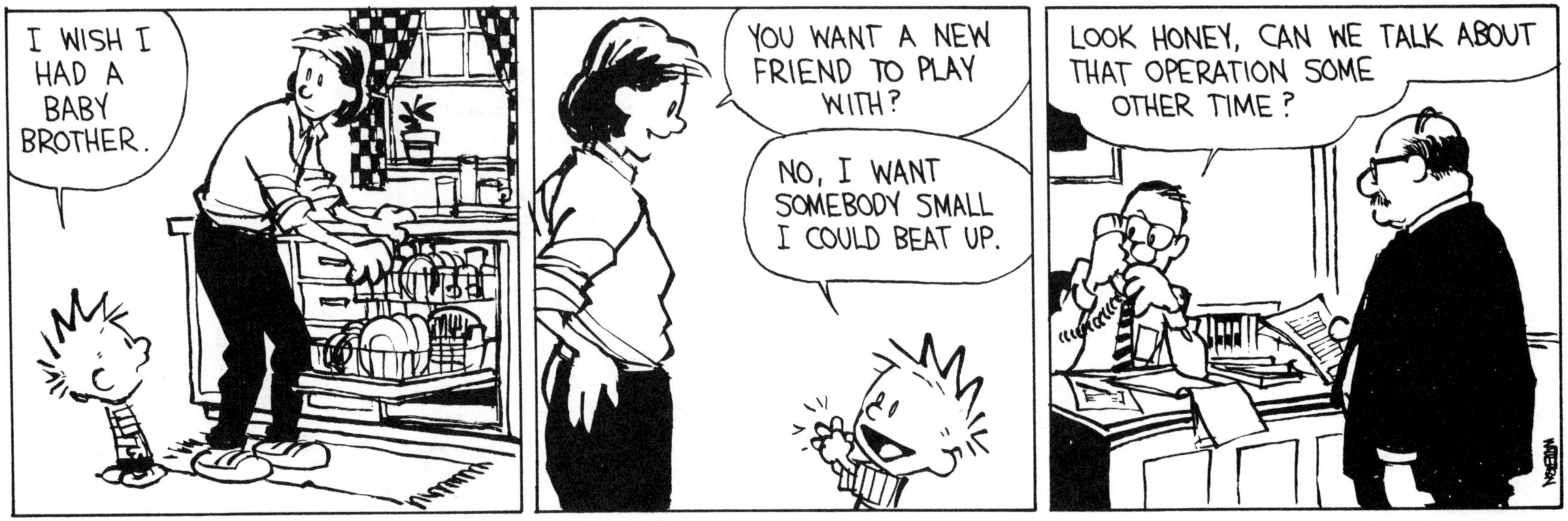
I WISH I HAD A BABY BROTHER.
YOU WANT A NEW FRIEND TO PLAY WITH?
NO, I WANT SOMEBODY SMALL I COULD BEAT UP.
LOOK HONEY, CAN WE TALK ABOUT THAT OPERATION SOME OTHER TIME?

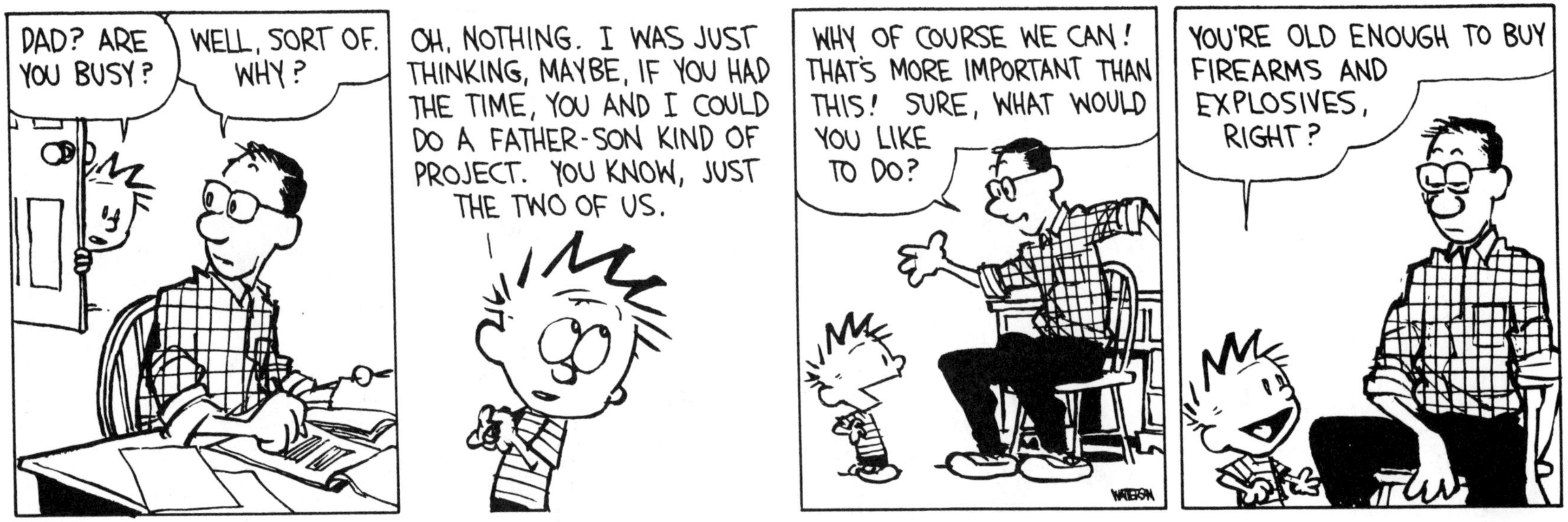
DAD? ARE YOU BUSY?
WELL, SORT OF. WHY?
OH, NOTHING. I WAS JUST THINKING, MAYBE, IF YOU HAD THE TIME, YOU AND I COULD DO A FATHER-SON KIND OF PROJECT. YOU KNOW, JUST THE TWO OF US.
WHY OF COURSE WE CAN! THAT'S MORE IMPORTANT THAN THIS! SURE, WHAT WOULD YOU LIKE TO DO?
YOU'RE OLD ENOUGH TO BUY FIREARMS AND EXPLOSIVES, RIGHT?

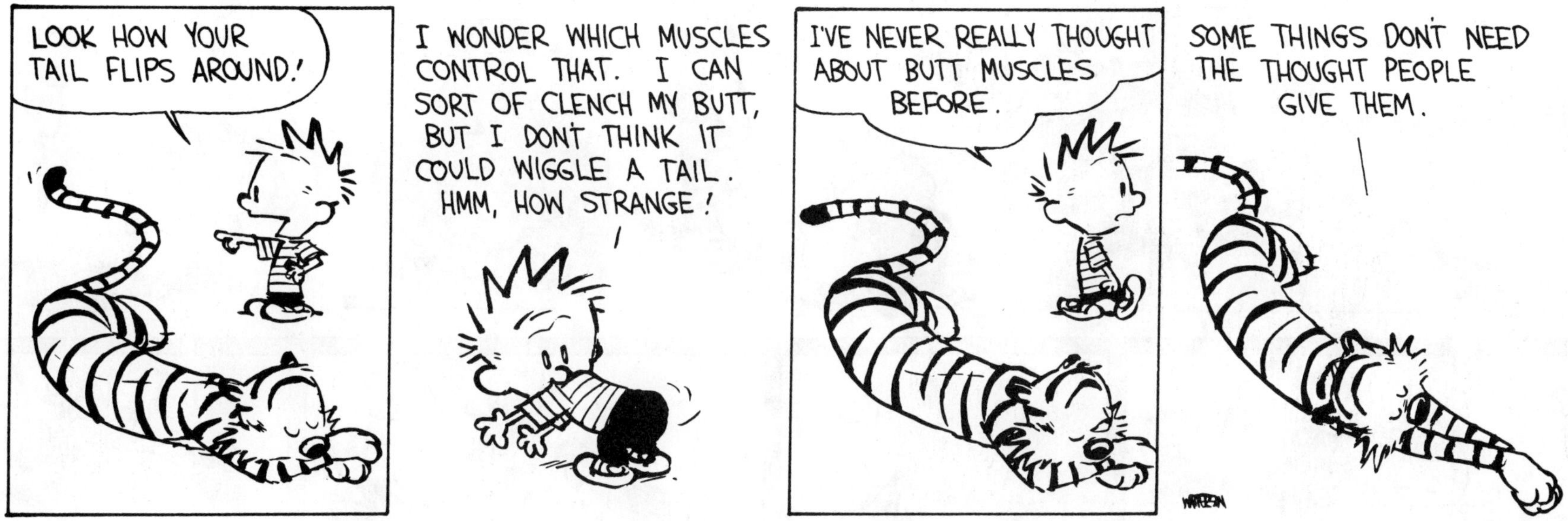
LOOK HOW YOUR TAIL FLIPS AROUND!
I WONDER WHICH MUSCLES CONTROL THAT. I CAN SORT OF CLENCH MY BUTT, BUT I DON'T THINK IT COULD WIGGLE A TAIL. HMM, HOW STRANGE!
I'VE NEVER REALLY THOUGHT ABOUT BUTT MUSCLES BEFORE.
SOME THINGS DON'T NEED THE THOUGHT PEOPLE GIVE THEM.

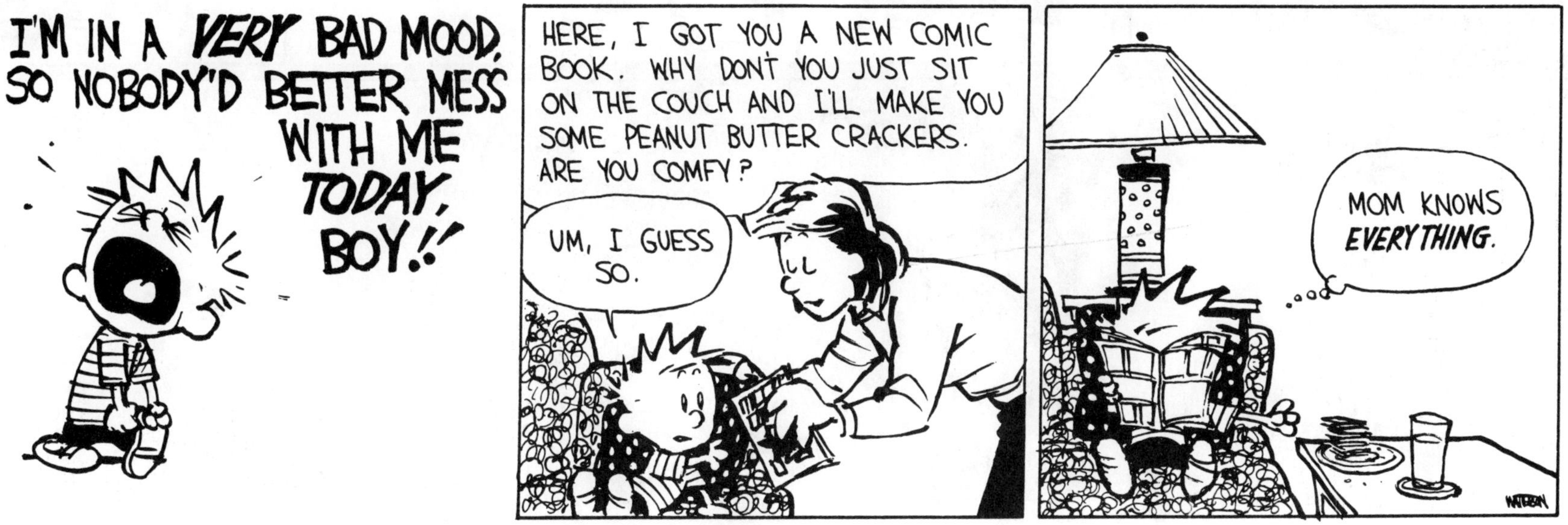
I'M IN A *VERY* BAD MOOD, SO NOBODY'D BETTER MESS WITH ME *TODAY*, BOY!!
HERE, I GOT YOU A NEW COMIC BOOK. WHY DON'T YOU JUST SIT ON THE COUCH AND I'LL MAKE YOU SOME PEANUT BUTTER CRACKERS. ARE YOU COMFY?
UM, I GUESS SO.
MOM KNOWS *EVERYTHING*.

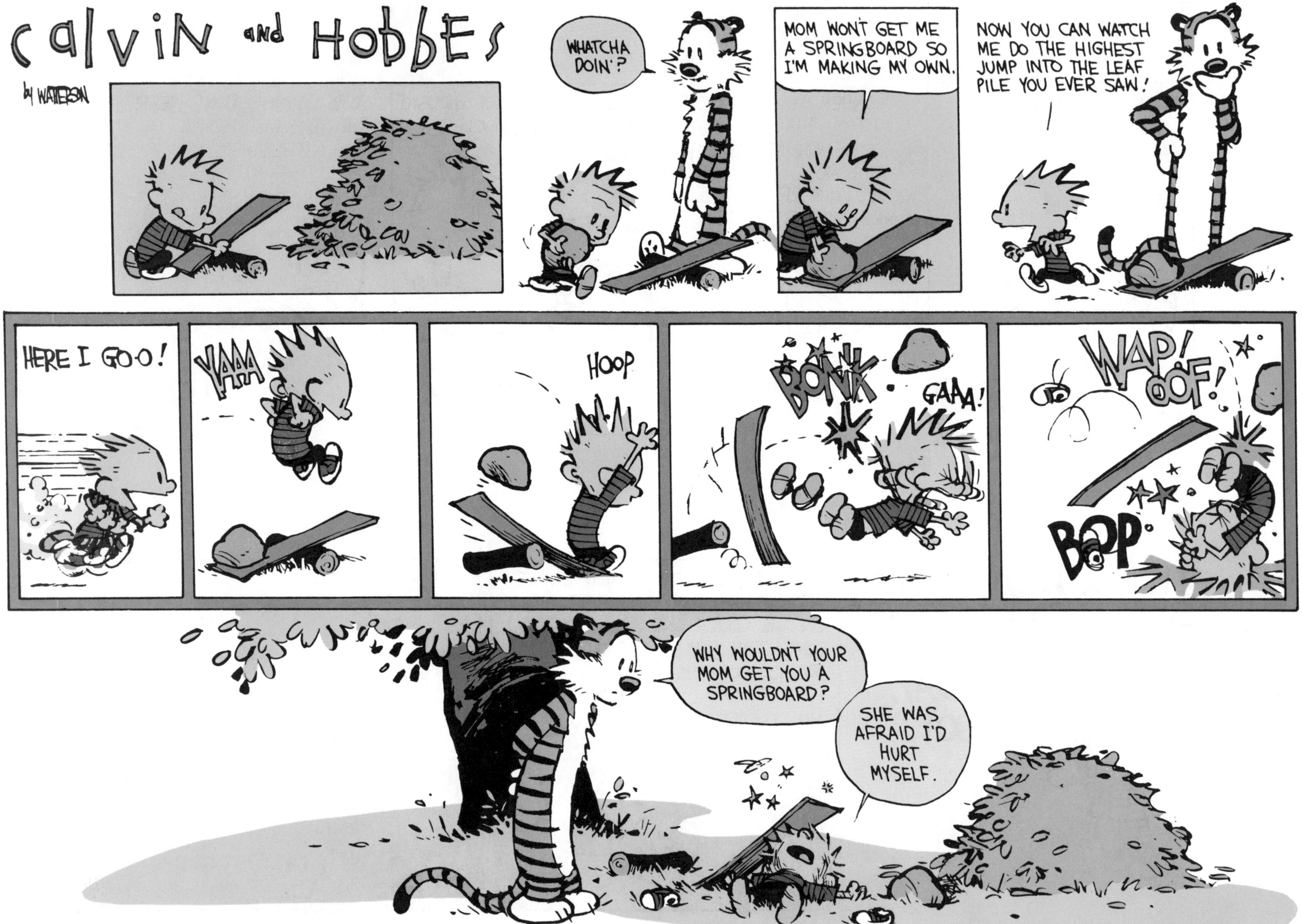
Calvin and Hobbes
by WATTERSON
WHATCHA DOIN'?
MOM WON'T GET ME A SPRINGBOARD SO I'M MAKING MY OWN.
NOW YOU CAN WATCH ME DO THE HIGHEST JUMP INTO THE LEAF PILE YOU EVER SAW!
HERE I GO-O!
YAAA
HOOP
BONK
GAAA!
WAP!
OOF!
BOP
WHY WOULDN'T YOUR MOM GET YOU A SPRINGBOARD?
SHE WAS AFRAID I'D HURT MYSELF.

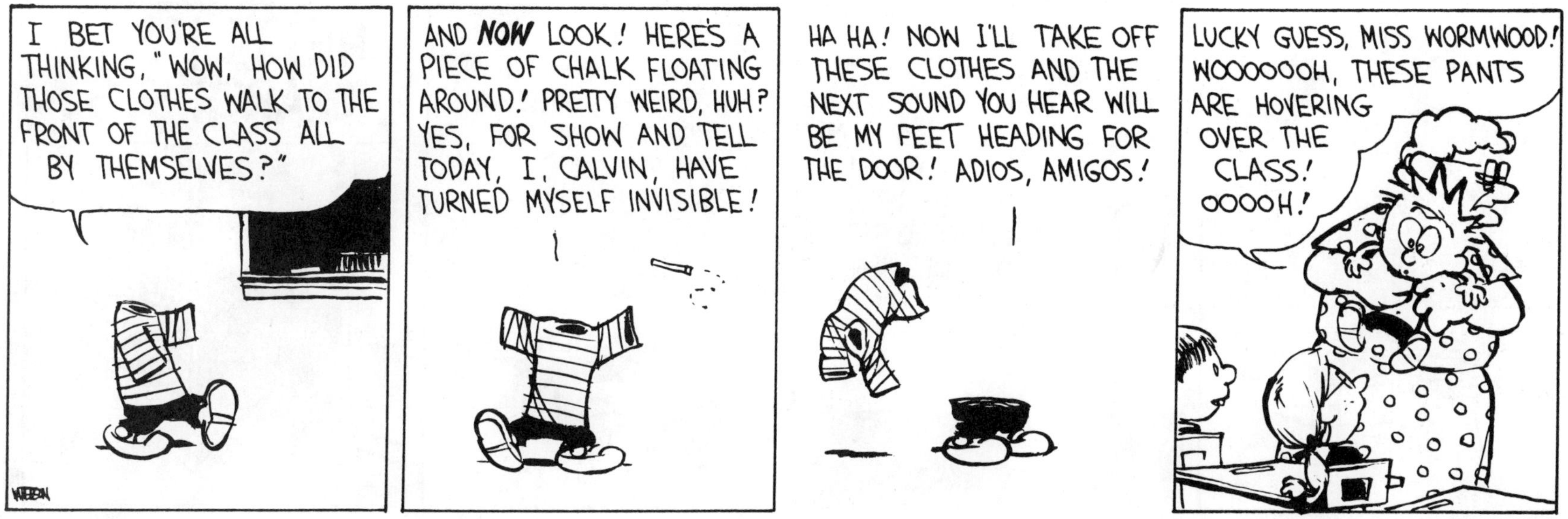
I BET YOU'RE ALL THINKING, "WOW, HOW DID THOSE CLOTHES WALK TO THE FRONT OF THE CLASS ALL BY THEMSELVES?"
AND NOW LOOK! HERE'S A PIECE OF CHALK FLOATING AROUND! PRETTY WEIRD, HUH? YES, FOR SHOW AND TELL TODAY, I, CALVIN, HAVE TURNED MYSELF INVISIBLE!
HA HA! NOW I'LL TAKE OFF THESE CLOTHES AND THE NEXT SOUND YOU HEAR WILL BE MY FEET HEADING FOR THE DOOR! ADIOS, AMIGOS!
LUCKY GUESS, MISS WORMWOOD! WOOOOOOH, THESE PANTS ARE HOVERING OVER THE CLASS! OOOOH!

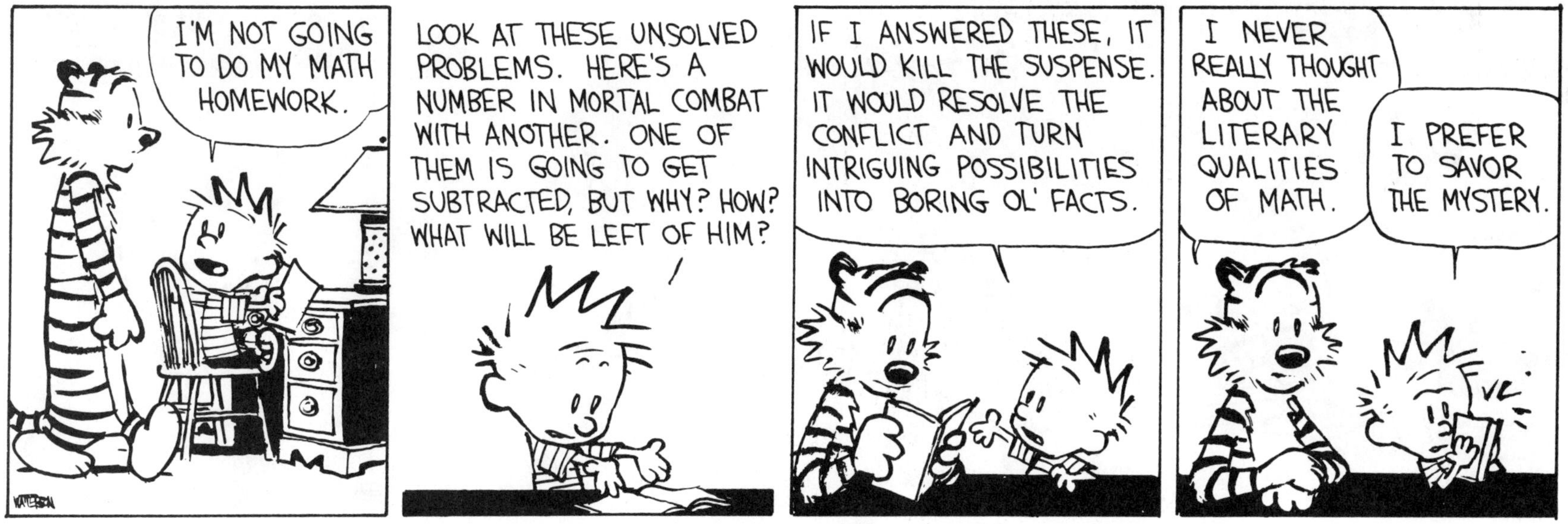
I'M NOT GOING TO DO MY MATH HOMEWORK.
LOOK AT THESE UNSOLVED PROBLEMS. HERE'S A NUMBER IN MORTAL COMBAT WITH ANOTHER. ONE OF THEM IS GOING TO GET SUBTRACTED, BUT WHY? HOW? WHAT WILL BE LEFT OF HIM?
IF I ANSWERED THESE, IT WOULD KILL THE SUSPENSE. IT WOULD RESOLVE THE CONFLICT AND TURN INTRIGUING POSSIBILITIES INTO BORING OL' FACTS.
I NEVER REALLY THOUGHT ABOUT THE LITERARY QUALITIES OF MATH.
I PREFER TO SAVOR THE MYSTERY.

MISS WORMWOOD?

YES, CALVIN?

IF IGNORANCE IS BLISS, THIS LESSON WOULD APPEAR TO BE A DELIBERATE ATTEMPT ON YOUR PART TO DEPRIVE ME OF HAPPINESS, THE PURSUIT OF WHICH IS MY UNALIENABLE RIGHT ACCORDING TO THE DECLARATION OF INDEPENDENCE.

I THEREFORE ASSERT MY PATRIOTIC PREROGATIVE NOT TO KNOW THIS MATERIAL. I'LL BE OUT ON THE PLAYGROUND.

HELLLPP! MONARCHISTS!

I'm gonna pound you in gym class, Twinky.

OH YEAH?? I'D LIKE TO SEE YOU TRY IT!

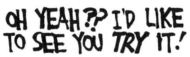

MY BRAIN WISHES MY EGO HAD CALL-WAITING.

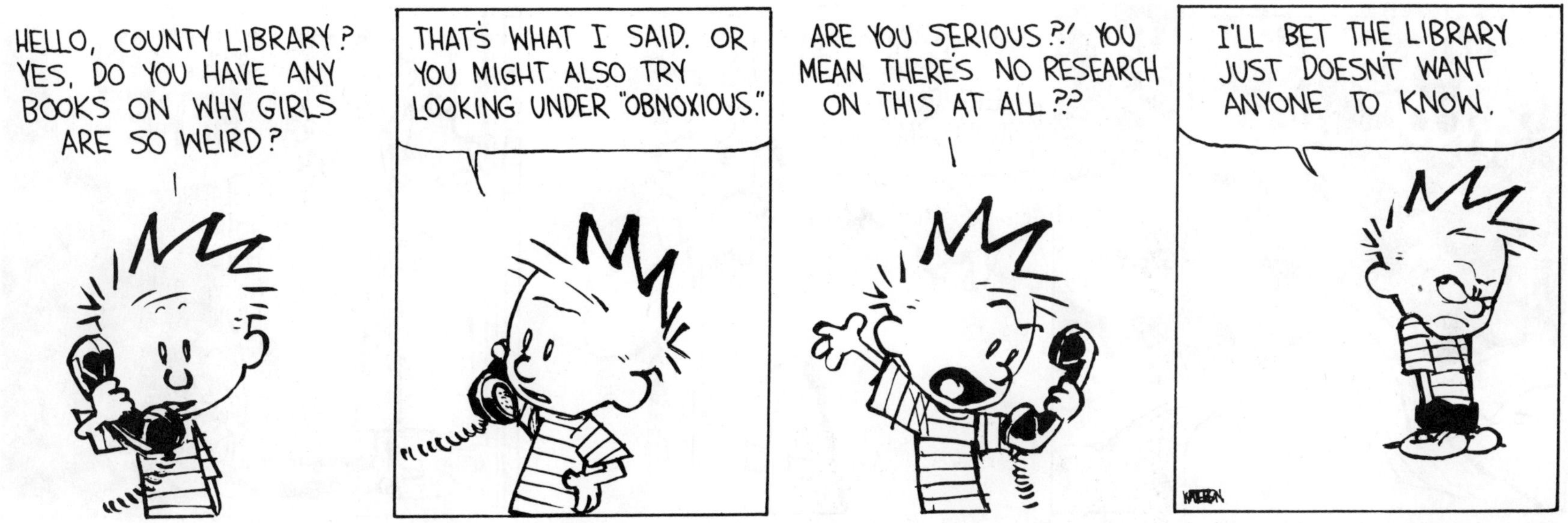
HELLO, COUNTY LIBRARY? YES, DO YOU HAVE ANY BOOKS ON WHY GIRLS ARE SO WEIRD?
THAT'S WHAT I SAID. OR YOU MIGHT ALSO TRY LOOKING UNDER "OBNOXIOUS."
ARE YOU SERIOUS?! YOU MEAN THERE'S NO RESEARCH ON THIS AT ALL??
I'LL BET THE LIBRARY JUST DOESN'T WANT ANYONE TO KNOW.

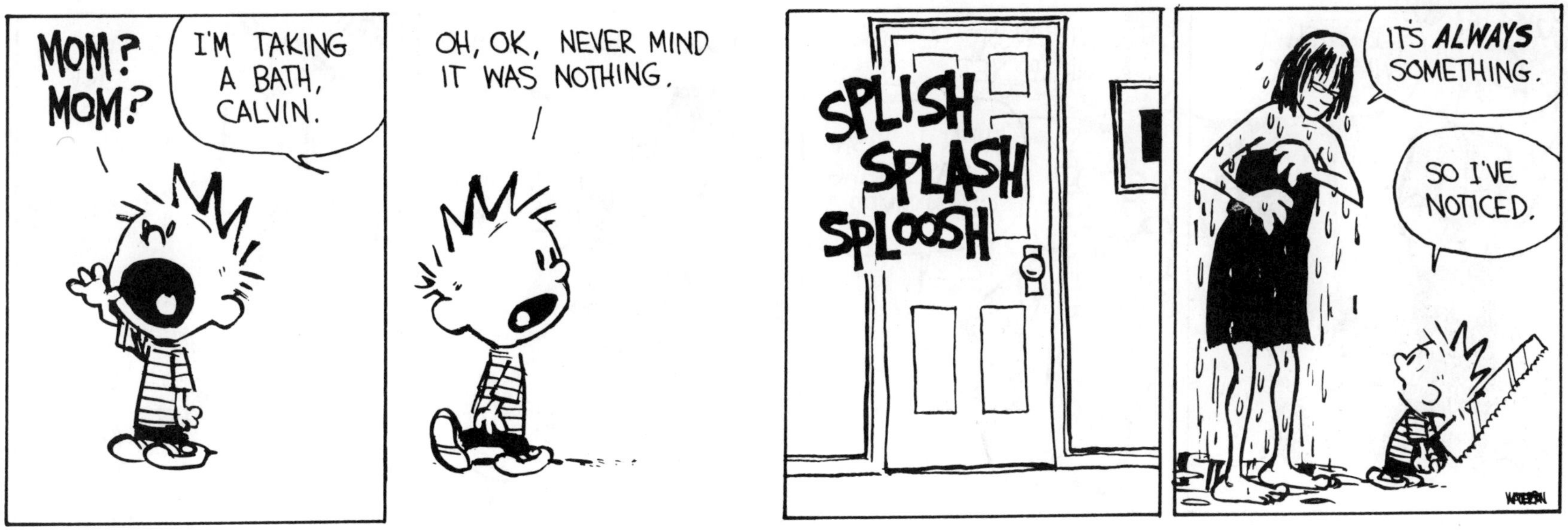
MOM? MOM?
I'M TAKING A BATH, CALVIN.
OH, OK, NEVER MIND IT WAS NOTHING.
SPLISH
SPLASH
SPLOOSH
IT'S ALWAYS SOMETHING.
SO I'VE NOTICED.

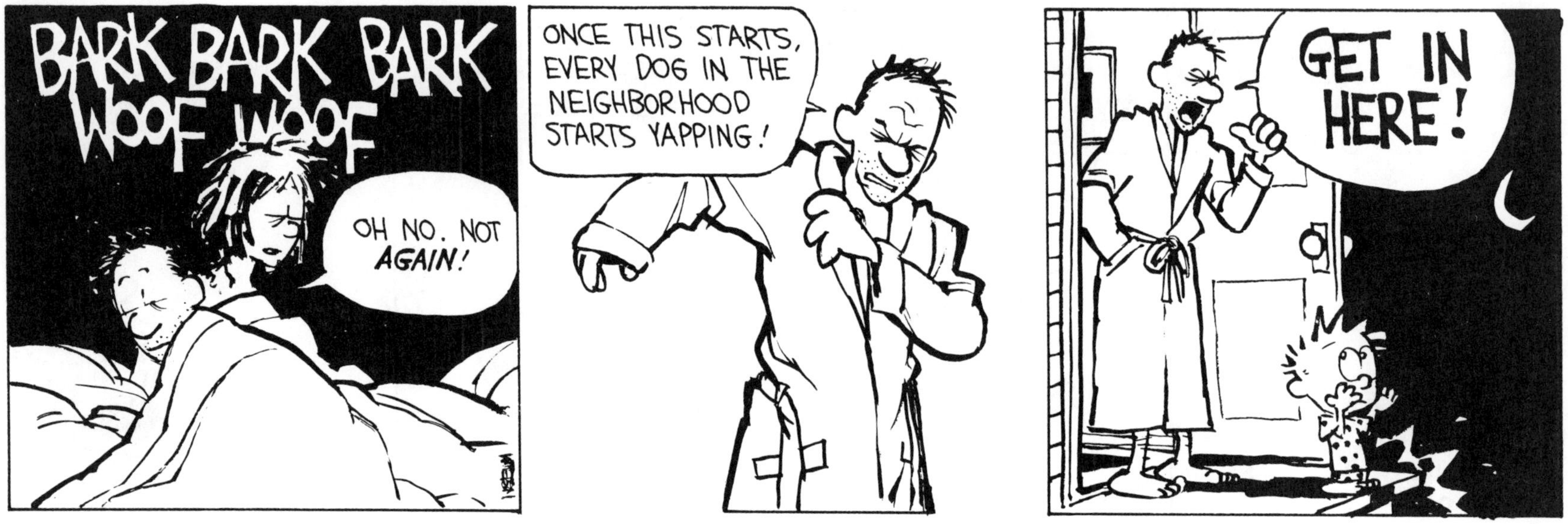
BARK BARK BARK BARK
WOOF WOOF
OH NO. NOT *AGAIN!*
ONCE THIS STARTS, EVERY DOG IN THE NEIGHBORHOOD STARTS YAPPING!
GET IN HERE!

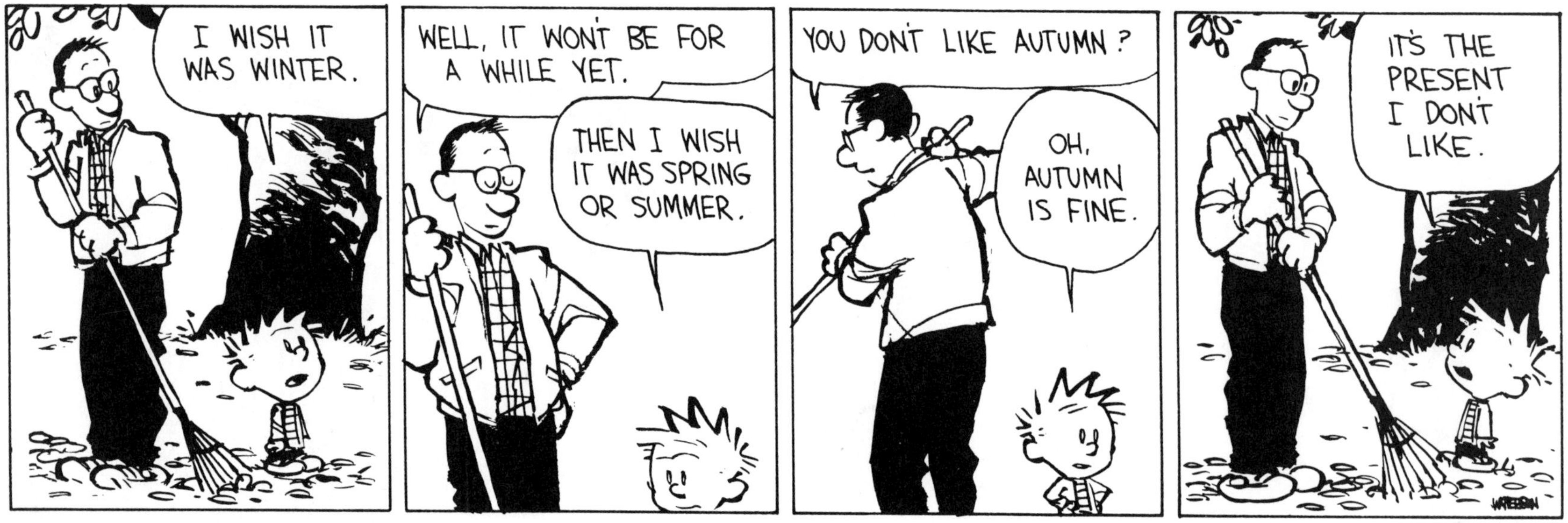
I WISH IT WAS WINTER.
WELL, IT WON'T BE FOR A WHILE YET.
THEN I WISH IT WAS SPRING OR SUMMER.
YOU DON'T LIKE AUTUMN?
OH, AUTUMN IS FINE.
IT'S THE PRESENT I DON'T LIKE.

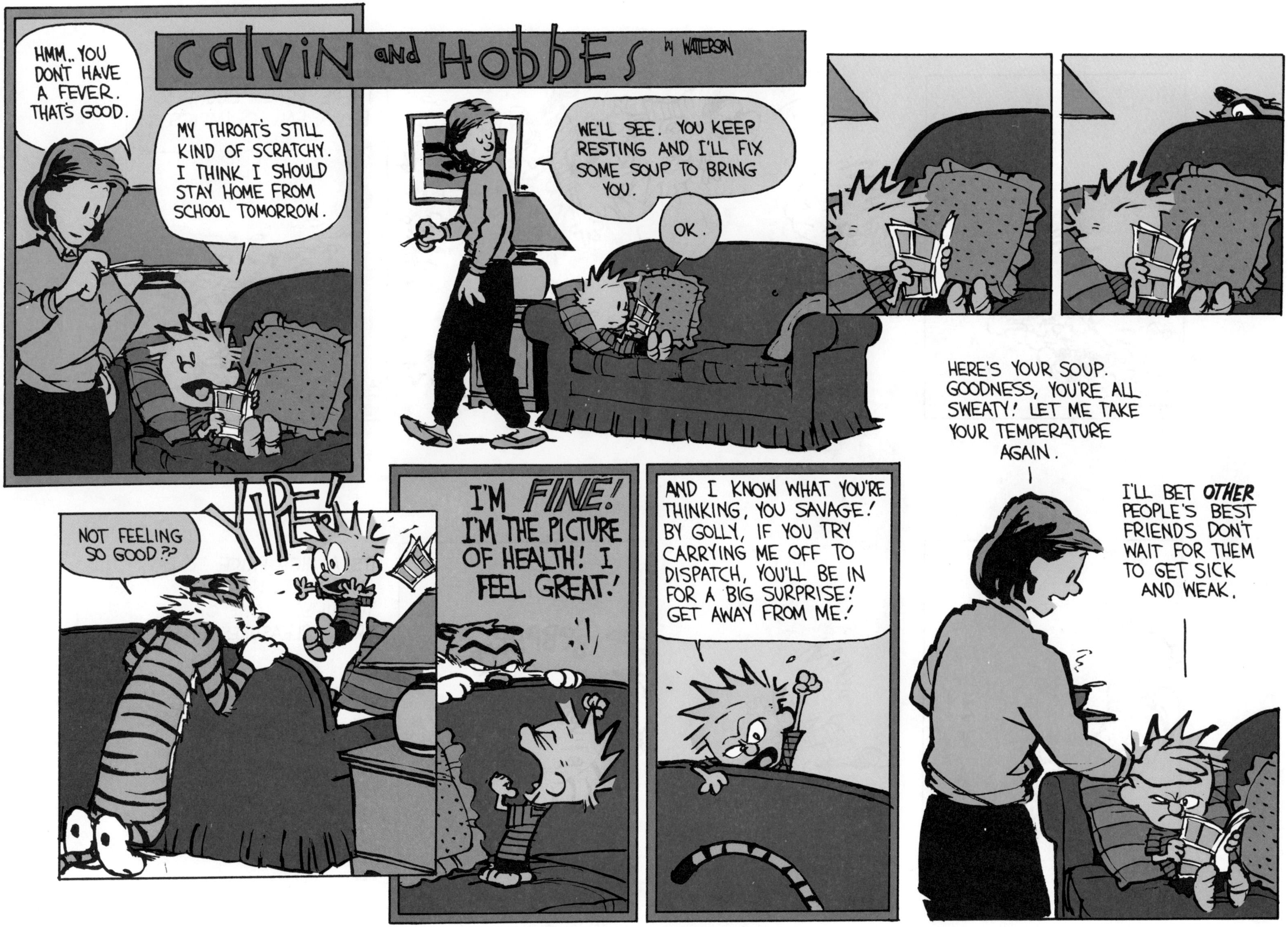
Calvin and Hobbes
by WATTERSON
HMM.. YOU DON'T HAVE A FEVER. THAT'S GOOD.
MY THROAT'S STILL KIND OF SCRATCHY. I THINK I SHOULD STAY HOME FROM SCHOOL TOMORROW.
WE'LL SEE. YOU KEEP RESTING AND I'LL FIX SOME SOUP TO BRING YOU.
OK.
NOT FEELING SO GOOD ??
YIPE!
I'M FINE! I'M THE PICTURE OF HEALTH! I FEEL GREAT!
AND I KNOW WHAT YOU'RE THINKING, YOU SAVAGE! BY GOLLY, IF YOU TRY CARRYING ME OFF TO DISPATCH, YOU'LL BE IN FOR A BIG SURPRISE! GET AWAY FROM ME!
HERE'S YOUR SOUP. GOODNESS, YOU'RE ALL SWEATY! LET ME TAKE YOUR TEMPERATURE AGAIN.
I'LL BET OTHER PEOPLE'S BEST FRIENDS DON'T WAIT FOR THEM TO GET SICK AND WEAK.

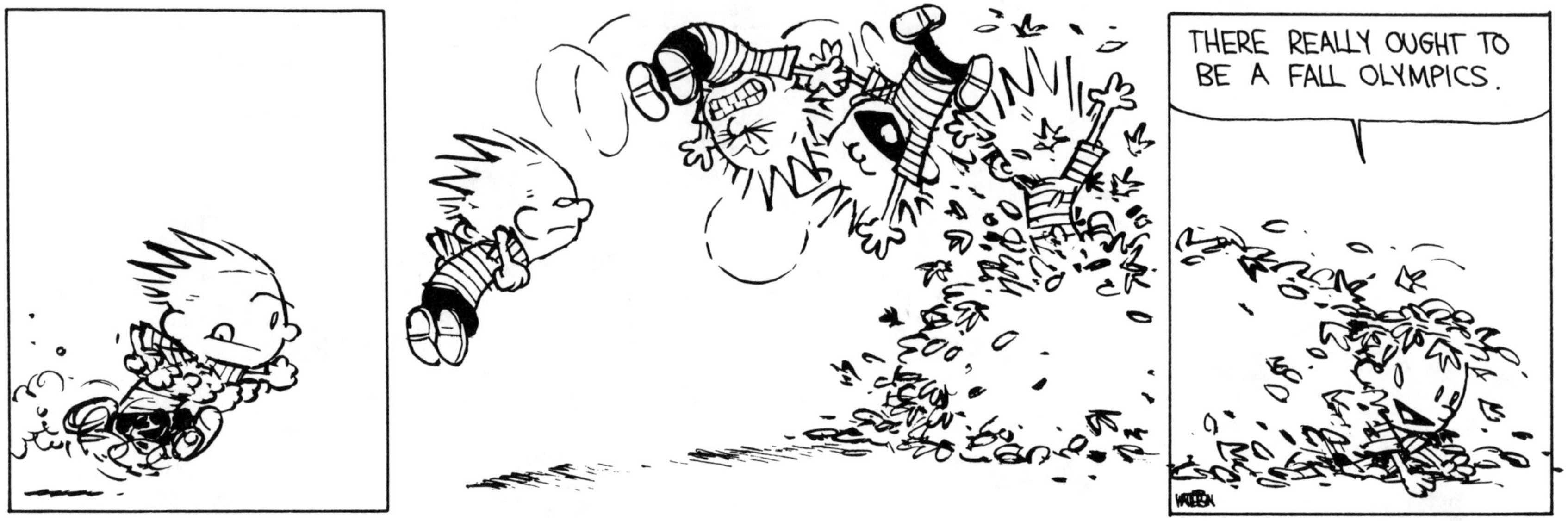
THERE REALLY OUGHT TO BE A FALL OLYMPICS.

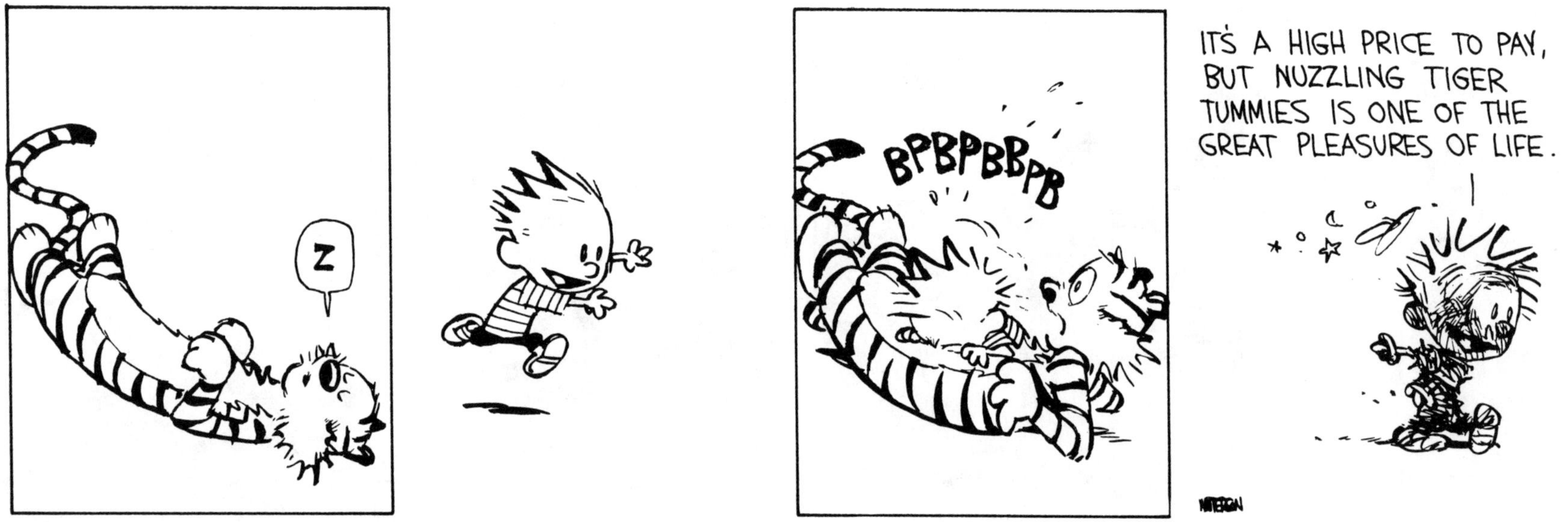
Z
BPBPBBPB
IT'S A HIGH PRICE TO PAY, BUT NUZZLING TIGER TUMMIES IS ONE OF THE GREAT PLEASURES OF LIFE.

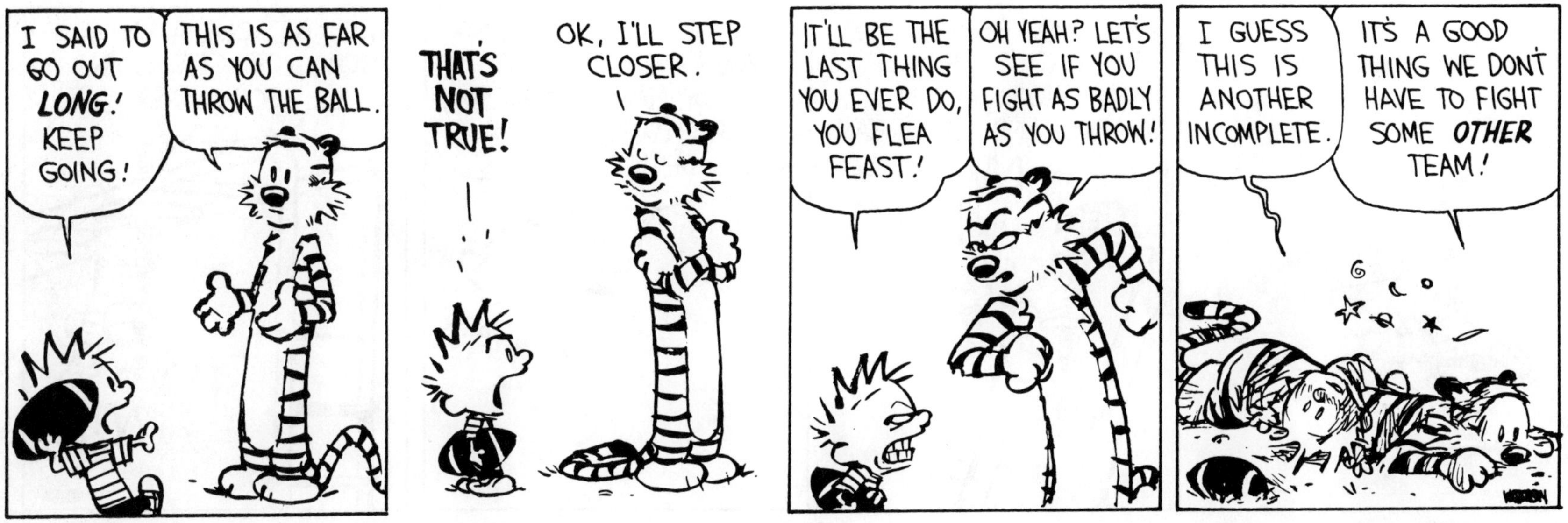
I SAID TO GO OUT LONG! KEEP GOING!
THIS IS AS FAR AS YOU CAN THROW THE BALL.
THAT'S NOT TRUE!
OK, I'LL STEP CLOSER.
IT'LL BE THE LAST THING YOU EVER DO, YOU FLEA FEAST!
OH YEAH? LET'S SEE IF YOU FIGHT AS BADLY AS YOU THROW!
I GUESS THIS IS ANOTHER INCOMPLETE.
IT'S A GOOD THING WE DON'T HAVE TO FIGHT SOME OTHER TEAM!

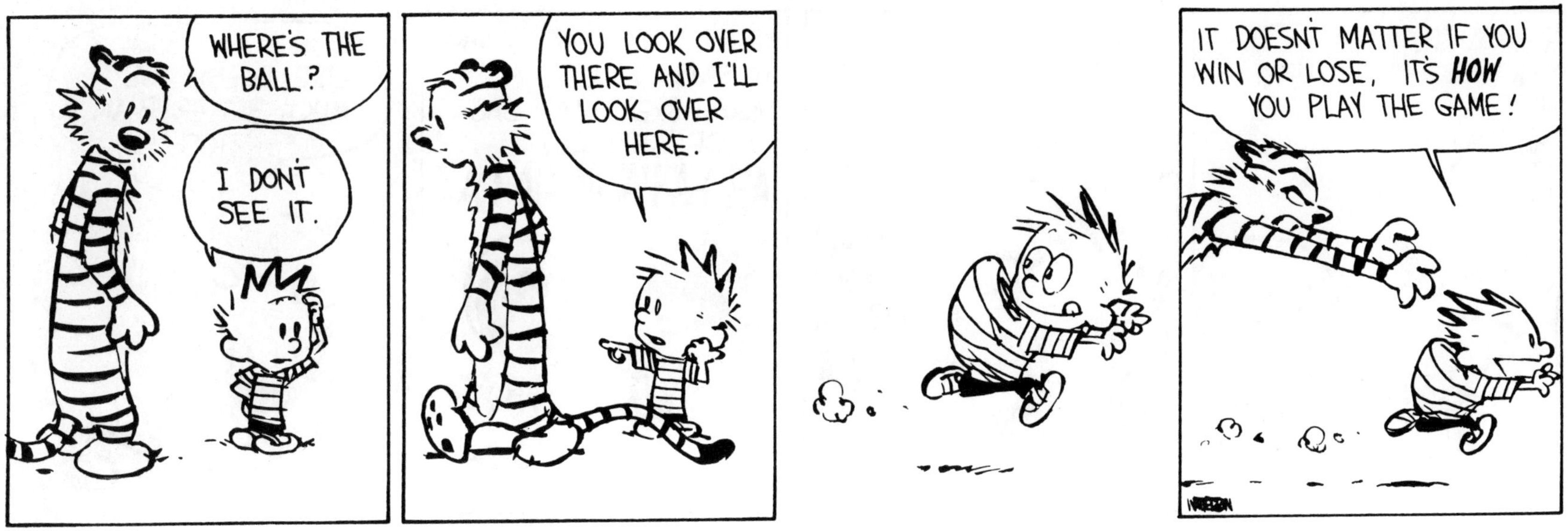
WHERE'S THE BALL?
I DON'T SEE IT.
YOU LOOK OVER THERE AND I'LL LOOK OVER HERE.
IT DOESN'T MATTER IF YOU WIN OR LOSE, IT'S HOW YOU PLAY THE GAME!

I LOVE RECESS!

TWO MINUTES AGO, I WAS EATING DEVILED HAM, CHOCOLATE MILK, GRAPES, AND ICE CREAM.

AND NOW I'M RUNNING AROUND ON A PLAYGROUND FULL OF NAUSEA-INDUCING, DISORIENTING MOTION DEVICES.

IT'S THE ONE TIME AT SCHOOL I GET SOME SOLITUDE.

HEY SUSIE, PICK A NUMBER IN THE FORTUNE TELLER.

UM... THREE.

ONE, TWO, THREE! NOW PICK A LETTER.

"B."

WE LIFT UP FLAP "B" AND IT SAYS, " YOU'RE A MOUTH-BREATHING BAG OF BOOGERS!"

AH HA HA HA HA HA!

LIFE DOESN'T GET MUCH BETTER THAN THIS.

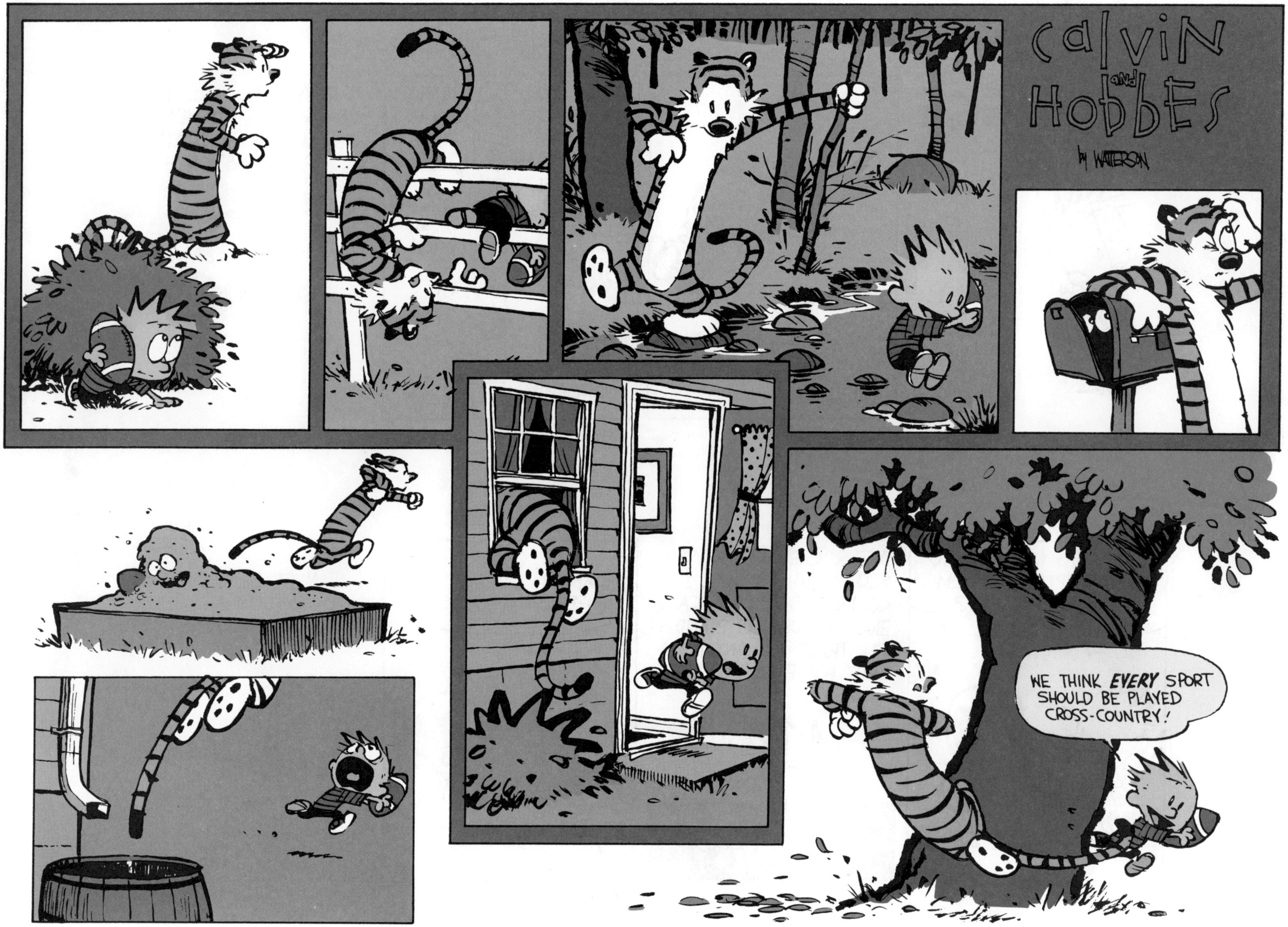
Calvin and Hobbes
by WATTERSON
WE THINK EVERY SPORT SHOULD BE PLAYED CROSS-COUNTRY!

RRINNGGG

DIDN'T YOU HEAR THE BELL? RECESS IS OVER. IT'S TIME TO GO IN.

I'M NOT DONE YET.

IT TAKES ME MORE THAN ONE RECESS TO WEAR MYSELF INTO A STATE OF SUBMISSION.

SUSIE, DO YOU WANT TO TRADE CAPTAIN NAPALM BUBBLE GUM CARDS?

AFTER CHEWING ALMOST $20 WORTH OF GUM, I'VE COLLECTED ALL THE CARDS EXCEPT NUMBERS 8 AND 34. I'LL TRADE YOU ANY DUPLICATE FOR EITHER OF THOSE.

I DON'T COLLECT CAPTAIN NAPALM BUBBLE GUM CARDS.

IT MUST BE DEPRESSING TO GO THROUGH LIFE WITH NO PURPOSE.

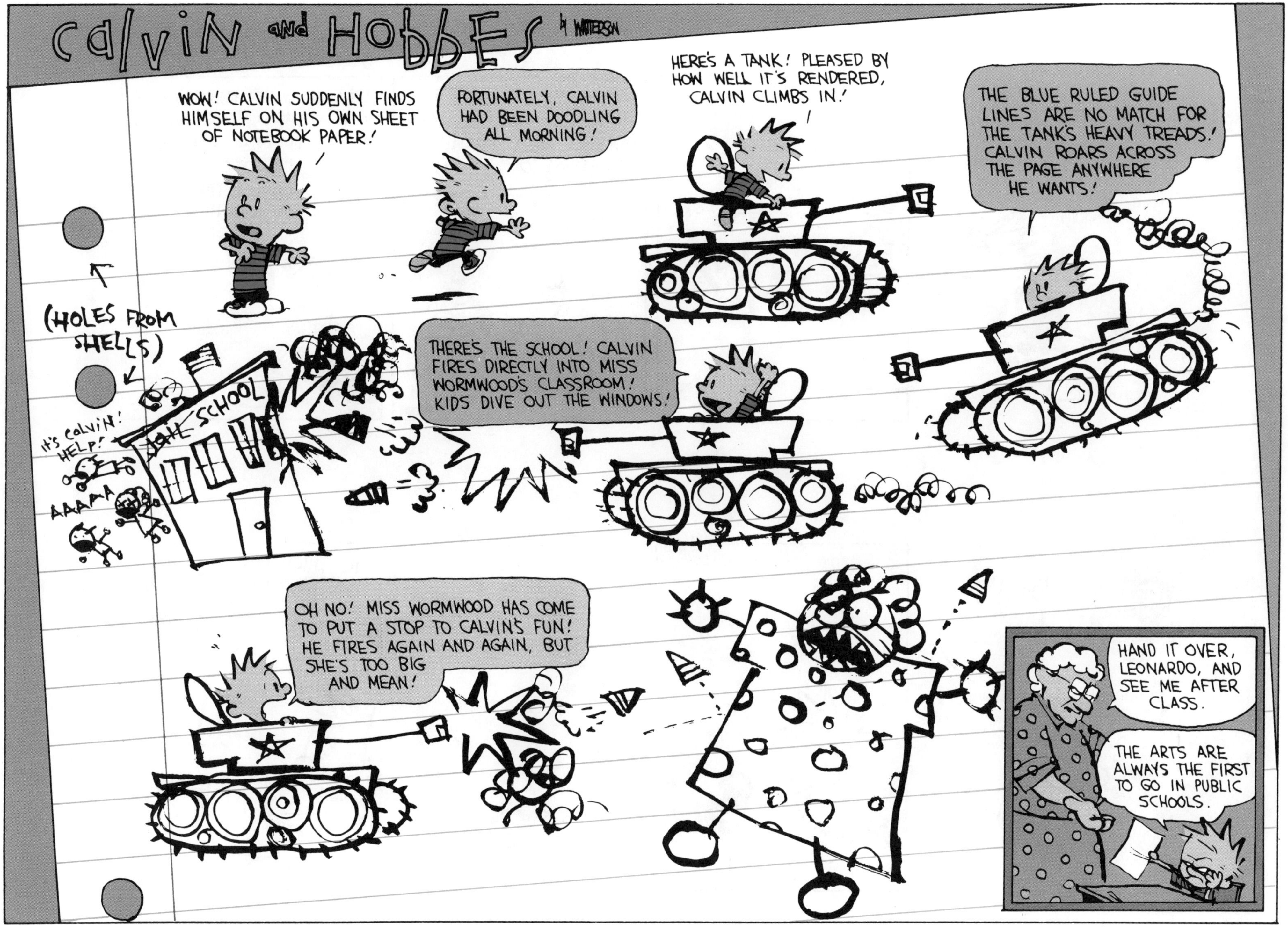

CALVIN and HOBBES by WATTERSON
WOW! CALVIN SUDDENLY FINDS HIMSELF ON HIS OWN SHEET OF NOTEBOOK PAPER!
FORTUNATELY, CALVIN HAD BEEN DOODLING ALL MORNING!
HERE'S A TANK! PLEASED BY HOW WELL IT'S RENDERED, CALVIN CLIMBS IN!
THE BLUE RULED GUIDE LINES ARE NO MATCH FOR THE TANK'S HEAVY TREADS! CALVIN ROARS ACROSS THE PAGE ANYWHERE HE WANTS!
(HOLES FROM SHELLS)
SCHOOL
IT'S CALVIN! HELP!
AAAA
THERE'S THE SCHOOL! CALVIN FIRES DIRECTLY INTO MISS WORMWOOD'S CLASSROOM! KIDS DIVE OUT THE WINDOWS!
OH NO! MISS WORMWOOD HAS COME TO PUT A STOP TO CALVIN'S FUN! HE FIRES AGAIN AND AGAIN, BUT SHE'S TOO BIG AND MEAN!
HAND IT OVER, LEONARDO, AND SEE ME AFTER CLASS.
THE ARTS ARE ALWAYS THE FIRST TO GO IN PUBLIC SCHOOLS.

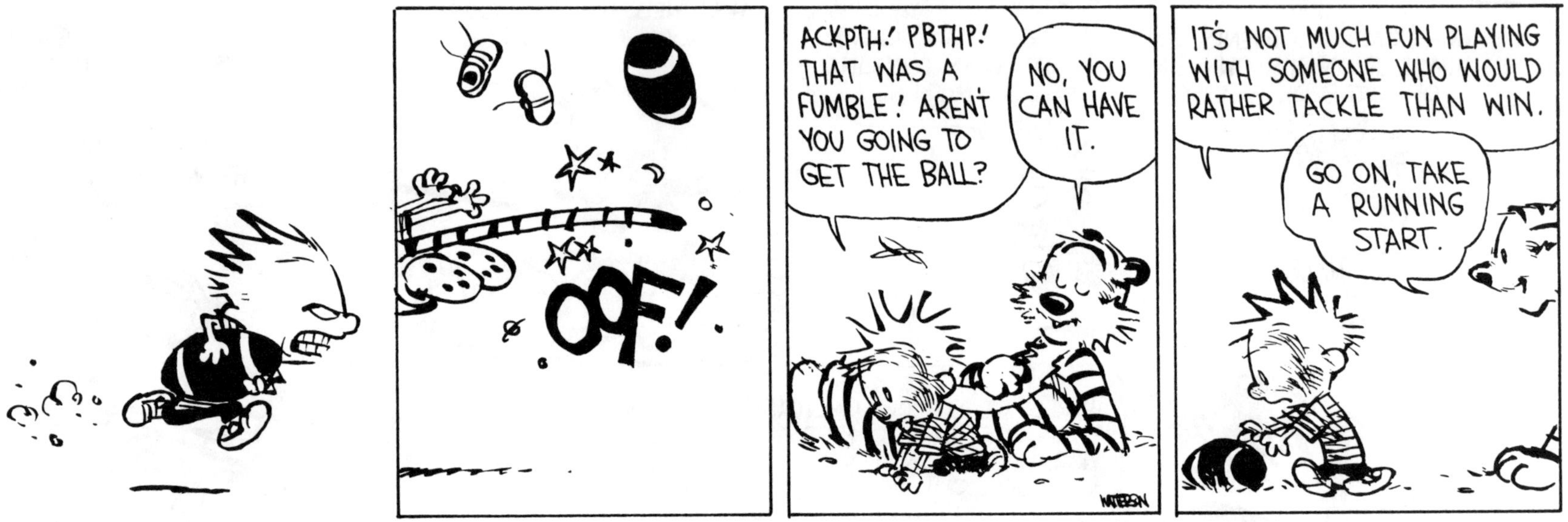
OOF!
ACKPTH! PBTHP! THAT WAS A FUMBLE! AREN'T YOU GOING TO GET THE BALL?
NO, YOU CAN HAVE IT.
IT'S NOT MUCH FUN PLAYING WITH SOMEONE WHO WOULD RATHER TACKLE THAN WIN.
GO ON, TAKE A RUNNING START.

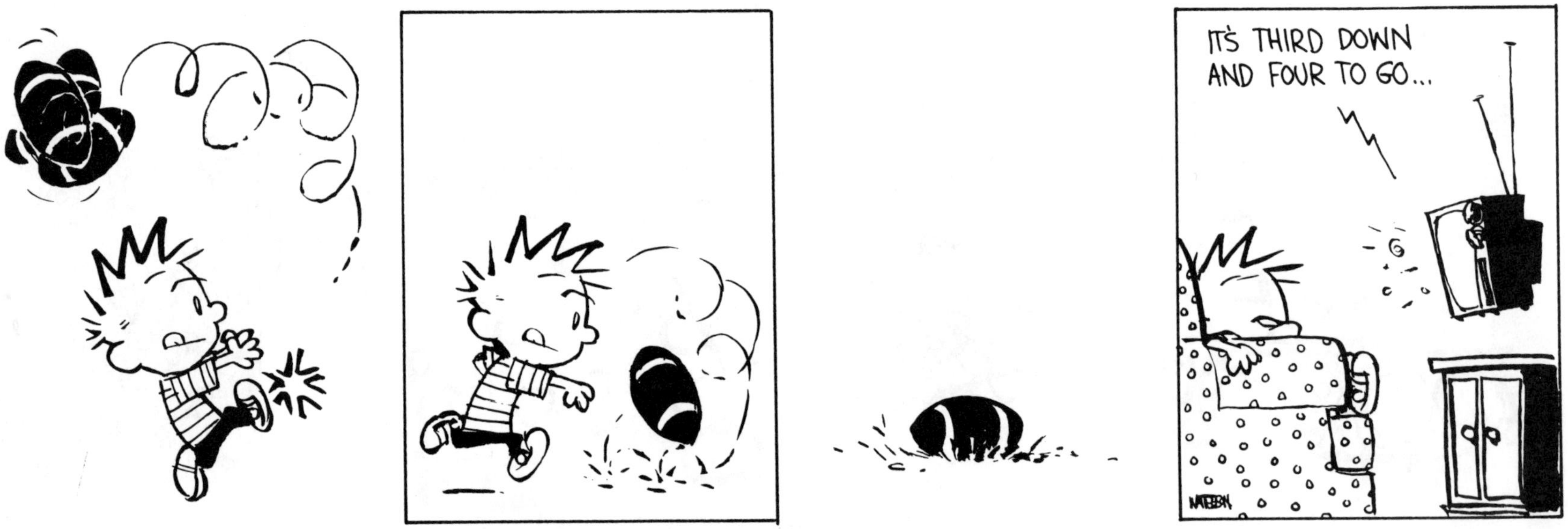
IT'S THIRD DOWN AND FOUR TO GO...

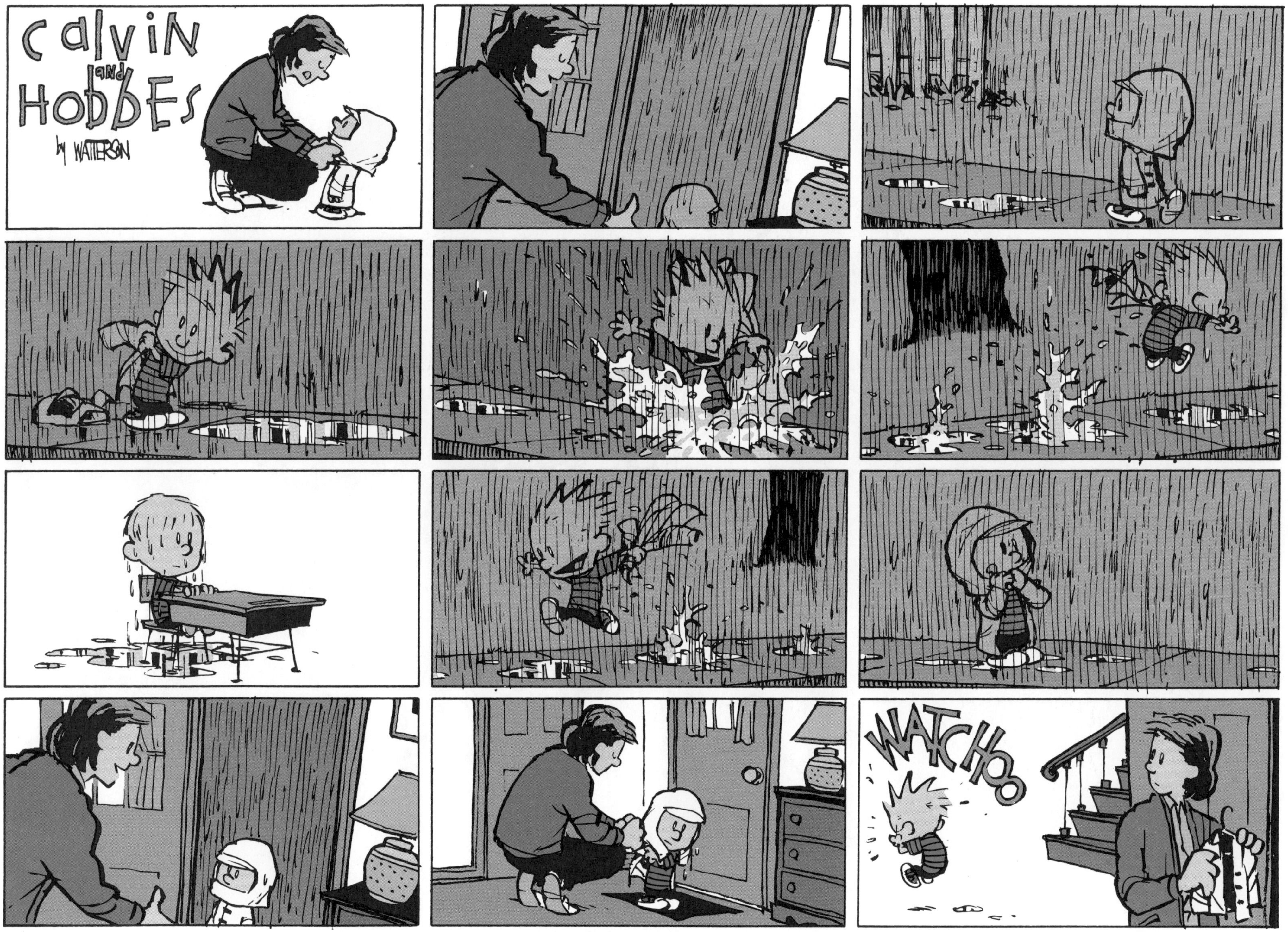
Calvin and Hobbes
by WATTERSON
WATCHOO

THE DAYS ARE JUST PACKED

Other Books by Bill Watterson

Calvin and Hobbes
Something Under the Bed Is Drooling
Yukon Ho!
Weirdos from Another Planet
The Revenge of the Baby-Sat
Scientific Progress Goes "Boink"
Attack of the Deranged Mutant Killer Monster Snow Goons

Treasury Collections

The Essential Calvin and Hobbes
The Calvin and Hobbes Lazy Sunday Book
The Authoritative Calvin and Hobbes
The Indispensable Calvin and Hobbes